WASHINGTON ROEBLING'S CIVIL WAR

From the Bloody Battlefield at Gettysburg to the Brooklyn Bridge

DIANE MONROE SMITH

STACKPOLE
BOOKS

Guilford, Connecticut

Published by Stackpole Books

An imprint of The Rowman & Littlefield Publishing Group, Inc.
4501 Forbes Blvd., Ste. 200
Lanham, MD 20706
www.rowman.com

Distributed by NATIONAL BOOK NETWORK
800-462-6420

British Library Cataloguing in Publication Information available

Library of Congress Cataloging-in-Publication Data available

Names: Smith, Diane Monroe, author.
Title: Washington Roebling's Civil War : from the bloody battlefield at
    Gettysburg to the Brooklyn Bridge / Diane Monroe Smith.
Description: Guilford, Connecticut : Stackpole Books, [2019] | Includes
    bibliographical references and index.
Identifiers: LCCN 2018058278 (print) | LCCN 2019001069 (ebook) | ISBN
    9780811767828 (electronic) | ISBN 9780811737883 (cloth : alk. paper) |
    ISBN 9780811767828 (e-book)
Subjects: LCSH: Roebling, Washington Augustus, 1837–1926. | United States.
    Army. New York Artillery. Independent Battery, 6th (1861–1865) |
    Gettysburg, Battle of, Gettysburg, Pa., 1863. | Soldiers—United
    States—Biography. | Military engineers—United States—Biography. |
    United States. Army—Officers—Biography. | United States—History—Civil
    War, 1861–1865—Artillery operations. | United States—History—Civil War,
    1861–1865—Balloons. | United States—History—Civil War,
    1861–1865—Regimental histories. | Civil engineers—United
    States—Biography.
Classification: LCC E523.8 6th (ebook) | LCC E523.8 6th .S65 2919 (print) |
    DDC 973.7092 [B] —dc23
LC record available at https://lccn.loc.gov/2018058278

Printed in the United States of America

*To my mother, Irene Kells Monroe, who nurtured my interest
in the Civil War and my love of learning.*

Washington Roebling.
Rutgers Special Collections.

Contents

Maps

*Maps created and adapted by Ned Smith

Introduction

Washington Roebling was the first-born son of a man who became a German American icon, a real-life example of an immigrant achieving the "American dream." For John Roebling, his new country promised what his native Germany had withheld. There, all engineering projects were controlled by government officials who seemingly discouraged innovation and initiative, while the United States embraced new ideas that would allow him to found the Roebling dynasty. Not only was John recognized as an outstanding engineer, but he had also invented machinery and perfected the processes for manufacturing "wire rope," just as the country became enthusiastic, with John's encouragement, about suspension bridges. There would also be the exploding demand for cables for the elevators that made America's skyscrapers possible.

Washington had followed his father into engineering, graduating in 1857 from Rensselaer Polytechnic Institute, then the premier engineering school in the country. But when the American Civil War came along, Washington volunteered, as did so many other patriotic young men, to fight to preserve the Union. If the other soldiers who served with the tall, blonde Roebling thought him some sort of elite who had grown up with the proverbial "silver spoon" you hear about, they were dead wrong. While his father, John, had acquired immense prestige and wealth, he shared little of it with his immediate family. Far from spoiling his son, the father imposed a childhood on Washington and his siblings far better described as Dickensian than as luxurious. His father's severe parsimony and frequent bouts of violent temper created an upbringing that frequently left Washington with no one to depend on but himself. It was a strange training ground for the man and soldier he would become, for while he was cynical and skeptical in his expectations of and experiences with the Union army, his faithful service to his fellow soldiers knew no bounds.

Like many other engineers in the army, Roebling was pressed into service as a scout, courier, mapmaker, and even one of our country's early "aeronauts," making balloon ascents to observe enemy positions and movements. In short, Washington Roebling became the sort of soldier who refused to allow his comrades to go somewhere that he would not go himself. In a war that had the Unionists often moving through enemy territory with faulty maps, men like Roebling rode out to find and chart roads, bridges, rivers, fords, and canals. But most important, he went out to find Confederates, an enemy with the distinct advantage of having soldiers who most often knew the territory in question intimately.

Again and again, all too frequently at the risk of his own life, Roebling went out, often alone in the dark of night, to search for the enemy. He pinpointed their positions and the nature of their fortifications or looked to discover the costly traps they set out for their blue-clad opponents. Roebling took pride in finding those hazards before his comrades walked into them. What inspired this kind of self-sacrifice in a man with Washington Roebling's background? It was a trait he would display again after the war when he engineered and tested the deep caissons sunk into the East River for the foundations of the engineering achievement of the nineteenth century, the Brooklyn Bridge. Testing the limits of what a man could safely endure while working in the caissons, Washington came near to dying from "caisson disease," more commonly known as "the bends." It condemned him to a pain-filled decade as an invalid, but his sacrifice, his refusal once again to send a man where he would not go himself, saved many of his workers from a similar fate. Much has been written about Washington Roebling, the bridge builder. Let us now consider Washington Roebling the soldier, the topographical engineer, scout, and courier, and, in all but name, the spy. He saw a great deal of the war and its many controversies and lived to tell about it in his own outspoken way.

At age eighty-six in 1922, Roebling told a correspondent asking for autobiographical information that during the Civil War, "through chance as much as merit, I was thrown into positions where campaigns and battles were planned and as often reduced to naught by an enemy who always had to be reckoned with. Perhaps I should have contributed to the avalanche of memoirs that have been printed and reprinted perpetuating the same errors and biased statements. To write a report of an action which shall be literally true as regards every phase of it is as impossible as [it is] inadvisable. It only creates enemies and, later on, jealousies, which are the curse of all wars."[1] But Roebling apparently did succumb to some extent, whatever his misgivings, to the temptation to write about the part he played in a number of battles and controversies. In 1898, he told another correspondent that he had written his recollections of the Battle of Chancellorsville[2] and a dozen others in which he had participated in significant ways. The elderly Roebling left the manuscript in his desk, unpublished, to be edited by his son after he was gone. His son, John A. Roebling II, for unknown reasons, did not fulfill that mission. Nor, to my knowledge, has the manuscript or any part of it been found.

In many ways, the disappearance of his military remembrances is a great loss, for while Washington Roebling became famous for building one of the wonders of the modern world, the Brooklyn Bridge, thanks to his and his brothers' business sagacity he also became a very wealthy man. He therefore was beholden to no man or institution, unlike so many of his fellow veterans who were writing about the war. Career military officers, politicians, or businessmen under obligation to the government were all unlikely to write critically of their former commanders, who held the reins of power for decades after the war, men such as President U. S. Grant and U.S. Army commanders in chief General William Tecumseh Sherman and General Philip Sheridan. While we don't have a military memoir from Washington Roebling's pen, we still, most fortunately, have many opportunities to experience the complete freedom with which he expressed himself, for he frequently corresponded with fellow veterans and historians in the years after the war. These candid letters, along with Roebling's wartime reports and correspondence, can in great part help make up for the unfortunate loss of his wartime memoir and, at the very least, give us an invaluable window into many of the most perplexing and frequently debated events of the war as seen through his astute eyes.

While Roebling is, for the most part, an articulate and literate subject, the reader should be aware that I have edited his writings to a certain extent. Where Roebling's meaning and intent are perfectly clear, I've avoided subjecting the reader to interruption with a *sic* and have corrected any misspelling or erroneous punctuation.

I

Gone for a Soldier

"WASHINGTON, YOU HAVE KICKED YOUR LEGS UNDER MY TABLE LONG enough, now you clear out this minute." Thus was twenty-four-year-old Washington Roebling propelled into military service by his father in early May 1861. The paterfamilias who caused Washington's sudden expulsion from his home was the brilliant, cantankerous engineer John A. Roebling, who, being well into his fifties, considered himself too old to follow the flag. But if the German immigrant had anything to do with it, a Roebling would be in the fight to preserve the Union, and that meant his firstborn son, Washington Augustus Roebling, a first-generation American citizen, was going to become a soldier. Ironically, young Washington had been contemplating just that calling but had hesitated to approach his autocratic father with the idea, fearing that he would reject any plan that took his son away from his many duties at his father's Trenton wire mill. In fact, Washington had been at his father's beck and call, as a worker at his factory or as his assistant on engineering projects, since his childhood. Seemingly controlling every aspect of his family's life, John had decided that his son would be an engineer just like him when Washington was still in his cradle. But for once, as far as the younger Roebling serving his country was concerned, John and Washington shared the same goal, though a less sudden and dramatic leave-taking would no doubt have been desirable.[1]

Both bitter and broke, Washington stopped at the nearby home of his father's mill superintendent, Charles Swan, who in many ways had acted as a surrogate father to him, and borrowed a few dollars that would get him on the next train out of Trenton to New York City. Roebling saw in the papers that the 9th New York still needed men, and after he'd been sworn in that evening and eaten a meal, he slept on the armory floor. We do not know

Roebling home and factory from a drawing by Washington Roebling.
Schuyler, *The Roeblings.*

whether Roebling had to convince the powers that be in the 9th New York that their designated artillery company was just the right place for him, but young Washington likely recognized that all the mathematics he had stuffed in his head while training at Rensselaer as an engineer might well be applied to such things as calculating trajectory or determining how far to elevate a muzzle to shoot over intervening men or barriers. And beyond getting to load and fire field artillery with his New Jersey mates, the challenge of providing effective fire likely had real attraction for the young engineer. Whatever the circumstances, Washington ended up in the 9th New York's Company K, its artillery unit, which left for Washington, DC, well before the rest of the regiment to acquire guns and the training to fire them. The company's members therefore missed the grand send-off New York City gave the men of the 9th as they left for the seat of war with their newly presented flags flying. There had been no grand send-off for the train that carried Company K's fledgling artillerymen to the nation's capital, and as the cars passed through Trenton, Roebling observed that his former home looked "silent and deserted." In a considerable understatement, he also commented, "Many stirring events passed before I saw it again."[2]

The newly minted artillerymen, most of them recruited from the New Jersey town of Rahway, had the thrill of seeing Abraham Lincoln on their arrival in Washington, when the president came out onto the rear portico of the White House to give a brief welcome to the incoming troops. The recruits had yet to be sworn in to the U.S. service and were free to roam about and see the sights of the city, but since young Roebling had traveled rather extensively with his engineer father, and the Roeblings had friends in the city, perhaps he

John Roebling.
Brooklyn Museum.

viewed the landmarks of Washington with rather less awe than the Rahway boys did. By May 30, the company was sent for artillery training on 14th Street at Camp Cameron. On arrival, Company K saw off the thirty-day men of the 7th New York State Militia, inheriting their wall tents with nice wooden floors, some mattresses, and even some wash basins. While the conditions may have been "posh" compared to what lay ahead, the men nonetheless got their first taste of regulated army life, up at dawn with a long list of rules to follow and at least a few duties to perform, until taps brought silence to the camp at 9:30 p.m. The fledging artillerymen chaffed at this seeming delay in the beginning of their active service, and Roebling observed that several months were "wasted" at Camp Cameron while they waited for their guns and training before they could rejoin the 9th New York Volunteers. As one of his fellow artillerymen commented while at Camp Cameron, there was "nothing much to do in the day time but eat our meals and write letters." Likely while in Washington, Private Roebling made a notebook, a sort of Artillery 101, regarding the training he received at Camp Cameron, laying down the positions and responsibilities of each eight-member team servicing a gun, as well as the basic principles regarding the most effective use of artillery and the all-important cooperation between artillery and infantry. His carefully written artillery notebook indicates that Private Roebling had his eye on the number one spot on each gun's eight-member team: the man who got to direct the gun's fire. Then, too, he acknowledged that the only way to advance in the artillery was if one of the officers left.[3]

The number of artillery units pouring into the capital far outpaced the number of guns the government had available, but eventually Company K's long wait at Camp Cameron was rewarded with two small, disappointing pieces, "both old and almost unserviceable." But while the artillerymen waited restlessly for equipment, the insistent drumbeat of an actual fighting war brought men of the North and South closer to inevitable collision. The fledgling entity calling itself the Confederate States of America funneled the many men rallying to its cause to the two areas deemed likely routes for anticipated Northern aggression: the Shenandoah Valley and the strategically important railroad terminus at Manassas Junction with its two crucial railroads. General Pierre Toutant Beauregard oversaw the burgeoning defense at Manassas, busily preparing defensive positions. Beauregard dreamed of destroying the Federal army that would come to confront his forces before going on to capture Washington. To the northwest, the less charismatic but more experienced General Joseph E. Johnston commanded a lesser army charged with guarding the Shenandoah Valley, the Confederacy's breadbasket and the easiest way for a Unionist aggressor to get at the Confederacy's new capital at Richmond. Meanwhile, the Union's answer to its countrymen's rebellion was General Irvin McDowell, a protégé of General Winfield Scott, commander of the Union's forces. Despite McDowell's protests that they were rushing into war with an army of untrained men, by July 16, for better or worse, the Federal advance began with McDowell's force, as predicted, headed toward a then unimaginable fate on the banks of Bull Run. As a second part of the Federals' two-pronged offensive, General Robert Patterson, another, much older protégé of Scott's, was expected to fulfill his somewhat less than clear assignment of assaulting Johnston or, if that proved problematic, at least holding Johnston's ten thousand or so soldiers away from McDowell's impending attack on Beauregard.[4]

In the weeks before First Bull Run, General Scott sent the clear message that he wanted movement, not excuses, and discounted any impediments his commanders' might be perceiving. But these orders urging action were copiously interspersed with expressions of Scott's desire that his commanders

General Winfield Scott.
Library of Congress.

exercise extreme caution, allowing no possibility of failure or embarrassing missteps. It isn't surprising that Patterson feared his first confrontations with Johnston's force, which, ironically, turned into nothing more than the rebels abandoning Harpers Ferry and ceding it without bloodshed to the Federals in mid-June. Patterson hoped that by intimidation he had forced the enemy into avoiding an armed confrontation with him over Harpers Ferry. But when General Scott stripped Patterson of his regular troops, leaving him with green three-month regiments who would soon be going home, it did nothing to keep Patterson's spirits up. Nor did it help when Scott removed Ambrose Burnside's Rhode Island infantry and artillery, leaving Patterson with no batteries. And in response to Patterson's extreme lack of transportation to supply his force, Washington instructed Patterson to be "self-reliant," despite the unlikelihood that he could rent wagons from unfriendly locals. In mid-June,

General Robert Patterson.
Library of Congress.

Congressman John Sherman, brother to another who was on a rocky road to military fame, wrote to Secretary of War Simon Cameron about the demoralization within Patterson's command. He attributed this not to any fault of Patterson but to Washington's withdrawal of all the resources needed to do what he was being asked to do: assault the enemy and/or prevent Johnston's force from joining Beauregard at Manassas. In this atmosphere of continuing uncertainty regarding missions and possible outcomes, when Company K at last rejoined its regiment, the 9th New York, its men found themselves heading for General Charles P. Stone's brigade, General James S. Negley's division, in General Patterson's command, the Department of Pennsylvania, which confronted, to some extent, Johnston's Army of the Shenandoah. It was General Stone's assignment to guard a number of fords and ferries on the Potomac below Leesburg. Meanwhile, General McDowell's Army of Northeastern Virginia began a slow approach toward Beauregard's Army of the Potomac. No one, least of all these fledgling artillerymen, knew what lay ahead and what would come of the impending collision between the armed might of the North and South.[5]

On July 9, 1861, Company K finally caught up with the 9th New York at Martinsburg, Virginia. Struggling to maintain control over Harpers Ferry, General Patterson had turned his efforts to securing the surrounding area and protecting the Baltimore and Ohio (B&O) Railroad, a key to keeping essential Federal communications open to the west. With his regulars and the Rhode Island contingent of his command having been taken for what General Scott described as the urgent defense of Washington, Patterson began deploying what was left of his troops to towns outside Harpers Ferry. As it happened, many of the citizens of Martinsburg were delighted when the Federals occupied the town on July 4 after it was abandoned by the rebels, for Martinsburg was the only town of any size in the Shenandoah Valley that had opposed secession during that state's recent referendum. The Unionists had replaced a punitive and costly occupation by Stonewall Jackson that had seen the destruction and confiscation of much of the rolling stock of the B&O railway hub there. But the artillerymen had little time to enjoy the friendly atmosphere of Martinsburg, for at a council of war Patterson's subordinates proved uniformly unhappy and uneasy with their current position. Thus, on July 14, the 9th and Company K, with their two guns of doubtful value, joined a movement of Patterson's forces toward Harpers Ferry, passing through Bunker Hill, Virginia, on the way. It was with some apprehension that the men of the 9th New York advanced, for, in that mysterious way in which rumor sometimes based on fact travels through an army, Company K had gotten wind that there might be a sizable enemy force on the route they were traveling. One of Scott's spies, Captain John Newton, had reported to Patterson that General Jackson was at Bunker Hill with forty-five hundred men, twenty-four guns, and a large cavalry force. And when contemplating what might be their first experience with the enemy, did that Southern town's name strike the raw troops as rather too reminiscent of that costly and bloody battle of yesteryear? In any event, their fears proved mostly baseless, and after a one-day stay at Bunker Hill passed, Roebling and Company K continued on, unopposed, to the strongly secessionist town of Charlestown. There they got quite a different reception from the women, who taunted the artillerymen with promises of what the Southerners would do to them. Not this time, however, for, as the artillerymen discovered (no doubt to varying degrees of relief or frustration), the enemy was retreating as fast as the Unionists advanced.[6]

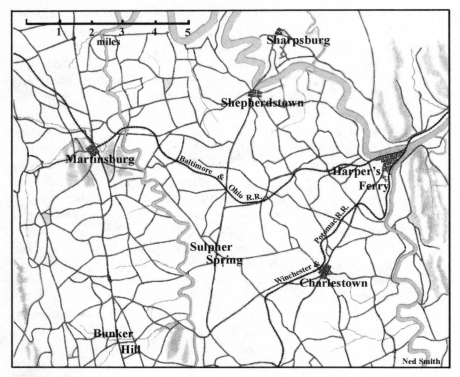

Serving with Patterson.
Adapted from plate LXIX, 1 OR Atlas.

In mid-July, it seemed like Patterson's Federals were trying to march off in all directions at once, and as the 9th New York made another march (in this case, a soon-aborted one toward Winchester), Roebling commented that the rebels were "running with alacrity." He also shared the rumors flying that Federal cavalry were killing large numbers of the foe. The wholesale slaughter of hapless fleeing rebels was somewhat wishful thinking on Roebling's part, for, as had happened when the Federals were entering Bunker Hill, Confederate cavalry provided slight resistance, resulting in one enemy killed and five taken prisoner. But it was hardly the wholesale slaughter Roebling was contemplating. Quite the contrary: Rather than confronting Patterson, the Confederates were preparing for something quite different. The 1st Virginia Cavalry, led by the soon to be famous J. E. B. Stuart, would be screening General Johnston's July 18 removal from Patterson's front.

So how did exaggerated estimates of Johnston's troop strength, sometimes inflated three to four times above what the general actually had in hand, come about? One source was one of Scott's spies, single operatives and a team led by Captain John Newton, who was responsible for the report that placed Stuart at Bunker Hill with a sizable force. Despite these rather dire reports of the enemy, Lieutenant General Scott nonetheless, periodically but with many cautious caveats and no direct orders, encouraged Patterson to attack Johnston's force. Just what, Patterson queried Scott at one point, would an attack on Johnston accomplish except perhaps to drive him to the very place they least wanted him to go, to join Beauregard? Patterson, in his June 28, 1861, response to Scott's query about whether he had crossed the river to confront Johnston, reminded his general in chief that he had no artillery and no cavalry, but if Scott wanted him to attack, he would do so cheerfully upon receiving Scott's explicit order to that effect. Keeping a close eye on Patterson at this time, Confederate commander Johnston reported that he recognized what Patterson tried next, a sidling to the Federal left, for just what it was: a Federal feint attempting to glue Johnston in place while McDowell attacked Beauregard at Manassas. It didn't work. But, in a way, Patterson did surprise Johnston when the rebel commander finally removed the bulk of his army from Patterson's front, for Unionists made no attempt to follow Johnston as expected.

In the next chapter, we'll consider why. Some very astute Civil War scholars have spent a lifetime considering the First Battle of Bull Run, and there is still so much to weigh, speculate about, and argue over regarding the momentous first major collision between the green armies of the North and South. But our mission is to follow the fates of Washington Roebling and the fledgling artillerymen of Company K, who remained with Patterson while the flawed drama of First Bull Run played out.[7]

2

For Want of a Wagon . . .

SERVING WITH GENERAL ROBERT PATTERSON'S ARMY IN JUNE AND JULY 1861, the men and horses of the 9th New York, including their artillery company, Company K, were starving. While any organization for supplying large armies in the field with food and forage clearly did not yet exist, there was an additional problem: no transportation. Then, too, the eyes of the military leadership were focused on the movements and needs of Irvin McDowell's army, which apparently had to come first. But even McDowell's army, begging for wagons, was trying to hire them from the local population—as if the hostile locals would go along with that. Not only were rebels at heart unlikely to cooperate with this perceived invading horde, but only a fool would let a wily Yankee make off with his farm wagon![1]

As Washington Roebling wrote on July 19 to his favorite sister, Elvira, from Charlestown, Virginia, "Dinner will be one hard cracker (Uncle Sam's pies) & a piece of salt pork." On July 14, Company K had marched three miles toward Harpers Ferry from Martinsburg, before they were to turn around and go back. Rumor had it that the reported July 11 victory of General George B. McClellan's forces at Rich Mountain in western Virginia had put a stop to Patterson's movement. The collective hypothesis was the mistaken belief that victorious McClellan was going to come and do what Patterson, it seemed, couldn't: confront and control General Joseph Johnston. But before long, the New York artillerymen were again on the move, this time, they believed, toward Winchester, though, as Roebling observed, no one really knew where, and an uncertain destination was about the only thing that added charm to a march. All pinned their hopes on going to Winchester, where they'd be "less likely to starve than in this miserable little hole," as Roebling referred to Charlestown. But for better or worse, instead of having their first brush with the rebels, Company K was stopped well before Winchester. It's hard to say which was the

Washington Roebling, Company K, 9th New York Volunteer Infantry (6th New York Independent Battery).
Rensselaer Polytechnic Institute Library, Special Collections.

greater disappointment: another denied crack at the enemy or being kept from Winchester and its promise of food.[2]

The artillerymen's short march took them through a region of devastated wheat fields, the crops rotting for lack of anyone to harvest them. In fact, Roebling observed there were no men, "only women and niggers." While it's disappointing to find the subject of your work (in this case, Washington Roebling) flinging the disparaging epithet "nigger" with great frequency, there's no temptation on my part to ignore or modify the facts, as one Roebling biographer did by changing the word to "negro" without letting on that he had done so. It is admittedly hard to reconcile Washington's habitual use of the word with a man whose life often demonstrated a remarkably well-developed belief that he had definite responsibilities for the well-being of his fellow men. And despite having been brought up in a family reputed to have been staunchly antislavery, Roebling's fellow feeling did not extend to the contrabands and servant class he encountered while in the army. As Randall Kennedy points out in *Nigger: The Strange Career of a Troublesome Word*, the use of the word began well before the Civil War, but there's little doubt that by the mid-1800s it was meant to be pejorative. In Roebling's encounters with former slaves in the coming months, one is unable to determine whether his demonstrated distaste for contrabands is merely racist or a reaction to his first brush with the population he saw as woefully uneducated and unskilled.[3]

In his letter to Elvira, Washington recounted the 9th New York's brief stay in the sorry village of Bunker Hill, described as three houses and three pig pens, in order, as they believed, to await the arrival of McClellan. There were still plenty of rumors about large bodies of rebels in the neighborhood, but they soon gave way to bored artillerymen casting about for something of interest in the ruined landscape. Unlike its Massachusetts namesake, the town had no battles in its past, but it did have one claim to fame. Before his soul went marching on, John Brown had been hung in a field in the town, now a cornfield next to Company K's encampment. The site of the hanging was marked by cornstalks, and pieces of the gallows were available for purchase at $1 a pound. Perhaps such local color took their mind off their hunger, for although they had been provided with six days' rations when they left Martinsburg for the second time, the boys ate them up in four days, and then they starved. Roebling also said that he hadn't once taken off the clothes he had left Washington in and was sleeping on the ground in a blanket in the open. He suggested that such a life was very healthy if you had plenty to eat, which they did not.[4]

The fact that the troops had devoured their six days of rations in four days wasn't the only reason for deprivation within the ranks. The great lack of supplies for Patterson's army was generated for the most part by the continuing scarcity of wagons and horses to haul what provisions were available. Nor was there sufficient forage for the horses, of which twenty-six tons were needed daily. The problem was severe enough that, Patterson informed Winfield Scott, it was bringing his army nearly to a standstill. Among the many other supplies lacking were shoes, with many of his three-month men barefoot and even without pants, Patterson reported. While addressing the collapse of his overwhelmed supply lines, Patterson also responded to Scott's warning that Johnston was reportedly about to make an assault on Patterson's exposed line of communication. Patterson asked for reinforcements that would allow him to transfer his depot to Harpers Ferry and eliminate the strain and risk of his now lengthy line of supply back to Hagerstown, Maryland. Into this pickle of want and frustration Scott dropped the suggestion that, if strong enough, Patterson could attack Johnston early the next week, or at least make

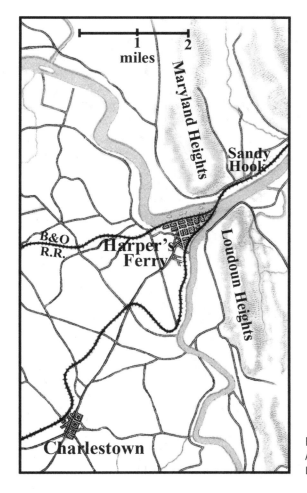

Harpers Ferry.
Adapted and enlarged from plate
LXIX, 1 OR Atlas.

a demonstration. Interestingly, Scott also expressed concerns that, if Johnston should retreat in force to Manassas, it might be too hazardous for Patterson to follow him.[5]

From both Bunker Hill and Charlestown, on July 16 and 17, respectively, Patterson had also reminded Scott that the term of service of a large part of his force was expiring in the next few days, and it was Patterson's opinion that the three-month men, half starved, unpaid, barefoot, and without a darn thing to brag about when they got home, would lay down their arms the very day their terms expired. Patterson again requested reinforcement by three-year troops, but Scott responded instead with a directive not to let the enemy "amuse and delay you with a small force" lest they reinforce General P. T. Beauregard. Scott chided Patterson for not attacking Johnston at Winchester, to which Patterson responded that he had indeed advanced to Bunker Hill and carried out Scott's alternative suggestion, to demonstrate toward Winchester. But, Patterson reported, though he had hoped their approach toward the enemy would inspire the three-month regiments to agree to extend their stay by a week or ten days, he was generally pleading in vain. While three regiments agreed to stay for another ten days, Patterson made preparations to send the rest of those who wanted no further part of army life home to be mustered out. Another response from the army's hierarchy came on July 19, with General Order No. 46 announcing Major General Patterson's discharge from the service on July 27. General Nathaniel Banks, who would be relieved of his duties in the Department of Maryland, would assume command of the army formerly under Patterson, which would now be called the Army of the Shenandoah. So Banks, not McClellan, came to take over from the beleaguered Patterson, while McClellan, taking credit for General William Rosecrans's victory at Rich Mountain and riding high in the administration's estimates, was called to Washington to see to the defense of the capital. One can't help but wonder how much of this toxic situation was generally known to those troops left at Charlestown just days before the impending battle at Bull Run, but Roebling commented at the time that everybody was glad of the change in command. Did the rank and file, wearied by weeks of seemingly aimless marching, no chance at confronting the enemy, and severe shortages of food and material, place all the blame on Patterson?[6]

Many years later, Roebling, with the war well behind him, looked back and remembered. He'd had years to consider the events of those first tumultuous months of the war and many opportunities to talk and correspond with other veterans. It is clear that Roebling placed the responsibility for what happened with Patterson and at Bull Run primarily on General Scott, with his ambiguous orders and the questionable intelligence he supplied to Patterson, which imparted falsely daunting reports on the enemy's strength. Scott's directives, never the direct orders Patterson requested, vacillated, with the lieutenant general sometimes encouraging aggression, then caution, but clearly indicating his own unwillingness to take risks or responsibility. Last of all, and perhaps most important, Scott, by surrendering to groundless fears of an impending rebel attack on Washington in the weeks before the coming collision at Bull Run, stripped Patterson of the only reliable troops he had at a critical time. Years afterward, Washington wrote with bitterness regarding the Federal advance on Bunker Hill, ten miles short of Winchester, "Gen.

Patterson had secret orders in his pocket from Gen. Scott, not to attack on any account; some of his troops might get hurt which might impair their efficiency to protect Washington. So we carefully crawled towards Winchester and when in sight of it, turned around and went back to Harper's Ferry. (The wicked flee where no man pursueth.) Simultaneously Johns[t]on went to Bull Run and defeated McDowell, which the United States richly deserved."[7]

Whatever upheavals were taking place in Washington and various army headquarters, on his personal front, Roebling was thrown bodily into the battle to feed and clothe his own contingent of troops serving with Patterson, for while at the unloved Charlestown, he was appointed commissary for Company K. While attending to acquiring provisions and seeing that each man's ration was weighed exactly and given out, he was excused from guard duty but retained his position on his gun. When on the march, it was his responsibility to stay up all night to supervise the preparatory cooking, and he expressed a new appreciation for the difficulties of the quartermaster's job by suggesting that it was next in line of difficulty to the commanding general's! While remarking on a soldier whose head was shaved in preparation for his drumming out for stealing a watch, Washington also said that several of his own hungry comrades had come near being shot after they were wrongfully accused of stealing sheep. But, perhaps inspired by his own weary nights of duty, he expressed pity for another soldier who was drummed out for sleeping at his post. If food was still in short supply, water was another problem for Company K. Roebling said that things were so strict that one needed a pass from the captain to get a drink of water, remarking that the artillery units were the worst off since they were always stationed on the highest ground, where water was scarcest.[8]

A much-needed distraction from thirst and empty bellies was provided by a copy of the *New York Herald* sent from home that reported a so-called battle at Bunker Hill in which their forces were said to have been engaged. Roebling commented, "It was all news to us and was read amid the greatest laughter." It duly reported that upon entering Bunker Hill, George Thomas's Federal cavalry, accompanied by a Rhode Island battery, had met some slight resistance from a body of Confederate horsemen. But this article was reporting a much more dramatic encounter with Thomas and the Rhode Islanders, who "opened with powerful effect with shot, shell and grape," speedily sending J. E. B. Stuart's rebel horsemen on their way out of the hamlet. Roebling and the men of the 9th New York would be treated to additional, likely imaginary, tales of derring-do by the Rhode Island Artillery.

Washington Roebling eagerly awaited letters and more papers from home, and with the company's ever-changing position, knowing which address would get his mail to him in a timely fashion was a challenge. Beyond letters, he was also eagerly awaiting a package from home bringing him a pair of shoes, for he, like many of his fellow soldiers, was almost barefoot. When the promised footwear failed to arrive, he quipped in a letter to his brother, "You must have forgotten to pray for their safe delivery." Roebling's references to religion were often irreverent, and he referred to himself as a "conceited skeptic."[9]

At the end of July, Company K was shifted to Weaverton, Maryland, and then to Pine Hill near Harpers Ferry, bringing it into contact with that Rhode Island battery that had seen a far different side of the war than the New York artillerymen had experienced so far. The Rhode Island battery had organized early and was among the first units to arrive in the capital, and Washington, short on defense, was more than glad to see them. Visits from the president, members of Congress, foreign dignitaries, and cabinet members were every-day occurrences for this battery. Accompanied by the ever-popular William Sprague IV, governor of Rhode Island, who was wooing the famous belle of Washington, Kate Chase, the Rhode Island battery got a generous share of the capital's attention, where it was enthusiastically feted and fed. Though the Rhode Islanders had initially been posted with Patterson, with the scare that the rebels were going to try to capture Washington, that same alarm that saw the regulars pulled away from Patterson also saw the Rhode Island bat-tery removed as well. Patterson bemoaned the loss of the Rhode Island guns, claiming they had been his only effective battery. So while Roebling's untried Company K sat out the dark days of Manassas sidelined with Patterson's army, the Rhode Island guns ended up in the thick of things at Bull Run, the only volunteer artillery to lend assistance to the nine regular army batteries at First Bull Run.[10]

Despite the disastrous results of that battle, at the end of which the Rhode Islanders lost their guns, the artillerymen remained apparently unchastened, for they entertained Company K with accounts of their sterling debut in combat. The now battle-scarred veterans gave their no doubt rapt audience, the untested artillerymen of Company K, the usual scenes of such prolonged rapid fire that the guns were too hot to touch for hours afterward. There were recriminations about how, if they had just had proper support and enough ammunition, things would have ended far differently. But the Rhode Islanders got quite carried away with their tales of derring-do when they proclaimed how much better their battery had performed in a tight spot in comparison with the four rifled and two smoothbore guns of Charles Griffin's West Point Battery. Telling how much more accurate their own fire had been, the novice gunners gave short shrift to what most historians concede are among the most vaunted artillerymen of the war and their famous fight at Henry's Hill. The novice gunners proclaimed that, unlike their own accurate fire, which had silenced two of the rebel's batteries, the West Pointers' shots consistently fell a half mile short of the enemy! Then, too, the Rhode Islanders were undoubtedly cheerful when the guns they had lost were replaced by those of their state's three-month battery, which left for home.[11]

By the end of July, the three-month men had gone home, and the five to six thousand men who constituted Banks's newly named Army of the Shenandoah were experiencing some anxiety over their reduced numbers. The members of Company K, who had signed on for three years, remained at their post. Rumor once more proclaimed the proximity of large bodies of the enemy in the area, and Roebling and his fellows felt their vulnerable position well in advance of the main Federal force. They suspected that the enemy was likely

Wrecked locomotive, Harpers Ferry.
Harper's Weekly, July 20, 1861, artist Alfred Wordsworth Thompson.

to try to take advantage of the Unionists' feeble numbers in the weeks before they could be reinforced with new recruits. Their new commander, General Banks, was apparently apprehensive as well, having for safety's sake sent what baggage the army had to the rear. The all-too-precious wagons sought safer ground by lumbering over rough tracks and crossing the Potomac at the wholly inadequate ford at Williamsport, Maryland. Roebling, who was still fighting the good fight of trying to feed the hungry troops of his company, had traveled to Sandy Hook, a mile east of Harpers Ferry, in search of rations. But in trying to return, he found the route completely blocked by the retreating wagons. He finally arrived back with Company K in time to join his battery, whose turn it was to man the picket line with their two guns. A contingent of regular cavalry accompanied them and patrolled the area for five miles around, lending some semblance of security to the battery's advanced position.[12]

But one senses that, for Washington Roebling at this time, other aspects of being a member of a battery were beginning to take the shine off the idea of being an artilleryman. Commenting that they had ten times more work to do than the infantry, what with always having to mount their guns on the highest hill, he described the awful job of getting their guns and caissons up to and into position on Maryland Heights opposite Harpers Ferry. Getting there, almost on top of Blue Ridge, required ten horses to pull the guns up a road with an angle of twenty degrees. Then, too, rising at daybreak made for a long day, and he observed that hardly a man even knew what day it was. And it seemed like a year since he had left home, rather than few months. With this increasingly jaded eye, Roebling noticed a party removing an old bridge, piece by piece, from a nearby river bed. He had spent many hours with his engineer father, assisting him in the planning and building of bridges, so there's nothing surprising about this sort of activity catching his attention. But there was the added novelty of a wrecked locomotive down in the river, one of nearly fifty that the rebels had destroyed in Harpers Ferry, Martinsburg, and the surrounding area. And as he told his friend and mentor Charles Swan, manager of the Roebling factory back in Trenton, timbers were arriving for trestle work to begin. One is tempted to say that Roebling's distraction by this scene of bridge building was an omen of things to come. In the months ahead bridges would once again play a big part in Washington Roebling's life, and in the not too distant future they would take him away from his life with the guns of Company K for good.[13]

3

Seeing the Elephant

With the reduction in federal numbers in general robert Patterson's former division and a belated recognition of the woeful lack of supplies and equipment the remaining troops possessed, someone in the Federal army's hierarchy decided that in order to hold onto Harpers Ferry, something would have to be done to correct these problems. It wasn't until August 1 that Company K received another four guns, bringing them up to a full battery of six, which would require doubling the number of men manning them. Was it a bit of loneliness that caused Washington Roebling to tell his friend at home, Charles Swan, that he hoped some of new men coming into the company would be Trenton men? The battery's hilltop posting was near a rocky outcrop that the locals aptly called Buzzard Rock; there Roebling had been watching the less than cheery display of a great number of turkey buzzards circling overhead. The heat and dust up there were, unfortunately, intense, for they'd had to cut down all the trees to allow a clean sweep for the guns, resulting in no shade. But by good fortune, a spring of ice-cold water came out of the mountainside near their artillerymen's camp. Writing to his sister Elvira, Washington said that even if one could find a cool place to lie down, an army of red ants attacked immediately. Another considerable cause of discomfort was an outbreak of chicken pox among the men, though unfortunately, he quipped, with no chickens. The boys, he said, joked that their itchy rashes were actually bristles trying to erupt from their having eaten so much salt pork. That highly contagious disease may have felled Roebling for a week, for there was a noticeable gap in his correspondence, later explained by his having spent time in the division's hospital. Being sent home to recover was hardly an option for him, since his autocratic father, who embraced every hydropathic craze that came along, wouldn't allow a regular doctor to treat anyone in his house. Meanwhile, though some of Company K's men were

General Charles Stone.
Library of Congress.

getting short furloughs to go home, Washington commented that he wasn't going to pursue that, since his tentmates had given him a haircut so short that he looked like a man they had recently seen drummed out of the army. Roebling commented that he wouldn't want to make a bad impression on the young lady friend Elvira had staying with her "or any other visitor who may bless our usually deserted house with their presence." It seems likely that, beyond a bad haircut, Washington was not ready to confront his father, for though he was corresponding with John Roebling, he was not likely to forget that his father had ordered him out of his home rather than discuss the subject of volunteering for the army with him.[1]

The uneventful days while their force remained at Harpers Ferry had been, Roebling declared in retrospect, an exercise in being "fortified against nobody." And as Roebling remembered it, the next movement, the withdrawal of General Nathaniel Banks's forces on July 28, had seemed as if they had "retired for no reason." "[They then] crawled through Maryland to Poolesville ostensibly to guard the fords of the upper Potomac." In fact, General Winfield Scott was once again playing it safe, urging caution upon Banks until the newly recruited three-year men could be brought in and trained, a directive Banks embraced. As the fall approached, the Federals wanted to keep what little artillery they had at Harpers Ferry; thus Roebling and the Company K battery parted ways with the 9th New York Volunteers, who prepared to accompany General Benjamin Butler's expedition to North Carolina. Officially detached from their parent regiment, the battery also acquired a new sergeant when Washington Roebling won his longed-for promotion. The batteries remained with their brigade commander, Charles Stone, who on August 3 won his own promotion to the rank of brigadier general. The newly designated 6th New York Independent Battery, as Company K came to be known, followed Stone into his new assignment with Major General George B. McClellan, who by August 15 was commanding the force now designated the Army of the Potomac. Roebling would later remember that, relatively speaking, the battery's early days in the service had been more like "a picnic" than a war, but that was about to change. However demoralizing the Federal experience at Bull Run had been, the New York battery no doubt felt sorely its having been sidelined with Patterson. But the 6th New York Independent Battery's upcoming introduction to combat was going to be a tough one. You might even say it more than made up for missing Manassas.[2]

In the fall of 1861, McClellan, as commander of the newly organized Army of the Potomac, maintained that his green troops simply weren't ready for combat. As Roebling would later remember, the Federals had the opportunity to spend a little time watching the enemy through glasses parading at Leesburg. But in October, after Stone reported to McClellan that his troops were now ready for more than just watching, McClellan saw a low-risk opportunity to mollify the apparently forgetful "On to Richmond" crowd. Believing the rebels were about to abandon Leesburg anyway, McClellan gave orders for several movements, feints, or reconnaissances in force on the enemy on his front that might push things along for a bloodless "victory." Stone's division, made up of mostly raw recruits with little training, received the grandiose designation "corps of observation." It consisted of three brigades, with the 6th New York Independent Battery assigned to the corps's 3rd Brigade, known as the California Brigade. There were, however, precious few Californians in it, for most of the men had been recruited from Pennsylvania and New York. The brigade was under the command of Colonel Edward Baker, a Mexican

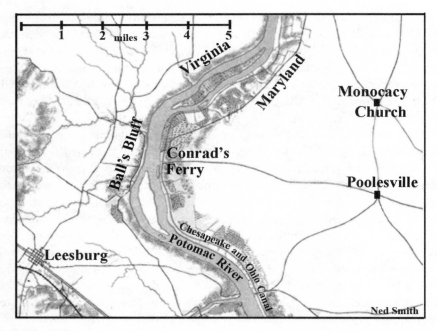

Ball's Bluff.
Adapted from Plate VII, OR Atlas.

War veteran and sitting senator from Oregon. Most important, Baker was a close friend of President Abraham Lincoln, so close that one of Lincoln's sons had been named after him. That relationship would make the reporting and interpretation of the role Baker played and where the real responsibilities lay more than a little difficult in the controversial days ahead.[3]

On October 20, McClellan ordered Stone to investigate just what rebel force lay opposite him across the river with the idea that an advance by a division ten miles beyond Stone's, under the command of General George McCall, might be able to push the rebels out of Leesburg. Leesburg was an objective much to be desired, for possession would give the Federals control of the Potomac from Washington to Harpers Ferry. And hadn't there been reports that the Confederates had abandoned Leesburg only to mysteriously reappear? Roebling apparently had been sent on reconnaissance, for he reported having interrogated two contrabands he captured on the other side of the river, who said that the rebels had left but returned again after three days. This disappearing act was the result of a restless rebel commander abandoning Leesburg, only to be told to get on back there. Stone, perhaps releasing the pent-up frustration of months of fruitless inactivity, swung into action, organizing what McClellan hoped would be a convincing feint toward the enemy across the river, one several miles away that would distract the enemy's attention from McCall's simultaneous advance. Stone shelled the rebels and even loaded troops into boats at what was locally known as Conrad's Ferry, sending them to an island in the river between the Federal position on the eastern shore of the river and that of the enemy on the western shore, with its towering cliff known as Ball's Bluff. For all his efforts, Stone was unable to provoke any response from the seemingly invisible enemy, and becoming more determined to learn something of the foe's position, he sent a small scouting party across the river in the night, which delivered a flawed report of a small rebel camp. Stone, emboldened by the supposed diminutive nature of the enemy's encampment and feeling secure in having McCall's division to call on if need be, ordered a raid across the river for the next night. With all the great benefits of hindsight, it is a scenario all too reminiscent of the first Federal attempts at reconnaissance prior to First Bull Run, when little or no rebel reply to their probing left Unionist commanders puzzled. Lack of an immediate rebel response resulted in many wrong assumptions, and when it provoked a more aggressive prodding by the Federals, it all too often ended in disaster.[4]

Therefore, three to four hundred untested soldiers, some carrying less-than-adequate smoothbore muskets, crossed the Potomac, which recent rains had running high and swift. They'd only been able to locate three boats with limited capacity, necessitating many trips. After climbing single file to the top of Ball's Bluff on a rough path, they found nothing. The report of a rebel camp proved false, and when the raid's leader relayed his disappointing discovery to Stone, orders came back to press on toward that most desirable Confederate stronghold at Leesburg. It didn't take long for the rebels to notice enemy activity at Ball's Bluff, and it was the hapless Federals' misfortune that the enemy brigade commander who would soon be confronting them was the aggressive, experienced Colonel Nathan Evans, who had already passed his test in combat at First Bull Run. But when the Unionists were at first confronted by an inferior number of the enemy, the raiders made the fatal decision to stand their ground. Though they could have withdrawn, trailing back down the cliff and crossing in shifts back to their own side of the river, their commander chose to stay with his back to the cliff and send word to Stone. Meanwhile, Colonel Edward Baker's brigade had earlier been placed in a position of support on the eastern shore of the river, and upon receiving no orders, Baker grew impatient. Before Stone received word from his raiding party, Baker arrived at Stone's headquarters, and before he left, he had secured Stone's written orders to cross the river and take command of the operation at Ball's Bluff. Stone was also ignorant of the fact that one of the supports he was counting on, McCall's division, had been withdrawn beyond reach by McClellan. Had Stone, having no reason as yet to be apprehensive, been intimidated by the famous senator, a close friend of the president, prompting him to give command of the mission to the impetuous Baker? Whatever the case, Sergeant Roebling and the 6th New York Independent Battery would be accompanying Baker on his mission. It was their misfortune that this, their first experience in combat, is still remembered as one of more tragic and controversial events of what would prove to be a long and eventful war.[5]

On October 21, 1861, Baker had nearly sixteen hundred troops to deploy against the enemy, his own brigade, the original raiders, still across the river, and the guard for a nearby ford that was to have been an escape route should retreat be necessary. The latter, in their eagerness to assist their comrades, crossed the river without orders and instead helped seal their fate by failing in their mission to protect what proved to be a vital ford. As for the crossing they were utilizing, Roebling would later write that its only advantage was its impracticality, making it one that the enemy would never dream they would try to use. Though Baker had been able to find one other boat, his troops' crossing of nearly a quarter mile of water was painfully slow. And while a scow had been brought over from a nearby canal, the Rhode Island Artillery's having pushed ahead of Roebling's guns proved to be a lucky thing, as he would later remember, for none of the Rhode Islanders or their guns returned. But at last it was the 6th New York's turn to cross to the island, and the guns were taken down the steep bank of the river by hand and loaded with the horses on a twenty-by-eight-foot scow found in the nearby canal. The scow had to be poled over, as a makeshift rope of tied-together corral ropes kept breaking. On reaching the island, the men hitched the horses up to take the guns to face the Virginia shore, where they came under heavy enemy fire. In waiting to cross, infantry received preference, and Roebling remembered witnessing the Tammany Regiment's initially "showing the white feather" when they refused to cross. Roebling and the 6th New York were among the many who made it only partway across the river to the intervening island, and after Colonel Baker, the leader of the hapless expedition, was killed, the hopelessness of the Federal position at the top of Ball's Bluff, with no viable means of retreat, became clear. The Ball's Bluff debacle resulted in less than half of Baker's force making it back across the river alive. All four of the Federal boats sank or were damaged and floated away, and many of the Federals died, either shot by the

Death of Colonel Edward D. Baker.
Currier & Ives, Library of Congress.

rebels at the top of the bluff or drowned trying to swim to the island or the opposite bank.[6]

Their position on the island was far from a refuge, for they came under heavy fire from the rebels at the top of Ball's Bluff. Roebling had the first of many close calls during his service when a bullet hit the pommel of his saddle and was deflected by a brass fitting from its intended path toward his body. When it became clear they weren't going to cross to the Virginia shore, and as the number of New York artillerymen being shot down mounted, the battery withdrew to the center of the island near a brick house being used as a hospital. Roebling in his later account refused to speak of what he saw there. The island soon became crowded with soldiers, those already on the island joined by the dazed survivors of the fight at the top of the bluff and the disaster of a near impossible retreat. Hundreds of bodies of the less fortunate who tried to swim to safety floated in the river, with rain adding to the already fast-flowing waters. When word came to withdraw during the night, the exhausted men of the battery hauled the three guns they had brought to the island up onto the Maryland shore through knee-deep mud.[7]

At the time, Roebling seemed to see the battle for what it was—"The whole concern is another Bull Run affair, of smaller proportions, but far bloodier as regards the numbers engaged"—but he was mistaken in his assessment of what would happen next: "The leaves will soon be off the trees and then such things will not happen again at least for this season." Nor could he imagine the fate of his brigade commander, General Stone. Believing that Stone had had pressing business with his command three or four miles away at Edwards Ferry, Roebling wrote, "If Gen. Stone had been present it would not have happened. . . . I guess Stone will be Banks' fighting general." The disaster at Ball's Bluff led to the formation of a congressional investigative body, the Joint Committee on the Conduct of the War, with its first business being whom to hold responsible for both Bull Run and Ball's Bluff. Within months, General Stone would be charged with treason and imprisoned for six months without trial or legal representation. While there is evidence that Baker and officers in his command made any number of mistakes, many were reluctant to place any blame on the president's dead, impetuous friend. Baker was increasingly eulogized, and the disgust of the general public grew as bodies of drowned soldiers from Ball's Bluff continued to wash up on the very shores of the capital. Meanwhile, any attempts by Stone to clarify what had happened or to defend himself only further inflamed Baker's defenders. So, if a scapegoat had to be found, it would not be Colonel Baker, while Stone, a Democrat who could be portrayed as having questionable loyalty for allegedly returning escaped slaves to their owners, would do nicely.[8]

Years later, Roebling remembered Ball's Bluff as his "first experience of a real battle with its hopes and fears, excitements and exhaustions and disappointments at the result and other wrongs." Roebling and the 6th New York's men had had an unenviable but perhaps eye-opening introduction to the confusion and unpredictability of combat. They hadn't made it across the last stretch of river onto Virginia's shore, but they nonetheless received their first casualties on the island and elsewhere. The battery's brigade commander, Colonel Baker, was dead, while their own first lieutenant, Walter M. Bramhall, who had despaired of getting to where the action was with his own battery, had crossed over with the Rhode Islanders and been shot twice through the leg. There's no question of where Roebling placed the blame for Ball's Bluff. It was upon that "ass," General George McClellan, who, Roebling offered, had lost nothing, while Stone's command lost a great deal in men and morale. "In all this Gen. Stone literally obeyed the peremptory orders of Little Mac," who, as Roebling noted, at first had defended Stone, but when investigative eyes turned toward McClellan, his support for Stone grew tepid. Roebling remembered all too well that General Stone's career was destroyed "to cover the asinine incompetence of McClellan." Ultimately it seemed that McClellan incurred no responsibility or criticism for the debacle at Ball's Bluff, as the month after the battle he became commander in chief of the U.S. Army.[9]

At the time of their first experience of combat at the front, Sergeant Roebling and the men of his battery began to see what happens when control and command give way to the chaos of war and started learning to contend with the painful results of others' incompetence. Their fledgling army had yet to recognize the dire consequences of the lack of a viable means of communication. Then there was the harsh lesson of which of their leaders would or would not pay for their mistakes based upon just how much influence they could wield. It is tempting to consider that, for General George McClellan, this was the first of future attempts to seek a bloodless victory. His desire to capture Leesburg by maneuvering men like chess pieces instead reaped disaster, one for which many in Stone's brigade paid a very heavy price.

4

Dueling with the Rebels

THE FALL OF 1861 SAW THE 6TH NEW YORK INDEPENDENT BATTERY IN southern Maryland opposite a rebel installation at Shipping Point at the mouth of Quantico Creek, with the opposing forces contending for control of the Potomac. The rebels had another battery nearby at Cockpit Point that was armed with English Blakelys, and the one directly opposite contained smoothbore sixty-four pounders said to have been taken from the former USS *Merrimac*, now the rebel ship *Virginia*. The Federals, when not at the shoreline taking potshots at the enemy, retired a short distance to within the precincts of the town of Poolesville, Maryland. There was pretty constant fire back and forth across the river, most often without result. Nor did the enemy's efforts do much to intimidate the Federals, for, as Washington Roebling pointed out, "a large round ball can be seen coming and is easily dodged." But the 6th New York soon had something to crow about when one of two British long-barreled, rifled Whitworths sent over by Union supporters in London was assigned to the 6th. When the guns had first arrived, they were given to the 3rd Division of the 3rd Corps, General Joseph Hooker's division, and a trial was made under Roebling's direction to see whether his artillerymen could hit the rebels' Shipping Point battery some two miles off with the Whitworth's hexagonal shot. With Roebling aiming, they hit it every time, and though they couldn't be sure just how much damage they had done, they could confirm seeing an unfortunate ox team topple over. Though some allowances were no doubt made for the Whitworth's remarkable accuracy, this impressive demonstration by Roebling and his gun crew most likely won them possession of one of the new guns. A demonstration for generals and dignitaries attempted by Roebling and his crew went less well, for the enthusiastic commanders monopolized the shooting for themselves. Roebling, in addition to studying up on the science and mathematics of trajectory, was apparently

Whitworth cannon and ammunition.
National Park Service.

familiarizing himself with the jargon of his new calling, for he described the earthwork protecting his gun when it was brought into action on the shoreline as an *épaulement*, the French military term for a barricade or rough parapet of earth used mainly as cover to protect a battery from flanking fire. A less savvy private in the battery merely said the gun was positioned in a pit in the sand, which Roebling freely admitted was just what it was.[1]

The battery would spend the next four months on the Potomac River attempting to control the rebels' efforts to impede shipping to and from Washington. Their days were spent drilling or out on picket, with the only excitement, other than exchanging shots with their foe across the river, the almost daily Unionist ship running past the Confederate battery. One such ship, the three-masted screw-propeller, steam-powered USS *Pensacola*, was such a substantial target that it is hard to understand how she sailed past the rebel batteries unscathed. Yet, despite the rebels' best efforts, with few exceptions, most ships passed successfully. In many cases, the enemy's efforts to hit ships posed more of a threat to the Federals on the opposite shore than to the passing mariners.

As winter approached and day after day of low temperatures ensued, rebels and Federals alike intensified their quest for firewood. This pursuit brought 6th New York soldiers a warning and reminder that stealing fence rails from the

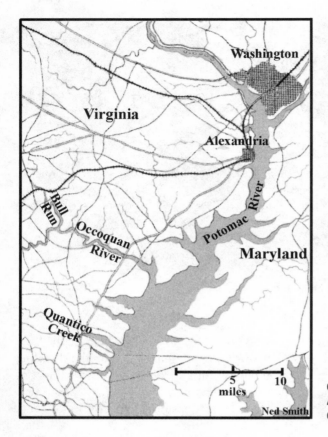

Control of the Potomac.
Adapted from Plate X,
OR Atlas.

locals was a court-martialing offense. Roebling suffered some minor illnesses in those first cold days at Poolesville; though he commented that "sleeping on the ground with the thermometer at 10 degrees is no fun," he also allowed that "neither does it kill you." The battery was eventually supplied with circular Sibley tents, which, though they had a hole for ventilation, did little to allow smoke to escape when a fire was built within. At least his battery's food supply showed slight improvement over their days with General Robert Patterson, and although the men often had to be satisfied with a meal of coffee and hard-tack, meat appeared on the menu with a bit more regularity. The camp where they trained and lived when not on duty was much exposed to the winds and weather of an increasingly harsh winter. It likely seemed a relief to Roebling when he was sent to Washington in November on company business, taking down payrolls and picking up fuzes and ammunition. But heavy rains had brought intervening rivers to flood stage, and he was forced to swim across several creeks. His horse, by the time he reached Washington, had completely foundered, and on turning the animal in to a horse hospital, he was able to obtain another mount. On his return, Roebling found that the 6th's camp had been moved to a new position near Budd's Ferry, Maryland, and while they now had better shelter and access to water than at their previous camp, the ground was decidedly damp. The battery had heard the rumors that their parent organization, the 9th New York, was about to join Ambrose Burnside's expedition to the Carolinas, where, Roebling hypothesized, "We would have pleasant winter quarters." But balmy southern weather was not for the New York artillerymen, who would never again serve with the 9th. And Roebling doubted there was any intention of their army going into winter quarters while they remained with George McClellan, for he had just seen several Federal divisions reported to be marching toward the lower Potomac with the goal of reopening navigation. Meanwhile, they would spend more cold winter days watching the enemy across the mile and a half of river that separated them.[2]

Not bothering to waste his newly acquired French military terms on his younger brother, in a letter written in the last month of that eventful year, Roebling described their dueling with the enemy and the pit of sand that housed their gun:

USS *Pensacola*.
Library of Congress.

We had lots of sport yesterday firing into the rebel batteries at Shipping point opposite. It was my turn to go down yesterday with my piece and another one on picket on the river; we left at 3 in the morning and return[ed] at 8 in the evening. A sort of pit has been dug out of the sand, say 4 feet deep—the dirt has been thrown up in front for protection, openings are left for the guns to fire throu [sic] there is no covering on top. To this exposed little hole one section comes down daily being relieved the next day by a section from one of the other 3 batteries.

Saying that they fired in all about forty rounds, he commented,

It required some time before we got the range of the [enemy's] battery the distance being about two miles, after that we hit them every pop. Usually the rebels do not think it worth while to answer to our shots from the light batteries—but this time they got mad and opened fire on us with 9 inch shell—the moment the guard sees the flash from their gun he cries out here she comes and all hands tumble head over heels for the hole, where they lie in a heap until the shell has passed over or burst. The first shell burst in the ground a few hundred feet past us, a piece of some 8 lb. weight flying back to where we were and striking within 10 ft of the Captain [Thomas B. Bunting]. The next shell burst in the water in front of us. The balance of their shells went over us bursting after they had passed us.[3]

Demonstrating that seemingly irresistible impulse to take some souvenir by which to remember your enemy, the artillerymen scrambled after rebel armaments that landed nearby. Roebling described one instance: "Two [shells] did not go off, these we dug up together with a solid shot and took them to camp; while the boys were digging up the first one another shell came along striking in the same place, fortunately it did not burst else their cake would have been dough. The report reaches us about 4 seconds before the shell. Then the shell comes whizzing along slowly—with the fuze burning; if they should happen to burst over the pit we would all go to the devil." But, Roebling remarked, luckily for them, the enemy's poor fuzes were not infrequently the cause of their shells failing to explode. As for those who refused to take cover, Washington told of one hapless lieutenant on the picket line who gave them all quite a laugh. He had declared that he would never run for cover when a shell came over, when one went through the roof of a slave cabin directly behind him. The formerly boastful fellow's more than apparent fright provided real enjoyment for all present. Some days a Federal gunboat running the rebel

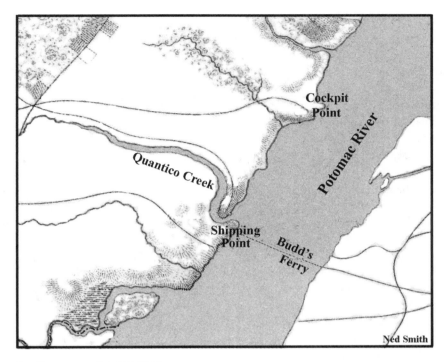

Dueling across the Potomac.
Adapted from Plate VIII, OR Atlas.

gauntlet would provide brief excitement; not infrequently, a rebel deserter would come over, telling of the discontent among the Alabama and Mississippi troops in the batteries across the way. One rather remarkable Southerner with a gift for topographical detail made a three-dimensional model of the surrounding countryside for General Hooker's headquarters. A local delicacy provided another welcome diversion: "Oysters in the shell are very cheap here, 25 for 10cts; the negroes bring them around in ox carts." The shellfish made a delicious change from the artillerymen's regular fare. Then there was the memorable day when a small schooner carrying oysters, its crew anxious to stay as far away from the rebel batteries as possible, ran aground. When spotted by the Federals ashore, the boat's cargo was quickly unloaded, and while the lightening of the load allowed the unlucky schooner to escape, oysters aplenty disappeared into the delighted Unionists' camp.

But the battery's brief moments of excitement were interspersed with long hours of tedium, unrelieved by any whisper of an impending military movement, so it is no wonder that the artillerymen's days tended to blur together. Washington's life, when he was not on the Potomac shore with his gun crew, was spent in the camp at Budd's Ferry, where he shared a Sibley tent with, as one of his tentmates described it, "ten choice sports and their time occupied, when not on duty, in playing cards and writing letters." "Nearly every one could, or thought he could, play some kind of musical instrument," but none, the old comrade remembered, could come within a mile of Washington Roebling, "who could make a violin talk." When this last was written in 1926, the joy Washington's music brought to his tentmates during that winter of 1861–1862 remained a vivid memory. While the miserly John Roebling had at times harshly denied his family adequate food and clothing over the years, he had never skimped on Washington's musical education. John's great love of music inspired him to provide his son with the best teachers that money could buy.[4]

January's incessant cold rains gave way to February, during which the 6th New York saw the sudden departure of the battery's original commander, Captain Thomas B. Bunting, who left, bag and baggage, with no explanation to the men. A panel of regular army artillerists, including then major Charles S. Wainwright, had examined Bunting and found him sadly wanting in what it took to command a battery. Wainwright commented that Bunting "did not know the first thing; could not tell the proper intervals and distance in line; nor where the different cannoneers should sit on the boxes; indeed he at last admitted that he had never studied the tactics, so his was a very short and decided case." Given the panel's findings, Bunting was apparently allowed to resign.

The company's men then chose one of their lieutenants, Walter M. Bramhall, as their captain. Washington Roebling was elected on the third ballot in an apparently hot contest for the newly open lieutenant's position. That left only the necessary confirmation by Governor Edwin D. Morgan of New York, which caused Washington some concern. There were suspicions that Wainwright might use his influence as head of artillery of their division to push some of his friends into the battery. But Major Wainwright not only approved of the newly elected officers but also offered to write to the New York governor endorsing them. As for the departure of Bunting and the advent of Bramhall, Roebling commented, "The change in officers is highly satisfactory to the great majority of the men, and we all expect to get along finely hereafter." What Bunting had lacked in artillery skills, Bramhall could offer, but the new captain also had to spend time in Washington straightening out the company's finances. Bunting had also apparently been haphazard in his record keeping and left the battery's accounts in a sorry state.

On the subject of money, by mid-February 1862, Roebling had apparently reconciled with his father, for he approached his remarkably tightfisted parent for a loan. With his new appointment as second lieutenant came expenses, and he wrote, "My outfit will cost considerable; the uniform is more expensive than that of an infantry officer; according to Law Art[illery] off[icers] have to buy their own horses & saddles—but this is practically a dead letter, being never followed. I would thank you to send me about $75.00 which will be ample as I have a little money left of my own." By the end of the month, the money was forthcoming, but Washington had doubts he'd be able to reach the city to get outfitted, for there'd been an apparent tightening on leaves of absence, prompting rumors of a possible movement. The arrival of a full corps of signal officers also prompted talk of a move, but heavy rains soon dampened those hopes. In one heavy storm, the Confederate steamer *Page* broke loose of its mooring at the mouth of the Quantico and drifted across the river, where it was "captured" by the gleeful artillerymen. Hungry for good news, the 6th New York's little victory could be celebrated right along with word of General U. S. Grant's capture of Fort Donelson. Meanwhile, the artillerymen had to confine their own warfare to a fierce intersquad snowball fight, featuring the "Guerillas" versus the "Israelites."

Washington eventually made it to the city, where he spent all that his father had advanced to him. It is unknown whether, after he explained that the government was woefully behind in paying its troops, his request for an additional $25 from his parsimonious father was granted. By the end of March, the weather was fulfilling the promise of spring, and the arrival of a great number of scows, flatboats and even confiscated mail boats excited the conviction that a large movement of the Federal forces was coming soon. As Roebling and the battery chaffed at remaining "confined to this forsaken spot of Maryland," the Confederates' voluntary evacuation of troops from their batteries along the Potomac caused some disappointment, for it had been hoped that the Federals' new wonder weapon, the *Monitor*, would come clear the rebels out. But the enemy's departure was followed by what became the daily passing of troops on the river to Fortress Monroe, their bands playing gaily. While the artillerymen watched a fleet of some forty steamers carrying the troops of Generals Samuel Heintzelman, Irvin McDowell, and Erasmus Keyes, they began to suspect that if they got to leave at all, they would be the last to go. The young lieutenant pondered just what McClellan's plans might be and how the rebels would respond, but in a burst of optimism, he offered hopefully, if naively, "Our troops will therefore be in Richmond very soon."[5]

After an Unexpected Naval Adventure, the 6th New York Battery Joins McClellan on the Peninsula

IT SEEMED TO THE IMPATIENT ARTILLERYMEN THAT EVERYONE ELSE in the Federal army had left for Fortress Monroe on their way to join General George B. McClellan's growing army. But in early April, word finally came for the 6th New York Independent Battery to pack up and, with Joseph Hooker's division, head for McClellan's encampments on the Virginian peninsula. A five-mile march in the pouring rain brought them to their place of embarkation, Liverpool Point, but on their arrival, no transportation was available, leaving them with nothing to do but wait. To add to the uncertainty, their brigade commander, Colonel Daniel Sickles, in a fit of pique at having had his confirmation as brigadier general rejected by the Senate, left for Washington to pursue another nomination with the president, leaving his brigade to go to the front without him. Washington Roebling said that there was "great excitement" over the departure of their idolized commander, who, the men believed, had been removed from command because of his past notoriety. The dominant opinion within the brigade was that he was a brave man and a passable general, and "no one will ever have such command of the men as he had."[1]

Roebling would remember in later years that, as they awaited orders that would take them from their upper Potomac backwater to the front, news reached them of the furor caused by the first appearance of the ironclad *Virginia*. While the havoc the rebel vessel wrought upon the seemingly helpless Union warships caused something akin to panic in some circles, Roebling suggested that the 6th New York didn't take that much interest, for as they packed

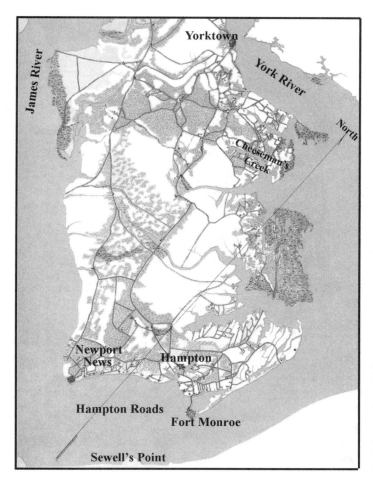

Meeting the CSS *Virginia* and joining McClellan on the Yorktown Peninsula. Adapted from Plate XVIII, 2 OR Atlas.

to leave, the artillerymen were soon fighting another sort of battle: getting the battery's recalcitrant horses and mules onto the schooners. Roebling commented that he and his comrades were "too busily employed in twisting the tails of mules to make them go into the boats, and had not time to get much excited." Tongue in cheek, he further offered, "I have always noticed that honest employment is an antidote to nervous apprehension." But on their passage away from their Budd's Ferry position, the men of the 6th New York noticed the ships of the "Stone Fleet," old ships and barges that the government had purchased and loaded with stones, with a plan to either scuttle the ships or have them dump their loads to prevent the *Virginia* from attacking the capital or other ports. For all the panic in the precincts of Washington, interestingly, the *Virginia* never strayed away from Norfolk and the James River, instead serving the Confederacy with protection for its capital.[2]

Eventually a tug brought a barge, the *Wallkill of Newburgh*, whose fancy name belied its humble amenities. Roebling saw it for what it was, writing, "The tub we are on is one of the Newburgh [New York] cattle barges and pitches like the dickens." But anchored for the night as they were at Liverpool Point, the men of the 6th slept comfortably enough in bunks on board the barge, little dreaming what adventures lay immediately ahead of them. With the steamer *Vanderbilt* towing their barge as well as the schooners bearing the horses, the battery was on its way the next day, April 10, and as the weather grew stormier, Roebling pitied the battery's horses packed tightly on the decks of the schooners. He had noticed that their legs were already swelling and worried that, after four days under the conditions they would endure, it would take a week after landing to get them back in shape. But by midday, when they reached the Chesapeake Bay, conditions worsened to the point that the cable from the *Vanderbilt* to the schooner behind the barge carrying the battery parted, and the schooner disappeared in the fog and rain behind them. As Roebling had predicted, the barge was rocking badly, and, beyond the seasickness that overcame all but a few, the men realized that they were in real danger. As Roebling said, "We expected to become food for fishes in place of food for rebel powder and ball. In entering the bay and as far down as the mouth of the Rappahannock our course was such that the barge had to roll in the trough of the sea which was very heavy under a North East storm; This old tub, flatbottomed with an empty hold and 2 batteries of artillery on her deck commenced to roll and pitch at an alarming rate, as might be expected with so much top weight." Roebling was among the few not disabled by seasickness, and while holding on for dear life, he and a few others stood by with axes, ready to cut away the barge's badly damaged cabin. As if things weren't bad enough, Roebling wrote, "the skipper at the helm lost his head entirely, and had sense enough to give up the helm to one of our sergeants who is a mate of 6 years standing and I may well say that to his skill in steering we owe our lives." Having cut loose all its tows except the 6th's barge, the *Vanderbilt* reached Fortress Monroe, to considerable relief, and moored just as darkness fell. The men of the battery had been looking forward to getting to Fortress Monroe, with its promise of markets with the delectable edibles denied them all winter, but few in the company wanted to even think about food. And if the artillerymen thought their troubles were over, they were wrong.[3]

USS *Vanderbilt*.
Library of Congress.

On their arrival at Hampton Roads, the site of that famous recent encounter between the *Merrimac* and the *Monitor* on March 8 and 9, the artillerymen were treated to a closeup view of the *Monitor* as they were towed past Fortress Monroe. Noting that the *Monitor* had her steam up, Roebling later learned that all the steam-powered vessels were kept in that state of readiness. He, as had many others, expressed surprise at just how small the "cheesebox on a board" was. They also spotted that other must-see at the fortress, the famous Lincoln Gun; then, continuing on, the *Vanderbilt* towed the *Wallkill* to the middle of Hampton Roads and left her there. After the terrors of the storm, the battery could be said to have spent a relatively peaceful night onboard the barge *Wallkill*, but for the preponderance of every sort of shipping that made the surrounding anchorage look like New York Harbor. But on the morning of April 11, after the mist lifted, "a curious sight presented itself; every vessel that had sails or steam seemed to be running away. The big boats out to sea, the smaller ones up Chesapeake Bay. Presently we noticed in the direction of Norfolk the black roof of a huge barn floating towards us. Then we realized that we were looking at the now famous *Merrimac*, which the Confederates had refitted and christened the *Virginia*. We were helpless and could not run away." The amazed artillerymen soon found themselves in the middle of an impending naval battle, for their barge was between the warships that

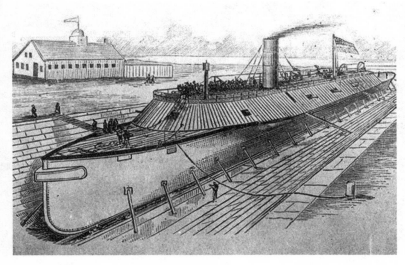

CSS *Virginia*.
Naval History and Heritage Command (history.navy.mil).

accompanied the *Virginia* and the USS *Naugatuck* with its single big gun. As cannonballs began splashing all around the *Wallkill*, the men of the 6th New York loaded one of their six-pounders and trained it on the *Virginia*. Apparently they thought better of firing it, or, as Roebling quipped, they "refrained from sinking her!"[4]

The *Virginia*'s escorts captured three of the ships hired by the Federals to transport men and equipment, though they had already discharged their cargoes. One of the ships' captured crew, on being closely questioned, told the captain of the *Virginia* that a Union ram, the *Vanderbilt*, was waiting for her. Finally, several U.S. gunboats and a warship, with one of the Federal ships, its sailors at their guns, ready to take on the enemy, came up right alongside the *Wallkill*, though neither the *Monitor* nor the *Vanderbilt* joined them. It seems that, as her previous month's engagement with the *Virginia* had been considered a stalemate, the *Monitor* was forbidden to enter Hampton Roads and engage the *Virginia*; instead, she was to act as bait, in hopes of drawing the enemy ironclad out into the water where the *Vanderbilt* would have an opportunity to ram her. Then, too, the Federals harbored real fears that, should the *Monitor* be sunk or captured, any restraint upon the *Virginia* would be gone. Unaware of his government's strategy and fears, and having fully expected the nearby *Monitor* to join the fray, Roebling commented at the time, "The result was very disappointing to us. We could see no reason why the *Monitor* should not have taken a position opposite the stern of the *Merrimac* and rake her fore and aft. But a Farragut was not on board. Our people were taken by surprise." Years later, Roebling acknowledged that the former commander of the *Monitor* had been seriously injured in the boat's initial fight and no longer commanded the *Monitor*, but he still felt that the ship had missed an important opportunity when the Union allowed the *Virginia* and its escorts to withdraw unchallenged and unscathed. Meanwhile, the 6th's artillerymen were likely more than happy to relinquish their front-row seat when the steamer *Hero* came to rescue them. In later years, Roebling would suggest that, though no fierce battle between the *Monitor* and the *Merrimac* took place on April 11, 1861, the *Virginia*'s sudden and largely unchallenged reappearance in Hampton Roads was a victory for the South, for, he suggested, the mere threat of the rebel ironclad's ability to interfere had further paralyzed the Army of the Potomac for an additional two weeks. McClellan's plan focused on the peninsula that lay between the James and York Rivers, and it called for his troops to land on both sides of the peninsula. The *Virginia*'s perceived threat to Federal use of the James River restricted McClellan's base of operations to the York. Nor could any hoped-for support or active role on the part of the Federal navy be expected in the advance up the peninsula, as all its attention was focused on the *Virginia* with its accompanying cloud of rebel warships.[5]

While the men of the 6th New York waited impatiently for their turn to go to the front, Roebling doubted they would get there before Yorktown was taken. In that, he was very mistaken, for although McClellan's initial advance toward Richmond had begun on April 4, and despite his outnumbering the rebels four to one, he allowed Confederate general John B. Magruder to bamboozle him into believing a much larger enemy force defended Yorktown than was actually the case. Instead of attacking Yorktown, McClellan therefore lay siege unsuccessfully to it, and not until May 3, 1862, and only when General Joseph E. Johnston had withdrawn his army, did the city fall into Federal hands. The 6th was a very small cog in General McClellan's slowly grinding machinery, and although the battery did move a short distance inland from its landing at Cheeseman's Creek, Roebling got his first glimpse of the front only by making an unofficial visit to the headquarters of 3rd Corps's commander, General Samuel Heintzelman, where he got a look at the enemy's line, saw some of the other Federal batteries in action, and experienced the incessant firing that went on day and night. Here, Roebling learned about the enemy's snipers, whose targeting of Unionist artillerymen exacted a heavy toll.[6]

The 6th New York would eventually get its share of hazardous duty on the picket line. The men had a particularly satisfying encounter with the enemy near one of the many dams on the rivers, all of which were protected by Confederate forts. With the surrounding low countryside intentionally flooded for miles around, a Federal work crew was attempting to build a road over what little dry land could be found, and the 6th New York had been called upon to provide support. The men of 6th had the pleasure, from their masked position, of surprising and driving off two rebel guns that had incautiously advanced with the intention of making the Federal road builders' lives a misery. But apparently such rewarding activities were few and far between, for Roebling would later describe the battery's experience there as "a month wasted lying in a trench dug by Gen. Washington." Here he also ran into an old acquaintance who was acting as a topographical engineer on the peninsula, and he acknowledged that there seemed little difference between the engineers' assignments and those of a spy. Their job, for the most part, was supplying the knowledge that the army so desperately needed in this territory of rivers, dams, and canals, all perfectly familiar to the enemy. Getting the vital information on roads, rivers, bridges, fords, enemy positions, and troop strengths required scouting close to and beyond enemy lines. The dangers of the occupation were hammered home when two of the engineers had their left arms taken off by a telling shot from a Confederate battery. As Roebling mused on this situation, he was watching a squad of rebel prisoners going by. "They look horrid and are entirely ununiformed," he observed, "but they can handle cannon well." The rebels at Yorktown were also more than adept at pulling the wool over the eyes of McClellan and his supposed spymaster, Allan Pinkerton, for these ragged rebels with their commander, General Magruder, had paraded in circles to disguise their small numbers. The well-executed charade brought McClellan's planned attack to a halt and caused the much larger Unionist army to bring in a number of twelve-inch mortars before settling into an ineffective siege. Lieutenant Roebling was also likely considering the lifestyles and chances of longevity of the army's topographical engineers, with their dangerous scouting missions, versus the lives of the army's artillerymen, prey to Confederate sharpshooters as they served their guns. The weeks at Yorktown likely gave him a lot to think about. He also had reason to appreciate, as justification for all the risks the engineers took, just how vital the information they gathered was to their army's chances of success, as he would come to know himself only too well in the future.[7]

McClellan's laborious buildup for the culmination of his monthlong siege became redundant on May 3, when someone finally pointed out that if the

Federals moved against the Confederates' communications, the Confederates would have to move. This proved true, with General Johnston withdrawing from Yorktown and leaving it to the Yankees. With the Federals finally making something resembling an advance, on May 5, the day that culminated in the Battle of Williamsburg, Lieutenant Roebling received the surprise of a lifetime. On April 30, 1862, a special order had been issued directing him to report immediately to the Quartermaster General's Office in Washington, DC. Unbeknownst to young Roebling, his father, John Roebling, had been called in to consult with General Montgomery Meigs, head of the Federal quartermaster's department, on the feasibility of stringing wire cables across the Potomac to prevent the CSS *Virginia* from assailing the capital. But the subject of suspension bridges, a Roebling specialty, also came up, and when Meigs expressed enthusiasm for these engineering marvels as a necessity for a modern army, John reminded the general that he already had a trained bridge

General Montgomery Meigs.
Library of Congress.

engineer in the service: Lieutenant Washington Roebling of the 6th New York Independent Battery. So, with the stroke of a pen, young Roebling was unexpectedly parted from his artillery comrades. In the weeks and months that followed, he would occasionally run into them again, but their fates would follow much different paths. The 6th went on to active service, with many battles to its name, including the Peninsula Campaign, Kelly's Ford, and Chancellorsville, and then, after it became a horse artillery battery in 1863, Brandy Station, the Bristoe Campaign, Mine Run, and the Overland Campaign.[8]

On arriving in Washington, Lieutenant Roebling met with General Meigs, whom he had met once before when still a student at Rensselaer. At that time, he'd accompanied his father, who had been called in as a consultant to supply wire ropes for Meigs's current engineering project: lifting massive stonework into place while constructing the Capitol dome. But bridges were on Meigs's mind in 1862: he wanted a manual for building military suspension bridges, and Lieutenant Roebling was going to write it. In six weeks' time, Washington produced a manual with technical drawings, all the while assembling all the equipment and specialized impedimenta needed to begin the business of bridge building. The government promptly published five hundred copies of his manual, and Lieutenant Roebling couldn't help but notice that, while General Meigs's name appeared prominently in its front, his own did not appear anywhere in the manual, a lesson in military customs and procedure for the young lieutenant. He commented, with the sense of humor that carried him through many hard times, "In my whole life I have never met an honorable man and therefore do not complain." With the manual complete and three sets of equipment made ready, Washington was ordered to join General Irvin McDowell's staff on the Rappahannock, where he would take charge of assembling the wire rope equipage needed to start building bridges for the Union army.[9]

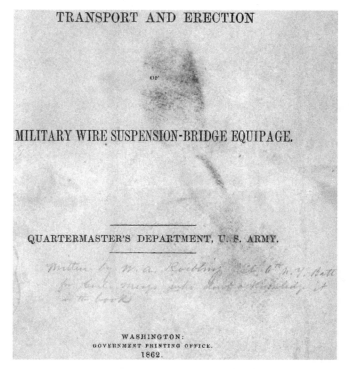

Cover of Roebling's *Military Suspension Bridge Handbook*
with handwritten notation by the author, "W. A. Roebling,
Lt. 6th N.Y. Batt. for Gen. Meigs who doesn't acknowledge
it in the book."
Rensselaer Special Collections.

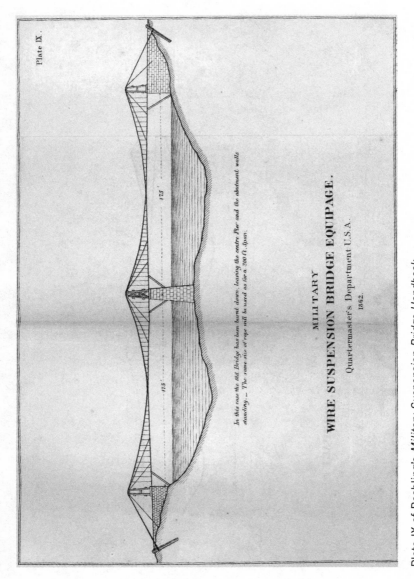

Plate IX.

MILITARY
WIRE SUSPENSION BRIDGE EQUIPAGE.
Quartermaster's Department U.S.A.
1862.

In this case the old Bridge has been burnt down, leaving the centre Pier and the abutment walls
standing.— The same size of rope will be used as for a 300 ft. Span.

175'

175'

Plate IX of Roebling's *Military Suspension Bridge Handbook*.
Rensselaer Special Collections.

6

Lieutenant Roebling, Bridge Builder and Sole Guardian to One Hundred Contraband

ALTHOUGH THERE WAS NO ENEMY OTHER THAN A FEW SCOUTS BETWEEN Irvin McDowell's corps and George McClellan's engagements on the peninsula, McDowell's Army of the Rappahannock sat in absolute idleness "protecting Washington." As the ever-outspoken Washington Roebling would later write, "When the time came to really protect Washington, they were swept away like chaff. This idea of protecting Washington prolonged the war a year, cost us millions and billions and was the outcome of a cowardly sentiment at the capital." Whatever else Roebling would think of U. S. Grant— and it wasn't much—he applauded the fact that once Grant came east, the obsession with "protecting Washington" was finally exploded, for before that, Roebling lamented, "it had governed all the movements of the Army of the Potomac. It required three years for the country to learn that the only way to protect a capital is to beat the enemy in the field." But in the summer of 1862, McDowell was at Falmouth, opposite Fredericksburg on the Rappahannock, where Lieutenant Roebling was ordered to join the general's staff. Prepared to "astonish the world with military suspension bridges," Washington served initially under Major David C. Houston for the next year. "He looked upon me as a sort of nuisance that he would have liked to get rid of," Roebling remembered in later years, also recalling that Houston had not stood very high in the corps of engineers and rather went downhill years later, being transferred with General Nathaniel Banks to that backwater of the unwanted: Louisiana. And yet, though he would have preferred not to be bothered, Major Houston was just curious enough to want to see with his own eyes one of the whippersnapper's suspension bridges. An old highway bridge crossing the Rappahannock at Fredericksburg, the Chatham Bridge, had been destroyed, but a number of piers, eight or ten, had been left standing. What, Houston posed, could the young bridge builder do with that?[1]

Of this, his first engineering project for the army, Washington was to remember, "Here I stood in an utterly false position, without a man or mechanic or a tool or material to accomplish anything with. A pontoon bridge by comparison is child's play. There you see a regiment of 1200 drilled men with 50 experienced officers and every imaginable tool and implement and a complete organization and commissariat under military drill, whereas I stood entirely alone with nothing." Nonetheless, Roebling carried on, making drawings, surveys, and estimates for supplies. There was material to be ordered and a train load of cables to be shipped. His requisitions for tools from the quartermasters' department were grudgingly filled, but only after the young lieutenant unsnarled miles of red tape. But he then hit one seemingly insurmountable snag when the local commander, General Rufus King, turned Roebling's request for men down flat. While Roebling was talking with him, General King suffered an epileptic seizure, falling to the ground—a lucky break for Roebling, as it turned out, for King's second in command gave the engineer a crew (just to get rid of him, he suspected). But the crew he was given consisted of one hundred contraband, "50 niggers and 50 wenches," as Roebling described them. It was his and the newly escaped slaves' misfortune that he apparently hadn't yet had a good experience with fugitives from slavery. He had just witnessed a party of contraband having a battle royale over material left behind by the 9th New York at the Budd's Ferry winter camp, and Roebling apparently found little to admire in these newly arrived refugees from the South. Many of them, one suspects, were untrained, uneducated field slaves, who now became Roebling's sole responsibility to feed, clothe, and shelter. Unskilled as many of them were, the young engineer perhaps unsurprisingly came to feel they were more trouble than they were worth for his bridge-building project. Roebling would grudgingly admit that even though the crew had neither mechanics nor "any skill whatever," nonetheless "some of the darkies were better than the white bums from the regiments." He set his crew to work in the woods of King George County, cutting wood for the bridge's towers. He also found a rarity: two Southern white men who had not joined the Confederate army who were trained carpenters. For many of his specialized needs, the latter two proved to be, he remembered, worth all the others put together. Then, too, Washington hired a deserter from the rebel army, despite his being one of the enemy who "amused himself last winter firing across the river at me at Budds Ferry—he is a good fellow though."[2]

Among other things, Washington needed boats to go back and forth between the piers in the river, so he built them. When the cables came, he managed to get use of a team of oxen and the blessed assistance for one day of twenty men from the construction corps to pull the cables over the river. But then it was time to start sending men aloft, and rather than face climbing high above the fast-running river below, many of his impressed workers ran away. They were, it seems, the lucky ones, for a number of the remaining men fell, broken legs being the most common result. The project had apparently become a nightmare for Roebling, for when floodwaters capsized a boatload of workers, all twenty drowned, and not one body was recovered. Remembering the horror and his own demoralized bitterness and anger, Washington wrote, "I had become so callous that I did not care one damn." Yet one contraband worker did manage to get his boss's grudging appreciation, for Roebling learned the name of "nigger George" while not bothering with those of the other workmen. Having no boards for the floor of the bridge, they dismantled nearby houses. When his white workers, some of whom came voluntarily from the 11th Indiana for extra pay, refused to occupy the same camp as his contrabands, Roebling withdrew from the whole lot, taking up residence on his own in the abandoned stone jail by the river bank. In it was a large long box, and when his curiosity got best of him, he pried a board loose and reached in. A cold face met his fingertips. It proved to be a statue of Mary, mother of George Washington, placed in the old jail for safekeeping, and the rather startled lieutenant packed his marble roommate safely away to await her resurrection after the war.[3]

Roebling later wrote a report for General Montgomery Meigs detailing some of his trials and tribulations while building this bridge, saying that with proper workmen he could have built it half the time. But, against all odds, all obstacles were met and overcome, and in just six weeks, from start to finish, the bridge, more than a thousand feet long, was opened to military traffic, with General George Thomas's brigade of cavalry one of the first to cross. Other minds and hands built two other bridges nearby, a canal boat bridge and a railroad bridge, both of which were swept away by the Rappahannock in flood stage. With some modicum of satisfaction, Roebling remembered, "The little suspension bridge remained intact." Looking back, Roebling would doubt the bridge had been worth the trouble to build, adding "certainly not as far as I was concerned personally." He later commented, "I look upon this job more with disgust than with pride; but more was to come; one never knows at what moment military exigencies may compel the abandonment of such structures, so it is best not to take the matter too much to heart." What floods could not do, General Ambrose Burnside did, when, as the Federals evacuated Fredericksburg a month later, anxious to deny the use of the bridge to the rebels, he had its anchorages blown up, dropping the bridge and cables into the river. Washington would hear that the cables, later fished out of the river, ended up as ferry ropes somewhere down South. Trying to find some value in this stress-filled venture, he realized that while constructing the bridge, he had learned much about the terrain of the surrounding area—knowledge that would come in mighty handy later on.[4]

Though matters were moving slowly on the peninsula, the presence of General John Pope's reorganized Army of Virginia enabled General R. E. Lee to consider a two-pronged attack on his army. Once again, Lee took the initiative, and it was soon learned that Stonewall Jackson was moving on McDowell's left, a situation that caused much excitement. Yet, in the midst of this uncertainty, Major Houston suggested that Roebling build a bridge at Waterloo, known also as Warrenton Springs, but before he could bring his equipment and material to the bridge site, the town was reoccupied by the enemy. Jackson was next reported at Manassas Gap, aiming to get past McDowell's flank to strike at the capital. McDowell marched to the gap and through it; then he crossed over the Shenandoah to Front Royal only to find Jackson gone. Both bridges at Front Royal had been swept away by a flood, but the piers of one remained standing, and Houston again suggested building a suspension bridge—two, in fact. Though Roebling found the masonry of the piers in poor shape, once again, the wheels were set in motion to bring material to the bridge site, while timber was cut for the towers and anchorage. Though the water was running like a mill race, when no boat could be found, Washington swam across the river with a tape in his mouth to get a measurement. But as he prepared to begin swinging the cables upon the newly rebuilt towers, it was discovered that Jackson had gotten around McDowell and gone on into the southern end of Culpeper County. It was time, once again, for the Federals to take up the chase, and so ended any thoughts of bridge building at Front Royal. Washington wrote to his brother at the time, "My cake is dough again for a bridge at Front Royal; I had no sooner started, when an order came for the greater part of the forces here to leave the place, leaving only a sufficient guard to protect the place, and since it is not worth while to build bridges for the seceshionists [sic] it was concluded to abandon it." Washington was somewhat reluctant to leave Front Royal, which he found a picturesque Virginia town compared to some he had been in. He did, however, find the women more than a little "secesh" and described to his brother, Ferdie, how

General Irvin McDowell.
Library of Congress.

one such damsel called him a "Northern Vandal" while accepting twenty-five cents for a very small pie. After safely disposing of equipages and materials, Roebling headed to McDowell's headquarters, on his way passing the battle-field of First Manassas, noting that the area was still horribly redolent of the smell of death and "the stink which is horrible." He arrived at McDowell's Culpeper position on August 7, the day following General Banks's unsuccessful strike at the enemy at Cedar Mountain. As the Federal commanders now had much else on their minds besides bridges, Roebling joyfully wrote home, "Bridge building was hung up for a while, thank God!"[5]

At the end of June, frustration with McClellan's lack of progress on the peninsula reached a high point. Fears mounted as the Confederates appeared to be flexing increasingly aggressive muscle. And there appeared a candidate for higher command in the army whose views met with the administration's

General John Pope.
Library of Congress.

and the radical Republicans' approval. Substantial political pressure brought General John Pope from the West to show the eastern soldiery how war was supposed to be fought. Declaring this one of the many great mistakes made by those holding the reins of power in the nation's capital, Roebling didn't hold back when describing what he and many others thought of General Pope: "A bombastic, vainglorious, self-boaster, with no ability or experience, new to his troops, and hated by the other commanders, especially by McDowell, whom he superseded; he lacked foresight, caution, and had no initiative; waited until it was too late and underrated Jackson." An additional boost was given to the opinion that Pope could accomplish something with the arrival of General Henry Halleck, who had been brought to Washington to take command of the armies and advise the administration. With General in Chief Halleck's stamp of approval for Pope, the administration put all its eggs in one basket.

On August 4, General McClellan was ordered to wrap things up on the peninsula and begin sending his troops to Pope. The already supplanted General McDowell now served as commander of Pope's 3rd Corps; nonetheless, Roebling relished his new duties on McDowell's staff, declaring, "I now had staff duty of a most agreeable kind. I was very expert in reconnoitering, in making sketches and maps of the country as I went along, of finding the enemy's position, and getting a knowledge of the terrain." His delight at not having to build bridges under all but impossible conditions was more than a little obvious. And what may seem like immodest self-praise regarding his skill as a topographical engineer was, in fact, an accurate assessment, as the commanders' reliance on him in the coming months confirms. But Washington also relished his newfound freedom, for he was able to get out from under the eyes of those at headquarters. He was now charged with exploring and mapping the terrain, plotting the roads and the river fords, and, most important, finding the enemy: "I had carte blanche to go anywhere I wanted in the whole army or surrounding country." His first reconnaissance with the horsemen of the intrepid General John Buford's cavalry through enemy lines to Madison Court House came near being his last. It was another of the many close calls Roebling would have with the enemy.[6]

Aide and Topographical Engineer
to General Irvin McDowell

ONE OF THE MOST COMPLETE SOURCES OF INFORMATION REGARDING what Washington Roebling witnessed in the days leading up to the Battle of Second Bull Run proper, which took place on August 29 and 30, was a letter he wrote to his father on August 24, a chronicle of what he had experienced and observed from August 17 to 24, 1862. The letter begins with the statement that General John Pope had banned all mail in and out of the Army of Virginia, a prohibition that countless soldiers, including Roebling, overcame by having someone carry their letters outside the restricted area to be mailed elsewhere. The other intriguing aspect of his very long letter, in which he reveals his innermost feelings and worries, is that he wrote it not to his favorite brother, Ferdie, or to his friend and father figure Charles Swan, but to the father with whom he shared a particularly strained relationship. Whatever his incentive for baring his soul to John Roebling regarding the tumultuous scenes he was seeing, it provides a most valuable window into Washington's Second Bull Run experience. Although a humble second lieutenant, Roebling was an engineer and aide on General Irvin McDowell's staff and a witness to a number of events worthy of consideration.[1]

By August 13, General R. E. Lee was convinced that the threat of George McClellan's Peninsula Campaign was essentially over, and the troops of the Army of the Potomac were being withdrawn and transferred to Pope's Army of Virginia. This freed Lee to send all his troops to confront Pope. As tensions grew and Confederate and Federal forces shifted, jockeying for position, Roebling said, everybody was on the "qui vive," on high alert. Hungry for news of the enemy, Washington was sent out on August 17 for a "survey of the road" to the town of Madison, a once sleepy Virginia county seat that had already

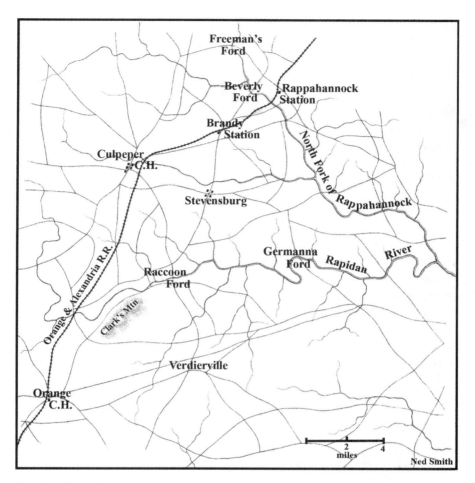

Scouting for McDowell.
Adapted from Plate XXIII, 4 OR Atlas.

seen one inconsequential incursion by Federal horsemen the previous month. While the ongoing uncertainty regarding the enemy's whereabouts was the impetus for his reconnaissance, that uncertainty likely caused him to ponder what the enemy would do to him if he was captured. "I'm almost a spy," he realized, and he must have asked himself whether the uniform he wore would save him from the well-known fate of spies. After a ride of twenty-five miles, he returned unscathed late at night to General McDowell's encampment near Culpeper. There he received orders to make himself available in the wee hours of the next morning to accompany a cavalry expedition to Louisa Court House, another county seat located some twenty miles within the ever-shifting enemy lines.[2]

Without a pause for breath, Washington rode five miles to report to General John Buford's headquarters at Stevensburg for this incursion into rebeldom, attaching himself to a force consisting of two regiments from Buford's brigade, some one thousand troopers who provided Roebling with a lot more company than he'd had on his lone venture the day before. The reconnaissance was led by Colonel Thornton Brodhead, commanding his own 1st Michigan and the 5th New York. On leaving Buford's encampment, the expedition rode five miles to cross the Rapidan at Raccoon Ford, and there occurred one of those quirks of fate that could lead one to believe that Roebling and his fellow soldiers were living under a lucky star. Confederate general James Longstreet, cautious fellow that he was, had ordered troops under the command of General Robert Toombs to guard that very ford. But when the prickly Toombs found out that Longstreet had moved some of his troops without his permission, Toombs ordered them back to camp, leaving the ford unguarded. Thus, our intrepid Federal reconnaissance crossed the Rapidan unimpeded and, traveling on byroads, penetrated twenty-one miles into enemy territory to within five miles of Louisa Court House. Though the Federal troopers were blissfully unaware of it, the countryside was swarming with rebels. As luck would have it, however, they saw little of the enemy, except for ten or so unlucky stragglers, whom they took prisoner. The party was unconcerned enough to take a half hour break before continuing on.[3]

Having rather miraculously met with no opposition, the Federals began their return to their own lines, boldly choosing a main thoroughfare to bring them back to Raccoon Ford and Fredericksburg. But their plans changed when, in the gathering light at 5 a.m., they quite unexpectedly came upon General J. E. B. Stuart and his staff at breakfast at Verdiersville, a few miles from their nearby cavalry camp. Surprise, in this case, was apparently mutual for both parties, as, to Roebling's great disgust, one of the Federal officers, a major, had an opportunity to shoot Stuart and didn't. Considering the consequences of the major's hesitation, Washington was unsurprisingly more than a little critical of the "stupidity of the Major, he being afraid to shoot him." It was apparently a mistake Roebling was confident he wouldn't have made. While some of Stuart's staff were captured, Stuart himself pelted away "with lightning speed," no doubt toward his cavalry's encampment. How nonplussed would the Yankee horsemen have been if they'd known that, on reaching the woods and some semblance of safety, Stuart stood and watched

Colonel Thornton F. Brodhead,
1st Michigan Cavalry.
Library of Congress

as the Unionist troopers confiscated his cloak and plumed hat? These prizes, though highly treasured, were hardly the most valuable items captured by the Unionists that morning. Previously, on hearing a large body of horsemen approaching, Stuart had sent one of his aides out to welcome the expected General Lee and the overdue Fitzhugh Lee and his brigade of cavalry. Instead, Brodhead had captured the aide along with two dispatch pouches crammed with important papers, including Lee's detailed orders for the attack he was about to make upon General Pope and his army.[4]

It didn't take long for Brodhead and his party, with their already tired horses, to realize that they were in a tight spot. Cut off from their planned route of return over Raccoon Ford, they did not know how long they had before Stuart's cavalry showed up with an eye to wreaking a little vengeance on the Yankee intruders. Knowing the rebel horsemen would soon be in close pursuit, the party, in desperation, made a beeline dash in the direction of Fredericksburg, though with grave doubts that they would be able to outrun

J. E. B. Stuart.
Library of Congress.

the fresh horses and irate troopers of Stuart's cavalry. To their great relief, the worried Federals managed to cross the Rapidan at Germanna Ford, though they were still some fifteen miles from Fredericksburg. To their surprise, they had reached the crossing before the enemy caught up with them, and once they were across the river, the danger for that day was for the most part averted, though they knew they'd had a close call. The information they had gained and the knowledge of the roads they had surveyed were more than valuable, but they had to make it back alive to pass this intelligence on to their commanders. Though Washington Roebling beat the odds against capture, his troubles were far from over. Roebling's horse had gotten him through but, at the end, broke down completely so that he'd had to abandon his mount. Thirty-six hours later, carrying his saddle, Roebling returned to where he had left McDowell's headquarters, only to find the camp, and the whole army for that matter, gone. Too exhausted to pursue answers, he wrapped himself in his blanket and slept. On going into Culpeper the next day, he discovered that the entire army had retreated "for no apparent reason whatever." "I was about the last man left," Roebling commented. He did, however, manage to get himself on the last train to Rappahannock Station, where Pope's army was now posted, for the most part, on the north shore of the river, ready to make a stand against the enemy. Unaware of the reasoning behind the move, Roebling commented disparagingly that the enemy "was perfectly justified in supposing that we had left from fear."[5]

If Washington had missed out on some of the excitement at McDowell's headquarters, he was about to make up for it. On the day following his return, Roebling, crediting the enemy's cavalry with having routed their Federal counterparts, saw all Union presence driven from McDowell's front on the south side of the Rappahannock except for two batteries positioned upon two small hills. This small Union presence on the south side of the river would prove a bone of contention between the antagonists. While one battery's line of communication was a railroad bridge defended by the batteries of McDowell's corps on both shores, the battery on the other hill had to rely on a low, 160-foot trestle bridge that McDowell's engineers put up overnight. The Federal position was considered quite strong, rather an ideal place to await the reinforcements expected from McClellan's army. But the luck of the Union batteries across the river ran out in the days to come, when heavy rains brought the Rappahannock to flood stage, threatening the bridges that were their only lifeline. But the rampaging river wouldn't be the only problem that the Unionists at Rappahannock Station faced, for General Lee saw their batteries on the south side of the river as a *tête-de-pont*, a possible bridgehead, that McDowell's force might exploit to attack across the river. Lee's response to this Federal annoyance resulted in what has been called "one of the fiercest small artillery duels of the war," but still the Federal batteries clung to the south shore. Only when threatened by an earnest attack by Longstreet's infantry did the Union guns withdraw across the river, the Federals burning the railroad bridge while under heavy fire from the rebels. It took no time at all for the enemy to claim the abandoned hills. Thus, as two more Federal bridges bit the dust, with both the new trestle bridge and the old railroad bridge destroyed, at least Lee and McDowell could rest easier regarding the worries that the batteries and the bridges engendered.[6]

The situation on McDowell's front at the center of Pope's defensive line along the Rappahannock settled into little more than mutual glaring and some skirmishing, but all was not well. General Lee was determined to find a way around the Federal right flank. The situation on McDowell's right heated up decidedly and resulted in yet another of the minor "battles" fought in the days leading up to the Battle of Second Bull Run proper on August 29 and 30. Rappahannock Station was far from the only crossing point on the Rappahannock, for ranging from south to north were Beverly Ford, Freeman's Ford, Fox's Ford, Warrenton, Sulphur Springs, and Waterloo Bridge. While Pope seemed content to defend most of the fords with only strong pickets, McDowell remained wary. On August 22, when intense firing signaled trouble at Beverly Ford, McDowell and Roebling rode up to where Kennedy's 1st New York Battery and the 3rd Maryland Infantry were defending the crossing. When ordered to test the waters at the crossing here, Colonel Thomas Rosser's Confederate cavalry had first opened with two guns from the other side of the river. When the Yankees quickly gave way, Rosser made a dash that netted him several slow Federals and a stack of abandoned Unionist muskets. When McDowell arrived, he discovered, much to his disgust, that the deadly accuracy of the rebel guns had not only silenced the Federal battery of six guns but also driven it and its supporting regiment of infantry away. At the time, Roebling noted that a Maryland regiment had given way and added its members to his mental list of who could or could not be depended upon. McDowell and company managed to stop the fleeing battery at one point, but another spot-on solid shot from the enemy, and they were away again. Here the conspiracy theory cooked up by the Unionist soldiery who most disliked McDowell was seemingly disproved. It had been suggested that the absurd hat McDowell wore, described as "an immense Japanese washbowl," was a secret signal to the enemy that the traitorous McDowell was on their front. But although McDowell was wearing his silly hat, the rebels put a shot near enough to the general for gravel from its ricochet to knock off his well-known headgear.[7]

Luckily, other troops were available to defend Beverly Ford, and McDowell brought General Marsena Patrick's brigade of Rufus King's division to send the rebels back across the river. General John Reynolds's New York battery, despite lacking experience, held its own in the ensuing artillery duel, but James Hall's 2nd Maine Battery came along to finish the job, silencing the rebel battery in a few minutes and sending Stonewall Jackson's rebels, who had hazarded a crossing at Beverly, back where they had come from. As Roebling would later observe, "'The result of the little affair [was that] 800 Rebel cavalry and 4 guns held in check 12,000 [Federal] infantry, 16 guns and 2,000 cavalry,' and the [rebels'] main body 'moved around our right 20 miles up.'"[8]

While Roebling accompanied McDowell to Beverly Ford, he was also in a position to observe an unfortunate encounter involving General Franz Sigel's troops. Sigel, whose division was holding the Federal right, became aware of the Confederate incursion and sent General Carl Schurz with a brigade to nearby Freeman's Ford. Sigel pushed his force across the river, which ended in disaster. The debacle could only have reminded Roebling of the disaster befalling the Federals that he had witnessed at Ball's Bluff. A Confederate witness described the rebels "pouring a dreadful fire into their crowds of confused and broken lines, as they were huddling together to cross." Many were shot in the back, and others were drowned by the crushing crowd, which pressed for the opposite bank. Only a Federal battery on the other shore prevented the enemy from following the fleeing Yankees across the river. Both Sigel and Schurz were émigrés who had fled their fatherland during the 1848 revolutions, and while Sigel was given command in recognition of his military training, Schurz earned his appointment through his strong support for the abolitionist cause. But their strongly accented English, along with the preponderance of nativist prejudice at headquarters, made these transplanted

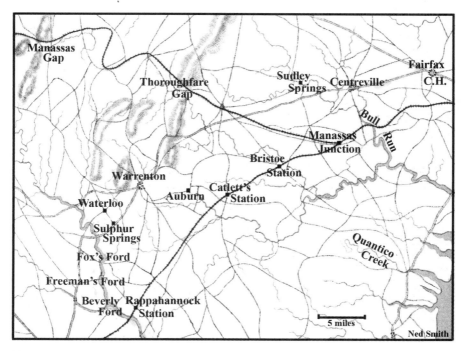

Face-off at the Rappahannock.
Adapted from Plate X, 1 OR Atlas.

Germans very handy scapegoats. It's hard to know what Roebling made of the prejudice he saw, for he acknowledged that Sigel was treated differently from his American counterparts. Yet Washington did at times express harsh criticism for what he deemed the too excitable German temperament.[9]

J. E. B. Stuart, after the diversion at Beverly Ford, made his way further up the river, crossed the Rappahannock, and embarked on his ambitious raid upon Catlett's Station. Though it likely soothed Stuart's ruffled feathers over his brush with the Federal cavalry at Verdiersville, it caused little harm to the Unionists except for some serious embarrassment. But what was the meaning of all these small-scale scrapes, a division here and a division there? Roebling was among those who suspected, based on mounting evidence, that these squabbles with Longstreet's soldiers were a distraction from what the rebels were carrying out elsewhere. Roebling suggested that Pope at this point had two choices: "Our force was say 45,000 effectives and the question was shall we cross the river, whip this division and fall on the enemy's flank or shall we retreat and give up this point of the R[a]pp[a]h[annoc]k. Pope decided on the latter course, the man, you remember who snubbed McDowell about lines of retreat." No one, including Washington, was going to let Pope forget his previous disparaging remarks when comparing the pugnacity of the western versus the eastern soldiery. Meanwhile, the men and horses of Pope's army were going hungry. Washington admitted that he "stole some green corn, begged a cup of coffee from a soldier, got a bite from the table of a resident. We were much like dogs sitting around on their haunches, waiting for scraps from the table."

On the afternoon of August 23, orders came from Pope that illustrated his indecision and hesitancy. While Sigel went further up the river to Waterloo, two divisions of McDowell's corps and three thousand cavalrymen retired to Warrenton, King's division went to Sulphur Springs, and Banks's and Jesse Reno's divisions hovered nearby within five miles of the Rappahannock. The enemy's failure to cross over after McDowell withdrew from the Rappahannock further convinced Roebling and others that the enemy had other fish to fry elsewhere. At 10 p.m. that night, as McDowell's corps was still four miles from Warrenton, news came that Pope's headquarters train at Catlett's Station had been captured by J. E. B. Stuart. Roebling, who had availed himself of a "nigger" servant, said that his man had been left behind with others at Catlett's Station, where the headquarters wagons had been sent for safety. Though General Pope's belongings were lost, including his best dress uniform coat, which Stuart gleefully confiscated, Lieutenant Roebling's kit escaped untouched. And his servant, though he had been captured, "got off afterwards." It is known that one of the officer's servants, when offered by his rebel captors "kind treatment if faithful, and instant extermination if traitorous," chose to guide Stuart's fifteen hundred troopers into the station. It is pure speculation but amusing to think that it was Roebling's servant who, albeit unwillingly, assisted Stuart and was allowed to depart with his life and his master's belongings afterward. It was not a transaction, though made under extreme duress, that any contraband would confess to his employer.[10]

Things started to go from bad to worse as the Confederates completed the disruption of Pope's communications with Washington. Rumor became all the Federals had to rely on for intelligence about enemy movements or, for that matter, for word of the longed-for arrival of McClellan's army. As Roebling commented, McClellan's Army of the Potomac was said to be "somewhere in the neighborhood but where was not known; communication between Warrenton & Washington was interrupted and Pope had neither the brains for devising any plan of operation much less for executing it." Harsh words from the young lieutenant, but for someone as dependent for his survival as Pope was upon the Army of the Potomac's coming to join him, it was unforgivable that he had failed to leave orders or directions for McClellan's arriving soldiers. Thus when telegraphic communications between Pope and Washington were completely cut, Pope's only way of coordinating the joining of his and McClellan's armies was also lost. What followed was a period of confusion. Roebling stated, "A dozen orders were given & countermanded the same day and the troops subjected to a lot of useless marching which only fatigued them and lost 2 precious days and rations also which were running short." The army indeed was having trouble keeping its men supplied with food, and many a man was marching on a grumbling, empty stomach. Roebling and his immediate commander, Major Houston, were among the lucky few who could remedy this problem by visiting Warrenton's Warren Green Hotel for their dinner. But there was plenty of news to spoil their appetites, for it was discovered that somehow all the maps of Culpeper County, maps the topographical engineers had spent months gathering information for and preparing, had been lost. While not explaining the circumstances of the loss, Roebling was outspoken in blaming Pope and McDowell for the calamity. While dining, they also received orders to "rush down to the river and examine all fords, preparatory to all the troops crossing the Rpphk that night and falling in the enemy's rear. We returned at 1 o'clock in the morning only to find the order countermanded." While at the river, Washington viewed the ruins of the buildings at the famous resort at White Sulphur Springs. With a pang of regret, he declared, "Our men destroyed them the day before, an act only in keeping with all their other acts of vandalism. I have seen numerous instances myself where men with their families who considered themselves rich the day before, were homeless beggars the day after, not knowing where to get their next meal; most of the destruction is perfectly wanton, and not necessary, and only calculated to make the inhabitants your bitterest enemies." Having been denied their pleasant dinner in Warrenton, Roebling and Houston dined that day with General Banks. Washington found him "a perfect gentleman which you can say of no other general except Hooker," an opinion the young lieutenant would modify somewhat in the coming months. Meanwhile, the contemplative Roebling also observed of Banks, "He seems however to be pursued by bad luck."[11]

These observations of Roebling's regarding the destruction of civilian property are interesting in terms of not just the impact on those who saw all their earthly belongings swept away but also the effect that the license to steal and destroy had upon the perpetrators. And what could and should happen when an army's ability to feed its men and horses breaks down? Does morality start to shift in the eyes of starving men? And does a civilian's suspected support for the enemy justify destitution as punishment? It seems more than a little evident that, at this point in the war, the administration, Secretary of War Edwin Stanton, newly appointed general in chief Henry Halleck, and the Congressional Joint Committee on the Conduct of the War were all answering "yes" to the question of whether the war should be brought home to Southern civilians. It was this hardening that saw the like-minded General John Pope brought east, and in the months and years to come, it would see the elevation of men like U. S. Grant, William Sherman, and Philip Sheridan to the command of the Union armies.[12]

The Eventful Days Leading to the Battle of Second Bull Run

GENERAL JOHN POPE WAS FINALLY ABLE, RELUCTANTLY, TO TEAR HIS focus away from the Rappahannock, and he began to accept and respond to the reports of Stonewall Jackson having passed through Thoroughfare Gap. Washington Roebling later caustically observed, "The enemy's movements were mysterious to Pope and McDowell. Moreover, guided by false pride, they delayed to fall back to Centreville as being a retreat of the Army of . . . Virginia that would 'dim the then brilliant fame of John Pope.'" As Roebling and Major Houston returned to McDowell's corps, they found the general's troops leaving Warrenton on the main pike, which ran to Centreville, crossed the Manassas Road at Gainesville, and then passed through First Bull Run battlefield. Great agitation reigned in the Federal army, for news of Jackson's great destruction of the Federal stores at Manassas Junction had arrived. McDowell was in a savage state of mind and nearly knocked the head off one straggling soldier. While the rank and file muttered that they would shoot McDowell, Roebling overheard the general muttering, over and over, "Demain, nous avons une grande batallie, une grand bataille (Tomorrow there will be a great battle)." Did McDowell imagine the next day might give him a chance to redeem his shattered reputation? They encamped eight miles beyond Warrenton and were joined by Franz Sigel and the first arrivals from the Army of the Potomac, the soldiers of General John Reynolds of Fitz John Porter's 5th Corps. While most of the exhausted Federal cavalry had all but ceased to function, John Buford was still bringing information to McDowell, and startling information it was. It left McDowell as seemingly the only one in Pope's army who was worried about the imminent arrival of James Long-street. Early the next morning, McDowell sent one of his divisions, under the

General Fitz John Porter.
Library of Congress.

command of General James Ricketts, to Thoroughfare Gap in the Bull Run Mountains in hopes of preventing Longstreet's corps from passing through and reinforcing Jackson. Roebling had the impression that the rebels, finding Ricketts barring their way, merely sidestepped him and passed through Hopewell Gap four miles further on. Roebling found it difficult to understand how Ricketts could not have known about Hopewell Gap, for, he pointed out, it was "laid down on every map."[1]

McDowell, meanwhile, continued his advance toward Manassas with Reynolds's division following slowly, leaving General Rufus King's division to head for Centreville via the Warrenton Turnpike. General King was Roebling's nemesis from his bridge-building days, and the question as to whether epilepsy was impairing the general's ability to command could easily be answered in the affirmative. By this time, King was already commanding

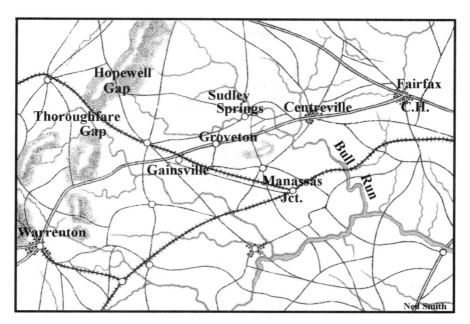

Lead-up to Second Bull Run.
Adapted from Plate XXII, 5 OR Atlas.

his division from an ambulance, and a severe seizure would soon leave his division essentially without a commander in a most desperate situation. As McDowell and his staff rode at the head of his column, they suddenly came upon a rebel battery that hurled a shell at them, killing five men with a shot that came near dispatching them all. Jackson, having captured one of McDowell's couriers, knew exactly where McDowell was and where he was going. As a delaying action, the enemy battery's activity was a great success, for McDowell's men were promptly ordered into line of battle, a move that took an hour to complete, by which time, as Washington pointed out, the rebel battery was long gone. But the deployment of the Union soldiery had another unforeseen result. Empty stomachs overruled any perceived need to pursue the enemy. The men had seen no rations for some time and discovered crops to be enjoyed. Roebling lamented, "Wasting 4 precious hours more, spent in robbing orchards & cornfields, and watching immense columns of dust in front of us." Then again, McDowell himself seemed somewhat disinclined to get back on the road, for he settled down in a nearby orchard, "munching on apples 'by the basket,'" while perusing maps and contemplating what this

General Rufus King.
Library of Congress.

ambush had meant. When once more on the move, McDowell divided his force again, sending King's division down the pike in the late afternoon, while McDowell, Roebling, and several other staff members followed the railroad line toward Manassas in hopes of finding the elusive Pope.[2]

Arriving at Manassas at dark, McDowell was disappointed in his search for Pope, for in this stunning example of command and control becoming completely unglued, Pope, he was told, had gone in the direction of Centreville. While McDowell was hunting for Pope, Pope was hunting for McDowell, and everybody was hunting for the uncooperative enemy, General Jackson. But on reaching Manassas, McDowell became aware of an ominous heavy cannonading from the direction of King's force, which had unknowingly stumbled upon Jackson's main body of some twenty-four thousand rebels. At the moment he was most needed, King was apparently struck with a seizure that left his brigade commanders without orders or direction. In this state of confusion, the first shots were fired in what came to be known as the Battle of Second Bull Run, and while King's division was like a rudderless ship, a surprising lack of coordination within Jackson's forces allowed the men of King's division, after hard fighting, to withdraw. They stumbled into Manassas at 3 a.m. but did not find McDowell there. Anxious to go to King's aid, McDowell started off cross-country in the dark and lost his way three times in the swamps of Flat Run, the particularly cold night adding to the misery. At midnight, he gave up, encamped, and later breakfasted with Reynolds, who had also had a brush with the formerly elusive Confederates. When McDowell returned to Manassas, he found General King's roughly used division, and though their commander was still far from well, King's decision to withdraw likely denied Jackson the opportunity to destroy the division completely. Luckily, an order from Pope directing the seriously outnumbered King to "hold his ground at all hazards" hadn't reached him. McDowell also found General Ricketts's division at Manassas, fresh from its inevitable failure to prevent Longstreet's passage through the Bull Run Mountains to join Jackson. It was not a good night's work. In fact, the only good news was that General Fitz John Porter had showed up with the Army of the Potomac's regulars. The obvious reason aside, McDowell had been hunting for Pope in hopes of putting his mind to rest as to just who would be commanding whom when the officers of the Army of the Potomac arrived. The first encounter did not go well, for when McDowell put Porter in a position facing the positions of King's and Reynolds's fights of the previous night, Roebling observed, "Porter obeyed none [of McDowell's instructions], running off as soon as the enemy opened fire with a battery." Though McDowell had spent most of the previous night looking for Pope, Pope placed all the blame on him for their not finding one another.[3]

After a night destined to leave everyone in bad fettle, McDowell, seemingly undaunted though still uneasy, led two divisions toward the old Bull Run battlefield, where the main body of Jackson's troops had taken up a superbly defendable position. As for Pope, when this news reached him on the night of August 28, he convinced himself, quite erroneously, that he had caught Jackson in mid-retreat and remained, for the most part, confident that, as far as the enemy was concerned, he could "bag the whole lot." Thus, as he issued his orders to his commanders that night to concentrate on Jackson at Groveton, Pope was in fact committing himself to fight on the ground of Stonewall Jackson's careful choosing. Nor did Pope seem concerned with the obvious threat posed by Longstreet's imminent arrival on the scene, for Longstreet would take up a position on Jackson's flank at the scene of King's fight the night before. As McDowell arrived early in the afternoon of August 29, he found the battle had commenced, with Joseph Hooker, Philip Kearny, and Franz Sigel already engaged and Sigel by far bearing the brunt of the fighting. Pope, fully believing that it was he who had done the stalking and was finally forcing a confrontation on the fleeing Jackson, instead walked unknowingly into a battle at a place especially chosen by the pugnacious rebel as one perfectly suited for him to take on and destroy a Federal force three times the size of his own.[4]

On the morning of August 29, Roebling tells, McDowell and his staff were in the saddle at daybreak and reached a house three-quarters of a mile from Henry House, where they found General Reynolds and his command. While Roebling watched the rebels on the road from Groveton to Sudley Springs, Reynolds and McDowell went out to reconnoiter. Returning by way of Bethlehem Church, they encountered the exhausted men of King's division; then, at King's headquarters at the Weir House, they found a great crowd of demoralized officers. Roebling opined that they had not covered themselves with glory in this, their first serious fight, and he expressed little sympathy for the pickle they had found themselves in the previous night. When McDowell encountered Fitz John Porter's column 2.5 miles beyond the church, after a conversation of some fifteen minutes, he took Porter aside for an earnest conversation of ten minutes more, unfortunately beyond the hearing of the staff. Thus, it was 2:30 p.m. before McDowell's force approached the loud cannonading the men had been hearing all afternoon. Upon reaching Henry House, McDowell left his staff, returning to instruct his aides that he was positioning King's and Ricketts's columns, as soon as they came up, in the valley of Young's Run alongside the pike. But it would be near dark before any of McDowell's troops became meaningfully engaged with the enemy. In a masterful demonstration of understatement, Washington said of the hapless divisions' attempts at assuming their positions, "They had very bad luck." While some lost their way, others were ambushed by the enemy, Roebling observed, and "the majority came back badly cut up and scattered." All evening the road to Manassas was filled with the straggling and demoralized men of Ricketts's command, hardly inspiring confidence in how things would go the next day. And though it seemed that Reynolds's men had fared better, many still felt the situation was dire.[5]

Upon McDowell's afternoon arrival at the fields that would comprise the Second Bull Run battlefield, Roebling had observed the rapid firing of the Federal artillery, their gunners proving an effective counterbalance to the lackluster performance of the blue-clad infantry already on the field. The Union batteries had been effective in silencing the enemy's guns as well, but in retrospect Roebling would remember, "Much valuable ammunition was however thrown away for which we paid dearly the next day." Though former artilleryman Roebling admired how Sigel had massed the guns together, they were on too high an elevation; accordingly, "every shot lodged where it struck, in place of glancing and bounding off to do more mischief." It was late in the day before McDowell got King's and Ricketts's divisions onto the left and center of the Federal line. It was fully dark when the rebels opened a cross-fire on King's tired division, which had gotten lost while seeking its position. Half the Unionists were killed or wounded. The other half wisely ran off. As the day drew to a close, Washington overheard General Sigel comment that his 1st Corps would have been victorious if only McDowell had arrived earlier. What could better communications and some semblance of command and control have accomplished, without McDowell having had to search for the armies' commander with the subsequent hope of receiving orders? McDowell finally met with Pope on the night of August 29 for the first time in four days.[6]

On the morning of August 30, most of the generals gathered at Pope's headquarters, including McDowell and his staff. Despite having received reports of Longstreet's arrival on the scene, Pope chose, inexplicably, to disbelieve or ignore the evidence. When fighting had not recommenced by 10 a.m., rumor ran riot at the Federal headquarters, quite mistakenly supposing that the rebels had run away. In fact, R. E. Lee was thinking, as historian B. F. Cooling aptly explains, that it was "better to let Pope batter himself against Jackson's resolute defense and then counterstrike at the opportune moment." Roebling describes Pope as bragging and overconfident and noted that "some of Pope's staff officers, low Western fellows, were preparing to get drunk, when at once the fight reopened with artillery, principally on the Union center." He also observed that no disposition had been made to meet such an attack. While the enemy had been repulsed on the Federal right, he could rightly be expected to attack some other point. But the Unionists' mass of artillery remained on their right, where it would be useless. As Roebling commented, "Our general seemed perfectly content to sit still and allow the enemy to do what he pleased."[7]

Roebling wrote that as the rebel fire on the Federal center grew hotter and hotter, every moment seemed to prove that the enemy was then hurling his entire force against the Union left. Roebling recounted that eventually, too little and too late, "McDowell saw it plainly enough and tried his best to avert the blow, but was unable to do it with his own troops alone." Several scouts had warned McDowell earlier in the day that the enemy was trying to turn his left, but even when General Reynolds tried to give him that same warning, McDowell refused to believe him. The day's action played out much as General Lee had hoped it would, with Pope making a futile assault on the enemy until even he could no longer deny the truth. Roebling, in a position to observe the unfortunately critical role McDowell had played in the calamity of August 30, describing the chaos and McDowell's subsequent actions.

> The running of our men had already commenced, at least 10,000 were on the full go. Many had not even heard the whistle of a shot before they ran. This was a most humiliating spectacle showing the utterly demoralized condition of the men. A lot of reinforcements had come in, composed of raw troops, the mere sound of firing sufficed to set them off. In the mean time the troops on our right had been brought over to the left, principally regulars and 9 months [regiments], and McDowell put himself at their head & succeeded in repulsing the rebels some distance, more troops came up in support enabling us to hold our line with security.

To a large degree, McDowell's mistakes that afternoon had an important bearing on this, his second great defeat at Bull Run, and he bore the brunt of the disaster as Pope, after issuing orders at 8 p.m. for his army to retreat to Centreville, turned command over to him and rode off. Though Lee and Longstreet urged their tired soldiers unsuccessfully to pursue the vanquished Yankees, a cavalry fight by Buford late in the day allowed what was left of the Pope's defeated Army of Virginia to retire in some semblance of order.[8]

While the Federals regrouped to confront whatever else the rebels meant to throw at them, a distraught brigade commander General Robert H. Milroy, whose men were giving way before the rebel onslaught, appeared before McDowell, howling for assistance. As an indication of his state of mind, Milroy later said of that day, "I felt that the crises [sic] of the nation was on hand, and that the happiness of unborn millions and the progress of the world depended upon our success." Roebling witnessed that mad apparition of Milroy and would in fact have to testify at a future date regarding Milroy's accusation that McDowell refused to assist his beleaguered brigade. As Roebling would later relate, though McDowell did not respond to what seemed like Milroy's hysterics, when word came from General George Meade that assistance was indeed necessary, McDowell sent aid. Thankfully, the fighting ended when night sent in, and Roebling was sent to find General Pope. But, as happened so frequently when trying to coordinate with that general, he could not be found, and Roebling was then unable to relocate McDowell. After searching all night, Roebling eventually caught up with McDowell and the rest of the army, which, to his surprise, had withdrawn to Centreville. Despite the decidedly discouraging events of August 30, Roebling and others had thought their army in fair condition to recommence the fight on August 31. Rebel prisoners had been saying that they had been living on mule and horse flesh for the last two days, though it is difficult to believe this was accurate given Jackson's capture of Pope's supply depot at Manassas Junction. Their statement that they were so short of ammunition that they were firing stones in place of lead from their muskets was only somewhat more plausible. So Roebling and others were game for the fight they expected the next morning, August 31. But the Army of Virginia's commander was not. Roebling says

General Robert Milroy.
Library of Congress.

of the night of August 30, "It was at this juncture that a certain *** General by the name of P**e ordered a retreat; the rebels were of course so utterly surprised that they did not even offer to pursue." With considerable anguish, Roebling declared himself "prepared to be surprised at nothing under such commanders," and he raged at remembering that just two hours before Pope's withdrawal from the battlefield, when the rumor of the Confederates having retreated was at its height, the fools at Pope's headquarters had telegraphed Washington, DC, announcing their great victory.[9]

At least this retreat, unlike the one after First Bull Run, could be said to have been conducted in some semblance of order, without the panic and loss of equipment that attended the aftermath of the earlier disaster. The army withdrew to Centreville, to Fairfax, and finally to Munson's Hill, where McDowell encamped. Here Roebling proclaimed,

> As for myself, I am completely tired out and used up; I have not had one meal a day for the last 3 weeks, have slept on the ground every night generally without blankets and been in the saddle constantly; I have also been lucky in not getting shot—McDowell is a brave and courageous man who don't hesitate a moment to expose himself when necessary, and I followed him closely. It is true there is something wrong about McDowell but he is a jewel compared with the commander who was never to be found when wanted and did not even expose himself enough to get a general view of the battleground and see how affairs went on. McDowell in many cases acted for him. As for the future I have no hope whatever; I assure you on Saturday night last I felt utterly sick disgusted and tired of the war; being somewhat rested now I feel more hopeful. Our men are sick of the war, they fight without an aim and without enthusiasm, they have no confidence in their leaders except one or two; I overheard Hooker give his opinion of McClellan and have little hopes of him. Sigel is physically unable to do much, because he does everything himself so as to be certain. Franklin & Hooker are looked on with most favor, but Franklin lost his golden opportunity on Saturday when he might have marched up and changed the tide to victory, orders or no orders.

Thoroughly discouraged by what he was witnessing of the demoralized Federal troops, Roebling closed this letter to his father with a damning assertion: "In the next place one Rebel is equal to 5 Union men in bravery that is about the proportion."[10]

To put Roebling's experiences into context, a brief overview of the battle allows us to consider Pope's unfortunate conduct before, during, and after the conflict. The Battle of Second Bull Run is remembered as one of the most daring and risky maneuvers of the war, orchestrated by the Confederates to pry Pope loose from his strong position on the Rappahannock and send him reeling back toward Washington. In a game of risk that ended up paying great dividends, Lee, confronting a larger opponent and flying in the face of all conventional wisdom, chose to split his army, sending Jackson on a fifty-mile march to outflank Pope's army, attack its vulnerable rear, and destroy Pope's communications. Longstreet's assignment, to distract and entertain the Federals on their line on the Rappahannock, was worked to perfection. Once Pope turned to confront Jackson's threat, which he was surprisingly slow to do, Longstreet could then join Jackson to finish him off. With a thorough knowledge of the territory they sped through and a cheering welcome from the locals, by dusk on August 25, Jackson, after a march of twenty-five miles, was twelve miles north of Pope, who was still lingering at the now famous Waterloo Bridge. But where were the Army of the Potomac reinforcements, and when George McClellan came, who would command? As two large Federal armies struggled to combine in a control-and-command disaster in the making, these were important questions, ones that General in Chief Henry Halleck was either unable or unwilling to answer. As more and more of McClellan's forces arrived, Halleck's protests that he was too busy to answer the many questions that needed answering became more strident. And when most needed, the overused Federal cavalry more or less ceased to function. As a further indication of Pope's misunderstanding of his enemy's intentions and his dilatory reactions, on the morning of August 26, as Jackson completed his march into Pope's rear, McDowell was inexplicably ordered to return to the Rappahannock and cross the river for a reconnaissance in force. As Jackson's incursion preceded unchecked, Longstreet's aggressive show of force at the river stalemated McDowell at Sulphur Springs and Waterloo Bridge. Though McDowell decided against crossing the river, that afternoon's confrontation seemingly became the focus of all Pope's attention, with Pope offering to send McDowell substantial numbers of reinforcements. Longstreet's mission of distracting Pope from Jackson's movements achieving complete success, it was time for Lee to reunite the two wings of his army. Longstreet would follow Jackson's route north through Thoroughfare Gap. Unchallenged, Jackson and the cavalry that accompanied him prepared to sever Pope's lifeline, the Orange and Alexandria Railroad. After waylaying several of the Federal trains, Jackson and his hungry men turned their eyes toward Pope's stockpile

General Henry Halleck.
Library of Congress.

of food and materials at Manassas Junction, its capture culminating in two of Jackson's finest days: a fifty-mile march, two wrecked Federal trains, and an astonishing amount of supplies for his men, supplies that would be denied to Pope's hungry soldiers. Nor would any more of the approaching Army of the Potomac reinforcements be able to reach Pope by train as planned. The cutting of Pope's telegraph communications added insult to injury.[11]

In its aftermath, the Confederate victory at Second Bull Run brought the Federal war effort to its knees. Roebling later wrote a damning assessment of the battle and its outcome:

That the Pope campaign would fail was a forgone conclusion; all elements of success were wanting. McDowell's corps composed one-half of this army; he hated Pope, so there was no possibility of co-operation.

The other troops were incompatible. Siegel's [sic, General Franz Sigel] excitable Germans were always an uncertain quantity. What cavalry we had was good, but was divided into small detachments, without a head to make it an efficient body. Banks was a political commander, although a very fine man personally, his troops accomplished more afterwards under other leaders. Lee's flank movement on the West was anticipated, nothing was done to head it off in time; hence when it did come it was in the nature of a surprise which demoralized the whole army. When the news of Stuart's capture of Manassas came the scene was like the feast of Balshazzar. We were just a day too late with our retreat or else Lee was a day ahead. Our day ahead backward [movement] would have enabled us to form a junction with the tired troops of McClellan. Even then the result would probably have been the same. McDowell was so jealous of Pope that he would rather lose the battle than have him win it. He purposely handled his command in a manner to bring this about. Pope again knew that McClellan was waiting to profit by his certain failure. McDowell's soldiers were a demoralized lot, they all hated him personally; he was brutal and domineering, without any other qualities to offset it. He would have made a good chief of staff.

As we shall consider in the next chapter, when McDowell was replaced by General Joseph Hooker, Roebling observed, "The change was most marked; the soldiers were fond of him and would go anywhere." But Washington also added a caveat regarding their new commander: "Hooker should have remained a corps commander, that was his limit." While everyone in the Federal army could only have been anxious to leave behind the trials and tribulations of General John Pope's fractured, costly venture into army command, that was not to be. In the months and years ahead, where to lay the blame for what happened at Second Bull Run would be investigated and hotly debated again and again.[12]

If Roebling ever felt any respect for or loyalty to General Irvin McDowell, it likely died with his experience of being called upon to testify the next spring at the inquiry regarding the general's role at the Battle of Second Bull Run. He wrote,

I was summoned to testify before the Congressional Court of Inquiry as to the defeat at Bull Run, especially McDowell's part in it. I no sooner arrived in Washington when McDowell buttonholed me, told me exactly what to say in the court. He told me in advance just what questions would be asked and warned me especially not to volunteer any information or opinions beyond what I was asked. I was the only staff officer who stuck to him through the fight, his own having disappeared, and therefore was the only one who had seen certain occurrences. Everything went off as he had fixed it, showing that such inquiries are a farce, everything being arranged in advance. But I noticed that McDowell never got another command. He was a man of a false heart.[13]

Roebling would later add another sad postscript to his experiences at Second Bull Run. One year after the battle, in August 1863, he revisited the battlefield with his commander at that time, General Gouverneur K. Warren. They were there to map the field, and Roebling wrote, "There being no enemy around and no one to interfere, there was ample time to study the various positions of the combatants, much better than during the actual battle, when everything is excitement." In the aftermath of the battle, Pope's blame for the outcome rested heavily upon McDowell and the commander of the Army of the Potomac's 5th Corps, Fitz John Porter. Roebling observed,

We also noted the position of Porter's 5th Corps, nearly two miles to the East. While at this point he was ordered by Pope to attack the enemy's flank instantly, and because he did not or could not do it he was dismissed in disgrace and was to be shot, all to cover up Gen. Pope's incapacity. Pope falsely or ignorantly assured that Porter was two miles nearer and in touch with the enemy's flank. Had this been so, then the dismissal would have been proper. Neither Pope or McDowell would ever acknowledge that they were wrong and were making false charges purposely to screen themselves.

For the 13,830 Federal casualties, it was a moot point.[14]

To some extent, Washington's return visit to Second Bull Run afforded him a most unpleasant glimpse of the harsh realities that most of the Federals who marched toward Centreville with the retreating Federal army had been able to avoid. The rebels, however victorious, woke up on the morning of August 31, 1862, to three thousand dead and fifteen thousand wounded lying upon the battlefield. The evidence of this tragedy remained a year later, as Roebling described:

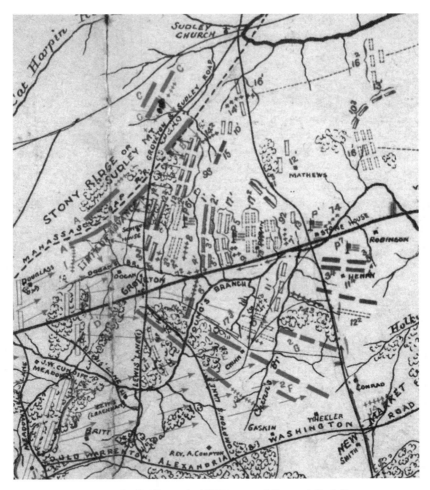

Portions of General G. K. Warren's 1878 map of Second Bull Run.
Library of Congress.

On the right of the field was the railroad cut occupied by the enemy, perfectly shielded. This position was almost carried by Butterfield's brigade of regulars (Porter's corps, who did all the real hard fighting). The leading soldier was shot dead within twenty feet of the cut. The ants had polished the 6-foot skeleton to a brilliant whiteness; a colony of wasps had established their nest within the skull and were flying in and out of the eye holes—a sad commentary on the glories of the martial field, but hardened as I was I could not resist shedding a tear. In various directions the wild Virginia hog was still busy rooting up corpses from their shallow graves. As we had abandoned the field the year before, the burying was poorly done. In such a survey one always sees too late what should have been done and what should have been left undone. There are always moments in a battle when it can be won!

That men like Roebling and his comrades could, after such devastating experiences, continue on in the face of what seemed futile carnage and sacrifice is remarkable, to put it mildly. For Washington Roebling, the Battle of Second Bull Run marked a point little more than a year into his military service. In the month to come, his and General Warren's fates would become irrevocably linked with that of the 5th Corps, which was, its members suspected, never entirely able to distance itself from the taint of its commander Fitz John Porter's supposed disloyalty at Second Bull Run. But after this battle, Roebling still had more than two years of hard service ahead of him, years marked by both triumphs and additional tragedies.[15]

9

With Hooker's Assault at South Mountain

THERE WAS LITTLE REST FOR EITHER ROBERT E. LEE'S OR JOHN POPE'S tired veterans, for the very day after this second momentous clash at Bull Run, Lee's ragged soldiers found themselves back on the march, this time in the pouring rain on a mission to once again outflank the Federals. On August 31, Pope remained at Centreville against the advice of his corps commanders, who strongly suspected Lee would attempt just such a flanking movement, once again severing Pope's communications with Washington and interposing his army between Pope and the capital. Pope was supported in his decision to remain at Centreville by General Halleck, who could hardly be fully aware of the condition of Pope's army and the predicament in which it found itself. And while Pope at first embraced Halleck's advice, he soon began to vacillate. Pope was left without information about the enemy, for his cavalry, their horses completely broken down, had ceased to function, a situation that would leave any commander uneasy. But this alone did not lead Pope to recommend to Halleck that his army be allowed to withdraw to the defenses of Washington. Pope accused the officers of the Army of the Potomac of nothing less than mutinous behavior and intent, claiming that they were inciting their men to disobedience and a refusal to fight. With no hint of the role he himself had played in the demoralized condition of his army, Pope instead blamed all on the "tools or parasites," as he labeled the adherents of George McClellan, who he alleged refused to take orders from him. As Halleck continued to dither, on September 1 Stonewall Jackson continued his flanking march, striving to attain what the Federals most feared, a position between Pope's army and Washington, DC.[1]

But Jackson was experiencing some disappointment, for his hope of staging another surprise attack upon the Yankees was being spoiled as Unionist soldiers kept popping up in his way. General Joseph Hooker in command of

James Ricketts's division and General Marsena Patrick's brigade were among those spoiling Jackson's plans. Jackson, having halted at Chantilly or Ox Hill to await support from James Longstreet, to his chagrin, found himself attacked, and the resulting battle, surrealistically fought amid violent thunder storms, ended with the deaths of two prominent Federal commanders, Generals Isaac Stevens and Philip Kearny. If nothing else, this proved that the Federals still had some fight left in them, and their surprisingly stubborn resistance bought Pope enough time on that cold, wet night to complete his withdrawal to the outskirts of Washington. If Pope was a defeated man, Halleck gave all appearance of also being at his wits' end. Taking Pope's advice that somebody must do something, Halleck urged the administration to call on General McClellan to come and take command of the defense of the capital. Though many in Washington wished to heap blame upon a disloyal McClellan and his minions for the disaster at Second Bull Run, the need for a savior of the army and the capital won out. Assuming that mantle, McClellan rode out to meet the beleaguered Union troops on the outskirts of Washington, and the cheer that arose from the vanguard carried resoundingly back through the ranks of the army. As a much-chastened General Pope rode off into military oblivion, Generals Lee, Jackson, and Longstreet began their incursion into Maryland. They had much to gain by maintaining the momentum of their campaign, which, beyond keeping the Unionists away from the Confederacy, might influence a discouraged Northern electorate to vote against support for the war in the upcoming midterm elections. And the seeming invincibility of the Army of Northern Virginia just might influence some of the Europeans who were still sitting on the fence regarding recognition of the Confederacy.[2]

Many of the despondent Unionist soldiers, on nearing the capital, found the news that they were going to be under McClellan's command something to cheer about. But it appears that few in the administration wanted to see McClellan, that odd combination of arrogance and seeming reluctance to fight, back in command of Federal forces. The job became his quite literally by default, though he was awarded the position of commander of the force defending Washington as opposed to being named commander of the armies. With the threat posed by the Army of Northern Virginia far from over, a leader who could invest the dispirited troops with a will to fight could not be discarded out of hand, however grave any doubts about his politics and tactical wisdom. With Pope leveling charges against Fitz John Porter, the administration was advocating for General Hooker to take over the command of Porter's 5th Corps, but on this, the eve of an impending advance, McClellan was able to stave off Porter's being replaced. Instead, Hooker replaced 3rd Corps commander General Irvin McDowell on September 6, with the corps now designated the 1st Corps in the "new" Army of the Potomac. As if they were tainted by their mere connection with their former commander, McClellan expressed his doubt about McDowell's old troops but his confidence in their new commander. "Hooker will however soon bring them out of the kinks and make them fight if anyone can." Overnight, Washington Roebling found himself working for both Hooker and McClellan. While McClellan was still negotiating with the administration regarding commanders, he ordered Hooker to begin the new 1st Corps's advance into Maryland. Moving north through the capital, McClellan ordered Hooker to bring the corps up the Seventh Street Road, which "conveniently brought them past McClellan's headquarters and enabled them to personally express their gratification at the general's restoration to command." Hooker would operate with the 9th Corps, commanded by General Jesse Reno, while General Ambrose Burnside took overall command of the right wing of the force McClellan intended to lead into Maryland.[3]

Washington Roebling was assigned to serve under McClellan's chief of engineers, Major James C. Duane, and would be attached to Hooker's head-quarters. McClellan had at his disposal the combined armies of the Army of the Potomac and Pope's Army of Virginia, in all six infantry corps of about eighty thousand men, a substantial portion of whom were green recruits. Though McClellan, thanks to the ever-inflated numbers brought to him by the unreliable Allan Pinkerton, believed the enemy had 110,000 men, Lee had 50,000 veterans in the field, though the grueling pace and lack of food continued to whittle down their numbers. On September 4, advance elements of the Army of Northern Virginia crossed into Maryland, with the main body entering Frederick, Maryland, on September 7. Desiring to increase Northern discontent and alarm by threatening Pennsylvania, Longstreet commanded a force sent to Hagerstown, Maryland, while Jackson was sent to Harpers Ferry to eliminate any possible threat to the Army of Northern Virginia from that quarter. Lee had to accept another disappointment on this score, for he had expected that, when threatened by Jackson and Company, the Harpers Ferry garrison would evacuate; instead, General Halleck ordered a Federal resis-tance. McClellan took the now combined Armies of Virginia and the Poto-mac in hand, and the new Army of the Potomac left the capital on September 7, the same day that found all of Lee's forces in Maryland near Frederick. That McClellan's new army was ready to follow him so soon after another bitter defeat provides convincing evidence that he could still inspire these soldiers. It also seems that McClellan, despite his reputation for slowness, may have

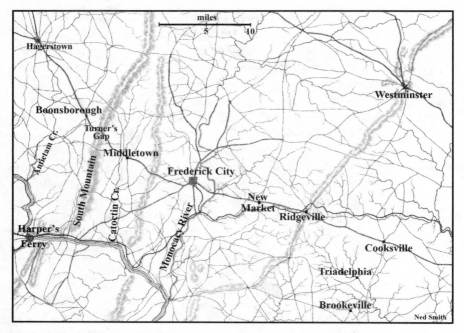

Assigned to Hooker's headquarters.
Adapted from Plate XXVII, OR Atlas.

surprised Lee, the Federal commander's somewhat more timely response to Lee's Maryland plans coming sooner than the rebel leader expected. But the onset of McClellan's approach did little to curb Lee's daring as he gave Jackson and Longstreet their orders. Within days, Lee would split his army into four parts, the larger of them leaving with Jackson to assist his envelopment of the Harpers Ferry garrison and negate its threat to Lee's communications. Longstreet and the remainder of the Army of Northern Virginia remained near Hagerstown and the passes through the South Mountain range.[4]

When Hooker's headquarters was established east of Frederick, the Federals were still in the dark as to what Lee was planning, but in the coming days, they learned that some portion of the Army of Northern Virginia was entrenched on South Mountain where the turnpike led over to Hagerstown. As McClellan left Washington, he had to decide whether his army was ready to drive Lee out of Maryland. Surprisingly, Lee seemed unconcerned, for believing that McClellan's army was still in Washington, he allowed Longstreet's force to remain at Frederick as a potential threat to both Baltimore and

Washington. On September 8, Burnside's force was ordered to march toward Cooksville on the National Pike that connected Baltimore and Frederick, though extensive straggling by Hooker's corps caused the right wing to come up short of that day's goal, the town of Brookeville. But the 1st Corps did better the next day, reaching Brookeville, where Burnside reported to McClellan that Hooker's leadership was reinvigorating McDowell's old corps. They were not only closing in on the Army of Northern Virginia but also curtailing the Confederates' ability to threaten Baltimore. By September 10, the Federals began to envelop Lee's position at Frederick, with Hooker's 1st Corps concentrating near Triadelphia, as the other corps of the Army of the Potomac concentrated nearby. On September 11, the Pennsylvania Reserves led the 1st Corps to its bivouac around Poplar Springs, about four miles southeast of Ridgeville on the National Pike, with the other divisions nearby. It seems that the soldiers of both armies were astonished by the well-tended fields of the region they were marching through, for the local men, mostly German immigrants, had, unlike the men of Virginia and elsewhere, stayed at home tending their farms. Their fields were full not of weeds, like the soldiers' own fields, but of tomatoes, potatoes, tobacco, fruit, and grain. Nor were these farmers likely to sympathize with the rebels who had passed through before the Yankees, for the ragged Southern invaders had stolen every workhorse they could get their hands on, paying the irate owners in worthless Confederate script. But even as the Federals pondered Lee's destination, few in his own army knew of their own commander's intentions. Though McClellan's pursuit would prove sluggish, it still provided enough pressure to convince Lee that perhaps, once his capture of Harpers Ferry had secured his rear and flanks, he could safely lead his army out of Maryland and back into Virginia.[5]

On the rainy night of September 11, Hooker was awakened by emissaries from his wing commander and superior, General Burnside. The two West Virginia cavalry officers found Hooker asleep in a wall tent in a nightshirt, all six feet of him, grey hair tousled and blue eyes sleepy, looking like anything but a general. They had come with word from General Burnside that he intended to make an early start to leading off the next day's march. Hooker, in a demonstration of the cheekiness and disrespect he was rather well known for, replied that if Burnside wanted to get his men on the road before Hooker got up in the morning, he would find "that we will strike the enemy's videttes at the Monocacy, will have a brush with Stewart's [sic] cavalry about Frederick City, a nice little fight at South mountain and hell on the Antietam." The two troopers had reason to later remember Hooker's all too prescient remarks, though his insights were based upon the latest intelligence received since the enemy had left Frederick. Although the rebel cavalry were screening their movement, Hooker had a pretty good idea what the next day would hold. Despite this reason to get up and get going, the 1st Corps fell behind schedule on the September 12, the rain posing one reason for a late start and subsequent substantial straggling. Nonetheless, by nightfall Frederick was occupied, and the citizens, glad to see the backs of the ragged and starving rebels, welcomed the Unionists. As the rebel cavalry, the Army of Northern Virginia's rear guard, reached the Catoctin Mountains, the administration in Washington again began to despair at seeming evidence of another bout of McClellan's "slows." On September 13, Hooker's 1st Corps remained at New Market awaiting McClellan's orders, which were not issued until 2 p.m. By 10 p.m., the 9th Corps had gone beyond Frederick and reached Middletown, where it received no further orders from McClellan regarding the next day. Although the other Army of the Potomac corps had come only seven miles on September 13, the 1st, 2nd, and 12th Corps and a division of the 5th bedded down around the eastern side of Frederick.[6]

The Army of the Potomac commander's seeming lack of urgency on September 13 is all the more puzzling since General McClellan had received a special gift that day. A courier or aide had carelessly dropped a copy of Lee's Special Orders #191, addressed to General D. H. Hill, orders detailing the movements of Hill, Jackson, Longstreet, and Lafayette McLaws for the campaign. Wrapped around two or three cigars, they were found by three delighted Yankees, who, more excited by the cigars than their wrapping, eventually realized the papers looked important. Luckily, the invaluable document was eventually passed up the line. Receiving the copy of Lee's orders before noon on September 13, McClellan, being McClellan, hesitated. Such a find seemed too good to be true. Was it a clever rebel trick? That day, in a message to Abraham Lincoln, McClellan, though he assured the president that he was rapidly swinging into action, added, "I have all the plans of the rebels, and will catch them in their own trap if my men are equal to the emergency. I feel I can count on them as of old." With this assertion to the president that if he should fail, it would surely be his men's fault, not his, no further illustration is needed to prove McClellan, above all, feared making decisions and being held responsible for them. McClellan's contemplation of taking action also was counterbalanced by his usual caution and persistent belief that his opponent had more than twice as many men as he actually did. Somehow, someway, McClellan believed he would be facing a force superior to his own, though even when Harpers Ferry surrendered on September 13, allowing Jackson to rejoin the Army of Northern Virginia, Lee still did not have anywhere near a numerical advantage. On the night of September 13, Lee, at his headquarters at Hagerstown, was determined to hold his position until word that Jackson's capture of Harpers Ferry was a certainty. Then a civilian who had overheard some of McClellan's aides enthusiastically discussing the capture of a copy of Lee's orders came to alert the Confederate commander. Lee responded by ordering Longstreet to send troops to Turner's Gap, and thus the die was cast for a confrontation at South Mountain. Longstreet would observe, "The hallucination that McClellan was not capable of serious work seemed to pervade our army even to this moment of dreadful threatening."[7]

Maintaining a screen for the Army of Northern Virginia, rebel cavalry abandoned Middletown on September 13, and Stuart called on D. H. Hill for infantry support for his horsemen. Hill sent, among others, Colonel Alfred Colquitt. Stuart assured the infantry commander that only Federal cavalry had followed his troopers out of Middletown and that Colquitt's brigade would have no trouble holding Turner's Gap. As for any cooperation from Stuart, when Colquitt asked for cavalrymen to act as pickets, Stuart informed him that his horsemen were needed elsewhere. Before dawn on September 14, Colquitt apprehensively watched the growing number of the enemy's campfires in his front, a force he estimated as two brigades of Federal cavalry between him and Middletown. Anxiously notifying General Hill of the precarious position Stuart had left him in, Colquitt deployed his fourteen hundred men on the eastern base of the mountain at Turner's Gap to meet whatever the Unionists were about to throw at him. Hill came to see for himself, resulting in his hurrying more of his division's brigades to Turner's Gap.[8]

Though the drummers in Hooker's 1st Corps beat reveille at 3 a.m. on September 14, there seemed little hurry to get under way. After breakfast and coffee, the drummers beat assembly at 6 a.m. While other divisions had to wait their turn on the National Pike, General George Meade's division had the corps's advance, and by 8 a.m. he began passing through Frederick. The generous welcome, by way of dippers of cold water and cakes and pies, must have seemed all the sweeter, given the previous hostility the Federals had met with elsewhere from the supporters of secession. By 11 a.m., Meade's 3rd Division, 1st Corps, began following the 9th Corps in a march to the west. They were traveling through the detritus of the previous day's horse artillery duel, and after the Unionists' made the steep climb to the top of the Catoctin range, they were greeted by the sounds and smoke of distant artillery fire. It was a clear announcement of what was happening ahead at South Mountain, with an added surreal touch of a crowd of civilians who had arrived to watch the spectacle of war that had come to their town. Meade passed through

Middletown and headed to the western bank of Catoctin Creek. By 1 p.m. ambulances and walking wounded from the fighting at nearby Fox's Gap met Meade's advancing Federals. By 2 p.m. McClellan and his staff were still well to the rear and had yet to reach the Catoctin Mountains. But Hooker seized the moment, and soon staff officers like Roebling were racing with orders from Hooker to his division commanders. The frenetic passage of couriers dashing to and fro panicked some of the sightseeing civilians, and their rush to the rear and safety began to impede the 1st Corps's progress. Meade, still in the vanguard, finally came within supporting distance of the 1st Massachusetts Cavalry, which, confronting the enemy at Turner's Gap, were in the midst of an artillery duel. To add to the confusion, here Hooker's division commander, the ailing General Rufus King, finally received the order relieving him of duty, and impending battle be damned, King turned the division over to General John P. Hatch and rode away. As the afternoon waned, McClellan finally arrived with a substantial cavalry escort, riding by many troops stalled in the road and unable to advance. McClellan's arrival at Middletown signaled his readiness to finally supervise a battle.[9]

As Hooker's 3rd Division commander, General Meade, reached the front, a courier from Hooker ordered him to deploy his men and confront the Confederate guardians of the north spur at South Mountain, Brigadier General Robert Rodes's Alabamians. As Meade positioned his men for the assault at Turner's Gap, Confederate general Hill had to spread thin what troops he had on hand to meet this impending Federal threat. Meade launched an assault at 4 p.m., and despite the steepness of the hill and intervening ravines and farm boundary walls that disrupted coordination of the attack, the rebels were driven further up the hill. Meade, riding behind his advancing second line, received word that the commander on his right believed he could outflank and take the rebel left wing, and Meade gave his approval. By dark, Meade's Pennsylvania Reserve Division and Abram Duryee's brigade had the rebels retiring south toward the National Pike. Meade's loss for the day was 413, including a disproportionate number of line officers, with seven captains and lieutenants killed and sixteen more wounded. Though it was costly, it was an indication that the officers of Meade's division and Hooker's corps were willing to set an example for their men. It was an example that Washington Roebling was about to show he was willing to follow.[10]

In another demonstration of leading from the front, when the vanguard of General Hatch's division advanced to the position they'd driven the enemy from around 3:30 p.m., they found their corps commander, General Hooker, already there. In this, his first battle as a corps commander, Hooker not only

General John P. Hatch.
Library of Congress.

had a presence at his front but also insisted on doing a good deal of his own reconnaissance. Hooker now sent skirmishers out to ascend the southern spur of the mountain, their job being to drive the rebels and provide what protection they could for Meade's left flank. General Hatch had three of his four brigades with him, and Roebling was sent to accompany Hatch's 3rd Brigade, under the command of Brigadier General Marsena Patrick. While two of Patrick's New York regiments were sent forward as skirmishers for the division, the rest comprised the first of three battle lines in Hatch's advance. Rebel commander D. H. Hill watched the ascension of Patrick's troops with foreboding, for he initially had little to meet them with. Hill would later comment on his troops overshooting that, between the steepness of the hill and the bad handling of the guns, the fire directed at the lucky New Yorkers "was as harmless as blank-cartridge salutes in honor of a militia general." Hill added, tongue in cheek, that the attackers didn't even have the decency to duck or dodge the rebels' ineffective missiles. But Hatch's luck was running out, for Confederate generals James Kemper, Richard Garnett, and Micah Jenkin's brigades came to Hill's rescue, though weary from having been rushed from their morning bivouac at Hagerstown to South Mountain. General Garnett, who commanded roughly four hundred Virginians, positioned his men behind a stone wall that separated a cornfield from a woodlot and prepared to confront Hatch's assault. The audacious Brigadier General Patrick, on horseback despite the steepness of the hill, was leading his main line as his skirmishers sought their rebel counterparts.[11]

The uneven ground raised havoc with Patrick's advancing lines, and at one point he rode forward to adjust them—too far forward, as it happened, for he suddenly found himself between his own skirmishers and those of the enemy. Washington Roebling, assigned to accompany General Patrick, may have been the one who cried "Gray Coats," for an accompanying aide alerted Patrick to his danger, and he plunged down the hill to safety. It was a close call, but Patrick now knew just where the enemy was. Patrick's second line caught up and merged with the first, and the Federals began to drive in the enemy skirmishers. Though advancing under a most galling fire from the enemy, posted above them behind trees and rocks, Patrick's line swept over the enemy's stone wall. General John P. Hatch would be counted among the casualties, having been shot in the leg. His leadership at South Mountain, as witnessed by Roebling, was later recognized with a Medal of Honor.[12]

Roebling would particularly remember the confrontation between the Zouaves of Hatch's 14th Brooklyn and Captain Henry Owen's 18th Virginia. Still wearing the red pants that had caused Stonewall Jackson to call them the "red-legged devils" at First Bull Run, the 14th Brooklyn, led by General Hatch, took exception to a volley the Virginians had fired their way. Though a feeble effort that went well over the New Yorkers' heads, it was still close enough that the antagonized Zouaves entered into a shot-for-shot slugfest with the enemy, losing more than a third of their members in fifteen minutes. On having stubbornly decided upon an attack as opposed to withdrawal, General Hatch was shot in the leg; yet, despite the severity of his wound, he refused to leave the field. The question of who would possess the ground was decided when Marsena Patrick brought up two additional New York regiments to reinforce the Red Legs, and the rebels finally, so it appeared, broke and ran.[13]

The Federals followed the rebels up a part of the mountain so steep that they had to hold onto stumps and branches to pull themselves up. Neither their dwindling supply of ammunition nor the thought of having to resort to bayonets stopped the Unionists' ascent. Hatch, weakened by his wound, finally

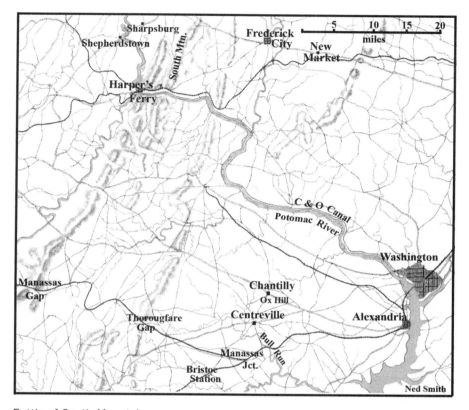

Battle of South Mountain.
Adapted from Plate X, 1 OR Atlas.

gave command of his division to General Abner Doubleday, but before he left the field, Hatch unfortunately ordered a cease-fire. This had the unexpected result of allowing the rebels to turn on their pursuers and fire a volley on surprised Yankees. The angry Unionists responded with a concentrated fire that completed the destruction of the 18th Virginia. Robert E. Lee, mounted on Traveler, had watched the Virginians' suicidal counterattack, and when the general himself came under heavy fire, he, as he would elsewhere, resisted all efforts by rebel officers to lead him out of danger, instead remaining to arrange for the troops in the area to retire and regroup. Though night had fallen, the fighting continued, with wild firing into the darkness that eventually sputtered to a stop, and the Federals found themselves in possession of nearly the entire crest of South Mountain. While the victory had come at a considerable cost, the Union troops had the thoroughly novel experience of what it felt like to win a fight. Holding the field on September 15, the day after the battle, proved quite a tonic for Hooker's men at South Mountain. The Federals would begin their movement to the east and south toward Antietam Creek, while the Army of Northern Virginia regrouped around the town of Sharpsburg and awaited Jackson and his troops after the highly anticipated capture of the garrison at Harpers Ferry. The Confederate plans would be dealt one more blow when Federal cavalry that escaped from Harpers Ferry the night before its capitulation, some twelve hundred troopers, captured sixty of Longstreet's wagons carrying ammunition. As for the significance of the clash at South Mountain, if the Confederates' primary aim there was to delay the Federals, it had been only a partial success. But, more important, after South Mountain, the Federals were advancing with a lighter step and a whisper of confidence.[14]

10

With Hooker at Antietam

AFTER RETIRING FROM SOUTH MOUNTAIN, ROBERT E. LEE MARCHED with his force in search of a good defensive line, while George McClellan was anxious to pursue (and, if possible, cut off) the Army of Northern Virginia's retreat. Joseph Hooker learned at dawn on September 15 of Lee's withdrawal and personally led General Israel Richardson's division, loaned to him from Edwin V. Sumner's 2nd Corps, down the west side of South Mountain. Preceded by Alfred Pleasonton's cavalry, when Hooker arrived at Boonsboro he learned that the Army of Northern Virginia was on its way to Shepherdstown Ferry, but Pleasonton also reported that the Army of Northern Virginia was "in a perfect panic," with Lee publicly admitting that they'd been "shockingly whipped." It was, one suspects, another case of relying too heavily upon the testimony of the prisoners and deserters captured by the cavalry. The report, however, apparently stimulated McClellan's sometimes dormant urge to forge ahead, for he dissolved his wing arrangement and turned Hooker loose to act independently of slow-moving Ambrose Burnside. A member of the inner circle at Hooker's headquarters, Washington Roebling, as he later confessed, was far from well, suffering the onset of a fever that would send him to the hospital after the upcoming confrontation, but the excitement of it all and the urgent need for scouts and couriers kept him in the saddle for the next few days.[1]

On September 15, Lee found what he was looking for on the west side of Antietam Creek. It was a strong position that banished Lee's thoughts of retreat and reignited Lee's will to do more than fight on the defensive, an idea further fanned to a flame by word from Stonewall Jackson that success at Harpers Ferry was imminent. While Hooker, with Richardson's division in the lead, was making an effort to follow Lee, such was not the case with Burnside and his 9th Corps, which, despite McClellan's urging, not only had

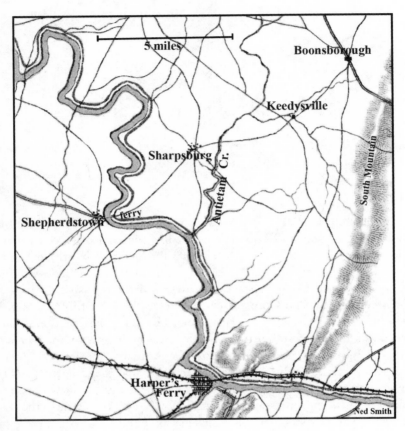

Antietam.
Adapted from Plate XXVII, 1 OR Atlas.

remained at South Mountain instead of marching but also was blocking the passage of other troops building up behind him. Nor had General William B. Franklin, whom McClellan was counting on to relieve the pressure on Harpers Ferry, made any progress. McClellan's faith in Franklin was sorely misplaced, for even when it became clear that Harpers Ferry was about to fall, Franklin found any number of excuses for not engaging the enemy. In fact, Jackson's bombardment at the ferry, much to Lee's satisfaction, finally produced the Federal garrison's surrender. Meanwhile, Hooker, having captured one thousand rebel stragglers, was baying like a hound on the chase, convinced of the demoralized condition of Lee's army—that is, until Hooker found the enemy halted behind Antietam Creek.[2]

Roebling wrote that on September 15, General Edwin Sumner was in nominal command of McClellan's advance, but Hooker was the first to arrive upon the scene of Lee's army deploying on the hills on the far side of Antietam Creek. In hopes that the Federals would be making an assault that day, Hooker's reconnaissance began at once, his engineers, including Roebling, discovering that Lee was assembling thirty to fifty thousand men and some one hundred pieces of artillery in a strong position on Sharpsburg Heights. Roebling would later remember that, in this pressure-filled situation, though he was increasingly feverish and sick, there was no time for such things, and the anticipation of critically needed duties kept him going. While Hooker had pressed his corps forward this day and then prepared for whatever came next, when General Sumner arrived on the front, as senior officer, he superseded Hooker and took command of the field. Apparently unaware of the intelligence Hooker had gathered, Sumner declared to McClellan that he knew little of the size or disposition of the enemy force, but Sumner nonetheless asked permission to dispose his forces in preparation for an attack. On McClellan's arrival, he, Sumner, Hooker, and Richardson met upon a hill that gave them a partial view of Lee's formidable position, for Lee had taken advantage of the rolling nature of the landscape to hide a good part of his force. Thanks to the scouting efforts of his engineering officers, Hooker was able to describe Lee's position in some detail, including the fords they had found above and below the Confederate position. With the day waning and many of his troops still on their way to the front, McClellan's innate caution kicked in, and little would be done other than orders to extend their lines, stretching out to feel for Lee's flank. McClellan placed Hooker's corps at the fork of the Big and Little Antietam Creeks on the extreme right of the position the Federals were assuming. Here Hooker would be in position to carry out the plan McClellan was contemplating, an attack on Lee's left. Meanwhile, the aim of simply forcing Lee back across the Potomac into Virginia was apparently still warring in McClellan's mind with the enthralling idea of possibly destroying his army. On September 16, Hooker had orders to cross over Antietam Creek in preparation for an assault the next morning. There being no bridge traversing the deep creek on Hooker's front, Roebling and Major David Houston built him one, and two hours later, at sunset, Hooker's corps was on the same side of the Antietam as their rebel foes.[3]

As historians Ethan Rafuse and B. F. Cooling point out, McClellan issued few written orders on September 16 and 17, nor did he provide much guidance to his subordinates or clarify what he actually wanted done prior to and during the Battle of Antietam on September 17. So there is some confusion,

General George Meade.
Library of Congress.

and therefore controversy, as to who was ordered to do what and when. It is known that Hooker received orders from McClellan between 1 and 2 p.m. on September 16 to cross the Antietam. Less clear is when McClellan first urged Burnside, verbally or otherwise, to cross the creek to threaten or assist with the assault of the Confederate right. Meanwhile, Roebling would relate that Burnside had been expected to cross over the stream on the night of September 16, just as Hooker's corps would do. While Hooker was unquestionably anxious to close with the enemy, was it Hooker's lack of confidence in Burnside's capacity to cooperate that caused him to express his concern that he might be the lone corps on the enemy's side of the creek with the Army of Northern Virginia? McClellan, instead of a concrete promise that at least one other corps would join him on the west bank, gave Hooker the feeble reassurance that, if needed, he was free to call upon Burnside for reinforcements. Roebling freely expressed his own frustration and bewilderment regarding the

General John B. Hood.
Library of Congress.

risky and ultimately costly position into which McClellan put Hooker's 1st Corps on the eve of the Battle of Antitiem.[4]

But regardless of the risks involved, shortly before 4 p.m. on September 16, Hooker sent the skirmishers of George Meade's 3rd Division and what cavalry he had across the creek to cover the rest of the 1st Corps's crossing, and when Meade advanced into the cornfield and a patch of woods, a sharp engagement ensued with John B. Hood's division of Jackson's corps, which was arriving from its conquest of Harpers Ferry. The fighting lasted until after sundown, but it was nothing compared to what would happen the next day among the stalks of corn and the trees of the "East Woods," both scenes of slaughter that would gain fearsome renown. When McClellan unexpectedly showed up to see what would happen when the corps crossed on the afternoon of September 16, Hooker, feeling he had a pretty good idea of what would happen, went to him and pointed out to McClellan that he "had ordered my small corps, now numbering between 12,000 and 13,000, across the river to attack the whole rebel army, and that if re-enforcement were not forwarded promptly, or if another attack was not made on the enemy's right, the rebels would eat me up." McClellan responded that, in addition to the promise of support from Burnside, he would order General Joseph K. F. Mansfield's 12th Corps to move to a position to support Hooker's movement. But McClellan, it seems, did not make clear to Hooker that it would take a night's march to bring Mansfield within supporting distance of the vulnerable 1st Corps. Without further consideration, McClellan then rode off with his staff to his headquarters at Keedysville, where he would sleep in the next morning through the early hours of Hooker's dawn attack. Later that morning, McClellan rode to a "commanding knoll" to view the ensuing battle. Again Roebling suggests that much misfortune could have been avoided had McClellan been at the front, where he could "easily have arranged simultaneous attacks." Though Washington wrote these words many years later, the emotions were still raw: "I was under fire and saw what was going on. He [Hooker] was driving the enemy most of the time." But without support, the ground they were gaining could not be retained.[5]

Washington and the 1st Corps were under fire that anxious night, about which he recounted an experience more than a little strange. If described by someone of more dubious judgment and intelligence or one known to resort too often to the bottle, the incident could be more easily discounted and disregarded. But in my view, considering Roebling's previous battlefield experience and seemingly unshakable aplomb, it would be difficult to find a witness more reliable and less given to exaggeration. On this night, while speaking with General James Ricketts in close proximity to the enemy, Washington related that a projectile passed so close to his face that "I was nearly killed by a cannon ball sucking the wind out of my mouth; the windage was too much for me." The event left a deep impression upon Roebling, and while others may have had similar experiences, the details remain difficult to explain. Yet if a shell's passage did indeed rob Washington of all the air from his lungs, perhaps those who have experienced having "the wind knocked out of them" and the alarm at being unable to breathe can appreciate just what a frightening experience it is. The American medical historians and those who have made a study of Civil War–era artillery whom I consulted knew of no similar corroborating accounts, and there was skepticism on their part that the ballistics of the guns of the period were capable of what today's much more powerful artillery can in fact inflict upon bystanders. But numerous accounts in British and French naval medical histories detail nineteenth-century injuries described as "Wind of the Ball," whereby projectiles passing in close proximity to victims left them unmarked but nonetheless injured, incapacitated, or mortally wounded.[6]

As previously stated, according to Roebling, Burnside had also been ordered to take his corps across on the night of September 16, but it is well known that the 9th Corps didn't manage to make its crossing of the Antietam at the infamous Burnside's Bridge until well into the afternoon of the next day. Burnside often failed to understand and carry out his orders, and given the way in which McClellan was directing his commanders at Antietam, it is unclear what his orders actually were for September 16. Years later Roebling would rail against Burnside's ineptitude at Antietam, declaring, "As to Burnside, everybody knows what he did—simply nothing, as usual. He could have crossed with ease on his first arrival, but stopped; he had no decision; began to mass artillery, fire to no purpose, only to arouse the enemy to renewed exertions. After he did get over the next day with heavy loss it was too late to act in conjunction with the other attacks. One brigade checkmated his whole corps." As for what opportunity was lost on this morning before Jackson arrival's, Roebling observed, "Lee's whole army was not up yet, and then was our chance." So although McClellan had apparently made clear his desire to attack the enemy on September 16, the foggy start to that day saw little more than dueling artillery. And his communications reveal clearly that McClellan was hoping that when the fog finally lifted, he would find Lee gone. The exception to all this hesitation on the part of the Federals was, of course, Hooker's small corps, already across Antietam Creek and ready to strike Lee's left. Of the harrowing experience the 1st Corps was about to experience that day, Roebling would comment, "McClellan always complained that Hooker took his orders too literally and got over and in place before any of the rest of the army could support him." Roebling further observed that McClellan "was not accustomed to have orders obeyed promptly." This certainly was the case with General Burnside's corps.[7]

On that rainy night of September 16, as McClellan rode off to his own comfortable billet, he had ordered that the men of Hooker's corps, in close confrontation with the enemy, have no fires, as if that would convince Robert E. Lee that they weren't really there. But the 1st Corps's crossing to the Army of Northern Virginia's side of the Antietam Creek had, of course, not gone unnoticed. Ample evidence for that was provided by the stand Hood's division had made against both Meade's and Ricketts's divisions that night, as well as the orders Lee gave for massing artillery and infantry on his left in preparation for the next day's fight. Jackson's forces had begun arriving at noon on September 16, and although Jackson had forewarned Lee that his troops were much fatigued by their efforts to take Harpers Ferry and their ensuing march to Sharpsburg after it fell, Jackson had personally led Hood's division to meet the Federal incursion on the Confederate left. Meanwhile, Lee sent orders to hurry along Lafayette McLaws's and A. P. Hill's passage from Harpers Ferry. In the days leading up to the battle, General Franklin's corps had been charged with preventing the force with which Jackson had successfully besieged Harpers Ferry from rejoining the Army of Northern Virginia, a task Franklin failed utterly to accomplish. As for Burnside, his position confronting the Confederate right could have been a promising one for an enterprising commander, but instead Burnside so clearly demonstrated that he was no threat that Lee could confidently send his troops to meet whatever the Federals had planned to throw at the Confederate left. In fact, the 9th Corps was having breakfast when the firing signaling Hooker's dawn attack on the Confederate left began. And though a considerable Federal force had now gathered at and near Antietam, Hooker alone would be making the assault, with McClellan and the other Federal corps standing relatively pat, awaiting the results. Having to be satisfied with the dubious reassurance that support was at hand, as soon as it was light enough to see, Hooker pushed his lead elements toward the soon to be infamous East Woods. After a night march General Mansfield, though new to command of the 12th Corps, which was top-heavy with green troops, was nonetheless game and had crossed two divisions over the stream in the early hours of September 17. But this promised support was still a mile away when Hooker assaulted the enemy at daybreak, and two hours would pass before any assistance arrived. Mansfield's corps attacked well after the 1st Corps's initial assault, and its men were going in on their own, exhausting themselves in much the same way as had Hooker's corps. By 10 a.m., Hooker had been shot in the foot and soon left the field. To the dubious criticism of his having made his assault too soon on the morning of September 17 was added criticism of him for leaving the field. But if Hooker was too early, McClellan left things until too late. Not until noon on September 17 did McClellan begin prodding his less ambitious commanders into action, sending Roebling's immediate commander, engineer Captain James C. Duane, to finally get Burnside's 9th Corps under way. The result was the debacle at Burnside's Bridge, where, for several critical hours, four hundred rebels prevented more than 12,000 soldiers of the 9th Corps from crossing the creek to threaten Lee's right flank.[8]

With Stuart's cavalry hovering on Hooker's right flank, on September 17 Stonewall Jackson sent two of his divisions to confront Hooker. They were posted just north of the Dunker Church in a northward-facing line from the West Woods to the East Woods. Hood's division, in consideration of the previous night's fight with Hooker, was allowed to fall back in reserve. On the night of September 16, Hooker had waited in vain for the promised arrival of Mansfield's division, but Mansfield would not even leave his Keedysville bivouac until 11 p.m. that night. Hooker, meanwhile, crossed the river to visit his men in the East Woods, where he was reassured by his officers' reports that darkness had brought their skirmish with Hood's division to a satisfactory conclusion. Uneasy picket firing, however, would continue through the night as both sides slept on their guns. Giving ample evidence that no one, especially McClellan, should have been surprised by the early hour of Hooker's assault, Hooker sent a courier to apprise McClellan of his position and to remind him that the 1st Corps would attack at dawn on September 17. With no further direction from McClellan, Hooker did just that, with Abner Doubleday's, Meade's, and Ricketts's divisions heading toward the only landmark visible on this morning of heavy fog, the Dunker Church. Mansfield had crossed the river late in the night, but his corps was not in position to make the assault, so Hooker's corps advanced alone into a thirty-acre cornfield and a confrontation that would go down in Civil War history as one of the most horrible of the war.[9]

Hooker was made aware of the presence of the rebels in the cornfield by way of the rising sun glinting off the bayonets of their muskets, visible above the crop. Apparently far enough away, McClellan was able to sleep on at his headquarters while the artilleries of both sides poured a deadly cross-fire into the combatants' ensuing struggle. Despite the fearful slaughter, Hooker's men began pushing rebel divisions from their position, and when McClellan finally arose and began to watch Hooker's fight from a distant hill, he chose to do nothing by way of supporting Hooker's struggle. He held Sumner's and Fitz John Porter's corps stationary, supposedly waiting to see what would come of Hooker's assault. With Burnside's Corps also on hold, Hooker fought on alone. Thus, when Jackson sent in his reserve, Hood's division was able to turn the tide against Hooker with a fierce assault on the Federal 1st Corps, and the Federals' exhausted lines began to break. When Hooker called upon Mansfield to come forward, the green troops he led did in fact advance, but Mansfield himself was cut down within minutes of arriving on the field with a gunshot to the chest that would prove mortal. Mansfield's corps, despite the loss of its leader and its inexperience, had some initial success but became fought out, much as the 1st Corps had been. When McClellan finally released Sumner to enter the fray on the Federal left, the 6th Corps met with misfortune when General John Sedgwick's division got a very rough handling

General Jacob Cox.
Library of Congress.

from McLaws's newly arrived division in the West Woods. As for the other division Sumner sent in, that of General William French, he first lost his way and, instead of joining the fight for the West Woods, hurled himself at the rebels in the Sunken Road, another landmark that would be remembered for the ferocity of the fighting and the heavy losses incurred.[10]

The events of September 16 and 17 remained vivid in Roebling's memory. While Hooker was driving the enemy on the morning of September 17, Washington remembered, "Burnside did nothing. He was practically behind the enemy—any other general would have won the battle in his position. The reason why McClellan did not relieve him is probably because he felt too insecure in his own position." Remembering how Hooker's 1st and then Mansfield's 12th Corps fought alone much of the day, Roebling commented, "About three or four in the afternoon was time to win the battle. The 5th Corps had been kept in reserve; stood in an excellent position to attack. Here came in McClellan's weakness about reserves. He could not bring himself

General Joseph Mansfield.
National Archives and Records Administration.

to throw them in at the decisive moment. So the golden opportunity passed away." Apparently Roebling did not realize that Hooker was fighting Hood's division of Jackson's command on the night of September 16: Roebling believed that the rebels they were fighting on the morning of September 17 were the first of Jackson's force to arrive on the battlefield. Roebling described the enemy they confronted near the Dunker Church: "They marched in brigade front as if on parade. That stopped further fighting on our part." He also observed, "Although Antietam was a drawn battle, the way in which it was fought was a great contrast to the wretched bungling at the second Bull Run. Troops who fought only half hearted at Bull Run, did splendidly at Antietam. Much of this change in morale must go to the credit of McClellan, aided of course by the absence of such marplots as McDowell, Pope, King and others." Roebling's faint praise makes for a sharp contrast compared with McClellan's

General Ambrose Burnside.
Library of Congress.

own assessment of how things went on September 17. As he wrote to his wife the next day, "The spectacle yesterday was the grandest I could conceive of, nothing could be more sublime. Those in whose judgement I rely tell me that I fought the battle splendidly & that it was a masterpiece of art." Of the battle that ended in what's most often described as a draw, James Longstreet commented that, by 1 p.m. on September 17, the men of the Army of Northern Virginia were so exhausted that if the Federals had put, say, ten thousand fresh men into the fight, the rebels would have been swept from the field. McClellan had sixteen thousand men standing by, Porter's 5th Corps and Franklin's 6th Corps less one brigade, which were never put into the fight. Thus Robert E. Lee's army lived to fight again and again.[11]

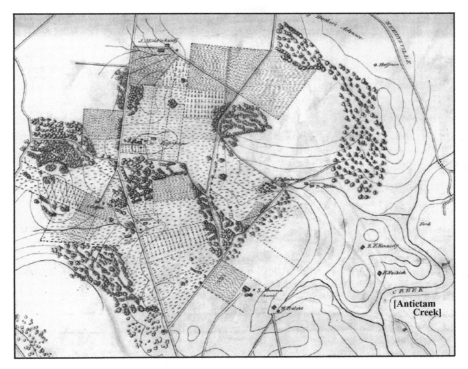

Portion of Houston/Roebling map of Antietam.
Library of Congress.

Roebling remembered the battlefield at Antietam with particular horror:

The appearance of the battlefield was horrible; the hot August sun changed a corpse into a swollen mass of putridity in a few hours—too rotten to be moved. Long trenches were dug, wide and deep, into which the bodies, thousands of them, were tumbled pell mell, carried on fence rails or yanked with ropes, unknown, unnamed, unrecognized. This is the kind of glory most people get who go to war. The next day it was discovered the Lee had withdrawn over night; feeble pursuit was instituted, but he recrossed the Potomac unmolested. Major Houston and myself made a field map of these part of the battle field in which Hooker's corps had fought. I still have the rough draft in my possession.

While memories of this particular battlefield provided fodder for many a veteran's nightmares, for Roebling was added the influence of a fever that, once the excitement of the battle was over, had him collapsing in delirium. "I crawled to a field hospital just established, and laid for ten days." Remembering all too well his father's daft ideas about being able to overcome all illness with willpower and eccentric water treatments, Roebling added sarcastically, "I could have avoided it all by more self-control; All diseases are unnecessary."[12]

A Bridge for McClellan
at Harpers Ferry

WHEN WASHINGTON ROEBLING HAD RECOVERED FROM HIS ILLNESS sufficiently to rejoin the 1st Corps, it and General Henry Slocum's 12th Corps had been ordered to Harpers Ferry. George McClellan was intent on making that location his new base of supplies, a move that the administration rightly saw as his settling in for the winter instead of moving against the enemy. Henry Halleck balked at McClellan's determination to repair the two bridges that had been destroyed, the railroad bridge over the Potomac and a wagon bridge over the Shenandoah, commenting that McClellan shouldn't be at Harpers Ferry long enough to need them. Regardless of Halleck's withholding approval, the superintendent of military railroads was assigned to rebuild the railroad bridge, while Washington Roebling was called upon to rebuild the wagon bridge after, according to Roebling, his direct superior, engineer officer Major David C. Houston, suggested the project to McClellan. Roebling was summoned to headquarters, where he described for McClellan what repairing the span would entail. Whether McClellan had official approval or no, he instructed Roebling to start organizing the rebuilding, and Roebling made a beginning by moving his meager baggage into an abandoned priest's house, while he stabled his horse in the adjoining church. Spending time at or near Harpers Ferry was not the only bone of contention between McClellan and the administration, for Abraham Lincoln also issued his Emancipation Proclamation, a position that so provoked McClellan that he remarked he would likely not remain in the army.[1]

When it became clear that McClellan had little inclination to leave Harpers Ferry, Lincoln paid a visit to him and the Army of the Potomac on October 3. Lincoln reiterated the pointed and direct questions that General Halleck had been asking: When was McClellan going to move, and what was his plan?

On October 6, shortly after Lincoln's visit, McClellan received a peremptory order: "The President directs that you cross the Potomac and give battle to the enemy or drive him south. Your army must move now while the roads are good." Within days, J. E. B. Stuart's October 9–12 Chambersburg raid added weight to the administration's growing exasperation. Stuart's one-thousand-man raiding party rode 130 miles through Maryland and Pennsylvania, destroying part of the Army of the Potomac's lifeline, the Cumberland Valley Railroad, and capturing livestock and hostages. But most of all, Stuart's raid was an enormous embarrassment to the Federal army and the administration. Though McClellan outnumbered the Confederates more than two to one, he responded with the usual excuses, citing inflated enemy numbers and his own lack of troops to both protect Washington and the Potomac crossings and retain a force large enough to take the offensive against the enemy. With winter weather closing in, on October 27 McClellan once more entered Virginia but failed to prevent Robert E. Lee from taking up secure positions behind the Rappahannock and Rapidan Rivers. It all came to end for McClellan at 11 p.m. on the snowy night of November 7, when Ambrose Burnside arrived at McClellan's headquarters with orders relieving McClellan and placing himself in command of the Army of the Potomac. Weeks earlier, when McClellan had written his report of the Maryland Campaign, he had commented regarding Burnside's performance, "I *ought* to rap Burnside *very* severely & probably will, yet I hate to do it. He is very slow & is not fit to command more than a regiment. If I rap him as he deserves he will be my mortal enemy hereafter—if I do not praise him as he thinks he deserves & as I know he does *not*, he will be at least a very lukewarm friend." Meanwhile, Lee, on hearing of the latest change in Federal commanders, commented, "I fear they may continue to make these changes till they find some one whom I don't understand."[2]

About this time, Roebling's immediate commander, Major Houston, "got tired of the Army of the Potomac," as Washington described it, and was transferred to New Orleans. It seems that Houston requested that Roebling go with him, but Quartermaster General Montgomery Meigs insisted he still had bridges for young Roebling to build. "I would have liked to go along," Roebling commented, but at least his lengthy bridge assignment at Harpers Ferry during the winter of 1862–1863 did spare him from serving with the Army of the Potomac under General Burnside's command. Roebling therefore did not have to endure the nightmarish Battle of Fredericksburg and the subsequent misfortunes of the Mud March. Major Houston was replaced by Major John M. Wilson (USMA 1860), who was charged with fortifying the heights around Harpers Ferry. Stonewall Jackson's successful

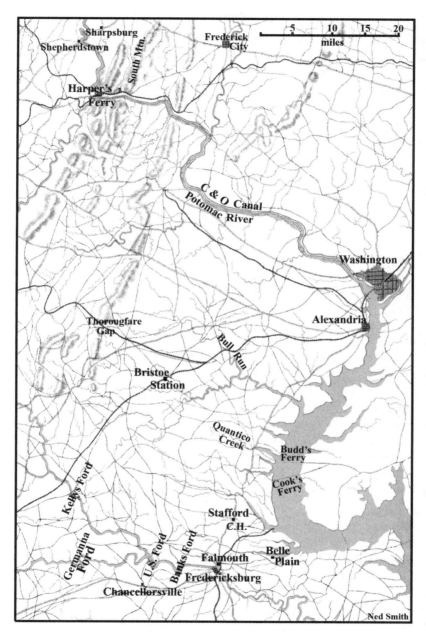

With McClellan at Harpers Ferry.
Adapted from Plate X, 1 OR Atlas.

taking of the town during the recent Maryland Campaign had made it abundantly clear that the surrounding heights had to be protected if the Federals intended to retain possession. Once again reporting directly to Quartermaster General Meigs, within a week Roebling had completed his plans for building the bridge over the Shenandoah. Wooden towers would be constructed on two of the old piers, and three spans would be laid. Anchorages were put in behind the old abutments, mostly timber posts, to which Roebling appended the purely pessimistic assessment "it being useless to make a [more] permanent structure." Though Washington was able to get some of the oak needed for the anchorages locally, lack of transportation forced him to requisition the rest of the needed timbers. The necessary dimensions were sent to a Baltimore sawmill, but it took so long to supply the needed lumber that several months passed before Roebling could proceed, the delay lengthening his stay at Harpers Ferry to more than four months, October 1862 through mid-February 1863. Yet another difference in the operation was that Washington was allowed to draw workers from various regiments of the 12th Corps, who, Roebling commented, "looked on it as a picnic and were glad to come; there were some good mechanics among them."[3]

Roebling was also allowed to hire an assistant engineer, and when one of his father's foreman, David Rhule, expressed interest in "doing something for his country," he was taken on as a "civilian expert." While awaiting the shipment of lumber, a battalion of U.S. engineers put at Roebling's disposal dug the excavation for the anchorage on the Harpers Ferry side. Meanwhile, on the Loudon end of the bridge, an anchorage was quarried out of a stratum of granite boulders by daily details of men from a prison camp. When these work parties were withdrawn, Roebling received his fifty men from General Slocum's 12th Corps, so when the lumber finally arrived on November 20, great progress was made. In two weeks the towers were in place on the piers and abutments. Cables were stretched across, and the joists were suspended, but this spurt of building progress came to an abrupt end when Slocum's corps was removed from Harpers Ferry on December 7, taking with it Washington's fifty-man workforce. While the engineer fortifying the heights around Harpers Ferry had been given funds to hire civilians, Washington had not, and when he applied to the new commander of the town, General John R. Kenly, for workers, he was initially denied. As Washington would discover, an apprehensive Kenly felt that "it would be very dangerous to have a bridge there because the rebels might cross on it." Kenly's jumpiness about possible enemy incursions is not particularly surprising, for he had been roughly handled by the enemy in the previous months. While he was commanding the 1st Maryland at Front Royal in May 1862, his regiment was surprised by Stonewall Jackson's army operating in the Shenandoah Valley, and there Kenly was severely wounded and captured, along with 691 soldiers of his 1,000-man command. Exchanged in August and made a brigadier general, Kenly was given command of the Maryland brigade, which joined the Army of the Potomac after Antietam. Though perhaps understandable, Kenly's anxiety about rebels sneaking up on him was making Roebling's completion of the bridge next to impossible.[4]

After a week of inactivity, Washington finally convinced Kenly that it wasn't safe to leave the bridge in its unfinished condition and persuaded Kenly to let him have a small workforce to complete the job to the point of putting the flooring on the bridge. But he, in turn, had to agree to Kenly's demand that every night every plank or gangway had to be removed. As Roebling commented regarding the much-feared Stonewall Jackson, "Some people tremble at the mere mention of his name" and "think it is about time for our army to get licked again." But he pointed out, "Scouting parties have been sent out 30 miles in all directions and no rebels found, whereas three nights ago the inhabitants here were turned out at one oclock at night and ordered to leave for Maryland because 30,000 rebels were surrounding the place, while the truth was that the nearest rebel force was 10 miles the other side of Winchester."[5]

Roebling made little progress until, thankfully, Kenly was replaced in command at Harpers Ferry by the wiser and calmer General Benjamin F. Kelley, who ordered the bridge completed at once and gave Washington the workforce with which to do it. Within in a few days, Federal army traffic was crossing the bridge, protected by the guns of a naval battery on Maryland Heights. At a cost of $9,000, Washington built a bridge with towers thirty feet above the water, safe from being carried away by the all too frequent rampaging floods. He reported that the finished bridge was a serviceable, useful structure, though it, too, would be destroyed by the rebels that summer of 1863 as Lee's forces marched toward their collision with the Federals at Gettysburg. In later years, Washington would lament that not a single sign of the bridge remained, and he had no photograph of it. His sole reminders of its existence were memories of how the Quartermaster's Corps had made his life a misery as the young engineer tried, often in vain, to keep track of every tool and bit of material he had utilized or requested. As many as eighteen years after the building of this bridge, the department was still demanding updated paperwork from Roebling, in one case regarding the loss of an old axe that had fallen into river. He also spent months ensuring that the men who had done extra duty building his bridge were paid as they had been promised.

The pursuit of getting the men their pay was made so difficult that a lesser man would have given up in disgust. For the most part, his work at Harpers Ferry ended Roebling's adventure in military bridge building. "It was cause of a year or two of hard, disagreeable, thankless, impossible work, because Meigs' ideas were all illusions. Suspension bridges can not be put up in a day across a stream, like pontoon bridges, especially as I had no force of men, no facilities, no tools, no nothing, except my honorable self."[6]

Though Roebling's bridge-building ventures were for the most part over, he remained unable to return to his duties with the 1st Corps, Army of the Potomac, for just before leaving Harpers Ferry, he was summoned on January 16, 1863, to appear as a witness before a court of inquiry in the case of Major General Irvin McDowell in session in Washington. When Roebling finally testified in early February 1863, he noted, "Everything went off as he [McDowell] had fixed it, showing that such inquiries are a farce, everything being arranged in advance." Roebling testified regarding the accusation by General Robert Milroy, who failed to appear in court, that McDowell refused to provide assistance when Milroy appealed to him during the battle. Roebling's testimony confirmed that Milroy had been in a highly excited state to the point of incoherence. Disgusted by the carefully prearranged nature of the questions and responses of the inquiry, Roebling was much relieved to finally be able to shake the soot and mud of the capital from his boots. In March, he applied for a new assignment and was sent to Fredericksburg to report to General Cyrus Comstock, chief engineer of the Army of the Potomac. Headquarters for the army was at Falmouth, where General Joseph Hooker, appointed commander of the Army of the Potomac on January 25, 1863, was seemingly infusing the men with spirit and optimism. The simple device of giving each corps a number and symbol was building much-needed esprit de corps as the army, recovering from its defeat at Fredericksburg, faced another year of fighting.[7]

With the spring would come mud season, and before the Army of the Potomac could go anywhere, corduroy roads had to be built for the many wagons needed to keep the army supplied. Roebling acknowledged that, for the vast number of soldiers put to work on building these roads, the labor was a welcome diversion from the monotony of winter camp. Washington took charge of a crew that built a road from General Daniel Sickles's headquarters to Stafford Court House and another from Falmouth to Belle Plain on the lower Potomac, where a succession of deep ravines and hogbacks provided challenges. After the road building came much surveying and mapping of the various fords, including Banks, U.S., Germanna, and Kelly's Fords, with consideration given to their suitability for the laying of pontoon bridges. The

General Cyrus Comstock.
Library of Congress.

coming campaign was discussed sub rosa, lest the ubiquitous reporters around headquarters should overhear and give away Federal plans. In some ways, the army's options were as obvious as they were limited. Repeating Burnside's mistake of crossing again at Fredericksburg was unthinkable, while crossing the river below the town would leave Lee in possession of the high ground. The only logical option, therefore, was to cross the Rappahannock farther up with the bulk of the army, leaving a small force to cross below by way of a diversion. Meanwhile, the army was in good shape, rejuvenated with new men and returning convalescents, and the cavalry were consolidated under the command of General George Stoneman (USMA 1846). Roebling noted that the suspension bridge he had built over the Rappahannock the year before had disappeared. He acknowledged, "So much useless work is done in a war!"[8]

The Chancellorsville Campaign, after torrential rains delayed its intended mid-April start, finally began on April 27, 1863, under a veil of secrecy. By the morning of May 1, the bulk of the Army of the Potomac was concentrated at Chancellorsville, where Washington Roebling, on Hooker's staff as an engineer, aide, and courier, would share, in part, in his commander's fate in the chaos of the upcoming battle.[9]

With Hooker at Chancellorsville

IN A LETTER WASHINGTON ROEBLING WROTE TO HIS FATHER IN THE weeks leading up to the start of General Joseph Hooker's Battle of Chancellorsville, he contemplated the discouraging state of affairs for the Union armies and, in particular, the role the Army of the Potomac would play:

> I begin to feel that our last hopes are centered in this Army of Potomac, and the results it may accomplish in the coming month; everything else is substantially a failure; our monitors have been whipped—Banks will probably be besieged in New Orleans in course of time. Grant's army having retired from Vicksburg will require months before it can be put into a position again to act effectively, and Rosecrans will do well if he holds his own. Our greatest difficulty will be in getting a fair start so as not to be obliged to attack the enemy in entrenched positions of their own selection; that can only be attained by an extensive flank movement and change of base, united with great celerity of movement. The latter we are in a condition to perform and the former will be shown in the coming few days—The severe storm of today probably interferes somewhat with operations—Our friends across the river are in status quo.

Roebling misjudged how quickly the Confederates of Louisiana would confront Nathaniel Banks and underestimated the time necessary for U. S. Grant to resume his siege upon Vicksburg, but his bleak assessment of the Federals' general lack of success reflected the worries of many of the country's Unionists. R. E. Lee's Army of Northern Virginia, already in desperate straits as far as essential supplies, could be forced from its strong entrenchments in the hills above Fredericksburg if a swift Unionist movement severed the rebels' precarious lifeline for food and forage. If Joseph Hooker could then force a battle upon the Confederates before Lee could take up another strong position, the tide could well be turned, at last, in favor of the Federals. Few would argue that success hung upon the alacrity of Hooker's intended flanking movement, but, as Roebling feared, the rains that April did substantially delay Hooker's advance, which, due to rising rivers and mud, ultimately did not get off until the end of the month.[1]

Should anyone wonder whether Roebling placed too much importance on the performance of the Army of the Potomac, consider historian James McPherson's assessment of the eastern versus the western armies and the role they played in the country's four years of Civil War. In *This Mighty Scourge*, McPherson reports,

> The war was won only by hard fighting, and the Army of the Potomac did most of that fighting. Of the ten largest battles in the war (each with combined Union and Confederate casualties of 23,000 or more) seven were fought between the Army of the Potomac and the Army of Northern Virginia. Of the fifty union regiments with the largest percentage of battle casualties, forty-one fought in the Eastern theater. Of course, in the grim calculus of war, sustaining casualties is less important than inflicting them, but there too the Army of the Potomac did far more than other Union armies. Of the fifty Confederate regiments with the highest percentage of combat casualties, forty were in the Army of Northern Virginia. In terms of fighting prowess, the "band box" soldiers in the Army of the Potomac more than held their own.[2]

On a more hopeful note, Washington went on to tell his father,

> Our long period of inaction bids fair before long to be changed into one of unusual activity. The body of the army has been in a state of readiness to move for some days and only awaits the signal to start. The manner in which we will march is upon an entirely new plan—no wagons will accompany us for the present—everyone will carry 6 days provisions in some way or other, and forage for horses is carried by pack mules—no clothes except what you have on your back can be carried, nor any baggage—my outfit consists of an oat bag containing a dozen pounds of crackers, a pound of coffee, some sugar & salt; meat is obtained from cattle that are driven along. No tents can be carried—Although the chances are that the move will take place tomorrow or next day, everybody is still in utter ignorance as to the direction of our march;

that fact alone speaks volumes in favor of Hooker's management and discretion, and is without a parallel in the previous history of the war.

Roebling clearly approved of Hooker's distrust of overly talkative officers and the ubiquitous journalists who would print whatever they heard regardless of the consequences for the army.[3]

Nor would Joseph Hooker be moving blindly through unknown territory, for he set General Gouverneur Warren and his topographical engineers to work scouting and mapping a wide swathe of the surrounding area. It was hoped that Hooker's army would not be wandering through uncharted regions looking for roads and fords, as Irvin McDowell had had to do in the days prior to and during the Battle of First Bull Run. And Hooker established his own intelligence network, avoiding the unreliable services of Allan Pinkerton and the flow of misinformation he and his operatives had supplied to George McClellan. Hooker also had another new tool that his predecessors did not possess, one of his own making. He formed the scattered fragments of his cavalry, previously distributed among and controlled by individual commanders, into a large independent unit capable of striking at the enemy in the manner that Lee's Confederate horsemen had subjected the Federals to all too often. Though Hooker kept his strategy for his upcoming campaign to himself, even a humble lieutenant like Roebling could see that the best option was to cut the Army of Northern Virginia's lifeline to its already meager food supplies and force Lee to relinquish his strong fortifications on the hills above Fredericksburg, thereby allowing the Army of the Potomac to accost Lee on ground of Hooker's choosing. Lee would have few options: either retreat toward Richmond or pull back toward Culpeper.[4]

Hooker had originally ordered cavalry commander George Stoneman and his near ten thousand troopers to begin a raid into rebeldom in mid-April 1863, with the intention of severing Lee's communications and forcing Lee away from his formidable fortifications. But as the rains of April 1863 continued, raising rivers to flood stage and turning many of Virginia's roads to mud, the cavalry were withdrawn, and Hooker began to reconsider the original details of his plan. While he retained the idea of Stoneman's cavalry making a raid, he decided that several corps of Federal infantry could do the work of severing Lee's supply lines. Stoneman's raid was a detail of Hooker's strategy that, in Roebling's opinion, hindered more than it helped, for while the distraction and destruction perpetrated by Stoneman's troopers gave temporary relief to the Federal efforts, Roebling rued the loss of the screening, intelligence gathering, and scouting the cavalry could have contributed had

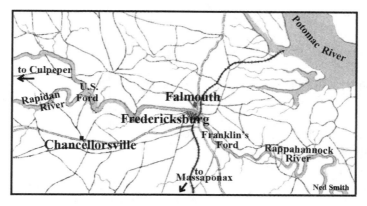

Chancellorsville.
Adapted from Plate X, 1 OR Atlas.

they been retained with the Army of the Potomac. The Federals' inability during the upcoming campaign to keep track of various elements of a daringly aggressive foe would have serious consequences for Hooker at Chancellorsville. The use of large cavalry raids in lieu of reconnaissance and screening was a mistake Roebling would witness again in Grant's Overland Campaign.[5]

Roebling's postwar commentary on the well-laid plans of the Chancellorsville Campaign and who was responsible for them makes for interesting reading. As for Roebling's credentials as an observer of his commanding officers and their strengths and weaknesses, he had been serving with the Federal armies since June 1861, including a stint on the staff of General McDowell before and during the Battle of Second Bull Run. He also served on General Hooker's staff at South Mountain, during the Battle of Antietam, and at Chancellorsville. His next assignment, and his longest term of service as a topographical engineer, aide, and courier, was with General Gouverneur Warren when he was the Army of the Potomac's chief engineer during the Battle of Gettysburg, then commander of the 2nd Corps at Bristoe Station and Mine Run, and finally commander of the 5th Corps during the Wilderness Campaign and siege of Petersburg. Roebling was an intelligent and resourceful individual, and he had one advantage after the war that many of his fellow officers did not have, especially those veterans who had continued with their U.S. Army careers or were reliant upon political favor: at the turn of the twentieth century, when Roebling did most of his writing, he was a wealthy man. The Roebling family's mill in Trenton, New Jersey, manufactured wire and wire rope for many purposes. Their products were essential not only for suspension bridges but also for the elevators that made the new skyscrapers possible; they also made wire and cables for ships and later for airplanes. The Roeblings were in the right place at the right time and became very wealthy, leaving Roebling beholden to no man. He was quite independent of his past commanders such as Grant and Philip Sheridan, who had wielded considerable power in the nation's government and military. In other words, Roebling was in the nearly unique position of being able to freely speak his mind and sometimes did. He had seen much, and much of it was not good, so unsurprisingly his observations were often critical with a hefty dose of cynicism. Here's what he had to say about Hooker as a corps commander and commander of the Army of the Potomac and his preparation for the impending battle.[6]

While Hooker's plans and preparations for his complex Chancellorsville campaign were shrewdly drawn, how much credit should be allotted to the Army of the Potomac's commanding general? In Roebling's opinion, not much. Roebling would write years later, "Gen. [Daniel] Butterfield, Hooker's chief of staff . . . was practically Hooker's brains, planned his campaign for him, prescribed orders of march, movements of troops, took all the responsibility, Hooker was simply the *beau sabrear*, posing before the rank and file, with whom he was a great favorite." Roebling also described Colonel Joseph Dickinson, Hooker's adjutant, as "a very good fellow in his way at cards, cocktails—but no real help." Roebling observed, "Hooker's mind was cloudy—he could not carry the position of every corps & division in his head, and in moving them he forgot where he had moved them. In short, he was unfit for the great task before him." Roebling added that instead of keeping Butterfield, the architect of the plan, with him during the Battle of Chancellorsville, Hooker left his chief of staff behind to coordinate communications and remain with John Sedgwick, who was to make a distracting feint against the enemy below Fredericksburg. When Hooker tried to implement the overall plan without Butterfield, he "failed miserably." While Stephen Sears has in many ways written an admirable account of Chancellorsville, he may be guilty of at times playing the part of overanxious apologist for Hooker, whom he describes in his introduction as having failed because of "inept lieutenants and simple happenstance." Sears also describes Roebling's testimony for Chancellorsville, particularly regarding Hooker's drinking, as "bitter, careless of fact, and twisted with self-importance." So much for giving unbiased consideration of Roebling's apparently conflicting, and therefore unwelcome, testimony. Let's consider what Roebling witnessed during the Battle of Chancellorsville, and we'll leave it for the reader to decide who is or is not a reliable witness.[7]

Roebling's prospective on the Battle of Chancellorsville is, of course, limited by his own assignments and duties on an extensive and often chaotic battlefield. This chapter, however, benefits greatly from Roebling's unpublished postwar writings, as well as his letters with a number of correspondents especially interested in Hooker and Chancellorsville. Therefore, this chapter takes advantage of Roebling's observations, often in his own words. Regarding the first day's advance, Roebling took particular exception to "the absence of the commander-in-chief at the critical point, so as to give positive orders." The critical point was, in Roebling's mind, with 12th Corps commander Henry Slocum's turning column. On the morning of April 29, Hooker accompanied Slocum's flanking force as far as Kelly's Ford, but then he inexplicably turned command of the right wing over to Slocum to oversee the crossing of some forty-seven thousand men in the next hours. By noon on April 30, George Meade's vanguard was in Chancellorsville, and Meade expressed his desire to march beyond the crossroads that afternoon. But Slocum made the orders Hooker had left him with known to Meade: the entire Federal force was to stop at the Chancellor crossroads to await the consolidation of all the corps and the return of General Hooker to take command. Hooker, meanwhile, had returned to his headquarters near Falmouth, congratulating himself on how well everything was going. Chancellorsville historian Sears describes how Hooker and Butterfield, with the absence of cavalry, were dependent upon being able to maintain communications with their two widely separated wings through telegraph and signal stations. But Hooker was now many miles from his right wing, leaving him with only imperfect knowledge of his turning column's situation on the ground. As Sears acknowledges, the army's telegraph communication was far from perfect and in fact broke down completely in the next critical days. Even the flag and night torch communication of the signalmen had to be discontinued upon the realization that the rebels had figured out the Federals' code.[8]

On the night of April 28–29, while Hooker's distant right wing was poised to begin its flank attack on the Army of Northern Virginia, Sedgwick's wing, not far from Hooker's headquarters, began the movement meant to confront and provide the distraction that would "entertain" Lee. It was dark and foggy, a night Roebling described as "weird and uncanny," with a surreal touch added by the partially inflated hot air balloon the column was dragging along with it. Though Roebling would become one of the army's daring "aeronauts" in the coming weeks, he said that this particular balloon proved "perfectly useless" and was "getting in everybody's way." A thick fog blanketed the countryside that night and the next morning, making an ascension for observation indeed useless. Before dawn, the army's Engineer Brigade struggled to lay the pontoon bridge that would enable Sedgwick's 6th Corps to cross the river at what was known to the Federals as Franklin's Ford, being the place of General William B. Franklin's crossing the previous year during the Battle of Fredericksburg. Here Roebling ran into an old classmate, Captain Charles Cross, a member of the independent brigade of engineers, and though Roebling likely needed no one to point out the danger of their situation and the fickle fortunes of war, he nonetheless got a stern reminder. As the Federals crossed in the dark and fog, the quiet was pierced by one word—"Fire"—followed by a volley from the pickets of the 54th North Carolina. Captain Cross, in the lead pontoon boat, was shot through the forehead and killed.[9]

After the Federals made their crossing, they camped near Massaponax and remained there all the next day. As Roebling commented, this sent a very clear signal to the rebels that Sedgwick's 6th Corps wasn't there to do anything significant—at least not for a while. Hooker's main thrust, it was not difficult for the enemy to ascertain, would be happening elsewhere. So, after a day of inactivity, Cyrus Comstock and Roebling left Sedgwick on the night of April 30, arriving at U.S. Ford on the morning of May 1.

> On reporting at headquarters, we noticed but little excitement. On inquiry among friends on the staff I learned that Gen. Hooker had been so elated over his wonderful success so far that he had taken a drop too much the previous evening and was still busy sleeping it off at 9 A.M. He was also tired from the long night ride to Chancellorsville—when he did rouse himself it was too late. He should have started with his army at daybreak en route for Fredericksburg, only seven miles off. There were only two brigades of the enemy in the way there; the road was clear, the country more and more open. Lee had started that same morning on his great turning movement so that the two armies would not have met in the early morning.[10]

On the morning of May 1, during Hooker's telegraphic and intelligence communications blackout, General Meade led a column of some ten thousand soldiers, while General George Sykes led another column of almost five thousand of the 5th Corps's regulars. Slocum, having returned to command of the 12th Corps, led his column of more than thirteen thousand men. These Federal columns were supposed to unite to carry the heights of Fredericksburg or, better yet, interrupt the expected flight of panicky rebels. But an uncooperative Lee left part of his force to confront a sedentary Sedgwick, while sending another large contingent to put paid to Hooker's flank attack. And the Confederates were already hatching plans to take the initiative by way of Stonewall Jackson making a flank attack of his own. Hooker mistakenly believed Lee had not moved and would be on the defensive. Instead, Sykes's and Meade's regulars ran into a determined struggle with the ever-aggressive Jackson. Hooker's plan came increasingly unglued, and by 2 p.m. the commander of the Army of the Potomac was ordering everyone back to Chancellorsville.[11]

While some debate the state of Hooker's head on the morning of May 1, there is no argument regarding that morning's late start. Roebling wrote, "It was 11 o clock before arrangements were finally perfected for the advance to begin." General Slocum's corps led on the road to Salem Church. Parallel columns moved on each side of him, going due east. Roebling says, "Shortly after noon Gen. Hooker sent for me, saying, 'I have determined to receive the enemy on my bayonets here at Chancellorsville. I want you to ride ahead to Gen. Slocum and tell him to stop the advance and return here with his command.'" Roebling wrote, "To hear was to obey," but, fully realizing that the order he was carrying would knock everything sideways, he remembered,

> I rode perhaps too fast. When I reached Slocum the steeple of Salem Church was already in view. When I gave my orders from Hooker, Slocum turned on me with fury, saying, "Roebling you are a damned liar, nobody but a crazy man would give such an order, when we have victory in sight. I shall go to Hooker myself, and if I find that you have spoken falsely, you shall be shot on my return." Off he went, the advance was stopped. The battle of Chancellorsville was lost right here. Subsequent events were only necessary sequences. In course of an hour Gen. Slocum returned, having labored in vain with Hooker to make him rescind his change of plan. Casting a scowl at me, he turned the head of his column. They marched to an overwhelming defeat.[12]

Roebling offers, by way of explanation for Hooker's sudden change of plans, that Hooker depended heavily upon his chief of staff, his right-hand man Daniel Butterfield, whom he had left to oversee the disintegrating communications between the scattered Federal forces and keep an eye on Sedgwick. Nor was General Gouverneur Warren, whom Roebling described as the best man (in some respects) on Hooker's staff, at headquarters that day. This left Hooker with the services of Colonel Dickinson, who, as we've previously acknowledged, was a good fellow, but his strong points extended to card playing and making cocktails. So when the distant Butterfield sent a dispatch to

General Daniel Butterfield.
Library of Congress.

Hooker after his commander arrived at Chancellorsville, advising him to fight the battle there because in his opinion it was the best ground and strongest position, it undoubtedly influenced Hooker's thinking. Regarding Butterfield's claim that his opinion was supported by General Warren, Roebling wrote,

> As a matter of fact neither Butterfield nor Warren had been at Chancellorsville and knew nothing of the locality from personal observation. Hooker had been so accustomed to receive Butterfield's opinions as infallible that he accepted the suggestion at once and gave orders in accordance. I happened to be the unfortunate selected to carry the news to Slocum. The five corps commanders received the new orders with consternation. They begged him almost on their knees to go forward. The high ground and commanding position had already been gained,

from which we could act offensively and defensively equally well, with plenty of open ground to watch the enemy; whereas Chancellorsville was low, indefensible and surrounded by higher ground already in Lee's possession. Hooker remained obdurate. He had that ugly streak in him, which a man gets when he is only half drunk. Gen. George Meade, of the 5th corps, became most violent in his demand to go ahead. Two months later when he relieved Hooker from his command of the army at Gettysburg his first act was to dismiss Butterfield and put in his place my friend, Gen. Andrew A. Humphreys [USMA 1831], an able, energetic and hard fighter, and [apparently unlike Butterfield] not a sneak.[13]

The regressive movements demanded by Hooker having been made, Roebling remembered, "an hour or more were consumed to put the troops in the new defensive positions. All enthusiasm had oozed out of the men. Towards evening Gen. Comstock and myself rode out to the position of the 11th corps, Howard's, at the request of Hooker who was getting suspicious. They occupied the extreme western end of the position, presumably the safest place on the whole line. Howard was away praying, but we saw Devens & Schurtz." Despite (or perhaps because of) Roebling's own German ancestry, he felt free to take verbal potshots at his fellow Germans:

The latter's [Howard's] German troops were jumping around in regular Dutch style, talking, gesticulating, fighting the air with their fists, with one eye on the coffee pot, arguing whether it took three or four men to carry a fence rail. In front of them was a thick cornfield. A reb could sneak up within 20 feet of their line without being seen. Occasionally a scattered shot was heard in the woods to the left. When we left headquarters a silly rumor gained ground that the enemy were retreating. Hooker beamed with delight. That was simply the tail end of Jackson's corps switching around in its circumgyration around our lines. I must confess that, I myself saw nothing of the enemy, although there were some ominous shots in the distance, making everyone feel anxious. Fifteen minutes after we left the blow fell.

Lee had taken up Jackson's suggestion of making a flank attack on the weak Federal right flank.[14]

Regarding Jackson's May 2 rout of the 11th Corps, Roebling noted that General Carl Schurz, second in command of the corps, in his posthumous memoir threw "the blame entirely, and justly so, on Howard who was not at the front and was not attending to his business." But Roebling added, "At the same time I must say that a practical soldier (not a political dilettante) would have placed videttes far enough in his own front to warn him in time." Roebling remembered, "It was dark when we returned to the Chancellor house. Not more than 15 or 20 minutes afterwards a confused roaring sound seemed to penetrate the air, ominous and alarming, but mysterious withal; I could not recall the like. On looking back over the road we had just returned on, a curious sight met the eye, for all the world like a stampeded herd of cattle, a multitude of yelling struggling men who had thrown away their muskets, panting for breath with faces distorted by fear, filled the road as far as the eye could reach." When the mob reached the Chancellor House, "Hooker and his staff rushed out with drawn sabres and began belaboring the leaders of Howard's cowards, all in vain." Roebling said that on hearing a German voice, he "stopped one fleeing man long enough to learn that an immense body of rebels had suddenly risen out of the cornfield in their front and overwhelmed them, he was the only man saved (as he thought)." Roebling passed his caustic judgment: "It is an old saying that the man who runs away may live to fight another day. But these same men ran away only to run away a second time at Gettysburg. Fortunately this Dutch panic did not affect the other corps in the least. It was confined to the 11th corps."[15]

"In the meantime the adjacent corps opened fire on the advance of Jackson. Sickles with the 3rd corps, threw himself in the breach, checking the rebel onslaught. The battle raged far into the night. Brave Berry was killed. Gen. Meade, brave and alert as ever, threw part of his 5th. Corps between Jackson's advance and the road to the U.S. Ford, thus saving our ultimate line of retreat." Unbeknownst to the Federals, the Confederates had paid a heavy price for their rout of the Federal 11th Corps, for in a night reconnaissance ride, Stonewall Jackson was mortally wounded by his own men when attempting to reenter his line. Roebling remembered, "There was little sleep that night, anxiety as to what the morn might bring forth kept us awake." Roebling relates that on May 3,

fighting began at daybreak, attack and counter-attack on the plain south of Chancellor's. Reynolds' 1st corps arrived and took position. All the fighting was done by three corps, Hooker refused to let the 1st, and 5th corps go in, notwithstanding their [commanders'] urgent entreaties. They numbered 44,000 men. We had two men to the enemy's one. Thirty-five thousand of our men had not fired a shot. Hooker acted like a jealous drunkard. When he had a drink he felt aggressive for half an hour, then he weakened, countermanded all forward movement, actually withdrawing troops who were driving the enemy! He could manage a corps. In command of a large army he lost his head.

After this scathing inditement of Joseph Hooker, a U.S. Military Academy graduate in the Class of 1837, Roebling made a surprising, yet defensible, pronouncement. Summing up his opinion of Hooker's rise to command the Army of the Potomac, he wrote, "He was a political general." Roebling no doubt remembered Hooker's advocates in Washington, who included, to varying degrees, Abraham Lincoln, Edwin Stanton, and members of the Radical Republican establishment.[16]

Roebling looked back on the battlefield at Chancellorsville as another place where bad dreams are born. "The view of the battlefield was a harrowing sight. Swept by cannon shot and bullet in all directions, encumbered by the dead and dying, affrighted fugitives running in all directions, not knowing which way to turn." As anyone who has experienced combat can likely relate, odd occurrences will remain vivid memories for witnesses, for Roebling wrote, "I recall a soldier with his knapsack torn off by a cannonball, the blow sent him in the air turning him twice before he fell dead from the shock." And he also remembered several close calls he himself had at Chancellorsville: "While riding over to the First Corps, a confederate came out of the woods close by and fired at me with deliberate aim—an excellent line shot, but too low, as the bullet passed through the sole of my boot and belly of the horse." Roebling also related, "On the porch of the Chancellor house a bullet struck me in the forehead. A very stiff visor on my cap deflected it into the cheek of a bystander, who cursed me with his other cheek."[17]

But the close call Washington would recollect most vividly occurred on May 3, 1863:

> I was leaning against a large wooden column of the Chancellor house porch, watching the fire of three rebel batteries who were making the house their target. Presently Hooker came out of the house and leaned against the same column. At that moment I saw a ball coming which bid fair to hit him. I yelled, "get back General!" He moved less than a foot, just enough not to be killed. But the shot hit the column in the middle splitting it into two parts, one of which knocked Hooker down with great force, stunning him at the same time. I thought surely Hooker was dead and rushed into the house crying, "Hooker is killed!" His staff came out, and seeing him lying unconscious thought so too. The body

was dragged off to a tent. I escaped unhurt. Oh, would that I had kept silent and allowed him to be killed. The battle Chancellorsville might still have been saved.

With Hooker lying insensible, believed dead, the appointment of another commander was imperative. While Roebling wished that Meade would be that commander, General Darius Couch (USMA 1846), because of his seniority, was called upon. Couch tried to refuse the command, but being the senior commander on the field, he was, for all practical purposes, stuck with it. Much to his relief and everyone else's surprise, Hooker revived. "Most preposterous conditions" then ensued, according to Roebling. Hooker refused to relinquish his role as commander in chief but wanted the reluctant Couch to serve as acting commander, giving the orders and taking responsibility for what happened next. But Hooker, Roebling witnessed, was also still insisting that the army position itself to retire across the river.[18]

While this drama played out at the Chancellor House, three of the Army of the Potomac's corps were still fighting, with the 1st and 5th Corps standing by in reserve. That afternoon, continued heavy Confederate fire upon the Chancellor House saw the Federal headquarters driven from the building. At midnight on the eighth day of his failed campaign, Hooker brought Butterfield, Warren, and the army's corps commanders together in his headquarters tent near the Bullock House crossroads. Roebling heard Sickles and Couch concur with Hooker's decision to withdraw back across the river, while others felt that "with Hooker in that dazed intractable condition it would be folly to attempt anything. It was tacitly agreed to do nothing." But Meade, despite his own desire for an advance on Fredericksburg the next morning, realized that Hooker had likely already made up his mind to withdraw his army across the river. The next morning, Roebling remembered, "Meade planted 56 cannon in line to protect our retreat. Lee respected that array. The engineers including myself, started in to lay out a hasty semi-circular entrenched line through the woods as a further safeguard. Here I lost myself in the thick underbrush for two long hours; could not believe my own compass, finally struck a small camp of runaways, who directed me to the U.S. Ford road, where I breathed more freely in spite of the heavy rain." Roebling discovered that he was only a few miles from Sedgwick's force, which had reached within a mile of the spot where Slocum's advance had been forced to stop and retreat.[19]

Torrential rain that had begun in the latter part of the afternoon of May 5 brought high water as another challenge the Army of the Potomac had to face in recrossing the Rapidan and Rappahannock that night.

Roebling recounted that they had to fight to keep the rampaging rivers from carrying their bridges away. Each corps acted for itself, for Hooker had preceded his army across the river.

> The army straggled back to the same old camping ground. The astounding farce had come to an end. You can search history in vain for a parallel case. If Hooker had gone bodily over to Lee he could not have helped him more than he did. How can it all be explained. Very easily I think. Hooker was simply a moral fraud. He had always posed. When it came to the supreme test, he failed utterly. He would have liked to hide in the bushes, but with thousands of eyes upon you the commander has not the privilege of the private. I well know how it racks one's nerves to stand up and be fired at. I also know that when a general has done his very best and is defeated fairly and squarely, he is entitled to a nervous collapse. But when a man breaks down absolutely before the battle has even begun, he does not deserve the name of soldier. It may be remarked that I have no right to criticize. But I underwent greater exposures, my life was threatened as often as his, and through his actions these sacrifices were all in vain, hence I have earned the right to criticize.

Roebling attributed Hooker's keeping his command for two months after the disaster to the political influence of Dan Sickles and Tammany Hall, among the general's other supporters.[20]

Remembering all too well the demoralizing effect yet another defeat had upon the Army of the Potomac, Roebling wrote many years later regarding the circumstances under which Lincoln replaced Hooker with George Meade on the eve of the Battle of Gettysburg: "And how did Lincoln do it! In the dead of the night, clandestinely, fearing that if the slightest hint of the proposed change leaked out, it might yet be frustrated by powerful enemies. War should be carried on by absolute despots. In a republic where everyone claims equal rights, progress is always checked by hates and jealousies." While Hooker would be sent west to serve with another army, Roebling would remain with the once again vanquished Army of the Potomac, an army that longed for better days and better leadership. Its head engineer, Comstock, abruptly went west as well to fortify a supposed threat to Pittsburgh. Roebling applied to go with him, for western Pennsylvania was full of childhood memories. He had been born and raised in the German American enclave his father, John Roebling, had founded, Saxonburg, and had gone to boarding school in Pittsburgh, but it was not to be. Comstock went on to serve as an engineer with Grant at the siege of Vicksburg, but Comstock and Roebling would meet again during the 1864 Overland Campaign. The circumstances they encountered then would be no less strenuous than their previous experience when serving under General Hooker.[21]

During the Battle of Chancellorsville, Roebling had been given a harsh introduction to the area known as the Wilderness and its surroundings. He would visit it again under equally unpleasant circumstances. Roebling's new direct commander was engineer General Gouverneur K. Warren, and their service together would change Washington's life forever. Under the command of Generals Warren and Meade, men Washington came to admire and respect, the next year and a half was one of great change and challenges for the Army of the Potomac and its soldiers.

On to Gettysburg with Meade and Warren

AFTER THE TRAUMA OF CHANCELLORSVILLE, WASHINGTON ROEBLING wrote that both the Army of the Potomac and the Army of Northern Virginia settled in for six weeks of mutual observation. While an unqualified Confederate victory, Chancellorsville had come at a heavy price. R. E. Lee had lost 13,460 men, or more than 20 percent of his army, including the irreplaceable Stonewall Jackson. The Federals had lost even more, 17,304 casualties, but were better able to repair their losses by bringing in new men. After a few weeks of calm, clerks at the Quartermaster's Department hunted Roebling down and subjected him to more demands, ranging from an accounting for a tent fly he lost at Chancellorsville to providing even more paperwork regarding the equipment and materials he had used to build bridges. The Roebling Collection at Rutgers University has many examples of such correspondence as well as Roebling's numerous lists of materials and men. Pay for the extra-duty men would be among the last things Roebling was able to clear up. Not only did different quartermaster officials demand different forms and endorsements, but the men who had worked on the bridges were now scattered everywhere that the Federal armies had troops. Meanwhile, some of the workers had died, or deserted, or (lucky enough to be discharged) gone home. But Roebling never gave up, and by the end of May 1863, every man who could be found was paid.[1]

Not all of Washington's days entailed such tedium, however, for with his assignment to serve under General Gouverneur Warren, now chief engineer of the Army of the Potomac, Roebling was selected as one of the Federals' "aeronauts" in the Military Balloon Corps. Washington had made a number of ascensions while still under the command of Cyrus Comstock before and during the Chancellorsville Campaign and rather inexplicably describes how Comstock, before leaving to go west at the end of April 1863, had "rehabilitated" the balloon service. By contrast, evidence suggests that Comstock had brought the whole balloon operation to its knees, to the point that it would cease to exist in the coming months. Regardless, Warren supported the daily balloon ascensions as valuable tools for mapping the countryside and keeping a close eye on the enemy. Roebling described how the first ascension "makes one a little nervous; the rest are easy." His willingness to be sent up as much as fifteen hundred feet in a tethered balloon while standing in a wicker basket that came up only to one's knees is just one example among many of his daring nature. These ascensions were not for the faint of heart, but when the weather cooperated and the ground crew was experienced, the ride was almost pleasant. Washington commented, "In clear weather the view was grand. The Blue Ridge slowly rose above the horizon in the west. The Potomac appeared as a silver thread; even the Chesapeake rose to sight." But when winds twisted the knee-high basket about, the experience bordered on terrifying. Roebling wrote, "The balloon turns around constantly, mixing up the points of the compass. In a high wind it slants so that you are almost thrown out. To use glasses and maps required dexterity and still more was needed to know what you were looking at." Put that together with the multiple times the balloons escaped their moorings and sailed away (in some cases, over Confederate-held territory and angry rebels), and one can see that the assignment was only for those with adventurous spirits.[2]

General Hooker took a great interest in the daily reports of the aeronauts, but despite Hooker's intense desire to keep such things secret, there were others who were following the reports of the Army of the Potomac's high-flying engineers. With a keen eye on the fiscal stability of the United States, the financiers of the country were much concerned with the success or failures of the Federal armies. In New York, the young J. P. Morgan was in fact the first to install a telegraph in his offices, and his telegrapher was close friends with one Jesse Bunnell, a civilian who frequently worked at Hooker's Army of Potomac headquarters. During one of the last balloon ascensions Washington Roebling made, he telegraphed his encrypted report to Hooker's headquarters that Lee's Army of Northern of Virginia was on the move. When Roebling's report of the movement, one that would culminate in the Battle of Gettysburg, arrived at Hooker's headquarters, it arrived at Morgan's offices in New York City a mere five minutes later.[3]

Despite evidence that the Balloon Service frequently provided valuable information to the Federal armies and their commanders, its days were

Balloon ascension.
Library of Congress.

numbered when the Quartermaster's Corps tried to make Thaddeus Lowe, the civilian who headed up the Balloon Service, a slave to the paperwork that plagued its military personnel. Lowe simply refused to gratify the quarter-master's insatiable demand for record keeping, stating that he was too busy supplying the commanders of the armies with information to waste time on paperwork. When some of Lowe's competitors and a disgruntled dismissed employee accused him of misusing and misappropriating government funds, Cyrus Comstock, overseeing the Balloon Corps in April 1863, apparently embraced the charges. While General A. A. Humphreys and others who had previously overseen Lowe's work had sensibly allowed him control of the bal-loons, Comstock demanded control over everything to do with the Balloon Corps, while questioning and cutting Lowe's funds. When General Warren became the Army of the Potomac's chief engineer, the relationship apparently improved, but the damage that Comstock and the Quartermaster's Corps had done had apparently proved the death knell for the Balloon Corps. The

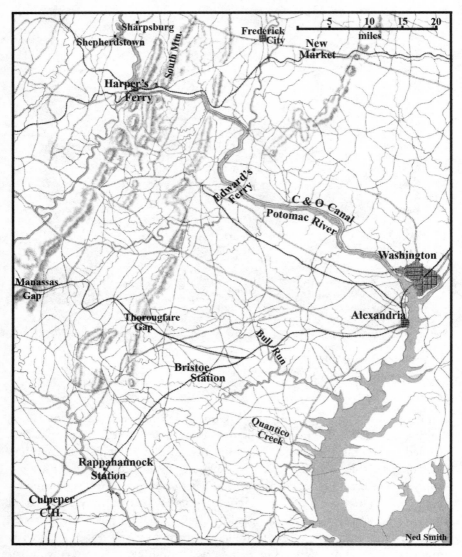

Scouting for the Army of the Potomac.
Adapted from Plate X, 1 OR Atlas.

aeronauts and their balloons would disappear from the skies above the armies, but not before Roebling had made many valuable ascensions, generally just before dawn, which enabled him to count the enemy's cookfires since their camps were generally hidden by trees during the day. While making one of his last ascents, Roebling noticed and reported that R. E. Lee and his army had disappeared from their front, one of many indications that the Army of Northern Virginia was on the move, heading westward toward an unimaginable collision with the Army of the Potomac in the sleepy town of Gettysburg, Pennsylvania.[4]

During his three and a half years of service during the war, Roebling had many near misses, and he sometimes believed he lived under a lucky star. He said that one of the last balloon ascensions before the Army of the Potomac began its pursuit of Lee was made by another fellow, and enemy fire sent fragments of shell through the balloon, letting out the gas. The unlucky aeronaut descended at great speed, barely living to tell about it. "That was my luck!" commented Washington. But during this period his luck also temporarily deserted him, for he told of how, when his horse was startled by a braying mule, he was thrown and landed on a stump. "I struck above the groin and felt as if I were injured internally," a wound from which he suffered pain for the next thirty-five years. After decades of pain, Washington mentioned the injury to a New York doctor, who, upon examining the site, suddenly struck the spot violently with his fist. He explained to his shocked patient that when the original injury healed, it had formed an unnatural adhesion that caused the pain. To Washington's amazement, the doctor was right, and he was freed from suffering. But that 1863 injury apparently did little to slow him down, for in the coming months of 1863 and 1864 Washington would tempt fate again and again.[5]

In mid-June 1863, the Army of the Potomac was shadowing Lee and the Army of Northern Virginia, and scouting duties led Roebling to ride forty miles to Rappahannock Station in one day. While fortifying the crossing there, he met and spent time with General A. A. Humphreys, who was commanding a division in General Sickles' 3rd Corps. Roebling said, "My admiration for Gen. Humphreys commenced then and ended only with his death." The two would have much contact in the coming year, and his admiration never dimmed. Meanwhile, uncertainty as to Lee's intentions found the Army of the Potomac following the railroad leading to Washington, until it was ascertained whether the Army of Northern Virginia would move east of the Blue Ridge or along the valley of Virginia. Roebling commented, "This uncertainty was soon dispelled by the capture of nearly all our troops in the valley. When Lee crossed the Potomac at Williamsport [Maryland] we knew that Washington was not the objective point, but rather Harrisburg or Baltimore." When the pursuing Federals crossed the Potomac at Edwards Ferry, Roebling remembered all too well his experiences there with the 6th New York Independent Battery in the ill-fated Battle of Ball's Bluff—one in what was becoming a long line of the Army of the Potomac's disasters.[6]

Among all the clamor and ongoing conjecture as to just what Lee's intentions were after he began his June 3 movement away from Fredericksburg, Roebling's immediate superior, General Gouverneur K. Warren, chief engineer of the Army of the Potomac, shared, nonplussed, with Roebling that he was supposed to be in Baltimore to get married on June 17 to one Miss Emily Chase. Warren had already postponed his wedding several times, and while no one doubted that another substantial battle was in the Army of the Potomac's future, it was agreed that the armies' reactive movements would not culminate in that clash for a while. With some difficulty, Warren got his furlough from General Joseph Hooker. While Roebling no doubt longed to accompany Warren on his brief respite away from the cares of the army and into the company of Baltimore's young ladies, the army's needs would dictate another plan for the young engineer. Roebling did travel as far as Baltimore with Warren, where, he wisecracked, he left his commander "to his fate." But Roebling traveled on to Philadelphia, where he'd been sent to acquire maps of southern Pennsylvania that Warren suspected they would soon urgently need. Roebling next stopped in Trenton for an hour and was somewhat shocked to find there "everything in despair and confusion. They were so prostrated with gloomy forebodings—that Philadelphia would be taken was a foregone conclusion." Surprised by the fear that Lee's movements could generate in the civilian population, Washington took the next train back to rejoin the army, "the only safe place I knew of." On a more serious note, he took leave of his weeping mother, whom, sadly, he would not see again until he found her on her deathbed.[7]

Roebling was supposed to have met General Warren in Baltimore, but, as a result of urgent requests for Warren to return to the army, Roebling found that he'd been left behind. He began his return with a long ride to Frederick, Maryland, where he found the church bells of the city ringing the alarm to summon the militia of the town to man the earthworks against invading rebels, reportedly nearby. Riding on along the main road toward New Market, he inexplicably met no one and could therefore get no news of where the Army of the Potomac or the enemy were at the moment. He later discovered that the day before, J. E. B. Stuart's cavalry had swept through the area; the local

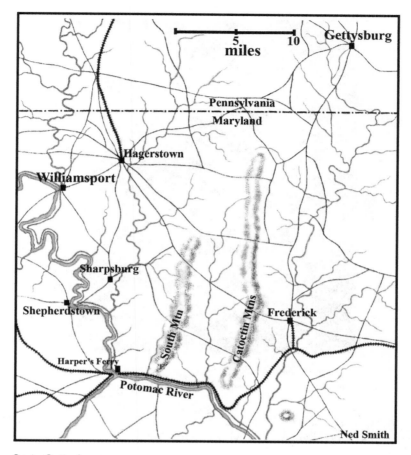

On to Gettysburg.
Adapted from Plate XXV, 6 OR Atlas.

population had gone into hiding and had yet to emerge. After a night spent under an apple tree, he decided the following morning to keep heading north by west. That afternoon, he thought he heard the report of cannon; putting an ear to the ground confirmed it. Upon gaining an elevation, he saw bursting shells some seven to eight miles away, for the first day of fighting at Gettysburg was under way. Roebling met up with the 5th Corps at Littlestown, Pennsylvania, joining them, eventually reaching the Army of the Potomac to find Warren and its new commander, General George Gordon Meade. Meade had arrived on the field at 1 a.m. on July 2, which would be the second day

General Gouverneur K. Warren.
National Archives and Records Administration.

of the battle. And although Meade realized that General Daniel Butterfield was a staunch Hooker partisan, Meade asked him to continue to serve as chief of staff at this critical time. It was an unavoidable decision that would cause General Meade considerable regret in the future.[8]

Having missed the first day of the battle, Roebling confessed that, although he listened to accounts of the previous day's fight, he would not entirely grasp what had happened until years later. Regarding the positions of the Army of the Potomac and the enemy, Roebling nonetheless joked, "Being an old campaigner by this time it did not take me long to grasp the situation." The Federal position was a now famous fishhook, and as General Warren commented, "We are now all in line of battle before the enemy in a position where we cannot be *beaten* but fear being turned." In fact, Roebling rode out in an effort to orient himself to Gettysburg and its surroundings, making a stop at Cemetery Hill, where, among other things, he found O. O. Howard's 11th Corps. Though Howard's soldiers had once again fled upon receiving a rebel

General A. A. Humphreys.
Library of Congress.

assault, Howard proceeded to argue with General Winfield Hancock over just who was in command of the field. Meade had sent Hancock ahead to take command of the field until his own arrival, but Howard, based on seniority, felt he should be in charge. Roebling also noticed another of Hooker's particular allies, General Daniel Sickles, whose 3rd Corps, despite considerable effort, had arrived too late on July 1 to participate in the first day's fighting. Sickles, whom Gettysburg historian Harry Pfanz describes as a frequent participant in Hooker's and Butterfield's "barroom and brothel" atmosphere at headquarters, was, Roebling declared, "bitterly aggrieved at the removal of Hooker." It was Sickles's animosity and resentment toward Meade, Roebling felt, that led to near disaster this day, July 2.[9]

General Sickles's orders for the second day of battle at Gettysburg, July 2, were to join the right of his 3rd Corps to the 2nd Corps's left and extend his line, putting his left at the field's dominating features, the Round Tops. Meade sent his son, George Jr., who had recently joined his staff, to check on Sickles's position and make the general aware of the location of Meade's headquarters. Young Meade soon returned with the unwelcome news that Sickles was not only not in position but also disputing where that position was. Sickles argued with anyone who would listen, and some who would not, including young Meade, Chief of Artillery Henry Hunt, Warren, and even Meade himself, and after an interview that Roebling described as "stormy and brief," Sickles had taken it upon himself to advance his corps almost a mile in advance of his assigned position. Having disobeyed orders, he notified neither Meade nor General Hancock, who commanded the 2nd Corps on his right. Sickles's poor judgment would result in terrible scenes of strife: the Peach Orchard, the Wheatfield, and Devil's Den, all remembered with horror, and that on a battlefield replete with many examples of unprecedented slaughter. Roebling, accompanying the 2nd Corps that morning, watched as Sickles, far in advance of the Federal line, became engaged. He believed that it was nothing more than a fit of pique at the removal of Hooker that caused Sickles to defy Meade. But instead of achieving some sort of vindication, Sickles found himself facing an enemy force double his strength while both of his flanks were in the air.[10]

Roebling recounted how "for several hours his [Sickles's] division commanders, Humphreys, Birney and their fellow soldiers made the bravest stand of the battle against overwhelming odds." The 3rd Corps faced destruction at the hands of the enemy unless immediately reinforced, and at this point Meade coolly and efficiently went to work to do what needed to be done. "Staff officers were sent flying in all directions to hurry up reinforcements," while Meade's calm demeanor and determination, according to Roebling, encouraged everyone around him. Roebling added the caustic comment, "In place of crying like Hooker 'I want to go home' he inspired everyone with some of his own vehement energy." Bringing in men from five different corps, Roebling told how Meade himself led some of his troops to the scenes of conflict where they were most needed. But another aspect of Sickles's disregard for his orders would impact quite specifically upon Roebling and Warren. Sickles's orders had been to occupy the Round Tops, and while the battle raged on the 3rd Corps's misplaced front, Little and Big Round Top lay undefended, an inviting target for an enemy that would like nothing better than to outflank the strongly positioned Army of the Potomac and take it from the rear.[11]

Little Round Top
and Pickett's Charge

ON THE AFTERNOON OF THE SECOND DAY OF THE BATTLE OF GETTYS-
burg, July 2, 1863, as Washington Roebling relates, "between 4 and 5 p.m.,
Gen. [George] Meade at his headquarters addressed us saying to Gen. [Gou-
verneur] Warren, 'I hear a lot of peppering going on over yonder about Little
Round Top. Suppose you ride over there and see what is going on, and if there
is any thing serious, see to it that it is met properly.'" Roebling commented
that, at the time, Meade had no suspicion that James Longstreet's turning
movement was already well under way. "Accordingly we mounted horse and
rode the mile and half or more, skirting the peach orchard and wheatfield
where hard fighting was still in progress. Arriving safely we encountered the
5th Corps at its [Little Round Top's] base, marching towards the Wheatfield—Warren stopped a moment to speak to them. I went on up, finding a
signal officer crouching behind the rocks—as soon as I showed my head above
the stones, bullets began to whistle about my ears. I could see confederates
in the woods in front. I rushed back to Warren and we both came up." On
the summit of Little Round Top, Warren would receive a similar greeting
from the Confederates, a bullet grazing his throat, for while Roebling was
summoning Warren, Roebling told, "In these few minutes the enemy had
approached in force. [John B.] Hood's Texans in solid column were marching
forward between the two Round Tops. Their advance had already crossed the
Taneytown pike and penetrated behind our lines." Roebling observed, "Had
Warren arrived five minutes later it would have been too late and we would
probably have lost the field." While much of the rebels' flanking force was
clearly visible, massing against Daniel Sickles's 3rd Corps, Warren suspected
that the woods between the Emmittsburg Road and Plum Run hid more,

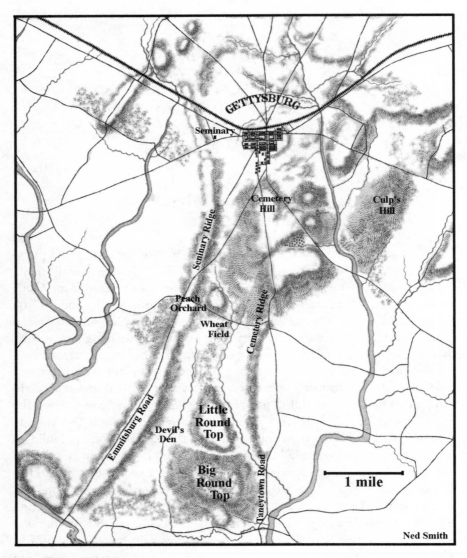

Second day at Gettysburg.
Adapted from Plate XCV, 1 OR Atlas.

and he said that, upon making a request to James E. Smith's 4th New York Independent Battery positioned above the Devil's Den, a shot lobbed into the woods revealed the hidden presence of a concealed rebel force.[1]

As Roebling later related, "Not a moment was to be lost. The summit of Little Round Top must be held at all hazards. Running down hill again Warren met [Colonel Patrick H.] O'Rorke's regiment, 140th N.Y. O'Rorke, USMA 1861, was a youthful friend of Warren's, having been his favorite pupil at West Point when the latter was a teacher there." O'Rorke, under orders to join the Federal effort to save the 3rd Corps, was persuaded to redirect his regiment and go to Warren's assistance. An impatient Roebling guided O'Rorke and the 140th's lieutenant, Porter Farley, riding their horses to the top of Little Round Top. But there was more to be done. Anxious to secure enough of a force to deny Little Round Top to the enemy, Washington began assisting Lieutenant Charles E. Hazlett's battery of six three-inch ten-pounder Parrott rifles to gain the summit: "The way was so steep that the horses could not pull the guns. We had to help pushing them up by hand. The moment a section got up it opened fire with good moral effect." While the arrival of the battery may well have cheered the beleaguered Federals on Little Round Top, in reality the barrels of the guns could not be sufficiently depressed to deal with the rebels who were swarming up the hill. As Roebling made another trip down Little Round Top's steep slope, seeking more infantry support to protect the battery, its commander, twenty-four-year-old Lieutenant Hazlett, was killed while kneeling over the mortally wounded brigade commander, General Stephen Weed. A newly minted brigadier general, the thirty-one-year-old Weed was shot by a Confederate sharpshooter near one of Hazlett's guns; paralyzed, he died within hours.[2]

In 1877, Roebling shared remembrances with Captain Porter Farley, a veteran of the 140th New York, explaining to Farley that he had been the mounted officer who accompanied General Warren on that day:

> I went with Colonel O'Rorke and your regiment to the top of the hill, where you at once became engaged with the enemy, who had almost reached the crest of the hill during the short interval which elapsed before we met your regiment, after we came down from the hill where the signal officer was. I had been on the summit of Little Round Top for half an hour with the signal officer, before we rushed down to call on you for help. I left Colonel O'Rorke as soon as he went into battle, and started with a message to General Meade, to inform him of what had been done. I passed through the remainder of Weed's brigade and along

George Gordon Meade.
Library of Congress.

the line of troops lying on the Peach Orchard road, who were already engaged with the enemy, and it seemed to me, before I had passed from one end of the line to the other, they had lost half their members, showing the severity of this onset and also the shortness of its duration, because it was all over in half an hour.[3]

The danger in showing oneself on Little Round Top that day in July was extreme, not only by way of the enemy's earnest assaults but also from their sharpshooters plying their deadly trade from nearby Devils Den. The enemy exacted a terrible toll from the commanders that answered General Warren's call for defenders of Little Round Top that day: Colonel O'Rorke lay dead, while battery commander Lieutenant Hazlett was killed while leaning over the dying brigade commander, General Stephen Weed. But Roebling also remembered the far luckier Colonel Joshua Chamberlain, crediting the men of his 20th Maine with giving the "first decisive check to the enemy, driving them

Charles E. Hazlett.
Public domain.

back through the ravine between the two Round Tops, into what was veritably a devil's den." When the worst of that terrible afternoon appeared to be over, Roebling remembered, "we remained masters of Little Round Top. The enemy's line was at its base. After we felt that we could hold it I quickly rode over to Gen. Meade, explained the situation, gave him at least a ray of comfort and then returned." The rebel force that had threatened Little Round Top and was driven off took refuge on the far side of Big Round Top, and although the 20th Maine had done a hard day's work, it was sent up in the night of July 2–3 to take possession of the bigger hill, thereby ensuring that the Round Tops stayed firmly under Federal control. Roebling related, "I returned to headquarters, too tired to eat, too exhausted to sleep, only to learn that equally severe fighting had raged around Culp's Hill and the cemetery. We had barely held our own." But as Roebling commented, while in the middle of desperate fighting, "a person forgets himself. The urgency of the moment overpowers everything. After it is all over then your nerves think about breaking down."[4]

Meade's Headquarters, Gettysburg.
Library of Congress.

"The morning of July 3rd broke bright and hot," Washington remembered. There was a lull in the fighting that, as often, he noted, "precedes the storm." With the benefit of hindsight, Roebling would later write, "We were not in condition to attack, so we rested, waiting for Lee's last onset. Gen. Meade said it would come in our centre. He was right, but it came late in the day, owing to divided counsels on the other side." Longstreet's preference for another flank attack, one that Roebling commented had some chance of success, was over-ruled in favor of an attack on the Federal center; Washington commented that Lee "had his way, to his own ruin as it turned out." One result of the fighting on the previous day, July 2, was that the organization of the Federal army was in much disarray: "Single regiments were scattered about, not knowing where their brigades were. Brigades had lost their divisions. It was essential that this universal mix-up be straightened out before Lee commenced his attack." Thus Daniel Butterfield, who was still Meade's chief of staff, sent Roebling on a mission to record the position of every unit on the field. "There was only one way to do it—namely to ride from the extreme left of the line, from Big Round Top along the entire front, passing Cemetery Hill and winding up with Culp's Hill, nearly three miles, and note down every regiment." This also meant a three-mile exposure to the enemy's sharpshooters, who were still busy with their infernal work. Roebling was particularly struck by the many dead on the field at Culp's Hill. He commented, "The task of the 12th Corps in holding their own and driving out the enemy who had taken their lines once, was fully equal to the 5th Corps' work at Little Round Top." A magnanimous comrade in arms was Washington Roebling, willing to recognize that another's fight had been every bit as terrible as his own.[5]

Roebling also described how, around noon on July 7, "Butterfield had another scare lest the supply of cannon ammunition would not hold out during a long battle. He could have had this information from Gen. [Henry] Hunt, Chief of Artillery," who was, Roebling remembered, "so deaf that he could scarcely hear a cannonshot." But instead of consulting Hunt, Butterfield, who Roebling believed was not on speaking terms with the artillery chief, instead ordered Roebling out again to count and report the artillery's supply of ammunition. "Ordinarily," Roebling observed, "this task takes several days as there were sixty batteries to be counted. One half of these were in reserve and had not fired a shot—that [half] took 10 minutes to count." As for the rest, a few had fired away their entire supply, and others some portion of it. But when Roebling reported to headquarters that there was plenty of ammunition, no one had time to care, for, he explained, "I had scarce returned to the absurd little two-room log house, misnamed headquarters, when two solitary cannonshots were heard. Instantaneously a hurricane of cannonshots fell upon, around and about us, accompanied by an appalling roar as of a thousand thunders. During that morning Gen. Lee had placed in position one hundred and thirty-eight cannon; they were discharged as one volley on hearing the signal of the two cannon, and each one made that little house its target."[6]

Roebling remembered,

The rain of destruction kept up for nearly an hour. We all felt that the great cannonade was merely the prelude to an infantry attack, with which Lee hoped to overwhelm our lines. He had pointed out to his gunners a small clump of trees, located several hundred feet in front of the little house. In their excitement, smoke and confusion they all overshot their mark, thus making this spot the real focus of countless shot and shell. Nearly forty-five years have elapsed since that day. The impressions left by that event are as vivid now as then. I fail to find words which would portray the absolute paralyzing horror of the situation. It was of no use to try and run away, all you could do was to stand still and commend your soul to God. Our little house was repeatedly hit, one ball through the garret, another carries away the steps, a third the posts of the porch.

A fragment of shell flying in through the door knocked down the table at which Col. Paine and myself were looking at some maps; we promptly ceased that occupation. Outside a string of horses were tied to the picket fence, a dozen were quickly killed. Another shot demolished the rest of the fence, setting my horse free. I had to run out to catch him. My horse was one of three unhurt.

Explaining why the Confederate bombardment was doing such damage, Roebling said, "The lay of the ground was such that the flying missiles would just skim the surface for a long distance, permitting nothing to escape." Then, too, "a perfect rain of shell fragments came down from above. As a rule the enemy's guns overshot their mark, hence the line of our troops lying flat on the ground behind a slight rise were reasonably protected. Many were killed a mile beyond us, as far back as Culp's Hill, and further."[7]

Finally, Meade's staff abandoned headquarters, for, as Roebling recounted,

At last it became a question of moments when we might all be killed, and those that were left retired to one side or the other, vainly seeking safer places. I rode up to Woodruff's and Cushing's batteries, where more ghastly sights met my gaze. They lost most of their horses and men, their guns were dismounted, but they held their ground; every moment the sickening thud of a ball passing through a horse was heard; neither was it an infrequent sight to see a poor beast fly to pieces from a shell exploding inside of it. We had as many guns as the enemy in position, but Gen. Hunt would allow only the half to reply; he certainly had ammunition enough and a sufficient number of reserve batteries. In such emergencies people sometimes lose their judgement.

But Roebling reconsidered, "Perhaps Hunt did not want to reveal the positions of our guns so as to lure Pickett's men on to surer destruction." He also remembered, "Under all this terrific fire Gen. Meade never lost his head nor did his judgment waver. Feeling sure that Lee would attack in the centre he made due provision by drawing troops from all available sources and massing them at the probable point of attack. This went on during the hottest fire. Had Pickett's men penetrated even farther than they did into our lines their defeat would have been only more overwhelming. There was also a possibility of Longstreet's making a flank attack on our left. That had also been attended to by a proper disposition of troops."[8]

Roebling continued,

After the cannonade had lasted about three quarters of an hour it suddenly abated and we felt that the infantry would commence its attack. Every available gun of ours, over a hundred in number, had orders to open on Pickett's line as soon as it appeared. After Pickett had started, the enemy's artillery began firing again over their head to cover the advance, but ceased soon after. Most of the battlefield was covered with thick smoke, making it difficult to see without a field glass. Gen. Meade had moved over behind the 2nd. Corps. My point of view was from near our batteries. As soon as the advance of the charge made its appearance all our batteries opened. Although not as numerous as the enemy's, they made more noise, which added to the general confusion of sound. Presently the [Federal] infantry opened fire. Pickett's men had a long distance to go, half a mile in some places, exposing them to a prolonged fire. Some of our troops were so disposed as to throw a flanking fire, than which nothing is more demoralizing. Gen. Meade's preparations to receive the enemy were so complete that no one felt any anxiety as to the result. Even if our first line were carried, there were two more lines behind them which were sure to repulse or capture them. Thus it was that the small force which did penetrate our first line were all captured. We were almost sorry that more had not been allowed to get that far. When the enemy had passed over half the ground their leading ranks already wavered and commenced to run back, but the main body reached the objective point, a small clump of trees, where Webb's Philadelphia Brigade held its ground pretty well, although some fell back. All of the enemy who actually penetrated our front were captured or killed. The field they had advanced on was strewn with the dead, the wounded and those who had thrown themselves on the ground to escape annihilation. No troops could have withstood our terrible fire. For once the Confederates found themselves in the same position that our army had been in so often, assaulting positions that could not be carried.[9]

Roebling considered,

Lee claimed that his arrangements had miscarried, but this is always the case, more or less. Anxiety gave way to exultation on our part, cheers were heard on all sides as the prisoners were gathered in by the thousand. We had a feeling that this was the last effort on [the] part of Lee, not because there was not plenty of fight left in his men, but because they had nothing to eat. The country had been ransacked of all available

General Warren.
Norton, *The Attack and Defense of Little Round Top*,
1913.

food supply, and as he had no railroad leading south to his own magazine, there was no alternative left but to starve or retreat. The Army of
Virginia always faced this predicament on their way north. Hundreds of
books have been written on the battle of Gettysburg, mostly by people
who were not there, and based upon facts that were slowly gathered
during months and years afterwards. It could not be otherwise. When
the last charge was in progress, we did not know that it was Pickett's
18,000 Virginians who were coming at us. We did not know that it was
Armistead, or Barksdale, or Kemper, or many, many others that were
losing their lives. These particular events are slowly realized from day to
day and finally woven into a connected narrative. The eye witness can
only describe the great events as they pass before his vision. He simply
sees the enemy and knows that it is a struggle for life or death.

With a cynicism inspired by hindsight, Roebling continued, "As for credit
and reputation, that is given by newspapers to the first man who strikes their

Alexander Webb.
Library of Congress.

fancy, and there it stays. For example, it is known that Gen. Pickett in person never crossed the Emmitsburg Road, full half a mile in the rear of his extreme advance, and yet in history he will go down forever as the leader of that charge!"[10]

Roebling concluded,

Night came at last. Everyone sought a soft spot of ground to recover from the extreme exhaustion and nervous tension of the previous week. I laid down in the furrow of a plowed field without cover. At eleven o'clock a terrific tempest burst upon us from the west (partly induced by the violent cannonade). I slept through it all. Gen. Meade, still weak from his old wound, was lying nearby; he got up and sat on a stone, drenched to the skin. This rain flooded everything, even drowning wounded men. To Lee's army, who were meditating a retreat, it was even more fearful. The great flood it caused in the Potomac, delayed his crossing over a week. The next day was the 4th of July. There was no fighting; picket firing also diminished. I took the occasion to ride over the battlefield, where you could almost step from corpse to corpse. Many bodies still moved spasmodically, showing they were not quite dead. Our little head quarters had become a surgeons' shambles, with a pile of legs and arms six feet high back of the little window. As we had remained masters of the field many of our wounded could be saved who would otherwise have perished. After you have seen a certain amount of misery and suffering one becomes hardened to it. There is room for only so much pity in the human breast.[11]

Roebling offered,

Who deserves the credit of winning Gettysburg? I say General Meade. There was not another man in that whole army who was his equal in the attributes that constitute a real commander. He made no mistake. He was equal to every emergency, meeting the enemy at every point. He had the confidence and esteem of every man in that army.

Regarding the nature of the Army of the Potomac's pursuit of Lee's retreating Army of Northern Virginia, Roebling stated, "On the night of July 4, we anticipated that the enemy might be gone the next morning, and so it proved. Preparations for pursuit, or following him, were begun." Roebling admitted, "Not much enthusiasm was manifested. We were still too tired. Gen. Meade sent for me and asked me to find Gen. A. A. Humphreys. I had an inkling of what was coming." Recognizing him as a messenger from General Meade, Roebling remembered, "Gen. Humphreys smiled. Arriving at headquarters, he was informed that he was appointed Chief of Staff to the Army of the Potomac in place of Butterfield, retired. This appointment created universal satisfaction as it marked the extinction of the last vestige of the old Hooker regime." News of U. S. Grant's victory at Vicksburg reached the Army of the Potomac as it took up its ponderous pursuit of General Lee and his Army of Northern Virginia.[12]

15

After Gettysburg and the
Path to Bristoe Station

WHILE U. S. GRANT CELEBRATED HAVING FINALLY CAPTURED VICKSBURG
after months of futile maneuvering, the soldiers of the Army of the Potomac
were slogging down muddy roads in pursuit of Lee's Army of Northern Virginia. What a very different "victory" was General Grant's compared with
General George Meade's. Grant's campaign, one not without a number of failures, such as the fiascos at Yazoo Pass and Steele's Bayou, lasted from October
1862 to July 1863, finally ending with an assault against a Confederate army
that had ultimately been starved into submission. Meade's victory, and a decisive victory it was, entailed three days of combat with combined casualties of
45,000 to 51,000, making it the bloodiest battle in the American Civil War. At
Vicksburg, Grant suffered 4,800 casualties, and while it might appear that the
"casualties" the Confederates endured, 32,697, were by comparison enormous,
one must consider that nearly 30,000 of those counted were surrendering
rebel soldiers whom Grant paroled after Vicksburg's capitulation. To be exact,
29,495 enemy soldiers were allowed to walk away from Vicksburg, the only
stipulation being that they must not take up arms again against the United
States until after they'd been officially exchanged. Grant did this despite his
awareness that a good number of the soldiers now being released from Vicksburg were parolees he'd set free after taking Forts Henry and Donelson the year
before. Meanwhile, Grant advocate General in Chief Henry Halleck, as well
as other rivals of Meade's, derided his victory at Gettysburg with accusations
that he mismanaged the battle and was fumbling the aftermath. Halleck, in a
mind-boggling masterpiece of hyperbole, declared of Grant's victory at Vicksburg, "In boldness of plan, rapidity of execution, and brilliancy of result, these
operations will compare most favorably with those of Napoleon about Ulm."[1]

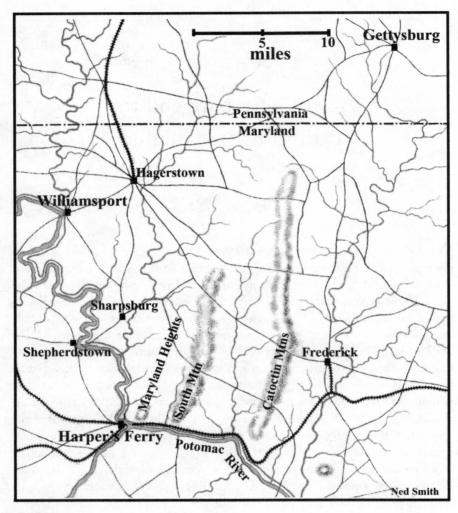

After Gettysburg.
Adapted from Plate XXV, 6 OR Atlas.

On July 4, while gathering up the wounded and beginning the burial of the dead, Meade ordered probes of the enemy's line still facing him from the Confederate position on Seminary Ridge, while Lee, meanwhile, was contracting his lines and entrenched in case of attack. A field return of the Army of the Potomac on July 5 showed that its seven infantry corps had, on average, the numbers usually found in a division, about five thousand men each. Torrential rains following the Battle of Gettysburg would make Lee's withdrawal and retreat, and Meade's subsequent attempts to follow him, a misery for all concerned. Exhaustion combined with impassable roads led Washington Roebling to later write of those days after Gettysburg, "The direct pursuit of Lee brought but scant return in the shape of part of his wagon train," a reference to the Union cavalry's capture of parts of the Army of Northern Virginia's column of wagons. Struggling along mud-bound roads, many were carrying the Confederate wounded who could be moved and what meager supplies Lee's army had left. Meade sent Gouverneur Warren and Roebling to ascertain Lee's route, accompanied by John Sedgwick's 6th Corps for a reconnaissance in force. The resulting reports put the Army of the Potomac on a course to follow the Army of Northern Virginia. Realizing that following directly in the rebels' rear would allow them to utilize delaying tactics upon the pursuing Federals, Meade chose what he hoped would be a faster flanking route. Heavy rains on the night of July 7 and all the next day posed their own challenges. Roebling wrote, "The main [Federal] army followed on the eastern flank of the Blue Ridge, floundering through mud all the way. I was with the advance of the 6th Corps, sending back reports of the terrible condition of the roads, retarding all rapid movements." After scouting both mountain gaps, Roebling reported to Warren on July 8,

The roads are frightful. Colonel Reynolds has been trying all day to get the Sixth Corps batteries over. It will take until to-morrow noon before he is entirely across, and then the horses will be unfit for use. The trains have all gone to Frederick. None attempted the Mountain road today.

Two days later we crossed the Blue Ridge above Maryland heights, only to find Lee strongly entrenched in an impregnable position, prepared by him a month before with his usual skill. As our army came up we tried in vain to find an assailable point. Lee was waiting for the Potomac to subside, and gathering canal boats for a new bridge. We drove in the pickets at various places to no avail. The enemy were only too anxious to have us attack as our defeat would be certain.[2]

Plans for an assault upon the Army of Northern Virginia's position at Williamsport were frustrated by the rugged nature of the surrounding countryside, full of ravines, ditches, and rock walls. But by far the most difficult problem was the inability of the Unionists' probes to find a weakness in Lee's well-chosen, increasingly well-fortified position. Former 3rd Corps division commander General Andrew Humphreys, now Meade's chief of staff, described Lee's position as one of extraordinary strength, made more formidable by skillful fortifications. Upon personal surveys, Meade, Humphreys, and Meade's engineer, General Warren, were unable to find vulnerable points. Nor did the reconnaissance in force carried out along the entire front on July 11 and 12 result in his corps commanders' finding a place that promised a breakthrough. Meanwhile, the continued falling level of the flood waters was a constant reminder that time was running out, though, as late as July 12, the ever-dependable General John Buford was reporting that only rebel wounded we're being taken over the river on a small ferry and that the water level still made the ford inaccessible. Buford reinforced this observation with reports that fully equipped Confederate horses, unfortunate beasts that had apparently been tried at the ford, had come floating past his troopers' picket post on the river. Meade, planning to order the whole army to make a reconnaissance in force the following day in hopes of uncovering a weakness in the Army of Northern Virginia's lines, called his corps commanders together on the night of July 12–13. Both Humphreys and Roebling recounted the adverse reaction of the corps commanders, with Roebling saying that five out of six were against an assault. This unfavorable response, Roebling felt, led to postponement of the Federal advance until early on the morning of July 14, when it was discovered, Roebling wrote, "that the bird had flown" in the night.[3]

After "Lee retired over the Potomac in safety," Roebling said, the chagrinned Federals had a chance to examine the Army of Northern Virginia's earthworks at length. Humphreys wrote, "A careful survey of the intrenched position of the enemy was made, and showed that an assault upon it would have resulted disastrously to us." Humphreys, a veteran of Ambrose Burnside's disaster of the previous year, further suggested that the enemy's earthworks at Williamsport were equal to (if not more formidable than) the rebel defenses the Federals had futilely hurled themselves against at Fredericksburg. Roebling, too, examined the enemy's works: "I rode along the [Lee's] entrenched line. It was built of logs and earth, well chosen, ditched in some places with strong abattis in front. We could not have taken it. That we did not make the attempt was a great disappointment to Gen. Lee." There's a certain irony here: In the aftermath of a great battle, the commanders of both the armies that fought at Gettysburg, the victor and the defeated, offered to resign, Lee because he felt that he had failed and Meade because his administration felt that he had failed. Neither resignation was accepted.[4]

Roebling acknowledged that much of the condemnation of Meade and the Army of the Potomac at the time flowed from the "vile, irresponsible, rascally newspaper, whose ignorance is only exceeded by its animosity." But Roebling also remembered the hourly dispatches from Halleck and the administration in Washington that arrived at Meade's headquarters. "Why don't you attack! Why don't you reap the profits of your victory! None of these people knew or cared about the real situation." Roebling declared Halleck "as unreasonable as any," though the general in chief, as usual, declined to take any responsibility or issue direct orders. The voices of the increasingly wide circle of promoters of U. S. Grant in Washington had been augmented by the dramatic and fabricated assertions and allegations of General Dan Sickles. The wounded "hero," now minus a leg, found a ready audience, which included President Abraham Lincoln, for his tales of how the inept General Meade had wanted to retreat instead of doing battle with Lee at Gettysburg. And hadn't he, Dan Sickles, saved the day by strategically moving his 3rd Corps, disrupting the rebel assault, and forcing Meade to fight? Most students and scholars of the battle, however, believe Sickles's intentional disregard of his orders resulted in a costly disaster for his own troops and for those who had to rescue them from the dangerous predicament in which their commander had placed them. But Sickles managed to get his story heard first, regaling Lincoln with his creative fictions. One such occasion comes down to us from a witness, James F. Rusling, a New Jersey man whom Roebling knew well and identified as a Joseph Hooker sycophant and adherent, much like Daniel Sickles. Truth never got in the way of a good Dan Sickles story, or a Rusling one for that matter. Rusling declared that it was Sickles's heroic accomplishments at Gettysburg that likely saved him from a court-martial. Though there is no evidence that a court-martial was considered, many believe it was Sickles's serious wounding that forestalled his being held accountable for his grievous disobedience of orders and the dire consequences.[5]

In the aftermath of the turmoil and disappointments of Williamsport, the Federals moved on, and with Warren and the Army of the Potomac, Roebling returned to familiar ground.

The army now moved on to Harper's Ferry, some crossing at that place by the railroad bridge which we had held, others lower down at Berlin. When we arrived within a mile or so I examined with a field glass the suspension bridge which I had built the winter before across the Shenandoah. I could see that the enemy had cut the suspenders and let the floor fall into the river, but the cables hung there apparently undamaged. I immediately got a detail of men and a number of wagons and commenced to load up timber and lumber and boards, obtained by tearing down houses and robbing the Baltimore and Ohio Railroad. When the troops arrived I was already busy rebuilding it. In two days I had it finished and part of our army crossed on it.

General Warren would say of Roebling's bridge work at Harpers Ferry that September, "Lt. Roebling built the wire suspension bridge over the Shenandoah, and has just repaired the serious damage done to it by our troops on evacuating Harper's Ferry, a delicate operation which no one but an expert in this kind of bridge could have safely performed."[6]

When the Army of the Potomac reentered the state of Virginia, the administration ordered it to take up a "threatening position, but not to advance against Lee, who was in position in vicinity of Culpeper Court House between the Rappahannock and the Rapidan." Meade and his army were fated to spend the fall in often futile and always frustrating sparring with Lee and the Army of Northern Virginia. With the loss of three of his corps commanders—Reynolds, Sickles, and Winfield Hancock, casualties at Gettysburg—Meade saw to one temporary replacement for command of the Army of the Potomac's 2nd Corps. He wrote to Halleck on July 19, "The very valuable services and most efficient assistance rendered me by Brigadier-General Warren induce me to nominate him for the commission of major-general to be assigned to the second Corps." Nor was Warren the only one whose services were recognized. On July 15, General Warren requested that Lieutenant Roebling be made his aide-de-camp. Warren would say of the engineer, who would spend the following months with him as a scout and courier, "Roebling was on my staff, and I think performed more able and brave services than anyone I knew." Francis Walker, 2nd Corps historian and later president of the Massachusetts Institute of Technology, also spoke well of Roebling, describing him as "an officer of rare topographical abilities." At the time Roebling served with Warren in the 2nd Corps, he came to know Lieutenant Frank Haskell of Gettysburg fame, who was also on Warren's headquarters staff.[7]

Early in September, rumors were flying that James Longstreet and his corps had left the Army of Northern Virginia and been sent to Tennessee. In response, Meade ordered a reconnaissance in force by Alfred Pleasonton's Cavalry Corps supported by Warren's 2nd Corps. On the night of September

11, Warren received orders to advance the next day to Rappahannock Station. On the morning of September 13, Pleasonton and Warren crossed the river, drove the enemy nine miles south, and took possession of Culpeper Court House, where the entire Army of the Potomac would soon follow.

Awaiting intelligence on the Army of Northern Virginia's positions, General Meade, pondering how much the transfer of Longstreet's corps had weakened Lee, considered his options. Meade shared his thoughts with Halleck; they included a change of supply base to Fredericksburg or the James River to strengthen the Army of the Potomac's hand for an advance upon Richmond. Halleck responded to his ideas with the reminder that he could give Meade no additional troops and the admonition "No rash movements can, therefore, be ventured." It is of considerable interest that while Halleck was discouraging the movements Meade contemplated, movement was just what President Lincoln wanted, and sooner rather than later. But Halleck emphatically refused to endorse Meade's ideas for engaging Lee, though within months the future lieutenant general Grant would be given a free hand to execute what was merely a variation on Meade's plan. Not only had Halleck put a stop to Meade's further advance, but he also transferred two of the Army of the Potomac's corps to Grant, who had been given command of William Rosecrans's army after the latter's defeat at Chickamauga. While there is no question that Longstreet's presence at the battle influenced the outcome, Halleck had refused Rosecrans's request for reinforcements, reinforcements that Halleck now sent to Grant. The Army of the Potomac's 11th and 12th Corps were detached on September 23 and sent, under General Joseph Hooker's command, to Grant at Chattanooga. The loss of these twenty thousand men seemingly froze the Army of the Potomac in place for a time, but luckily not much was heard from Lee's Army of Northern Virginia either.[8]

General Warren did all he could to keep Meade informed as to the condition of the roads, fords, and bridges, as well as the enemy's movements, and Roebling was Warren's eyes and ears. Meade demonstrated his confidence in Roebling's scouting by specifically requesting from Warren, "If you could spare Roebling for this purpose, I should be obliged to you." As Warren reported to Meade from Culpeper on September 15, 1863, "Lieutenant Roebling says the railroad is in good order all the way to Mitchell's Station, and the bridge over Cedar Run is all right." But even someone with Roebling's dedication and daring could not be available 24/7. While requesting an additional engineering officer, Warren also asked Meade if, since Roebling had already been scouting all night, he could send orders to General Pleasonton to have the cavalry take up the reconnaissance. Warren requested that Pleasonton assign the ever-reliable General David Gregg to this task, but, whoever Pleasonton sent out, not all the reports subsequently sent from the cavalry to headquarters were accurate. In fact, the cavalry's inaccuracies would prove all but fatal to the plans Meade was formulating to develop his next move.[9]

With plans he put forth for an advance rejected, Meade was understandably confused by the conflicting signals coming from Halleck and Lincoln regarding whether and where he should attack and what approach he should take. Meanwhile, it seemed, as Roebling would later caustically observe, that though deprived of two corps, Meade was "expected to do more with what he had left then before." The ensuing Federal inactivity preyed upon all in Culpeper and its vicinity, and it seems that Warren was beginning to feel the loneliness of command. A member of his headquarters "family" described a night of imbibing that left the general the worse for drink. Washington Roebling, it is said, took charge of his commander once they got him to the building housing his headquarters. With no memory of what had happened the night before, Warren swore off whiskey altogether. Roebling would later confide to his fiancée, Warren's sister Emily, that Warren "is a perfect gentleman when he is sober—but 2 glasses of ale Oh Lord!"[10]

A presentation sword sent to General Warren in early October from the citizens of his hometown, Cold Spring, New York, likely cheered the general up, although the hoopla of the presentation ceremony made him decidedly uneasy. Meade aide Theodore Lyman described finding Warren lodged in "Spartan simplicity, in a third-rate farmhouse. His dress even more spartan than his lodgment." Lyman described a slender, sunburnt man with piercing black eyes and declared him "one of the very best generals in the Army of the Potomac! He is a most kind man, and always taking care of hysterical old Secesh ladies and giving them coffee and sugar. As to Secesh *males*, in the army he is a standing terror to them." Lyman was much amused that "this valiant warrior, who don't care a button for missiles, was extremely nervous" regarding the ordeal of the sword presentation, attended by scores of the Army of the Potomac's generals and their staff. Much relieved when the formalities had finished, Warren commented, "The execution is over; now won't you come and eat something?" The "something" consisted of roast beef, baked ham, bread, and assorted pickles laid out on a table with newspapers for a cloth, washed down with whiskey punch. As this ceremony had taken place in full view of the rebels across the river, Lyman was grateful that the opponents were on such friendly terms, their pickets regularly conversing, that they didn't throw a shell into this gathering of the Army of the Potomac's elite.[11]

Part of Warren's problem was that he was also missing his new wife and, a slave to duty, he refused to take leave until he felt sure there would be no fighting or movement while he was gone. He snatched a few days in Baltimore, only to return to Culpeper to find that Lee and the Army of Northern Virginia were on the move. Lee had begun an advance on October 9 with the intention of turning the Federals' right flank; then he would position the Army of Northern Virginia between the Army of the Potomac and Washington and force a fight upon Meade regardless of any disadvantages of the Federals' position. In *George Gordon Meade and the War in the East*, Ethan Rafuse inexplicably declares that Meade was well informed regarding Lee's movements and intentions in the days leading up to Meade's move to Centreville and the Battle of Bristoe Station. However, ample evidence exists that conflicting Federal reconnaissance reports left Meade very much in the dark. Reports of variable accuracy from the Federal cavalry, completely erroneous and misleading in the extreme, first caused delay and confusion. But it soon became clear that Lee was once again attempting to threaten the Federal flank and cut the Army of the Potomac's communications. Alert to the danger and refusing to fight on ground of Lee's choosing, Meade issued orders on October 10 for the Army of the Potomac to withdraw to a more secure position on the Rappahannock, though those faulty reports from Pleasonton's cavalry, as well as those from Sykes's 5th Corps, confused and delayed the withdrawal. From October 11 to October 13, the 2nd Corps engaged in one of the most arduous marches of its history with little or no time to eat or sleep before reaching the village of Auburn. Bivouacking on the south side of Cedar Creek, Warren would have preferred to cross over to the north side the night before, but the slow-moving 3rd Corps blocked the narrow crossing. As Francis Walker, 2nd Corps historian, comments, any corps acting as rear guard, as Warren was for the Army of the Potomac, is doomed to frustration (if not outright danger) should it be unfortunate enough to be trailing after slow troops. Warren was in just such a situation and was forced to allow his men, dropping to the ground with fatigue, to encamp before crossing the steep-banked creek. They got scant rest before rising early on October 14, for while the Army of the Potomac continued on to Centreville, it fell to the 2nd Corps, with timely assistance from General David Gregg's 2nd Cavalry, to continue to act as the Army of the Potomac's rear guard.[12]

Heavy fog blanketed the area as Warren's lead division began crossing Cedar Run. Suddenly Gregg's cavalry, guarding the 2nd Corps's left flank and rear, were driven in by enemy cavalry. Upon Warren's earnest request, Gregg managed to hold the encroaching rebels at bay while the 2nd Corps began to

Gen David Gregg.
Library of Congress.

cross. Coming under severe pressure, Gregg called upon Warren for support and received it, but then danger threatened from another direction. After the first of the 2nd Corps's units made it across the creek, J. E. B. Stuart's cavalry, cut off from the Army of Northern Virginia, burst out of the murk upon the surprised Federals with guns and cannon blazing. These encounters led to a deadly comedy of errors for all participants, with the 2nd Corps caught between Stuart's cavalry on one flank and an unknown quantity of A. P. Hill's and Richard Ewell's corps, comprising half of Lee's Army of Northern Virginia, on the other. None of the commanders, Confederate or Federal, had any real knowledge at first of what numbers and whose troops they were facing. In the initial encounters, Gregg's cavalry's stubborn delaying action bought Warren the time he needed to deploy his men. Meanwhile, across the stream, the feisty resistance of the 2nd Corps elements surprised by Stuart sent the rebel horsemen on their way to a quieter, safer position. As he pivoted his column to the left, bringing the men of the 2nd Corps into a line of battle, Warren began to recognize an advantage that could be snatched from the threat he

General A. P. Hill.
Library of Congress.

was facing, a chance to turn a potential disaster into an opportunity. Despite operating on six or seven hours of sleep in the last forty-eight, the tired and hungry 2nd Corps, subject to Warren's imperative orders, performed miracles at the fight that became known as Bristoe Station. Confederate general Hill, in his enthusiasm to pursue the disappearing 5th Corps, which he mistakenly believed was the Army of the Potomac's rear guard, walked into a trap of his own making. Warren would take advantage of the unwary rebels, and as the hunters became the hunted, he gave Hill's command a sharp and embarrassing rebuke. It played out in this way.[13]

At midday on October 14, Warren received word from Meade that the Army of the Potomac's way to Centreville was clear, and if Warren's 2nd Corps, acting as rear guard, should need assistance, General Sykes's 5th Corps had been instructed to stay within supporting distance. Much, it turned out, was erroneous about Meade's reassurances, for General Judson Kilpatrick's cavalry's report—that the way to Centreville was clear—would prove gravely inaccurate. Nor would Sykes's 5th Corps wait around to see how the 2nd

Corps fared in catching up with the rest of the Army of the Potomac. Sykes, claiming that the head of Warren's column had been sighted, took his 5th Corps and scarpered. By 3 p.m., when a furious cannonade broke forth on the road ahead, Warren and staff rushed to the head of the 2nd Corps column only to find, not Sykes, but A. P. Hill's Confederate corps. Henry Heth's division led Hill's advance, and the hapless Heth was so focused on tearing after the disappearing Federal 5th Corps that he failed to notice Warren's forces. The rebels' frustrated firing of a few shells at the escaping Federal 5th Corps had alerted Warren that the enemy was quite startling near. Further investigation revealed that two battle lines of Confederate infantry were bearing down upon the flank of Warren's vanguard. While the conscientious cavalry of David Gregg remained with the 2nd Corps, General Warren, the brand-new commander of the smallest of the Army of the Potomac's corps, was left to his own devices to confront whatever part of the Army of Northern Virginia Lee would choose to throw at him. What followed is ample proof that, for Roebling, being on the staff of General Warren would seldom be dull.[14]

Warren was lucky to have two resourceful commanders at the head of his column that day, division commander General Alexander Webb and 2nd Corps chief of staff Colonel C. H. Morgan. They had already begun to deploy men into a defensive line when Warren and his staff arrived. Warren rushed Webb's men into a heaven-sent nearby railway cut. Some well-applied Federal artillery fire distracted and somewhat delayed the onrushing rebels from their pursuit of the 5th Corps, but reaction to this unknown quantity of Federals that had mysteriously appeared on their right flank would be a case of too little, too late. Webb's men were soon joined by comrades anxious to gain the limited shelter of the cut before the redirected charging rebel battle lines reached them. The enemy, on reaching the cut, was repelled by Federal rifles and bayonets. Generals Warren and Webb, with their staffs, galloped up and down along the track encouraging and steadying the men. Confederate prisoners revealed that these were men of Hill's corps, but Warren well knew that although the Federals had successfully repelled two of Hill's brigades, a lot more rebels were undoubtedly somewhere nearby. Then, too, the 2nd Corps was on the wrong side of a river from its own army and safety, and Confederate batteries commanded the river crossing that was the way out. While Warren and his staff brought up more troops, forming a line for the expected onslaught, the men of Gregg's cavalry, despite having expended their carbine ammunition after much hard fighting, joined the left of Warren's battle line and prepared to defend themselves with pistol and saber. When darkness provided a much-needed respite, Warren, taking his wounded and his prisoners

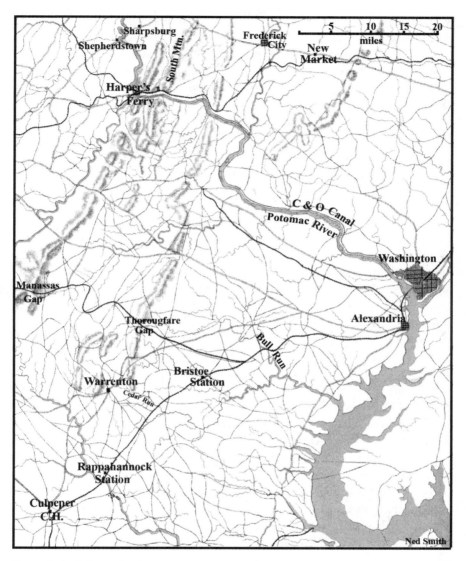

The path to Bristoe Station.
Adapted from Plate X, 1 OR Atlas.

with him, was able to withdraw, his weary soldiers marching an additional twenty-five miles to the safety of the Army of the Potomac's position at Centreville. Warren, his staff, and the men of the 2nd Corps could finally breathe more easily.[15]

Neither Meade nor Lee would get the battle each had sought that October, although the fighting season was not yet over. Meade's position at Centreville proved so well chosen that Lee chose not to attack. Instead, before recrossing the Rappahannock, Lee destroyed the railroad Meade depended upon to supply his army. Foiled while he reestablished his communications, Meade confided to his wife regarding his dealings with Lee, "This was a deep game, and I am free to admit that in the playing of it he has got the advantage of me." But there were those, Washington Roebling among them, who appreciated General Meade's intelligence and integrity, qualities that prevented him from sending the soldiers of his army into battles that, though they might please the administration, they could not hope to win, no matter how many men were sacrificed. While many of the men who served under him respected him, despite his gruff and often cantankerous ways, the administration expressed, often through Halleck's increasingly contemptuous voice, its disapproval of Meade's handling of the Army of the Potomac. Meanwhile, after the punishment he inflicted upon the Army of Northern Virginia at Bristoe Station, Warren's star was on the ascendant. Following hard upon the heels of his much-praised performance at Gettysburg, many were taking notice of Warren's quick thinking and reactions. It was, as one Hill biographer has described Warren's action at Bristoe, "one of the neatest traps arranged in the Civil War." Warren's aide, Frank Haskell, well known for his own courage and determination, said of Warren after that fight, "Such men as he are required to end this War—men who will not hesitate to strike when a chance occurs, and who still *hanker* after a chance and run forward to meet it."[16]

That same October, U. S. Grant would be granted a promotion to full major general in the regular army, backdated to his victory at Vicksburg on July 4, 1863. Meade would not be given the equivalent rank until August 1864, and then it would be at the request of Lieutenant General Grant. The tone of Halleck's dispatches to Meade, which previously had often cautioned the Army of the Potomac commander against rash advances, changed quite dramatically. Now they were taunting and goading. Halleck offered this to Meade in mid-October: "Lee is unquestionably bullying you. If you cannot ascertain his movements, I certainly cannot. If you pursue and fight him, I think you will find out where he is." It would be hard to find a man more duplicitous than Henry Halleck. He had no loyalties, not even doing all he could to ensure victories on the battlefield to secure the ultimate survival of the Union. While in the past he had treated U. S. Grant in a similar fashion, at some point Halleck eventually threw all his eggs into the Grant basket, assisting his ascension to command of the Union armies. But this also meant that anyone who stood in the way of his plans for Grant, including George Gordon Meade, would be treated with scorn and pushed aside.[17]

In 1915, Roebling received an unexpected honor from his 2nd Corps comrades of 1863. The executive committee of the 2nd Corps Society voted unanimously to elect him an honorary member. On the committee's letter of recognition, Roebling proudly noted that during the months that General Warren and he served with the 2nd Corps, between Gettysburg and the 1864 Overland Campaign, "the most important battle fought by the 2nd Corps during the time was the action at Bristoe Station, when the enemy was repulsed." As part of his military family, Washington Roebling would see much of General Warren, acting as his aide, scout, topographical engineer, and courier. He would also have much contact with General Meade, frequently carrying dispatches between him and Warren under the most critical and provoking circumstances. Having served under the likes of Generals Irvin McDowell and Joseph Hooker, in whom he lost all confidence, Roebling never lost his respect for Meade and Warren, even while enduring the great hardships and turmoil of the coming months. Roebling would remember those generals' many strengths and achievements even as he himself marched into old age and his old commanders were long gone.[18]

General French's Failures Deny the Army of the Potomac a Fight at Mine Run

At THE END OF OCTOBER 1863, IF THE SOLDIERS OF THE ARMY OF THE Potomac hoped that another year of fighting was coming to an end, they soon received sufficient signs to know this was not the case. Rumors abounded in camp that General George Meade was planning a movement, and his refusal to grant any leaves of absence seemingly confirmed it. Even though the weather had turned bitterly cold and Henry Halleck had denied Meade's request to change his base of operations to Fredericksburg, though his options were limited, on November 7 Meade moved the Army of the Potomac to the Rappahannock. Gouverneur Warren proposed a swift advance to Germanna Ford to prevent Robert E. Lee from withdrawing, but Meade was apparently fairly confident that Lee would give battle on the plains around Brandy Station. But a surprisingly easy Federal victory at Rappahannock Station that gave the Unionists a bridgehead in enemy territory, rather than bringing on a battle with the Army of Northern Virginia, prompted Lee to abruptly withdraw across the Rapidan. The rebels, no doubt reluctantly, left behind the well-built quarters where they had planned to spend the winter between the two rivers. And Meade was left having to formulate another plan, this time to attack Lee in his new position south of the Rapidan. As Meade pondered his next move, he called General Warren to headquarters, asking him to bring along the newly promoted Captain Roebling, whose knowledge of the area could prove helpful. The Army of the Potomac commander eventually decided upon a quick movement eastward to three fords on the Rapidan that would allow him to cross to the east of the Army of Northern Virginia's positions and subsequently swing south and west on the Orange Plank Road and the Orange Turnpike, with the intention of turning the enemy's works and forcing

Lee into an open field fight. On November 26, the 2nd Corps with the Army of the Potomac began the series of advances that would become known as the Mine Run Campaign, days that would have a lasting effect on many lives.[1]

On November 26, Warren's 2nd Corps commenced a movement intended, by means of a rapid march, to render Lee's line of defense at Mine Run untenable and force him to fight on Meade's terms. Speed was of the essence, for the Federals had intelligence that the corps of the Army of Northern Virginia were some distance from each other, and it was hoped they could be destroyed in detail before they could reunite. But from the start, delays and blunders hindered the Unionists' movements. Meade's options were few, consisting mainly of trying to turn one or the other of Lee's flanks. And weren't the lower fords of the Rapidan relatively unguarded, a seeming invitation to "cross here"? Though Warren's 2nd Corps reached its assigned crossing place, Germanna Ford, by midmorning, General William French's 3rd Corps did not. With orders that all corps would advance at the same time, Warren was halted to wait for the tardy French, who did not arrive at his crossing place until noon. Though Lee had apparently received intelligence that the Army of the Potomac was preparing to move before it took a single step, the appearance of several corps at crossings of the Rapidan undoubtedly, to quote Ambrose Bierce, "acquainted the enemy with our intention to surprise him." Then, too, recent heavy rains had raised the river to the point where several of the pontoon bridges employed were coming up embarrassingly short, causing additional delay. Despite all this, the Federals still believed they might make something of an admittedly bad start. If they could catch the separated elements of Lee's army before they came together, perhaps a decisive blow could still be struck.[2]

The morning of November 27 found the 2nd Corps again in motion, and by 10 a.m. Warren was confronting two divisions of Richard Ewell's rebels, only to be called upon to halt once again, to wait for French to bring up the 3rd Corps. Warren barely had time to deploy his corps before the enemy's battle line threatened to extend beyond his own, and he was under intense pressure from enemy infantry determined to challenge this isolated Federal incursion. Warren waited in vain for French to come up on his right as ordered, and the 2nd Corps fought on alone against an increasingly aggressive enemy. Only the fall of darkness brought an end to the fighting on Warren's front with still no sign of the 3rd Corps. French had, in a chronological list of his blunders, taken the wrong road, forgotten or misunderstood his orders, and, as a result, stopped and waited for Warren to come to him. Then, on encountering enemy resistance when he finally advanced, French stopped again for an elaborate deployment that allowed one rebel division to stop his entire corps in its tracks

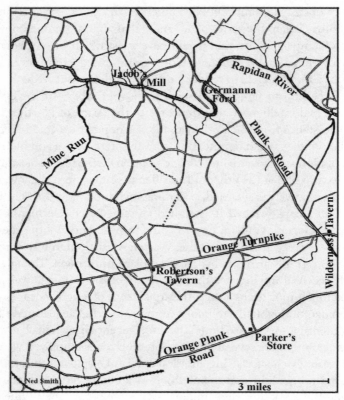

Mine Run.
Adapted from Plate XLVII, OR Atlas; map in Walker, *History of the Second Army Corps*, 371.

for the rest of the day. What Meade had most wanted to avoid—giving Lee time to bring together his scattered corps on ground of his choosing—had been handed to him by General French's inept handling of his corps. And as Francis Walker, 2nd Corps historian, suggests, the aggressiveness with which Lee confronted both Warren and French on November 27 gave Meade some apprehension that Lee would try to push a force between the Army of the Potomac's positions and the Rapidan, cutting the Federals off from their avenue of supply and retreat.[3]

Regardless of the rough handling the Federals had received, another commander would have perhaps packed up and gone home after two such days, but Meade was still determined to get a battle out of Lee. By daylight on November 28, when the five Union corps pushed forward in search of the enemy, as 2nd Corps historian Walker describes, they "came in sight of the valley of Mine Run, a very ugly looking line of hills had been rendered more repulsive in aspect by fallen trees and lines of freshly dug earth." Heavy rains had turned the run in many places into a marsh and hindered an accurate assessment of the enemy's position, but it became apparent that enough time had been lost that the rebels had had sufficient time to construct and improve their entrenchments. Faced with formidable enemy earthworks, strengthened with abatis and artillery emplacements, though Meade had five men to Lee's three, a frontal attack on such defenses would be foolhardy. But Warren thought he saw a chance. Meade therefore allowed him that night to withdraw the 2nd Corps and a division of the 6th Corps, accompanied by three hundred cavalrymen, with an eye to attempting to turn the enemy's right. Arriving on the Confederate right late on November 29, Warren had found the enemy's works were slight and thinly manned, and when he reported to Meade's headquarters that stormy night, Meade strengthened his expedition with two divisions from French's 3rd Corps. At 8 a.m. the following morning, Warren was to attack the Confederate right, while assaults would be made along the battle line in support of the flank attack. But unbeknownst to Warren, the rebels had, with speed and skills they were well on their way to perfecting, extended and fortified their right, manning it with, among others, the troops Warren had so roughly handled the month before at Bristoe Station, A. P. Hill's corps.[4]

The night of November 29–30 was bitterly cold, to the point that one commander declared that it resulted in more deaths from exposure than would have been suffered in battle. Before dawn, Warren and his staff gathered around a campfire to eat a meager breakfast, and the general made a prescient declaration: "If I succeed today I shall be the greatest man in the army; if I don't, all my sins will be remembered." Well before daybreak, Warren and Washington Roebling crawled across the moonlit landscape on their hands and knees to have a close-up look at the rebel earthworks they were about to attack. What they found was a very bad surprise. Forewarned by J. E. B. Stuart's scouting, the enemy had perfectly anticipated Warren's intentions and point of attack, for, frankly, few other options could have held any promise for the luckless Federals. The rebels, using their prodigious skills to dig in and fortify, skills that would prove the bane of the Army of the Potomac's existence in the year ahead, had overnight made the line Warren was to attack a defensive stronghold. They had reinforced their extended line with all the troops and artillery they could fit into the entrenchment. As Warren described, he discovered that "the breastworks, epaulements, and abatis [had been] perfected and that a run for eight minutes

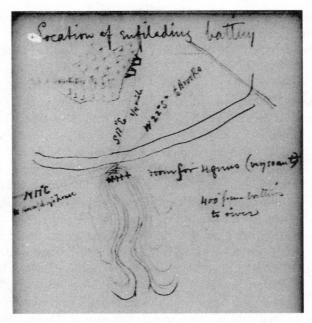

An image from Roebling's scouting notebook.
Rutgers Special Collections.

was the least time our line could have to close the space between us, during which we would be exposed to every species of fire." The enemy's earthworks, Roebling wrote, were "fully manned—high and strong," so strong that Roebling refused to believe they had been constructed overnight. General Gouverneur K. Warren, the thirty-two-year-old rising star in the Union army, then made a life-and career-changing decision, and since he was too far away to consult with the army's commander, he made the decision alone. Just as he received orders from Meade to attack immediately, Warren called off the assault.[5]

Once again, Roebling was chosen to carry wholly unwelcome news to a commander known to lash out when provoked at anyone present, let alone the bearer of the bad tidings. Warren sent Roebling to Meade with a terse message scribbled on a piece of paper: "Position and strength seem so formidable in my present front that I advise against making the attack here. The full light of the sun shows me that I cannot succeed." But it was Roebling's verbal message that Warren had suspended the attack on his front that visibly disconcerted Meade, who exclaimed, "My God! General Warren has half my army at this disposition." Without a moment to lose, Meade sent his aides to

General William French.
Library of Congress.

call off the supporting Federal assaults, as the general, reportedly looking "as savage as anyone could," rode to confront Warren. On seeing the situation for himself, despite Warren's expressed willingness to attack if ordered to do so, Meade decided not to overrule his young subordinate. As Meade returned to his headquarters, he was confronted by General French, who was smarting from having two of his divisions put under Warren's command that day. Throwing Warren's decision not to attack in Meade's face, French taunted him, "Where are your young Napoleon's guns; why doesn't he open?" It is hard to imagine accomplishing much in the way of teamwork with a teammate like General William French.[6]

In his report on the Mine Run Campaign, Meade mostly blamed its failure on French's bumbling command of the 3rd Corps, but despite his subsequent endorsement of Warren's decision to cancel his attack, Warren, too, came in for his share of criticism. Meade reported, "After the enemy, through these culpable delays, had been permitted to concentrate on Mine Run, I have reason to believe, but for the unfortunate error of judgment of Major-General Warren, my original plan of attack in three columns would have been successful, or at least under the view I took of it, would certainly have been tried." And describing the mishaps of Mine Run to his wife, while he mentioned French's delay, Meade referred to Warren's aborted attack as a mistake that cost him another day, robbing him of any hope of finding a weak spot on Lee's formidable line. It's hard to give Meade's description of a lost opportunity much credence, for Lee had apparently already put himself in an impregnable position before Warren's canceled advance. But perhaps of greatest importance as far as Meade and Warren's relationship was concerned were matters of subordination. While Meade agreed with Warren's decision to call off a futile attack, the circumstances under which the latter had taken it upon himself to halt the assault without first consulting his superior was perhaps, in his commander's eyes, an unpardonable sin. Both men expressed the same sentiment and conviction that launching an assault that would cost many lives and that they knew would fail, only to prove that it would fail, was unthinkable. Both men expressed anxiety that they would be replaced for failing to do battle with the Army of Northern Virginia, regardless of the cost in lives. And both expressed their willingness to pay that price for doing what they felt was not only right but also their duty as responsible commanders. Realistically, however, Meade, already under intense fire from critics and rivals for his command, would be held most responsible. In November 1863, though it had been only five months since Meade had replaced Hooker, 6th Corps commander John Sedgwick commented, "Meade is twenty years older than when he took command." Though Warren was Meade's trusted advisor at Gettysburg and had become a trusted corps commander at Bristoe Station, his independent decision to call off his assault at Mine Run raised issues for Meade, already known to be touchy regarding matters of subordination, chain of command, and obedience to orders. These increasingly sensitive issues would plague both Meade and Warren in the coming year.[7]

Before the soldiers Warren commanded on the Federal left were told that the assault at Mine Run on November 30, 1863, had been cancelled, they had already been more than a little apprehensive. They did something that only occurred when a situation looked particularly dire: wrote their names on slips of paper and fastened them to their coats so that their bodies would be identified. The pockets and haversacks of the 2nd Corps's chaplains were also filled with personal mementoes, watches, rings, and photographs left in their care by the men who would make the attack. Roebling of Mine Run many years later, "No assault could have succeeded—ten thousand men would have been slaughtered." He added, "Mine Run was lost the day before when the works were unoccupied and we could have walked in but waited for nothing." Overcome with a bitter cynicism inspired by such memories, he blustered, "Today I think different—Life is the cheapest thing there is!" It is a strange and disconcerting sentiment from a man who risked his own life, again and again, to save others from hazard. But because of the moral courage of Generals Warren and Meade, these soldiers would live to fight another day. Historian Francis Walker points out that the speed and thoroughness with which the rebels fortified their right flank in nothing more than a night at Mine Run was something new and rather unfathomable in the war up to that point. As the war progressed, the rebels and their Federal counterparts, inspired by instincts of self-preservation, would adopt to a great degree the habits of digging in and fortifying positions whenever they were under threat. It was a remarkably effective exercise in defense that the Confederates would employ against the Army of the Potomac many times in the months of conflict still to come.[8]

On December 1, Roebling was sent out to investigate the position of the rebel cavalry's picket line, the scene where the enemy had shot one of the Federals' most advanced troopers. Warren forwarded the sketch Roebling made of the enemy positions and the roads, reporting no significant change to the rebels' formidable defenses. The Federals continued their confrontation with Lee at Mine Run for several more days, with another plan for an attack on the enemy contemplated, then abandoned. With temperatures becoming so severe that several Federal pickets froze to death, on the night of December 1 the Army of the Potomac was finally withdrawn, the soldiers realizing that this time they were likely headed to their winter encampment at their former position north of the Rapidan. As at Bristoe Station, Meade had at least handed Lee a disappointment, having once again refused to make the futile attack upon formidable rebel entrenchments for which Lee hoped. Then, too, on the night of December 1, the attack on the Union left that Lee had directed A. P. Hill to prepare for was foiled. If Hill had been hoping to get his own back for the blow the Army of the Potomac had dealt him at Bristoe Station, he was out of luck: when day broke, Meade's army was gone. Hill followed the Federals but managed to do no more than scoop up Unionist stragglers. The Army of the Potomac arrived at the Rapidan and crossed before Hill could prevent it. Lee's frustration at the outcome of the confrontation at Mine Run is apparent in his comment "I am too old to command this army; we should never have permitted those people to get away." The Army of the Potomac's chief of staff and historian, General A. A. Humphreys, later wrote, "But for the restrictions imposed on General Meade from Washington, he would have fallen back toward Fredericksburg, taking up a position in front of that town.

Had he done so, the first battle with Lee, in May, 1864, would not have been fought in the Wilderness, but in a more open country."[9]

There was, it turned out, plenty of blame to go around regarding the Army of the Potomac's failure to bring the Army of Northern Virginia to battle. While Meade already had numerous enemies and competitors for his command, Warren, too, came in for his share of criticism. It was a difficult transition for Warren to go from trusted advisor to a subordinate who, in Meade's eyes, had embarrassed him and let him down. Nor, seemingly, was Warren entirely aware of how extreme the change in Meade's estimation of him would be. In early December, for example, Warren wrote a twelve-page letter to Humphreys, Meade's chief of staff, suggesting that he share it with General Meade. In it, Warren expounded on his ideas for conducting a campaign and organizing the army. He asserted that the army was hampered by the retention of inept corps commanders, with, unsurprisingly, General French and a few others who had performed badly during Mine Run heading the list of those to get rid of. Warren had apparently taken this theme up with Meade previously, for, in a letter to his wife, Warren suggested that he was not feeling very kindly toward Meade, since he could have gotten rid of French before the Mine Run debacle. His very understandable frustration at the mess made of the Army of the Potomac's most recent campaign notwithstanding, Warren was seemingly clueless regarding what Meade wished to hear from his former chief engineer at this point. As Roebling would spend the rest of his Civil War service as engineer and aide to General Gouverneur Warren, his fate was, to a great extent, tied to that of his commander.[10]

While the commanders and men of Army of the Potomac had again tried and failed to bring Lee to battle in the fall of 1863, U. S. Grant, with the help of his advocates and boosters in the army and in Washington, was adding luster to his already glowing and growing reputation. He glibly took credit for having won the Battle of Chattanooga. Though a decided victory, that battle in no way resembled or reflected what Grant had planned, nor the actual role he played there, but those were minor details lost in the loud praises sung by his promoters. Meanwhile, for Meade and the men of the Army of the Potomac, whatever glories Gettysburg had brought their army must have seemed to be fading very fast. Meade's reputation was taking such a beating in the press, which claimed that nearly everyone *but* he was responsible for the victory, that he eventually commented to his wife, "I suppose after awhile it will be discovered I was not at Gettysburg at all."[11]

Upheaval in the Army of the Potomac's Command Structure in No Way Prevents the Course of True Love

In MID-DECEMBER, BOTH GOUVERNEUR WARREN AND WASHINGTON Roebling were granted leaves of absence, and together they traveled homeward, Warren to Baltimore and his wife, Washington to his family's home in Trenton, New Jersey. It would be Washington's first visit home since his brief stop before Gettysburg, and it gave him an opportunity to spend Christmas with his family. As he would later declare that one can only have a really merry Christmas with a crowd of small children, spending time with his younger brothers, Edmund (nine) and Charles (fourteen), likely made for a happy reunion. Then, too, one assumes that these two young boys rather looked up to their big brother, the soldier. Music was also a special part of the Roeblings' holidays, and Washington no doubt joined in. While John Roebling had kept his family on such a tight budget that they often suffered for want of food and clothing, he was lavish in his expenditures for music lessons for his children.[1]

In the first week of January 1864, at the end of their leaves, Warren and Roebling traveled to Washington before heading back to the army, where they received permission to extend their furloughs if they could gain approval from Army of the Potomac headquarters. But on arriving back in Culpeper, they discovered that Winfield Hancock's return to the 2nd Corps had been premature, and, still suffering from his Gettysburg wound, he had gone back to the capital, leaving Warren, once again, temporarily in command of the corps. It was a time of great uncertainty. A reorganization of the Army of the Potomac was being contemplated, including a consolidation of the five corps into three. Heavy losses, especially in the 1st and 3rd Corps, made them candidates for dissolution. Distribution of their soldiers among the remaining corps would greatly increase the size of each. Then, of course, there was the matter of who would command them. There was no question that Hancock would return to the 2nd Corps, but what of the 5th and 6th? Roebling expressed doubt that Warren would get one of the corps, and if he didn't, Warren was apparently contemplating requesting an assignment in Texas. One incentive for duty there might have been the weather in Virginia that year; as Roebling wrote to his father, "The winter here is unusually severe for this section of the country, still it is preferable to the fathomless mud which will come before long." Nor were the Federals entirely free from anxiety as far as the Army of Northern Virginia was concerned. Roebling commented, "An advance of Lee is not unlikely with the present reduced condition of the army [Army of the Potomac]—all furloughs have been stopped."[2]

In mid-January, General George Meade tried to grab a rare leave with his family in Philadelphia, but the planned visit of several days unexpectedly lasted a month when he came down with pneumonia. But while he was recuperating, the game was afoot in Washington. Ambitious senator Benjamin Wade introduced a bill in the Senate to reconstitute the Joint Committee on the Conduct of the War, while U. S. Grant's staunch friend Congressman Elihu Washburne introduced the same measure in the House of Representatives. Its passage inaugurated the committee's campaign to reconstruct and enhance Joseph Hooker's and Daniel Sickles's reputations and destroy Meade's. As historian Bruce Tapp observes, it was hardly a process beneficial to the Union war effort. The committee's investigation of Meade exploited rivalries and jealousy within the army and unsurprisingly promoted distrust and hostility. Testimony began with known enemies of Meade or those who held grudges and were seeking vindication or possible restitution to former commands. After first attempting a rewrite of the Battle of Chancellorsville to put Hooker in a better light, the committee met privately with General Sickles to plan strategy. Testimony would be taken, first and foremost, from Sickles, who was very much annoyed at losing his command of the 3rd Corps and criticism of his performance at Gettysburg. But other disgruntled commanders were willing to join the chorus of disapproval against Meade, including displaced generals Abner Doubleday and Albion Howe. Doubleday had been replaced as commander of the 1st Corps, and Howe had been removed from division command after Mine Run due to conflicts with both Meade and John Sedgwick.[3]

Having recuperated sufficiently to return to the army, Meade made his way to Washington and paid a visit to Secretary of War Edwin Stanton, who, Meade recalled, assured him that "there was no other officer in command who had to so great a degree the implicit confidence of all parties as myself; but he [Stanton] said there were several officers in my army that did not have confidence of the country, and that I was injuring myself by retaining them. I told him I did not know who they were, but that if he was aware of this fact, I thought it was his duty to retire them, and I should not object." It's easy to believe Meade was being somewhat disingenuous regarding who needed retiring, but, meeting again the next day, he heard Stanton out regarding whom the secretary of war deemed incompetent and how reorganizing the army would make their dismissal easier. Disbanding the 1st and 3rd Corps could realistically be attributed to their depleted numbers and would also provide an opportunity to permanently sideline Generals William French and John Newton. Meanwhile, discussions of who would command the remaining three corps went on for the next month, with the final decisions dependent

Charles Dana.
Library of Congress.

Lieutenant General Grant.
Library of Congress.

upon how "Congress passed judgement on the confirmation of the various Major Generals in embryo." It was a given that Hancock would return to the 2nd Corps and that Warren would, as Roebling put it, again "be adrift." As early as the first week of January 1864, many in the Army of the Potomac were apparently aware of the planned downsizing, and Warren and Roebling thought that the chances of Warren's getting command of one of the remaining corps were "doubtful." But despite their pessimism, Warren was assigned the 5th Corps, replacing General George Sykes. Though Meade supposedly defended all his generals, even General French, he ultimately capitulated to Stanton, fighting only the war secretary's wish to replace General Sedgwick as commander of the 6th Corps. Meade lobbied, successfully, for Sedgwick to retain his command.[4]

Another key manipulator in the drama of spring 1864 was General in Chief Henry Halleck, one of the slipperiest (one is tempted to say slimiest) players in army politics. Halleck was perfectly capable of telling dramatically different things to different people (i.e., lying), to the point that it was impossible to take his word about anything. For example, Halleck had written to Grant in July 1863, "Meade has thus far proved an excellent general, the only one who has ever fought the Army of the Potomac well. He seems the right man in the right place." But this praise would have greatly surprised Meade, who was receiving only disparaging criticism from Halleck at that time. Nor had Halleck admitted to Meade, as he did to Grant, that "Lee's army is by far the best in the Rebel service and I regard him as their ablest general." By December 1863, unbeknownst to Meade, a meeting with Lincoln deciding his fate took place, attended by the duplicitous Halleck, Secretary of War Stanton, and Charles Dana. Dana was an assistant secretary of war and Stanton's eyes and ears at Grant's headquarters in the West. Dana's wildly biased reports from the field had helped clear away a number of Grant's rivals and position him for his upcoming promotion. It reveals much that Dana had for some time had plans for Grant to be the next president of the United States (with, of course, a nice political appointment for himself). Stanton, Halleck, and Dana met with Lincoln to discuss just who should replace Meade as commander of the Army of the Potomac, with Grant recommending two of his cronies, General William F. "Baldy" Smith or General William Tecumseh Sherman. With Halleck's encouragement, Grant had also written with suggestions regarding the movements of the eastern armies, and by February 1864 the House of Representatives was calling for Grant to come east, offering to elevate him to lieutenant general, a rank previously held only by George Washington and Winfield Scott. As for life in the surprisingly frigid state of Virginia, Roebling remarked, "Winter quarters in Culpeper were enlivened by speculations as to the new commander in chief from the west—by the reorganization and consolidation of the corps."[5]

But more than concerns about such changes "enlivened" the men of the 2nd Corps. In the first week of February, the entire corps was sent out to Morton's Ford on the Rapidan in response to General Benjamin Butler's request for a demonstration in support of his upcoming raid. When Butler's force failed to advance and attack, the 2nd Corps wasn't notified, and thus left in the lurch, its dash against the enemy, meant only to be a feint, resulting in needless casualties. Warren's report mentioned the bravery and patience displayed by many of his officers, including Roebling, who led a Rhode Island battery to its position during the fighting. Warren also included Roebling's map of Morton's Ford with his report. After the debacle at Morton's Ford, the officers of the 2nd Corps were relieved to turn their minds to something far more pleasant. That February, they held a ball, which they were determined would outshine one just held by the 3rd Corps. As fate would have it, the event would also turn Washington's life upside down. Her name was Emily.

Washington enthused to his sister that the 2nd Corps's gala was

the most successful ball ever given in any army or by anybody. I had complete charge of getting up the building, which was the main thing you know; I built a hall fifty feet wide and ninety feet long with a supper room attached 20 x 90; we had 2 reb saw mills and therefore had any quantity of boards and sawed lumber. The spring floor is a perfect success—just spring enough to avoid breaking through. In point of attendance nothing better could have been desired; at least 150 ladies graced the assemblage, from all quarters of the Union and at least 300 Gentlemen from General Meade down to myself. I received numerous congratulations upon the success of everything.

Washington recited a list of society ladies who attended—Miss Hamlin, Kate Chase, and the Misses Hale—but there was no doubt as to who was the belle of the ball for him: "Miss Emily Warren, sister of the General, who came specially from West Pt. to attend the ball; it was the first time I ever saw her and I am very much of the opinion that she has captured your brother Washy's heart at last. It was a real attack in force, it came without any warning or any previous realization on my part of such an occurrence taking place and it was therefore all the more successful and I assure you that it gives me the greatest pleasure to say that I have succumbed."[6]

In a letter to his favorite sister, Elvira (a.k.a. "Dear little Cuss"), Washington described his Emily as "dark-brown-eyed, slightly pug-nosed, lovely mouth & teeth, no dimples in her cheeks. and a most entertaining talker, which is a mighty good thing you know, I myself being so stupid. She is a little above medium size and has a most lovely complexion." Saying that tintypes simply didn't do her justice, he explained, "Some people's beauty lies not in the features but in the varied expressions that the countenance will assume under various emotion etc. etc." One supposes, therefore, that he liked her animation and the smiles she apparently bestowed upon him. Emily's Washington, meanwhile, stood five feet, nine inches and had a fair complexion, blonde hair, and blue eyes sometimes described as gray. We can, I assume, be confident that he cleaned up nicely for his appearance at the ball where he met Emily.

Descriptions of Washington's appearance in the upcoming campaign suggest a much more rugged and careless exterior than the one he presumably presented at the 2nd Corps's extravaganza. One can only imagine how much the taciturn Washington appreciated and enjoyed the constant intelligent conversation supplied by Emily. It was Emily's great good fortune that her brothers, Gouverneur and William, believed in a real education for women and were willing to pay for it. Emily had attended the Georgetown Academy for Young Ladies in Washington, DC, a Catholic institution run by the Visitation Sisters, where she received an exemplary education for a woman of her time. Her curriculum included ancient and modern secular history, geography, mythology, prose composition, rhetoric and grammar, French, algebra, geometry, bookkeeping, astronomy, botany, meteorology, chemistry, and geology. Emily was therefore quite capable of keeping a bright young man like Washington Roebling on his toes.[7]

Returning to the mundane matters of camp life that winter and spring, we can speculate about just how Roebling's assignment, as Warren's aide-de-camp in both the 2nd and the 5th Corps, put him in a position to know much of what was going on in the Army of the Potomac and beyond. With apparently no concern regarding sending sensitive information through the mail, on March 1 Washington wrote a detailed description to his father about the commencement of the Kilpatrick/Dahlgren Raid, which he described as "something in the Grierson or Streight style, his [General Judson Kilpatrick's] plan being to go by Richmond through Raleigh, Columbia, across Georgia and join Sherman." Washington commented, "He took with him almost one-half of our cavalry force and has been gone now several days, long enough to preclude the possibility of returning to our army directly; the chances of his entire command being captured are of course two to one against him." Apparently Army of the Potomac headquarters did not have a lot of confidence regarding the success of the raid, though infantry feints were made to distract the enemy from what the Federal horsemen were up to. There is a certain irony in Washington comparing the Kilpatrick/Dahlgren venture with Benjamin Grierson's and Abel Streight's raids, for Kilpatrick's raid would end in failure, as did the other two. What proved more successful than the raid by way of intelligence, however, was the return of several officers who had escaped from Libby Prison and taken good advantage of the maxim to be where your enemy least expects to find you: "Much valuable information has been obtained from some of our officers who recently escaped from Libby and have been staying within the lines of Lee's army, the safest place they could find, waiting for an opportunity to cross the Rapidan into our lines."[8]

On March 4, based solely on the testimonies of disgruntled generals Dan Sickles, Abner Doubleday, and Albion Howe, three members of the Joint Committee on the Conduct of the War—Benjamin Wade, Zachariah Chandler, and Benjamin Loan—met with President Lincoln and Secretary of War Stanton and demanded Meade's removal from command of the Army of the Potomac. The committee even threatened to make the testimony public if Lincoln did not cooperate, but the president, unmoved, recognized the testimony, drawn solely from Meade's enemies and competitors, for what it was. It was likely at his insistence that the committee went back to work and interviewed Meade himself and other, more impartial witnesses. Meade's first appearance before the committee took place on March 5, when he was called without warning or time to prepare to face a grilling regarding Gettysburg and the aftermath. Meade, to his credit, gave a satisfactory account of himself, dispelling the false accusation that he had not wanted to fight at Gettysburg. He also made clear that Sickles had disobeyed orders and nearly caused his corps to be annihilated. Meade also described his own desire to attack R. E. Lee at Williamsport, Maryland, and how he had deferred to and agreed with the opinion of his corps commanders that Lee's defenses were formidable and that the rebels, contrary to rumor, were not without ammunition. Meade's testimony before the committee was "leaked" to the press, whereupon his prosecution was continued in certain newspapers. Attacks on Meade in print included those by an anonymous writer, "Historicus," long believed to have been either Sickles himself or one of his staunch supporters. Though the committee continued to call witnesses hostile to Meade, it allowed him a second opportunity to testify, and this time he was prepared with copies of orders and reports. Meade also gave the committee a list of officers who could confirm his conduct during and after Gettysburg.[9]

Warren was one officer called upon to testify before the committee on March 9 and 10. As biographer David Jordan comments, "Warren's performance before the Committee won him few friends in the army. He dutifully defended Meade's performance at Gettysburg and after the battle, although admitting that he himself might have done things differently from Meade on occasion. Warren was critical of Sedgwick, Hooker, Sykes, Halleck, Howard, French, and Sickles as he answered questions from Senator Ben Wade, the committee chairman, about actions at Chancellorsville, Gettysburg, Williamsport, Bristoe Station, and Mine Run." Opining at one point that not all the corps commanders had "been equal to their positions," he suggested that the main fault lay with their not visiting their front often enough to accurately assess real situations. When Warren spoke about what a grave loss John

Reynolds and the wounded Hancock were to the Army of the Potomac, Wade tried to get him to add Sickles to that list, but Warren would not. He offered that Sickles was brave and well intentioned but an amateur in a military setting. On his way back to the army, Warren collected his wife and his sister Emily and brought both down to experience camp life for a week. Roebling, still much smitten with Warren's sister, was delighted.[10]

On March 23, Gouverneur Warren was appointed commander of the Army of the Potomac's 5th Corps, replacing General George Sykes. Having the thirty-four-year-old replace him and being himself sent to command a Kansas backwater was likely a hard pill for Sykes to swallow. Warren also realized that his division commanders were senior to him in age, if not rank, and he worried about men used to division command being relegated back to brigade command. Brigadier General Charles Griffin (USMA 1847) retained command of Warren's 1st Division, while Brigadier General John Robinson of the regular army took the 5th Corps's 2nd Division. General Samuel Crawford, a former army doctor and close friend of General Meade's, commanded Warren's 3rd Division, and General James Wadsworth, an independently wealthy New Yorker, commanded the 4th Division. Few of the officers and men of the dissolved 1st and 3rd Corps were happy about being thrust into different corps. Nor was former 1st Corps artillery commander General Charles Wainwright pleased to take up that position in the 5th Corps under Warren. There were many reasons why not everyone would be content with the new 5th Corps commander's meteoric rise and good fortune. As Roebling commented, Warren ascended to permanent corps command "in the face of bitter jealousies and opposition which pursued him and maligned him through the whole Wilderness Campaign."[11]

Various building projects apparently broke the monotony of winter camp, for as spring approached, bringing with it contemplation of another year of fighting, Washington commented, "Our rainy season commenced yesterday and will probably continue for several weeks; we are well prepared for it, our corps having built many miles of good corduroy road and half a dozen bridges over Mountain Run which is quite a creek during high water." But there had also been chances for entertainment, calling on what talent the 5th Corps and the locals had to offer. The building Washington took such pride in having planned and built for the 2nd Corps's ball was now a venue for other pleasures: "My ball room has been converted into a theatre where we have nightly minstrel performances, native talent, and Shakespearian readings etc." Every visit no doubt reminded Washington of the momentous night when he and his Emily had met. They wasted no time in improving their knowledge of one

Emily Roebling.
Rutgers University Library, Roebling Collection.

another, keeping up a brisk, almost daily stream of correspondence. While the letters to "Dearest Emmie," "Sweet Pet," and "My Dear Love" contain all one would expect by way of courtship from a seriously smitten young soldier, brief hints as to what was going on in the Army of the Potomac crept in on occasion. Our view of the upcoming Overland Campaign will therefore be enhanced by incongruous details of military significance that pop up in love letters but will rely primarily on the day-by-day report of the tumultuous Overland Campaign penned by Roebling in the autumn of 1864. The writings of Army of the Potomac chief of staff A. A. Humphreys provide reliable testimony, as do the Official Record and the statements of other witnesses. The admirable histories by Edward Steere and William Matter on the Battles of the Wilderness and Spotsylvania afford invaluable insights to our consideration of Grant's Overland Campaign.[12]

One particular change to the Army of the Potomac would have enormous consequences for both the army and the 5th Corps. The orders that came at the end of March regarding the reorganization included the dismissal of cavalry commander General Alfred Pleasonton. Secretary Stanton and Lieutenant General Grant had made the decision, with General Meade playing no part other than to remove his objection. Pleasonton's dismissal and John Buford's untimely death left vacancies at the top of the Cavalry Corps. While a capable candidate for cavalry head was at hand, acting commander General David Gregg, Grant instead installed his protégé, General Philip Sheridan. Though his experience with either cavalry or large commands was extremely limited, Sheridan nevertheless came to his new position with strong opinions about how the cavalry should be utilized. Another Grant favorite, General James Harrison "Harry" Wilson, would command Sheridan's 3rd Division, though he had no cavalry experience. Since any officer who had seniority over Wilson had to be pushed aside, numerous veteran cavalrymen, including David Gregg and J. Irvin Gregg, George Armstrong Custer, and Henry Davies, were displaced and transferred to make way for Wilson. Another Grant appointee to the cavalry without cavalry experience was Sheridan's new 1st Division commander, General Alfred Torbert. Torbert's assignment displaced the well-respected General Wesley Merritt, who had been commanding Buford's men since the latter's death. Merritt was sent down to brigade command, as were Custer and Thomas Devin; all would serve under Torbert. But of perhaps greatest importance in the coming weeks and months, beyond the placing of inexperienced leaders at the head of the Army of the Potomac's Cavalry Corps, was commanding general Sheridan's willful insubordination. The doting Grant would virtually ignore Sheridan's defiance of orders and defiance toward his superior, army commander General Meade. This, in combination with General Wilson's incompetence and duplicity, would have dire repercussions for the Army of the Potomac.[13]

18

A Relative Calm before the Storm

At THE END OF MARCH 1864, WHEN GENERAL GOUVERNEUR WARREN WAS appointed commander of the 5th Corps, he established his headquarters at the Virginia Hotel in Culpeper. Warren described the establishment unappetizingly as dirty and disorderly, and Washington Roebling related that it was owned by a "ferociously Secesh" mother and daughter. But whatever the inconveniences, Warren went to work with the help of Fred Locke, who had been chief of staff virtually since the corps's inception. Much of their work involved incorporating three of the former 1st Corps divisions into the 5th Corps, an onerous undertaking since many of the officers and men of the 1st deeply resented the dissolution of their corps and their subsequent displacement and reassignment among strangers. The resulting hostilities were likely far more challenging than the actual move from one headquarters to another, and Roebling at the time declared himself exhausted.[1]

Another obligation arose with the arrival of Lieutenant General U. S. Grant on April 25 to join the Army of the Potomac, which he had announced the month before he intended to accompany during the upcoming campaign. George Meade at the time commented that, with that announcement, Richmond would surely know where to look for active operation and would prepare to receive the Army of the Potomac accordingly. Generals Meade and Warren rode over to visit Grant, with Warren commenting that he "seems to be much more vivacious than I supposed and did not look *at* me with any apparent eye to discerning my qualities in my face." As Warren biographer David Jordan points out, the newly minted lieutenant general would have plenty of opportunities to judge Warren in the coming weeks, with many of his opinions colored by the poisonous comments of the scheming and manipulative General James H. "Harry" Wilson, whom Grant had installed as the new commander of the Cavalry Corps's 3rd Division. As the Army of the Potomac was to embark upon what became known as the Overland Campaign, Roebling received a letter from his father. It is hard to know how Washington received John Roebling's thorough embrace of the current conventional wisdom, an enthusiastic and optimistic appraisal of U. S. Grant, and his expressed belief that, now that Grant was in charge, they were going to see something. Meanwhile, Grant's military secretary, Ely Parker, leaves us with his (and perhaps Grant's) impressions of the Army of the Potomac, declaring it to be of "splendid material, in fine condition and well supplied with everything." But Parker added in a letter to a friend, "Its only shortcoming was the 'inefficiency and effeminacy' of its commanding officers, and General Grant rapidly weeded them out."[2]

Warren's headquarters at the Virginia Hotel left much to be desired, as did much of Culpeper, for it was apparently a less than a fair city. But Washington described the place where Warren and his staff had finally taken up residence to his fiancée, Emily, as much more upscale. "We occupy one of the finest houses on the Main Street of Culpeper, partly occupied by Mrs. Rixey and Miss Rixey, who charm Yankee ears with a guitar." Washington, who was sharing a room with Bob Warren, the general's brother and aide, had a fine view of the Blue Ridge from his window, "covered with snow & sending down the coldest kind of blasts across the plains." But when Lieutenant General Grant moved into a house just two doors down from Warren and Roebling, much needed attending to in apparently seedy Culpeper. One job Washington was given was putting the Culpeper Court House to rights, which he compared to the Herculean task of "cleaning out the Augean stable." He also described the holes in the street as being near big and deep enough to swallow a horse and rider whole. Roebling oversaw the soldiers put to work doing repairs, who protested against what they saw as cleaning up the streets for the "damned secesh." He compared trying to fill up all the holes in the Culpeper streets to the endless, futile task of Sisyphus. Washington quipped that if Emily didn't know who Sisyphus was, he was a fellow who "used to sell ale in the Bowery," which would likewise be an endless job. The Federals also found themselves under attack from a plague of rats, for which infestation Washington facetiously asked his Emily to mail him a cat. In Culpeper, Washington met and was favorably impressed by General Wesley Merritt, who came to town to deal with another kind of infestation. While Washington declared Merritt "a fine fellow" and said he had "a handsome fine open countenance and pleasant tone of voice," not everyone would have enjoyed the sound of Merritt's voice. Determined that his men would be where they were supposed to be, Merritt had come to Culpeper to drive all his quartermasters, commissioned orderlies,

Washington Roebling.
Rensselaer Special Collections.

and teamsters "out of their rat holes in town" and send them back to their assigned quarters in a tented field.[3]

When it came to topographical matters, it was also Roebling's job to interrogate knowledgeable locals. One black man who reputedly had once been General James Longstreet's body servant was said to have extensive knowledge of the territory across the Rapidan. Sent to Roebling for questioning, Washington wrote, "the poor fellow trembled so much that it looked more like a trial for capital punishment than a Topographical examination; it required 2 glasses of ale to pacify his nerves." After the informant's ordeal, Roebling got the fellow a job as a cook, while he himself put the information given him to good use by drawing up maps. On the subject of black men, Roebling commented that while the army was getting reinforcements of all sorts, they hadn't received any "colored" troops. He expected that they would, for he was under the impression that "Grant is well disposed towards them." U. S. Grant's approval of black soldiers is debatable. He would later testify regarding the prevention of the U.S. Colored Troops from leading the assault at the Battle of the Crater, for which they had trained, that he was merely deferring to Meade's decision, though it was clearly Grant's orders that made the change. There is also a question as to why Grant apparently approved the decision whereby not one of the two hundred thousand black soldiers who fought for the Union participated in the Grand Review, the parade in Washington celebrating the end of the war.[4]

Prior to the opening of the spring campaign, President Abraham Lincoln paid the Army of the Potomac a visit on April 1. A review was planned with the intent to provide a little pomp and circumstance for the commander in chief, but it didn't work out as planned. Part of the cavalcade of officers who accompanied Lincoln that day, Roebling recounted, "The President was mounted on a hard mouthed, fractious horse, and was evidently not a skilled horseman. Soon after the march began his tall hat fell off; next, his pantaloons which were not fastened on the bottom, slipped up to the knees, showing his white home-made drawers, secured below with some strings of white tape, which presently unraveled and slipped up also, revealing a long hairy leg." Roebling confessed that while inclined to smile, all were also chagrined that their president was enduring such an "unmerited and humiliating" experience. Lincoln was not the only one humiliated around that time, for Warren's servant at the 5th Corps headquarters received rough treatment from rowdy Federals. The servants were not happy about their move from the 2nd Corps headquarters to that of the 5th, but they were nowhere near as disgruntled as the men of the 14th Brooklyn, formerly of the 1st Corps. Not only had they endured having their corps disbanded and being sent, unwillingly, to the 5th Corps, but they had also seen the early recruits of the 14th, their time being up, going home while they must stay. The 14th Brooklyn, also known as the "Red Legged Devils," a sobriquet acquired at First Bull Run, were never known for their amiability and, as Roebling recounts, made a custom of abusing every negro that showed himself. They assaulted a 5th Corps headquarters servant that Roebling referred to as "his serene majesty Wolford," and far from garnering any sympathy from his employers, Roebling declared, the incident had probably been done him good. Employee/employer and race relations had much room for improvement in the Army of the Potomac.[5]

Meade, still under scrutiny by the joint committee and a hostile press, at least felt comfortable with what he was learning about Lieutenant General Grant. It was Meade's impression that pressure from the administration had resulted in Grant's traveling with the Army of the Potomac. Meade enthusiastically embraced what he saw as potential, now that the powers that be in

Washington were allowing Grant to carry on operations the way Meade had always wanted to do and been denied. He declared, "Cheerfully will I give him all credit if he can bring the war to a close." Meanwhile, Meade gave a revealing description of the lieutenant general to his wife. Having noticed that people were often disappointed on first meeting Grant, he wrote,

> Grant is not a striking man, is very reticent, has never mixed with the world, and has but little manner, indeed is somewhat ill at ease in the presence of strangers; hence a first impression is never favorable. His early education was undoubtedly very slight; in fact, I fancy his West Point course was pretty much all the education he ever had, as since his graduation I don't believe he has read or studied any. At the same time, he has natural qualities of a high order, and is a man whom, the more you see and know him, the better you like him. He puts me in mind of old [Zachary] Taylor, and sometimes I fancy he models himself on old Zac.

It would take months for Meade to realize that Grant, though he allowed Meade to retain nominal command of the Army of the Potomac, was not his friend. Grant's cadre of friends, mostly from the West, would always take precedence over Meade and the eastern commanders. An example of Grant's real estimate of Meade lies in a comment he made about the victor of Gettysburg well after the war: If "Sherman or Sheridan had commanded at Gettysburg, I think Lee would have been destroyed." But it is worth remembering that even once Grant had complete control of Federal forces, it took him a year, with the concerted efforts of four major armies (those of W. T. Sherman, Phil Sheridan, and George Thomas and Meade's Army of the Potomac), as well as numerous smaller forces at his command, to finally bring Robert E. Lee to heel.[6]

There can be little doubt that as Meade, commander of the Army of the Potomac, and Warren, commander of that army's 5th Corps, entered upon the spring campaign, their relationship was not what it had been. Warren was excited and optimistic about having been given permanent corps command, but one begins to wonder whether he was aware that the confidence Meade had placed in him as trusted advisor during Gettysburg, Bristoe Station, and Mine Run no longer existed. Then, too, to those who knew him well, Warren was showing signs of strain in the days before the first advance. Not only was he facing the challenge of his first real chance to prove himself with permanent command of a corps, but he was also trying to abstain from alcohol, realizing that his poor tolerance for drink was proving problematic. Roebling wrote to Emily, "Your brother is working quite hard; I feel sure he can't stand it long without stimulants, he gets along now by going to sleep at 6 o'clock on three chairs drawn up to the fire, whether he falls off during the night I don't know—So far from calling that a rest I should call it a mortification of the flesh worthy of a follower of La Trappe." That regime apparently did not last, for several nights later, the general, his brother Bob, Roebling, and another staff member stayed up well past midnight playing a card game called Muggins. Under the influence of two glasses of ale, Washington acknowledged, Warren got "darned mean."[7]

As the time neared when the 5th Corps would again be on the march, Roebling pondered what Grant must be thinking. After a review of the 2nd Corps late that April, Roebling offered, "I know it is the finest body of men for its numbers that he has ever seen, and when he comes to consider that the rebs have been usually a match for them, his heart will be apt to be filled with slight misgivings; at any rate he won't be guilty of [Joseph] Hooker's weakness of looking upon it as the finest army on the planet and allowing that thought to occupy his head to the exclusion of all others." But whatever Grant thought of the officers and men of the Army of the Potomac, his own expressed lack of concern regarding his enemies was problematic, especially considering the abilities of his new opponent, General Lee. Grant is quoted as saying in the first days of the Overland Campaign, "Oh, I am heartily tired of hearing about what Lee is going to do. Some of you always seem to think he is suddenly going to turn a double somersault, and land in our rear and on both of our flanks at the same time. Go back to your command, and try to think what we are going to do ourselves, instead of what Lee is going to do." Nor does Grant's philosophy that the enemy is just as scared of you as you are of him seem to hold much water in this case. Grant declared, "I never experienced trepidation upon confronting an enemy, though I always felt more or less anxiety. I never forgot that he had as much reason to fear my forces as I had his. The lesson was valuable." While such ideas undoubtedly boosted Grant's confidence, this seemingly carefree philosophy could arguably tend to encourage him to dangerously underestimate his opponent, a risky thing to do when his opponents of 1864 were Robert E. Lee and the Army of Northern Virginia. They would exact a very steep and often unnecessary price in blood and sacrifice from the Army of the Potomac during the Overland Campaign.[8]

As the spring campaign approached, Washington confessed to his Emily, "The time now still intervening before our movement is one of anxious anticipation; if we were once on the move every thing would be all right; one's spirits always rise with movement & action." Making light of his apprehension, he described an event that no doubt gave Emily no comfort regarding the grave uncertainties of soldiers' lives: "I had the pleasure of being thrown from my horse, head over heels; I am sure I would have broken my neck if you hadn't a mortgage on me; now I can't even do that much without asking your permission." But several days later, thoughts of the upcoming move were weighing heavily again. He observed,

> Everybody begins to feel fidgety & feverish about the move; it surely can't be three days before something happens; Grant is reticent & glum—Meade snappish. Gen. Meade intends to move down shortly; it will be a little livelier when his crowd comes along and will help to dissipate the blues which are settling on us deep and heavy; this business of squatting down in our camp so long is very bad; constant moving about is the excitement that a soldier needs; when he lies still in camp he becomes a prey to his own thoughts and anticipation.

"The poor fellows," he exclaimed, no doubt including himself, "who have a girl at home to think of are still more to be pitied." Nor was his Emily oblivious to the dangers the coming weeks would bring. As they had delayed any plans for their wedding until the following year, Washington offered, "I am glad your good spirits are returning, mind I want you to be in first rate condition next winter. So don't fret, darling. Your Wash."[9]

It is hard to know whether Emily would recognize her "Wash" that spring. Soon to be Major Roebling, he was becoming a far cry from the dapper young lieutenant she had fallen in love with at the 2nd Corps ball just a few months before. He would spend most of the months to come scouting for the 5th Corps, making notes and drawing hurried maps while in the saddle. When not acting as courier between Generals Warren, Meade, and Grant, Roebling was often leading various units of the Army of the Potomac to their positions on the front lines. He prepared for the upcoming campaign by getting a short haircut and close shave, not knowing when he would have time for his next. He was deeply tanned from his days in the saddle and quipped to Emily that he would be a fit companion for the subject of the old Scottish ballad "The Nut Brown Maiden." Theodore Lyman, a Harvard-trained scientist who acted as aide-de-camp for General Meade, has left us with a detailed and amusing description of young Major Roebling and his activities: "Roebling is a character. He is a light-haired, blue-eyed man, with a countenance as if all the world were an empty show. He stoops a good deal, when riding has the stirrups so long that the tips of his toes can just touch them; and, as he wears no boots, the bottoms of his pantaloons are always torn and ragged. He goes poking about in the most dangerous places, looking for the position of the enemy, and always with an air of entire indifference. His conversation is curt and not garnished with polite turnings." Lyman describes Washington as "the laconic one" even in verbal exchanges with his superior officers, including the often-alarming General Meade. Roebling was aware of his own reticence. Telling his Emily how love had changed him, he commented, "Neither am I more silent than usual, that would be impossible."[10]

But if Washington was a man of few words in the exchanges necessary for the business of soldiering, he apparently could hold his own when bantering with the staff members he fraternized with every day. Remarking that he found the 5th Corps staff much quieter than that of the 2nd Corps, Washington related to Emily that he came in for some teasing about his near daily correspondence with his fiancée. His friend General Andy Webb often greeted him with "How is she, Roebling, eh, old fellow?" and a punch in the ribs, whereupon Roebling would reply, "Last night's bulletin conveyed to me assurances of her most perfect well being." This would be followed by gales of Webb's well-known eccentric laughter. Emily, too, came in for her share of teasing from Washington, for he possessed a quirky, somewhat outrageous sense of humor. Sharing with her that he still looked at other girls, he explained that he only did so with an eye of comparison. He reassured her, exclaiming, "Not one possess that amiability, those mouth, them tooths, that eyes, in [fact] no one loves me as you do, that's the real secret is it not, dear, fun aside."

Even if sometimes reticent around his fellow soldiers, Washington poured out all his thoughts and yearnings to his Emily, with daily letters flying back and forth between the young lovers. The opportunities for such frequent correspondence would soon be coming to an end, however, as the Army of the Potomac prepared to advance. On the eve of the first day of the Overland Campaign, Washington wrote to Emily, "Dear Emmie, We suddenly got orders to decamp at midnight; didn't know it until evening—every thing is topsy turvy. Don't fret now or be uneasy, I guess we will all get through the fight safely—Goodbye my love; I guess there will [be] no mail for weeks & what a lot of sweet letters I will have from you. Your Wash."[11]

19

Into the Wilderness

IN THE WEE HOURS OF MAY 4, 1864, THE ARMY OF THE POTOMAC BEGAN moving out through the darkness, taking the first steps of the spring campaign with great enthusiasm. In this year, 1864, the term of service for many of the three-year regiments would expire, although, despite the eventful early years of the war, more than half of the veterans would reenlist. Then, too, they were leaving the boredom and discomforts of winter camp behind. They were still under the command of General George Gordon Meade, but they were also under the watchful eye of Lieutenant General Ulysses S. Grant, who had chosen to accompany the Army of the Potomac and was joined by his enthusiastic promoter in Congress, Representative Elihu B. Washburne. Without a hint of what lay ahead of them, General Meade and the Federal men and officers had high hopes of soon striking the blows that would end the long and costly war. Their optimism would be forcibly challenged in the coming weeks. Embarking on his first campaign in the east, Grant commented naively to the administration in Washington, "Forty Eight hours now will demonstrate whether the enemy intends giving battle this side of Richmond." The lieutenant general could scarcely have made clearer just how seriously he misjudged and underestimated Robert E. Lee. The Army of the Potomac's attempted passage from the Rapidan to Richmond, a campaign that Grant fully expected to complete in little more than a week, would in fact take a month and a half, with one bloody battle after another. And far from taking Petersburg or Richmond on arrival as planned, Grant's Overland Campaign, as it came to be known, culminated in what was called a siege, although it never managed to entirely encircle the rebels. The struggle would drag on for another ten months before Lee left Petersburg, Richmond fell, and the Army of Northern Virginia surrendered in April 1865 at Appomattox Court House.[1]

It is surprising that the history of the Battle of the Wilderness, that first terrible collision in a particularly brutal campaign, has come down to us with so many accounts of less than acceptable historical accuracy despite there being so many participants and witnesses. One major problem is the frequent (in some cases sole) reliance many historians have placed on the reports and memoirs of U. S. Grant, whose accounts are fraught with inaccuracies and an overabundance of self-justification. For instance, while we know that the Army of the Potomac crossed the Rapidan that spring day under the watchful eyes of the rebel signal station on Clark's Mountain, Grant would have us believe that he took Lee by surprise. He offers as proof of his catching Lee unaware the fact that the Army of Northern Virginia did not attack the Federals while they were crossing the Rapidan but waited until the next day. This indicates that Grant either never grasped or perhaps refused to admit the significance of Lee's waiting until the Army of the Potomac had crossed the river and he could challenge the Federals within the terrible confines of the Wilderness. Ample proof of how aware Lee was of the imminence of the Federal advance was the April 28 report of a rebel spy regarding Ambrose Burnside's 9th Corps marching from Washington, flags flying, bands playing, to join the Army of the Potomac. Then, too, thirty-six hours before the Army of the Potomac began its movement, Lee, while at the signal station on Clark's Mountain, announced to the gathering of corps and brigade commanders that he believed the Army of the Potomac would be coming that way, crossing the Rapidan at Germanna or Ely's Ford. Lee began to issue orders accordingly.[2]

Grant and Meade only compounded a bad situation by halting the movement of the 5th Corps hours before dark rather than advancing to a less vulnerable position. Concern for the Army of the Potomac's vast supply train offers some explanation, for the Federals were heavily reliant upon it until they could access their next base of supply. Concern for the trains was increased when, by 6 p.m. on the night of May 4, persistent requests from Philip Sheridan were rewarded by permission to advance David Gregg's and Alfred Torbert's divisions to Hamilton's Crossing to fight rebel cavalry. By the time the Federal troopers sent on this wild goose chase approached Hamilton's Crossing, they would find the Confederate horsemen long gone. But the unfortunate expedition, robbing the Army of the Potomac of its cavalry (and therefore its eyes, its screen, and the protection of its trains), placed severe hardship on Meade's infantry and its movement on May 5. Grant biographer Adam Badeau insists that Grant was not surprised by Lee's confrontation with the Army of the Potomac in the Wilderness but, on the contrary, had decided not to pass by Lee's flank and to provoke a battle there and then. General A. A. Humphreys,

General James H. Wilson.
Library of Congress.

Meade's chief of staff, suggested that no one would knowingly allow himself to be trapped into fighting on such a battleground. Intentionally inviting battle in the Wilderness also in no way explains why Grant and Meade would have separated the corps of the Army of the Potomac so widely as they advanced upon the enemy, as if expecting Lee to wait until Grant had chosen the field upon which he wished to fight. If Lee felt any surprise, it must have stemmed from an inability to believe Grant would make such stupid mistakes. These mistakes worked much in Lee's favor, throwing away all the advantages the Army of the Potomac enjoyed in numbers and artillery, which could not be used. Eventually even Grant would concede that fighting in the dense undergrowth of the Wilderness had meant "all the conditions were favorable for [Lee's] defensive operations"; yet Grant, here and elsewhere, would insist upon reckless, disorganized frontal attacks, again and again.[3]

On Wednesday, May 4, 1864, the four divisions of the 5th Corps left their different camps at precisely midnight, taking up a line of march to the Rapidan. General Charles Griffin's division took the lead, followed by Generals Samuel

General Charles Griffin.
Library of Congress.

Crawford, John Robinson, and James Wadsworth. While the 5th Corps was to cross at Germanna Ford, Winfield Hancock's 2nd Corps was to cross the Rapidan six miles upriver at Ely's Ford. The pontoon trains had been ordered from Rappahannock Station the day before, and General James Wilson's 3rd Division was to have installed a bridge and crossed ahead of the 5th Corps—in fact, Wilson had reported that they had done so. But when Gouverneur Warren's lead division arrived at the Rapidan, Wilson's horse batteries and trains were still on the north side of the river, and after installing its own bridge, the 5th Corps was then delayed an hour while Wilson used both bridges to complete his crossing. This was the first of a long list of Wilson's failures to fulfill his orders, coupled with his seeming belief that if he reported having done something, it was as good as having done it. Along with getting their bridge in position, the 5th Corps's engineers had plenty to attend to, for they built three roads ascending the hill on the far bank, hoping to minimize further delay. The 6th Corps would cross after the 5th, while Burnside, subject to Grant's orders rather than Meade's, was to bring the 9th Corps by a forced march from the Centreville area to the Rapidan at Germanna Ford.[4]

Warren and Roebling were, to some extent, familiar with the area known as the Wilderness from their experiences during the ill-fated campaigns at Chancellorsville and Mine Run. But Roebling had also spent a good part of the winter of 1863–1864 interviewing or interrogating anyone who had knowledge of the area and subsequently drawing maps from the information he had gathered. The 5th Corps was also accompanied by a local man Roebling referred to as the "little dutchman Girt." But despite an abundance of information that Roebling had in hand, by 4 p.m., though there was still a good four hours of daylight left, the entire 5th Corps went into camp around the Lacy House and Wilderness Run. It is perhaps indicative of Warren's apparent mistrust of Wilson's ability to screen and protect the army that after building three bridges over Wilderness Run, he directed Griffin's division to camp in line of battle across the Orange Turnpike about one mile west of 5th Corps headquarters at the Lacy house. Roebling would remember that the plan for the next day, May 5, apparently included the 5th Corps's advance to form a line of battle between the Orange Plank Road and the Orange Turnpike, while the 2nd Corps, marching from Chancellorsville toward Todd's Tavern, would come up on the 5th's left. The 6th Corps, meanwhile, would form on the 5th's right. Then, and only then, would the Army of the Potomac be in any way ready to engage the enemy. But General Lee and the Army of Northern Virginia had other ideas.[5]

Forever after, Washington Roebling would lament the fact that the 5th Corps, after crossing the Rapidan, was ordered to stop within a swampy hollow carved out by Wilderness Run when safer, higher ground was available just a half hour's march beyond. But neither Meade nor Grant, who had remained at Germanna Ford to watch the passage of the 6th Corps and await Burnside's 9th, could be located to change the order for the 5th Corps's mid-afternoon halt. A brief march ahead lay one of the few clearings in the Wilderness, an area known as the Chewning Farm, situated on a high plateau that offered a panorama of the surrounding second-growth forest. The Chewning Plateau overlooked and dominated the whole southern half of the what was to become the battlefield, as well as offering control of the few viable roads that traversed the dense woods. Apparently confident that his superior numbers made him immune to assault by the enemy, Grant showed little or no concern that Lee might strike the Army of the Potomac, for he had placed it in positions ready-made for exploitation by an aggressive foe. One of the few precautions taken by Grant and Meade was an order to cavalry commander General Wilson and his 3rd Division to maintain a presence on both the Orange Plank Road and the Orange Turnpike and provide fair warning should there be rebel

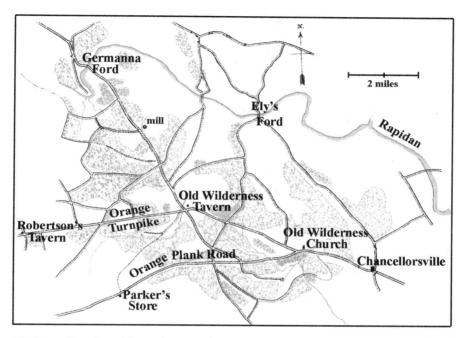

5th Corps May 4 positions at the Wilderness.
Adapted from Plate XCIV, 6 OR Atlas.

interference. The next day, when the rest of the 5th Corps began its advance, Griffin's division would remain behind to act as the 5th Corps's rear guard. It is hard to imagine what would have become of the 5th Corps if Warren hadn't taken these fundamental precautions on May 4 and 5.[6]

The relationship between Meade and Grant was curious, given the awkwardness of the command structure, with the lieutenant general always there to look over Meade's shoulder. Then, too, Meade was also very much aware of the continued pressure being applied by his enemies and competitors in Washington, a situation for which the lieutenant general had apparently expressed some sympathy. Meade's letters to his wife that spring are replete with praise for Grant and mounting confidence that his new superior intended to keep him in command of the Army of the Potomac; indeed, because of his seemingly respectful consideration of Meade's ideas and suggestions, Meade was convinced that Grant was a man with whom he could work successfully. A grateful Meade was anxious to please the lieutenant general and to respond promptly to all his wishes, whether expressed by direct order or merely intuited by Meade. He also realized that Grant was being given all the authority and resources needed to make the upcoming campaign a success, advantages Meade himself had been previously denied. Then there was also the Army of the Potomac's proximity to Mine Run, which could only have been a painful reminder to Meade of that embarrassing debacle. There would be no repeat of the inefficiency or of the hesitancy or disregard for orders that had brought on that disaster if Meade could help it.[7]

By 2 p.m. on May 4, General Wilson reported that he was following orders and had patrols out on the area's roads, but, contrary to his instructions, he did not maintain a presence on both major roads through the Wilderness forest. Instead, he pulled all his men off the turnpike and concentrated his division in a defensive position on the Orange Plank Road for the night, leaving the turnpike unguarded. It was a recipe for disaster, which was not long in coming. Wilson, far from contributing to reliable intelligence of the enemy's positions and intentions, added to the confusion. He reported, "[Enemy] Troops well down toward Mine Run, on all roads, except this one [Orange Plank Road]; none on this road nearer than 7 miles to this place. I have sent patrols out in all directions, but as yet hear of nothing, except a few light parties scattered through the by-roads." Wilson also reported what he believed were Lee's general dispositions based on his interrogation of a British subject who had traveled through the area and been brought into his head-quarters. Wilson's report, though based on negligent scouting, was nonetheless embraced at the army's headquarters, because it reinforced the conjecture that Lee would withdraw in the face of the Army of the Potomac's advance.[8]

Early on the morning of May 5, three divisions of the 5th Corps began their march in column toward that day's goal, Parker's Store, while Griffin remained ready to defend against any interference. With a seeming sense of impending trouble, Warren remained at his headquarters, choosing, with an interesting prescience, to stay with Griffin's 1st Division. Wilson had been ordered to maintain his position screening and protecting the 5th Corps's movement on both the Plank Road and the turnpike, but that morning, without notifying Warren or anyone else, Wilson rode away with his entire division. He would later try to justify this move by claiming never to have received the orders from Meade reiterating that he was to remain in his position. While Wilson had already abandoned the turnpike completely the previous night, the next morning the only indication that he was aware of any responsibility to protect the vulnerable column of the 5th Corps trailing through the Wilderness was his feeble gesture of leaving a single cavalry regiment on the Plank Road. The role that the rest of Sheridan's cavalry was to have played in shielding the army and its train was, of course, further weakened when erroneous reports of rebel cavalry won his permission to send Torbert's division away. Torbert's orders, thereby, were changed from assisting Wilson in shielding the infantry's passage to riding away with Gregg's division to Hamilton's Crossing. That fruitless expedition, as it happened, sent a large number of the Army of the Potomac's cavalrymen riding away from the encroaching enemy. This also curtailed the 5th Corps's marching orders and left it still well within the confines of the tangle known as the Wilderness.[9]

Early on the morning of May 5, Washington Roebling led a long, drawn-out column of three 5th Corps divisions along a narrow woods road heading toward Parker's Store. The day's march had been curtailed by the unavailability of Sheridan's cavalry to assist Wilson in screening the 5th Corps's advance. The changing of their goal for the day meant that, even when completed, it would have left them still within the confines of the Wilderness. The road they traveled was seldom used, and the corps's pioneers were sent ahead to build bridges and attempt to widen the road. The Chewning Plateau lived up to all of Roebling's expectations, providing overviews of the dense woods, with connection by two woods roads to the Plank Road on either side of Parker's Store. When firing was heard from the direction of Parker's Store, Roebling had Crawford's division begin to dig in and position its two batteries facing west and south. While they were entrenching, Roebling rode toward Parker's Store, where he found Colonel John Hammond's 5th New York Cavalry, the regiment Wilson had left behind, heavily engaged with what turned out to be A. P. Hill's entire corps. As the rebels streamed down the Orange Plank Road, the commander of the Army of Northern Virginia, General Robert E. Lee, was riding by Hill's side that day. By the time Roebling could bring up infantry support for the hard-pressed troopers, they had broken and were riding off toward Chancellorsville. General Crawford, meanwhile, had been able to send a communication by signal to 5th Corps headquarters but unfortunately added to the confusion. His erroneous report, that the encounter taking place at Parker's Store was merely a fight between the opposing cavalries, left Warren, and thereby Meade and Grant, inclined to dismiss the fighting at Parker's Store as nothing more than a cavalry skirmish.[10]

With the column he had been leading strung out for four miles along the roads leading to Parker's Store, Roebling rode in search of General Warren, anxious to alert him to the danger on their left flank. But when he found him, all the 5th Corps commander's attention was focused on the critical situation on General Griffin's front on his right flank. As Warren had been mounting to leave his headquarters and join the head of the column Roebling was leading to Parker's Store, a courier came from Griffin. While preparing to put his men into column to join the trek to Parker's Store, his 1st Division was still deployed in line of battle on either side of the Orange Turnpike, when a large force of the enemy began attacking his pickets. When Warren shared Griffin's report with Meade, newly arrived at Warren's headquarters, Meade ordered him to suspend his march and attack the enemy with his whole force—not an easy order to obey when your corps is strung out along miles of roads through the woods. At the start of the communications for that day that would strain the usually positive working relationship between Griffin and Warren, Griffin requested that he be allowed to discover the position and size of the enemy's force he was facing and deploy accordingly before he attacked. To Grant, still back at Germanna Ford, Meade sent the following:

> The enemy have appeared in force on the Orange pike, and are now reported forming line of battle in front of Griffin's division, Fifth Corps. I have directed General Griffin to attack them at once with his whole force. Until this movement of the enemy is developed, the march of the corps must be suspended. I have, therefore, sent word to Hancock not to advance beyond Todd's Tavern for the present. I think the enemy is trying to delay our movement, and will not give battle, but of this we shall soon see. For the present I will stop here.[11]

Meade's missive to Grant is an apt display of the inherent difficulty of responding to the actions of General Lee and his Army of Northern Virginia. Meade's memories of his failure the previous fall, when General William French succumbed to a rebel delaying action, were all too fresh. Meade was not about to let this campaign become a replay of Mine Run. Thus, he ordered an attack in force by Griffin. But apparently he had a niggling worry that this might be another of Lee's more substantially aggressive movements; thus Meade also chose to order Hancock to halt his march, which was taking him even further away from the 5th and 6th Corps. As Meade waited impatiently for an advance on the enemy, he contemplated, quite unrealistically, how soon the 6th Corps could come up on Warren's right flank. Writing again to Grant, Meade reverted to an uncharacteristically bellicose posturing regarding the possibility that Lee meant to fight them in the Wilderness: "I will, if such is the case punish him. If he is disposed to fight this side of Mine Run at once, he shall be accommodated." Things started to go sideways when, in his response, Grant directed that the 5th Corps "pitch in" without allowing any time for dispositions. Griffin, drawn up in line of battle with both flanks

General Samuel Wylie Crawford.
Library of Congress.

dangling in midair, wanted to know when he could expect the arrival of promised support. Crawford, encouraged by Roebling, clung to his position at the
Chewning Farm as long as he could, leaving him a mile and three-quarters
from Griffin's position.[12]

Meade still hoped to avoid delay and continue the proposed advance and
turning movement, while Grant, based on Meade's reports and his response
to them, believed Warren was about to attack in force the enemy that had
appeared before Griffin. Meade and Grant seemed disinterested in urgent
requests from Warren, Griffin, Crawford, and Roebling for time to allow
reconnaissance and deployment and to maintain their hold on essential
ground. Refusal of all their requests was about to lead to near disaster for the
5th Corps. Without any possibility of immediate support, Griffin's 1st Division
was facing Richard Ewell's corps, estimated at as many as nineteen thousand
effectives. Ironically, Meade was completely unaware that the screen the cavalry
were supposed to provide did not exist, and he responded to Griffin's description of a large force of the enemy in his front by trying to send an order to

John Hammond, 5th New York
Cavalry.
GettysburgDaily.com.

General Wilson to report on what was going on. Grant, knowing only what he had been hearing from Meade, when he finally arrived at 5th Corps headquarters, was dismayed to find that almost nothing had been done by way of a Federal assault, and he took his displeasure out on Warren. As Roebling would witness, when Warren did not order his men into the tangled undergrowth of the Wilderness quickly enough to suit the lieutenant general, Grant threatened Warren with cashiering on the spot in front of the whole army if he didn't attack immediately. This was an interesting display of command style by Grant, threatening one of Meade's corps commanders with removal on this, the morning of the second day of the spring campaign, while Warren's corps was facing disaster. It was at this point, as Wilderness historian Edward Steere has commented, that Grant took over control of the conduct of the battle. His willingness to let Meade maintain unimpeded command of his army hadn't lasted more than a day into the campaign. And the rumor that Grant had questioned the courage of the Army of the Potomac was being speedily repeated by that army's officers.[13]

At first the officers and men of Griffin's 1st Division, though unsupported, were able to push back rebel skirmishers, but they suddenly walked into a volley from the invisible enemy, whose double battle line, they soon realized, stretched well beyond both of Griffin's unprotected flanks. Griffin's division found itself attacking two divisions of Ewell's corps, whose men were dug in and waiting for them. Then things went from bad to worse. As the enemy was reinforced, the Federal units tried to stand their ground or began falling back in some order, but the enemy aggressively pursued them, and Saunders Field (see map on page 219) and the surrounding woods became a killing ground. As the rebels appeared on their flanks, the withdrawal of the soldiers of Griffin's division, who claimed never to have been beaten before, became a rout. Meanwhile, Robinson's 2nd Division and Wadsworth 4th Division were struggling to obey their orders to take up positions on Griffin's left; they, too, received instruction to immediately advance into the woods and attack the enemy wherever he was found. Wadsworth and Robinson found advancing through the undergrowth with any hint of unit cohesion next to impossible and were soon served up the same rough treatment that Griffin's men had endured. But most dismaying to Roebling were orders for Crawford to abandon the Chewning Farm and return to the 5th Corps's position to join the divisions already attempting to fight on Griffin's left. Roebling's plea to maintain a presence on the Chewning Plateau couldn't have been more suc-cinct: "It is of vital importance to hold the field where General Crawford is. Our whole line of battle is turned if the enemy get possession of it. There is a gap of half a mile between Wadsworth and Crawford. He cannot hold the line against an attack." The rebels, still coming down and forming along the Orange Plank Road, soon discovered that Wadsworth's battle line was forming on their front at right angles to the enemy's line, and they proceeded to pour a devas-tating flanking fire into that hapless division's flank. After obeying his orders to move to the right, Crawford would find the undergrowth so dense on his new front that to enter the woods there was to disappear almost immediately. Crawford's men became so disoriented that the two flanks curled toward each other, and many died in the resulting "friendly fire."[14]

In retrospect, Roebling remembered that retaining possession of the Chewning Plateau would have prevented Lee's successful drive between the 5th and 2nd Corps and potentially allowed the Federals to divide the lead ele-ments of Lee's army and destroy them in detail. Then, too, Roebling recalled that after Griffin's first disastrous assault, Warren had more knowledge of what they were facing. Far from being opposed to making another attack, Warren proposed another, but one further south, where the enemy was threat-ening to turn the 5th Corps's position. A rejection of Warren's suggestion was speedily returned, and it was at this point that Grant informed Warren that he would remove him from command if he did not immediately make a frontal assault on his current front. Therefore the opportunities lost that day remain, along with many others, among the Civil War's what-ifs. Not until 2:30 p.m. on May 5 did Meade and Grant come to the 5th Corps's front, but even then they were far more interested in what might be happening with the progress of the 2nd Corps, which had been ordered to make a forced march to assist in confronting what Grant and Meade were finally beginning to concede was something more than a delaying action. Firing from that direction, well to the 5th Corps's left, indicated that the unimpeded rebels who had flooded down the Plank Road were making things hot for the vanguard of Hancock's 2nd Corps, which would have to fight on its own much as Warren's 5th Corps had. While Warren had been given the unwarranted promise that the 6th Corps would be protecting his right flank, many hours would pass as the 6th's vanguard struggled through the impacted undergrowth searching for the 5th Corps's vulnerable right flank. Many years later, Roebling would sadly describe Griffin's assault as "a splendid attack, losing most of his Regulars, gaining a few hundred feet of worthless ground & inflicting small loss on the enemy."[15]

Still picturing the Chewning Plateau in his mind, Roebling would write, "We should have attacked towards the left—towards the Plank Road where the ground was open and higher. We virtually had possession of it in the early morning, but gave it up through inexcusable default because there was no general officer present to direct. Warren was over with Griffin on the Orange Pike. I myself had been at Parker's Store early in the morning. We could have occupied it at 3 P.M. That would have been a different battle."

In addition, Roebling would comment on the orders that placed Hancock's 2nd Corps such a distance from the other corps of the Army of the Potomac. Whereas some described it as a great flanking movement, Roebling believed that its purpose was based upon Grant's mistaken belief that he was cutting off Lee's probable retreat from the advancing Army of the Potomac: "Grant made a fatal blunder in ordering Hancock off on a wild goose chase towards Todd's Tavern, whereas he should have been ordered to take position near Parker's Store on the left of the line of the 5th Corps on the morning of the 5th. When Hancock did return in the afternoon we were already hard pressed."[16]

On the night of May 5, General Griffin, known admiringly to his men as "Fighting Jack," came into army headquarters, furious that he had been forced to send his men into battle only to incur heavy losses in "useless slaughter." When Griffin declared that it had been an inexcusable blunder to fight from such a disadvantageous position, Grant and his right-hand man, General John Rawlins, took offense and suggested Griffin should be placed under arrest for such insubordination. One would think that Grant was quite strict about such matters, but, as will be seen, it depended on just who was being insubordinate.

The Battle of the Wilderness held particularly bitter memories for Washington Roebling, for it was an alarming introduction to Grant's limited and costly approach to fighting. Roebling would write to a prospective historian of the battle in 1909, "The Wilderness was a useless battle, fought with great loss and no result—all on account of two fundamental mistakes." Pointing out that the first mistake was "Grant's fatuous assumption that Lee would be afraid to attack him," Roebling also cited the failure to seize the key point of the field when it was within easy reach. He also pointed to Grant initially positioning Hancock at such a distance with fully one-third of the army and remarked on Meade and Grant's absence at the front when they were most needed. Many years later, after Warren had been dead for many years, Roebling would write, "Warren's suggestions as to the conduct of the battle were right, but were purposely ignored." Roebling remembered the dismayed 5th Corps commander commenting that those suggestions had been received with "contumely and scorn that was positively insulting."[17]

Costly mistakes aside, the nightmarish fighting at the Wilderness would haunt Roebling for many years, as it would many another soldier who witnessed it: "The charge and countercharge, the swift repulse of small inadequate bodies of troops launched against the enemy—the constant cry for reinforcements—the indescribable roar of thousands & thousands of muskets (not so appalling but more intense than the cannonade at Gettysburg)—The impenetrable gloom of the forest seething with fire & smoke." He remembered, "The dry woods were on fire, almost suffocating the men with smoke, burning up corpses and the wounded trying to crawl away." Such vivid and terrible recollections refused to be forgotten. When recalling how Crawford's men, in the confusion and fear of the day, had fired into and killed their own men, Roebling offered, "I mention this incident because it marked the beginning of Grant's reckless, murderous methods of hurling troops at fortified positions and other impossible places, without regard to human life, when better results could be achieved by proper maneuvering on the field of battle."[18]

While many of the 5th Corps fought and died, let us consider the fate of General James Wilson and his unfortunate cavalry division that day. Ironically, though one suspects that a nervous Wilson was attempting on the morning of May 5 to ride away from where he perceived the rebels might be lurking, he instead inadvertently rode right into them. As a result, Wilson and his men were on the run and cut off from the Army of the Potomac for the rest of the day. At noon on May 5, Sheridan had absolutely no idea where Wilson was and sent David Gregg's division out to find him. By mid-afternoon, Gregg had found Wilson in the vicinity of Todd's Tavern under hot pursuit by Thomas Rosser's Confederate troopers, and it was noted that Wilson's designated rear guard was doing its very best to catch up with his fleeing vanguard. Gregg recounted that "under compulsion of clearing a way for the rear of the column, Troopers cruelly spurred their jaded, foam lathered horses to great speed. The spectacle gave semblance of panic which was alien to the situation."[19]

General Wilson, being one of the youngest commanders in the Army of the Potomac, would outlive most of his fellow commanders, and his 1912 memoir was written with few still living to contradict him. It offers a measure of Wilson's cheek and capacity for lying, for he says that on this day, May 5, at the Wilderness he had "perfectly screened Grant's advance," while engaging the enemy "wherever we encountered him and making good our hold on the important points of the field." We'll encounter Wilson's perfidy again in the days and weeks ahead and witness his creative condemnation of any commander who dared criticize him. As he was one of Grant's inner circle, the lieutenant general embraced Wilson's lies as truth. Wilson was ably abetted in glossing over his failures and embarrassments by his cavalry commander, General Philip Sheridan, whose report for this day read, "I have the honor to report that General Wilson was attacked to-day at Craig's Meeting House. At first he drove the enemy on the Catharpin Road for some distance, then they drove him back some distance to Todd's Tavern, where he was joined by General Gregg's command."[20]

20

The Battle of the Wilderness Rages On

As THINGS SPUN OUT OF FEDERAL CONTROL AT THE 5TH CORPS'S FRONT on May 5, George Meade called for Winfield Hancock to retrace his steps and come to the scene of the Confederate assaults. Confusing and delayed communications between Army of the Potomac headquarters and Hancock resulted in unrealistic expectations of when he could arrive in force and what he could accomplish. General George W. Getty's division of the 6th Corps had been trying to cope on its own with two divisions of A. P. Hill's corps on the Federal left, and it was greatly desired that Hancock would join Getty in an assault. But Hancock reported, much as Gouverneur Warren had previously that day, that it was more than a little difficult to bring up troops in these dense woods, and only part of his force had arrived. Getty was subsequently ordered to attack alone. Neither Getty nor Hancock would succeed in recapturing the Chewning Plateau, the high ground that Meade and U. S. Grant had earlier refused Warren permission to retain. That controlling eminence was now firmly under Confederate control and would remain so. While Washington Roebling credits Hancock's arrival with preventing a complete rout of the Army of the Potomac, additional worries were piling up for Meade and Grant. As the realization that R. E. Lee was apparently bringing the entire Army of Northern Virginia to bear against the Army of the Potomac's precarious positions in the Wilderness, concerns were growing about the vulnerability of the 6th Corps's position on Warren's right and the Federals' ability to control the Germanna Plank Road and the ford. Then, too, thoughts were being given regarding what dangers might present themselves on the Federal left, during and after Hancock's reunion with the Army of the Potomac. The Federal cavalry were found ever more sorely wanting in providing intelligence and protection, for while Hancock's arrival had complicated

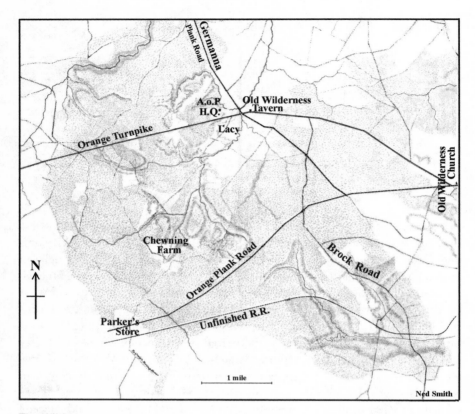

The Wilderness.
Adapted from Plate LV, 1 OR Atlas.

Lee's plans, Lee could count on the imminent arrival of James Longstreet's corps to provide welcome relief and support for his own struggling forces.[1]

When Hancock's newly arrived corps began to receive increasingly severe Confederate attention, Warren was ordered to provide relief by sending a force to assault Hill's left and rear. James Wadsworth's division was chosen for the mission, with its commander embracing this opportunity to compensate for the disastrous repulse and panic-impelled withdrawal his men had met with that morning. Wadsworth was to advance toward the swelling sound of the guns near the intersection of the Plank and Brock Roads. Roebling had likely been out there quite recently, for he gave a detailed description of what was occurring, reporting that "a column of the enemy was seen moving past Chewning's house towards Hancock; they came on a little wood-road, past a small block house west of Chewning's." At 4 p.m., Roebling accompanied Wadsworth's force, which entered the woods southeast of Warren's headquarters at the Lacy House. They were formed in two lines of battle with Wadsworth's division in the first and Henry Baxter's in the second, as the soldiers struggled through thick woods full of underbrush.[2]

Roebling accompanied Wadsworth and later confessed, "As soon as the thick underbrush was reached most of us were lost, including myself. Met some of the enemy who were equally lost." After advancing half a mile, they found a rebel skirmish line and drove the enemy steadily until it was too dark to see, the onset of night preventing Wadsworth from forming the hoped-for connection with Hancock's right. In fact, moving through the disorienting underbrush, Wadsworth's force had edged further to the left than planned and came up on the enemy's front rather than his flank and rear. Wadsworth's soldiers remained in their line of battle through the night, facing south, between the Widow Tapp's Field and the Brock Road. Prisoners they took proved to be newly arrived, like themselves, and were members of the column Roebling had seen earlier that had been sent from Hill's corps to confront the arrival of Hancock. Roebling described the nature of the fighting that evening, with Wadsworth's soldiers firing blindly into the forest at an invisible enemy whose presence was evidenced only by the hostile bullets swishing past their heads.[3]

Roebling, who had been in the saddle since dawn, returned to Warren's headquarters at the Lacy House at 9 p.m., where he tried to catch a few hours of sleep, but he was awakened to go to Grant's headquarters to share his knowledge of the situation of the Federal left around Parker's Store and the road leading to it. He first met with Grant's aide, Colonel Cyrus Comstock, known to Roebling as the engineer he had reported to when he was building the Harpers Ferry bridge. Comstock had come up in the world, for after he went west, he had become part of Grant's inner circle and was credited, along with General William Smith, as an architect of the plan the future lieutenant general Grant had sent to Henry Halleck as his overall strategy for the Federal armies that spring. Roebling wryly commented that it seemed Comstock, with his newfound prestige, was much jollier than the man he had known at Harpers Ferry. With Grant asleep, Comstock was handling consideration of just what to do with General Ambrose Burnside the following day, the 9th Corps still being subject to Grant's commands rather than Meade's. Proposals included sending him to join Wadsworth early the next day or for Burnside to make an attempt to recapture the Chewning Plateau. The latter forlorn hope was chosen. There seemed finally to be acceptance that the distance between

General Winfield Scott Hancock.
Library of Congress.

the Plank Road and the turnpike was too great for the 5th Corps to occupy alone and that the gap between the 5th and 2nd Corps was a real danger.[4]

Roebling was ordered to accompany Burnside the next morning and to direct his corps to the position he was to take up. Roebling recounts that, although Burnside had orders to start his movement at 4 a.m. on May 6, Roebling and fellow 5th Corps engineer Captain Emmor B. Cope waited all morning for Burnside to arrive, with each hour's passing making the ground he was to occupy more and more untenable. "When he did arrive, he and his staff made quite a show so that a rebel battery opened on him and made it so uncomfortable that he and his corps commenced to edge away to the left more & more." Roebling wrote, "A long consultation now ensued between Genls Burnside & Parke and Col Comstock. No one liked the idea of taking the hill by assault, and the reluctance was increased by an occasional cannonball coming down among the party." It was then decided to give up approaching the Chewning Plateau and instead move toward the left. While part of Thomas

General James Wadsworth.
Library of Congress.

Stevenson's division went over to assist the 2nd Corps, Orlando Willcox's division eventually managed to engage the enemy on Burnside's front, between Chewning and Wadsworth's position near the Widow Tapp's Field. Otherwise accomplishing little, as Roebling described, the afternoon saw "one 9th Corps division manage to intrench itself at right angles to Hancock's line and about opposite to the latter's right flank, and there they staid." While Roebling dealt with the 9th Corps, Wadsworth and his division were cutting a swath across the 2nd Corps's front and bearing the brunt of the enemy's fire, which would otherwise have been inflicted upon Hancock's 2nd Corps. It provided a much-needed relief for Hancock's beleaguered troops, who, with the arrival of Longstreet's vanguard to bolster the rebel battle line and threaten the 2nd Corps's left, were reaching the breaking point. But it was Wadsworth himself who would pay the ultimate price for his aggressive intercession. Early in the afternoon of May 6, while rallying his men after an enemy counterattack, he was shot in the head and subsequently fell into enemy hands; he died the next day. Roebling would later describe Wadsworth as "the real hero of the battle." Roebling witnessed some portion of the 2nd Corps's struggle, for after receiving a severe repulse, the enemy eventually counterattacked. Of the 2nd Corps's efforts to regroup at the Brock Road and prepare for the oncoming enemy's attack, Roebling said, "It is a matter of regret that there was not time for a movement forward by Hancock's right to the open ground of the Tap farm, which would have relieved the 2d corps from the horrible embarrassment of fighting later on in the narrow Brock Road, only ten feet wide, surrounded by flames and smoke and firing millions of bullets at an unseen enemy in the woods. I was there for several hours in the Brock Road on the afternoon of May 6th and shall never forget the sight."

There had been a delay before the enemy had followed up on its repulse of Hancock's assault, for some of the fight had gone out of the rebels with the accidental wounding of General Longstreet, but their attack was nonetheless made. Though the very breastworks the 2nd Corps was defending had caught fire in a number of places, the attack was repulsed while the flames and smoke added to the hellish confusion. Summing up Hancock's fight with exemplary understatement, Roebling would comment, "There certainly was a want of coordination in the various movements."[5]

While concerns at Army of the Potomac headquarters mounted on May 6 as Hancock and the 2nd Corps were receiving the bulk of the enemy's attention, where were Philip Sheridan and his cavalry, and what were they contributing to the Army of the Potomac's intelligence and protection? In his superlative consideration of the Battle of the Wilderness, Edward Steere gives considerable attention to the role of cavalry, both Federal and Confederate. In fact, Steere devotes an entire chapter to the "misadventures of Sheridan's cavalry." Would that James Wilson's abominable performance on May 4 and 5 had been Sheridan's only misstep, but May 6 would find the Federal troopers doing little other than fighting on the defensive. During the early-morning attack ordered by Grant to be made by every available Federal infantryman, the cavalry's assignment was to cover the left flank of Hancock's infantry and protect the army's trains, but it was also suggested that Sheridan attack and harass the enemy if he could do so without endangering the trains. Sheridan's immediate response was "Why cannot infantry be sent to guard the trains and let me take the offensive." Thus, Meade's orders to Hancock on May 6 explicitly instructed him, despite supposed cavalry presence, to watch for the enemy coming in on his left. Is it any wonder, after the nonexistent cavalry screen on May 5 and the resulting disaster, that Meade had little confidence in Sheridan's providing warning or protection? Finally sending his troopers out three hours

Sketch copied from original in Maj. Gen'l G. K. Warren's book of
official papers, marked Wilderness, May 1 to 7, 1864.

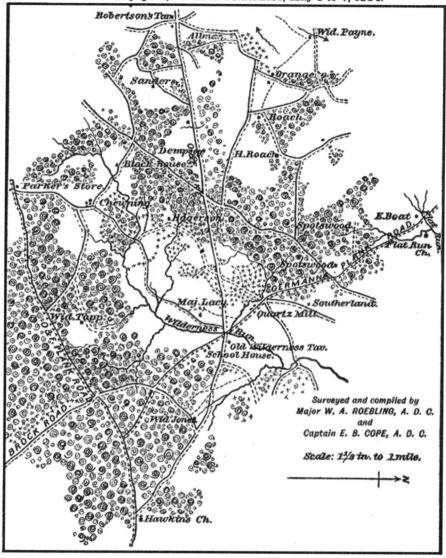

Roebling and Cope Wilderness map.
OR 36, I, 546.

after the infantry's assaults began, Sheridan provided none of the vital information that could have saved Hancock from a costly defeat.[6]

The day of May 6 had brought no joy to Federal hearts, but it was not yet over. That night, the 6th Corps on the Union right sustained an attack by the enemy that threatened to become a rout. At dusk, when Roebling rode over to Grant's headquarters on the Orange Turnpike, he arrived "just as the 6th Corps panic was in full swing." Though dire reports were flooding in, Roebling noticed that the lieutenant general's reaction was so subdued that he commented, "Grant apparently never noticed it & appeared utterly indifferent to what was going on. This surpassed my understanding." While initial reports first promoted the news that General John Sedgwick and a sizable portion of the 6th Corps had been captured, as time passed, more reliable reports came from the right, and Roebling reported that luckily "the panic stopped of itself shortly." But while there was the greatest excitement at both Meade's and Grant's headquarters, it was decided that someone should go out there to discover what was actually happening. Thus Roebling was chosen to lead Samuel Crawford's division, and as the men reached the Germanna Plank Road, "we found it filled with an excited crowd of soldiers apparently scared to death; There amounted in number to almost a division, and not a single one could tell why he was running; not a shot could be heard, as we moved towards Germanna Ford, the stragglers quickly ceased."[7]

Roebling and Crawford rode forward to investigate the situation at the 6th Corps front, where they discovered the army's hospitals lying undisturbed. After advancing another half mile, they received assurances that General Sedgwick had not been captured and that at least a portion of the 6th Corps's line remained intact. Therefore, by 11 p.m., Roebling and Crawford's division returned to the 5th Corps, whereupon they were regaled with a story by one of the colonels on the 5th Corps's right adjacent to the 6th Corps. He told Roebling that, fortunately for him and his regiment, the rebels had halted in their attack some one hundred yards before reaching his front. Then the Federals were inadvertently treated to the celebrations of the nearby vociferous rebels, who, while searching for water before settling down for the night, were giving themselves hearty congratulations "upon the way they had made the Yankees run."[8]

Compared with what happened to the 5th Corps on May 5, May 6 could be considered a day of relative quiet on Warren's front, but the fighting Warren's soldiers had done was enough to draw praise from 2nd Corps historian Francis Walker. The 5th Corps had received a much-needed reinforcement by way of newly arrived artillerymen, fresh from the defenses

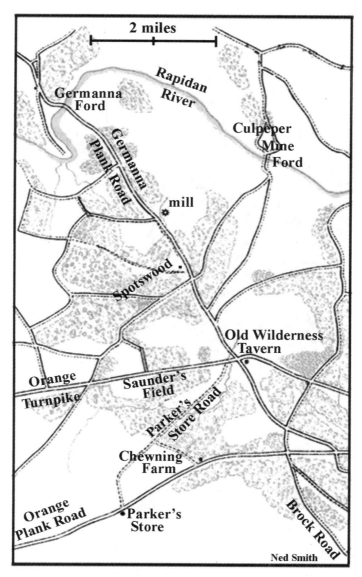

The 5th Corps in the Wilderness.
Adapted from Plate XCIV, 6 OR Atlas.

General John Sedgwick.
Library of Congress.

of Washington, DC. While previously all suggestions of taking troops from the capital's circle of fortifications had been rejected, Henry Halleck saw to it that Grant's urgent requests for men to replace the many casualties he was suffering were fulfilled. The artillerymen, whose training was mostly limited to handling the big guns outside Washington, suddenly found themselves being handed muskets and heading for the front under the guidance of Colonel John Howard Kitching. On their arrival, while with Hancock's 2nd Corps that morning, they had already been bloodied in a "little" fight that saw them lose "60 or 70 men." It likely was with some relief that the no doubt bewildered artillerymen were then commandeered to build breastworks on Charles Griffin's left and become a second line of support for the 1st Division. While many surely questioned what possible assistance these untrained, inexperienced cannoneers could offer the infantry, they would, in the days to come, prove their worth as well as their courage. On this night General Griffin apparently began to realize the full extent of his division's losses, and his anger of the previous day turned to sorrow. At 5th Corps headquarters, with tears streaming down his powder-begrimed face, Griffin remarked to Warren, "General, I have lost four thousand of my boys in that cursed hole."[9]

During the day of May 7, an uneasy quiet reinforced the view that the Army of Northern Virginia and the Army of the Potomac had reached a stalemate. Roebling was at the front first thing in the morning, and though the smoke of the fires in the dense woods obscured the enemy, he reported that on the 5th Corps's left "the rebels are cheering as if in considerable force in the direction of Parker's Store." Meanwhile, Griffin, on the 5th Corps's right, was shelling down the Orange Turnpike to deny the enemy use of the road. At about noon, orders came to Warren's headquarters to be ready for a movement that night to Spotsylvania Court House with the 5th Corps to take the advance. As Roebling reported, although preparation began immediately, to the corps's regret, five hundred of its casualties would end up being left behind for lack of transportation. With the battlefield eventually left in rebel hands, the wounded who survived long enough would be retrieved a week later under a flag of truce. While the Federals and the rebels halfheartedly strengthened earthworks on May 7, the commanders of both armies were considering what the coming days would bring. But many soldiers of the 5th Corps would never leave the Wilderness. The four corps that fought there reportedly lost 17,666 killed, wounded, or captured. The 5th Corps's loss was put at 5,132, but Wilderness veteran Morris Schaff asserts that Warren was ordered to under-report his casualties in an effort to mitigate the effect of the terrible losses. So while the real numbers for the Army of the Potomac at the Wilderness will never be known, when the wounded began pouring into northern hospitals from the battlefields of Grant's Overland Campaign, the truth would only be more shocking. But in the early days of the campaign, while the lieutenant general forbade reporters from using the military telegraph, in his reports to Washington Grant downplayed his losses while baselessly insisting, again and again, that Lee's Army of Northern Virginia was on its last legs, an assertion that would be glaringly disproved in the coming days.[10]

Roebling, as Warren's aide, if he was not scouting, was entrusted with carrying dispatches or leading troop movements. This duty frequently gave him the unique opportunity to witness events not only at 5th Corps Headquarters but also at the headquarters of Meade and Grant. His duties likewise brought him to the 2nd, 6th, and 9th Corps' fronts, as well as the battle lines of his own 5th Corps. Roebling's assignments in these first days of the campaign led Schaff to describe him and his fellow 5th Corps engineer Cope as "Warren's right hand men." At the Wilderness, Roebling, now a veteran of some experience in the field, was a man with quick intelligence as well as a fierce determination to provide his corps and his army, if it was in his power, with all they might need to ensure success and avoid calamity. This made him a formidable and astute observer often heedless of his own safety. In later years, when he remembered the Battle of the Wilderness, Crawford's losses by friendly fire on May 5 were a source of particular anguish. After Crawford was ordered to relinquish the key to the battlefield, the Chewning Plateau, his division had been ordered to enter the tangled undergrowth in an attempt to make a frontal attack on an unknown enemy position. Such events caused Roebling to condemn the lieutenant general, who insisted upon speed over coordination or intelligent disposition. Roebling suggested that this day's combat had been a prime example of Grant's recklessness, of his pitching men in without regard for human life, when judgment and patience and the use of informed maneuvering on the battlefield would have saved many lives.[11]

In his 1912 memoirs, James H. Wilson, who was largely responsible for the disaster that befell the 5th Corps and the Army of the Potomac on the first day of the Battle of the Wilderness, bragged of his complete success on May 5, the very day he had failed utterly to screen or provide warning to the Federals of the enemy's impending violent assaults. Wilson also claimed that he had fought three rebel brigades that day, when he and his division, though they outnumbered their opponent three to one, had in fact been routed by Thomas Rosser's Confederate brigade alone. Rather than hold him responsible for such incompetence, Grant believed all of Wilson's tall tales and recommended Wilson, already a brevet major general of volunteers, for promotion to the more prestigious rank of colonel in the regular army "in recognition for his service at the Wilderness."[12]

From the Wilderness to Spotsylvania

WHEN RESEARCHING U. S. GRANT'S OVERLAND CAMPAIGN, IT IS WITH reluctance that one finishes Edward Steere's thoroughly researched, even-handed, and succinctly written treatise *The Wilderness Campaign*, but it was my great good fortune to find William Matter's study of Spotsylvania, *If It Takes All Summer*. I was also lucky enough to enter into a correspondence with Bill and happily informed him that I found his work a much-needed continuation of Steere's exemplary research and writing. Bill was pleased, since it had been his goal to pick up where Steere left off at the end of the Battle of the Wilderness and to bring the Army of the Potomac and the Army of Northern Virginia on to the conflict at Spotsylvania.

By May 7, 1864, it was time for the Army of the Potomac to move, for there was nothing to be gained by renewing the fight in the confines of the Wilderness. Nor was there anywhere else for Grant to go but to the left, pursuing the unlikely hope that the Federals could get around R. E. Lee's right flank before his army could react. Since he had already relinquished his control of Germanna Ford and its environs to the rebels, Grant had no choice but to make a prompt advance to his next supply base. So while many insist that Grant's pluck and pugnacity put the Army of the Potomac on its path around the rebel right, Grant, more pragmatically, was trying to renew his communications and supply lifeline. And while he had apparently learned no lesson from his experience at the Wilderness, he was planning, after a quick trip through Spotsylvania, to arrive at the North Anna River the next day, May 9. It would be two weeks of ceaseless fighting before the Army of the Potomac saw the North Anna, only to find Lee's vanguard there to greet them as well.[1]

As for catching Lee unprepared for a Federal move from the Wilderness, that, too, was unrealistic, nor need it be ascribed to Lee's having some sort of special prescience, for, as historian Bill Matter commented, if intuition was

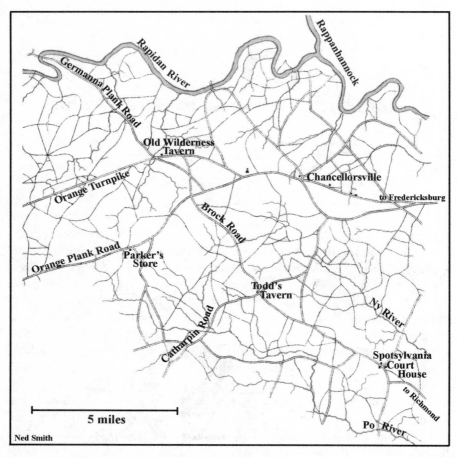

From the Wilderness to Spotsylvania.
Adapted from Plate LXXXI, 1 OR Atlas.

involved, it was "bolstered by clear, logical calculation." George Meade's chief of staff, General A. A. Humphreys, was apprehensive that when the Army of the Potomac sent its supply wagons, ambulances, and heavy guns away in preparation for the army's move, this would alert the enemy. Such was the case, for as the Federals' trains moved off, Lee was watching through a naval telescope that had been set up at the Confederate position on the Chewning Plateau. Then, too, the Union cavalry's withdrawal from (followed by its unexplained return to) Todd's Tavern had caught the rebels' attention and was duly reported to Lee by J. E. B. Stuart. Numerous reports from Stuart prompted

Lee to have a road cut from his front through the forest toward Spotsylvania and to send General Richard Anderson, appointed to command the wounded James Longstreet's corps, to start there on the afternoon of May 7. But beyond Lee's intention to deny the Federals access to the crossroads at Spotsylvania, much would hinder the Army of the Potomac's movement on the night of May 7. Lee obviously possessed a very active and effective cavalry, a valuable asset the Federals did not possess.[2]

Gouverneur Warren's 5th Corps was again chosen to lead the Army of the Potomac's movement to Spotsylvania, and after dark in the face of the enemy, the men quietly extricated themselves from their front. They were to move from the Army of the Potomac's center right, pass behind the 2nd Corps, and move on the Brock Road to Todd's Tavern and thus to Spotsylvania. The 2nd Corps would follow, while the 6th and 9th Corps would take a longer route toward Chancellorsville. The cavalry, now that General Edward Ferrero's U.S. Colored Troops (USCT) had assumed responsibility for guarding the trains, were freed from that much-resented responsibility. Philip Sheridan was thereby ordered to provide protection for the Army of the Potomac's right and left flanks and secure the routes for the infantry's upcoming move. Far from fulfilling that directive, Sheridan's cavalry, finding themselves unable to dislodge Confederate horsemen from the Brock Road, on the afternoon of May 7, at dusk, pulled back to Todd's Tavern, leaving the route Warren's 5th Corps was taking that night to Spotsylvania in the enemy's hands. Inexplicably, Sheridan reported that evening that he had driven the enemy in confusion all the way to Spotsylvania Court House and that the route of Warren's march, the Brock Road, was clear of the enemy.[3]

As Washington Roebling recorded, after sunset on May 7, the 5th Corps began its movement, with George Meade and U. S. Grant riding at the head of their column. The night was very dark, and the muddy condition of the roads made passage difficult. Led by Grant's engineer, Cyrus Comstock, they took the wrong road at a fork, one that led directly into rebel lines. Grant's military secretary, Ely Parker, later claimed to have pointed out to Grant that they were headed for trouble. Grant and Meade doubled back, leaving a guide at the fork to assist the 5th Corps in avoiding their mistake. This was hardly the last time that Cyrus Comstock led troops astray. Nor was it the last time the Army of the Potomac would be moving blindly with the enemy close by. The campaign became known for the poor quality and unreliability of the Federal maps, showing roads that didn't exist and not showing roads that did. Once again, Grant seemed unconcerned about the possible reaction of the Army of Northern Virginia, as indicated by Comstock, whose diary reflects the unrealistic belief at Grant's headquarters that Lee would fall back when the Federals advanced, the only question being how far. The Wilderness lesson had apparently not been learned. When Grant and Meade arrived at Todd's Tavern around midnight, they found David Gregg's division of Sheridan's cavalry. Gregg had no knowledge regarding the passage of the infantry that night, nor did he have orders to keep the road to Spotsylvania clear. When 1 a.m. arrived without orders forthcoming from Sheridan, Meade ordered General Wesley Merritt's cavalry to clear the Brock Road of enemy cavalry and sent Gregg to patrol between the 5th Corps column and the enemy. Though Sheridan could not be located, he was infuriated on learning that Meade had given orders to the Federal cavalry without consulting him. Meanwhile, Sheridan's utter failure to fulfill his orders regarding the Army of the Potomac's night march left Meade, not known for his patience at the best of times, let alone when he believed subordinates had failed him, seriously angry.[4]

At 1 a.m. on May 8, Meade sent orders to General Wesley Merritt, but as Roebling recorded, the vanguard of the 5th Corps arrived at Merritt's headquarters at 3 a.m. only to be told that Merritt had just received Meade's order and was still getting his cavalry under way to clear the Brock Road. Merritt's troopers failed to dislodge Fitzhugh Lee's Confederate cavalry blocking the road, and Warren and Merritt agreed that the infantrymen, though more than a little weary from their all-night march, would do the job themselves. The cavalry then took themselves off, while the pioneers of Robinson's division began removing the trees that the enemy had felled across the road, with several of the axmen losing their lives to the enemy's marksmen. When Robinson was able to advance to confront the enemy's skirmish line, whom should he find there but Sheridan, perhaps making a very belated effort to offer some assistance, however feeble, for Warren's advance. For a man who would take great exception to Meade giving direct orders to his men, Sheridan felt no such limitation applied to him. He ordered Robinson to deploy on either side of the road. Sheridan gave Robinson no forewarning that his division was facing a great deal more than enemy cavalry. The 5th Corps was about to have another very bad day courtesy of the Army of the Potomac's cavalry. Unbeknownst to any of the 5th Corps, beyond Stuart's cavalry lay Anderson's (Longstreet's) Corps. Having been notified by Stuart that the Federals were coming down the Brock Road, Anderson began to rush his men to the rebel horsemen's aid. Stuart personally placed the infantrymen as they arrived in the troopers' now beleaguered defensive line, and they were soon able to give the Federals a staggering and unexpected reception.[5]

Now advancing in full daylight, Roebling recorded, the men in Robinson's leading brigade, exhausted after a night of marching, were then asked to

General Wesley Merritt.
Library of Congress.

double-quick two miles, approaching the open field at the Alsop Farm very much "blown." General Warren, seeing that rushing into an unknown confrontation had made the men nervous and jumpy, went to the head of Colonel Peter Lyle's brigade to help steady them. As had all of Robinson's division, Lyle's brigade had already been seriously whittled down in the fighting at the Wilderness. Sure that they were facing only dismounted cavalry, some of the men failed to shed their knapsacks, but as they advanced this day, they ran headlong into the fire of entrenched infantry, and about halfway across the field, a sudden volley took the division's commander, General Robinson, and his second in command from their saddles, while the third and fourth officers, who tried to assume command, were shot down as well. When Warren realized what he was facing, he went back to hurry the rest of the 5th Corps to his front, a task complicated by his horse being shot out from under him. Roebling, too, tried to bring order to the chaos, guiding a battery that was unsure where to go up to the front to engage the enemy artillery. Eventually, part of Lyle's brigade broke and ran and could

General Philip Sheridan and his division commanders (left to right: Wesley Merritt, David Gregg, Sheridan, Henry Davies, James H. Wilson, Alfred Torbert).
Library of Congress.

not be regrouped until the men reached the woods at the entrance to the Brock Road. Despite that inglorious retreat of their comrades, part of Lyle's brigade tried to make a stand, and one of the men manning the rebel barricade declared he had never fought braver men than Lyle's. The rest of the 5th Corps had to defile off the narrow woods road, meaning they could only be brought up and fed into the fighting piecemeal on the battlefield that would become known as Laurel Hill, and additional divisions got similarly rough treatment as they entered the fight with Stuart's cavalry and Anderson's corps.[6]

Though historian Steere describes Sheridan's cavalry as more numerous, better mounted, and armed with finer weapons than the cavalry force at Lee's disposal, the Federal horsemen's performance does not bear up at all well compared to that of their Confederate counterparts. This is demonstrated by Lee's troopers' ability and willingness to do all that needed to be done: fighting and driving enemy cavalry, screening their army from enemy observation, mapping roads and appointing guides to lead infantry movements, scouting

General John C. Robinson.
Library of Congress.

and providing frequent reports to keep the Army of Northern Virginia headquarters apprised of Federal activities. And, when necessary, the cavalry would fight alongside Confederate infantry, as they did this first day at Spotsylvania. On May 8, Stuart's horsemen once again deserved accolades for successfully delaying the arrival of the 5th Corps at Spotsylvania, and when Warren was finally able to break through and deploy, the rebel troopers joined with Anderson's newly arrived infantrymen to fight the influx of Unionists. Stuart's support for Anderson's infantry provides a strong contrast to the actions of the Federal cavalry after they failed to break the enemy cavalry's blockade of the Brock Road. While the rebel troopers fought alongside their infantry comrades, the Unionist horsemen rode off, leaving Warren and the 5th Corps infantry to fight on alone. As Carswell McClellan, former aide to General Humphreys, asked in a scathing response in 1889 to Sheridan's memoirs, why, if the pugnacious Sheridan was so anxious to fight the rebel cavalry, did he utterly fail to do so on May 7 and 8 at Spotsylvania?[7]

We have followed the fumbles and failures of the Federal cavalry in some detail because of the tremendous impact the resulting confrontation between

Generals Meade and Sheridan would have upon the fate of the Army of the Potomac and every man in it. While it seems beyond question that Sheridan failed to carry out his orders for May 7 (orders he would claim he never received), he was unapologetic, even furiously confronting Meade for supposedly "changing" Sheridan's orders to his troopers. It being illogical to conclude that Meade "changed" orders that Sheridan had never issued, a shouting match erupted between Sheridan and Meade. Sheridan told Meade that since the commanding general felt free to issue orders to Sheridan's cavalry, he could go on doing it, for Sheridan wouldn't. Sheridan also declared that he saw "nothing to oppose the advance of the 5th Corps; that the behavior of the infantry was disgraceful." But when Meade went to Grant to report Sheridan's refusal to obey orders and his defiant and disrespectful insubordination, Grant demonstrated his willingness to disregard Sheridan's failures and offenses, for the only thing that caught Grant's attention was Meade's repetition of Sheridan's desire to go off and fight rebel cavalry. Grant's desire to fulfill his favorite's wish would leave the Army of the Potomac at a dangerous and costly disadvantage, without cavalry and without reliable maps in enemy territory.[8]

Warren's command was not the only corps which Sheridan failed this day. General Winfield Scott Hancock's passage to Spotsylvania had been interrupted by a false report of a large body of the enemy approaching his column. Colonel J. Irvin Gregg's cavalry brigade was assigned to patrol that sector, but Gregg came to Hancock on the afternoon of May 8 to warn him that his brigade was being withdrawn. Sheridan, with Grant's new orders in his pocket, promptly directed all his cavalry to return to his headquarters in preparation for their departure from the Army of the Potomac the following day. There would be no repercussions for General Philip Sheridan regarding his frequent failure to carry out orders or his insubordination to the commanding general of the Army of the Potomac. In fact, you could say that quite the opposite happened, for Sheridan was given an independent command with permission to gather up his entire force of troopers, some ten thousand men, and ride off to fight enemy cavalry, just as he had wanted to all along. Either it didn't occur to Grant or he considered it unimportant that in the coming weeks he was leaving the Army of the Potomac blind as it moved through unknown, poorly mapped enemy territory. While Sheridan's expedition was followed by half of Lee's cavalry, Lee wisely retained the other half, which would continue to scout for and screen his army. As for knowing the terrain, it seemed there was always a man in Lee's army who knew the area or sympathetic citizens who would come to his assistance.[9]

Sheridan did not write his report for the period of the Army of the Potomac's passage from the Wilderness to Spotsylvania until two years later, and the cavalry commander was still somehow blaming General Meade for the failure of his own cavalry to provide protection and intelligence. He stuck to his story that Meade's changing of his nonexistent orders had ruined everything. And while Meade had notified Sheridan of the orders he had issued to the idle cavalrymen, and they are in the Official Record, Sheridan nonetheless insisted Meade did not inform him. This was apparently another lost order in a long list of orders that never seemed to find General Sheridan. Grant, meanwhile, many years later in his memoirs, apparently drew upon the statements of Sheridan and the ever-unreliable Adam Badeau to reiterate and support the claim that Meade's "changing" of Sheridan's orders had denied the Army of the Potomac control of Spotsylvania. Historian Bill Matter suggests that we can be glad that Meade, who died in 1872, never had to endure reading what no doubt would have been painful versions of the night move to Spotsylvania as written by Sheridan and Grant in their memoirs. In a way it should come as no surprise that Grant, as he seemingly always did, took Sheridan's part, for didn't Grant, inexplicably, often express his irrational belief that Sheridan was a "genius"? By way of example, after the war, Grant publicly declared Sheridan "one of the greatest soldiers of the world, worthy to stand in the very highest rank," to be considered with "Napoleon and Frederick and the great commanders in history." Grant also stated that if Sheridan had been in command at Gettysburg instead of Meade, he would have destroyed Lee's Army of Northern Virginia.[10]

After enduring yet another surprise, courtesy of sudden volleys from a large, unreported body of the enemy's infantry, General Warren had also apparently brought his concerns regarding Sheridan's derelictions to Lieutenant General Grant, where he received no more attention than had Meade. Grant, however, likely remembered Warren's criticism of his favorite. In his memoirs, Grant placed the blame for not reaching Spotsylvania before the enemy upon Warren. Roebling would comment, many years later, that the ill will Sheridan bore toward Warren dated back to the latter's complaints over the cavalry commander's failure to safeguard the Brock Road on the night of May 7. Roebling, as scout and mapmaker for General Warren, would try to fulfill the immense unmet need of scouting and reporting for the 5th Corps and the Army of the Potomac. Again and again, he would risk his own life in order to see that no man was sent into a place he would not go himself. There were many hard days ahead for the 5th Corps at Spotsylvania and beyond, and Roebling would be called upon to lead troop movements and spot trouble before his corps marched into it.[11]

Laurel Hill, Again and Again

PHILIP SHERIDAN WAS NOT THE ONLY ENEMY GOUVERNEUR WARREN HAD to contend with during the Overland Campaign, for General James H. Wilson was always ready to put in a bad word when it came to the commander of the 5th Corps. On May 8 at Laurel Hill, in Spotsylvania, Warren's corps had endured another defeat from an unreported, unexpected enemy, but Warren was, it seems, far from losing heart. Having been forced to send his corps piecemeal into the fight on May 8 as the men came off the narrow Brock Road, he was anxiously awaiting the delayed arrival of the 6th Corps with some confidence that their combined force could dislodge the enemy gathering on his front. But Wilson, who wasn't anywhere near there, widely told a story that when George Meade urged Warren to "cooperate" with General John Sedgwick, as opposed to one or the other of the corps commanders being given command of the upcoming attack, Warren had thrown a fit. As Wilson would tell it, Warren responded, "Gen. Meade, I'll be damned if I'll cooperate with Sedgwick or anybody else. You are the commander of this army and can give your orders and I will obey them; or you can put Sedgwick in command and he can give the orders and I will obey them; or you can put me in command and I will give the orders and Sedgwick will obey them; but I'll be God damned if I'll cooperate with General Sedgwick or anybody else." It is a sentiment that any commander, especially one who had been through what Warren had just experienced, could creditably embrace. But Wilson, who could not have been there to witness this supposed tirade, is the only source for this story. When questioned, he would insist that Warren himself told him about it at a later date. That Warren made such a highly personal admission to James H. Wilson, whom he distrusted and held in considerable disdain, is unlikely in the extreme.[1]

The tired men of the 6th Corps arrived at Spotsylvania after an already circuitous march had been made longer. Their route had been unnecessarily changed to meet a nonexistent threat due to faulty or perhaps nonexistent cavalry reconnaissance. The matter of who would command once the 6th Corps reached Spotsylvania, if it had ever been an issue, had been settled, for Meade appointed the senior officer, Sedgwick, to command the battlefield. This, however, became a moot point, for Sedgwick sent a message with Washington Roebling that Warren should "go on and command his own corps as usual. I have perfect confidence that he will do what is right, and knows what to do with his corps as well as I do." But as the afternoon passed with Sedgwick slowly moving his troops into position, Warren's patience was tried as he observed the rebels busily strengthening their defenses. Not until 6 p.m. were the 6th and 5th Corps ready to make their assault, and although the two Federal corps were able to put six divisions on the field to Richard Anderson's two, between the rebels' improved fieldworks on Laurel Hill and the timely arrival of Richard Ewell's corps to reinforce Anderson, the enemy could not be dislodged, and Union losses were severe.[2]

On the next day, May 9, enemy sharpshooters were very active. About the time General Sedgwick was killed by a Confederate sniper, General Warren had been writing a confidential letter to his friend A. A. Humphreys, Meade's chief of staff. In this letter, which was never sent but was found many years later among his papers, Warren poured out his concerns and frustrations. After expressing a wish that the army could complete its marches without being subject to changes made upon every fleeting, often inaccurate report, he continued,

> I fought yesterday with all the rapidity possible, and know I could have kept going if supports had been close by, and when Genl Sedgwick came I urged my plan, which he took time to have explained and adopt. And here I would venture another opinion that Genl. Meade should accompany the column moving to *the desirable* point as I was yesterday. Whether he thinks I am capable or not, my want of rank makes me incompetent when two corps come together, and I don't think our other two corps commanders are capable. General S[edwick] does nothing of himself. I have lost confidence in Genl [Winfield] H[ancock]'s abilities to do it from his failing with all the force he had in our first and second days' battles, especially on the latter day when he gave to Genl. [James] Wadsworth the command of the column of the attack. I think if he had

moved out with his whole command directing near the head in person he could have won.

The entire Army of the Potomac mourned the popular "Uncle John" Sedgwick's death, and when Warren learned of it, he folded his letter and put it away, where it would not see the light of day for many years.[3]

Roebling spent May 9 in the saddle, moving along the 5th Corps line and beyond, as the army was making all efforts to secure its position by digging in and placing batteries on Charles Griffin's and Lysander Cutler's fronts. Keeping track of rebel movements, Roebling spotted an enemy wagon train accompanied by a small squad of cavalry moving on Warren's right. The brigade sent over to drive them off was then used to close up a gap in Warren's line. He watched the vanguard of Hancock's 2nd Corps finally arriving to come down on the 5th Corps's right, where Warren had assumed they would take up a position in the space the 5th Corps had left for them. Instead, the 2nd Corps began to cross the Po River for an ill-considered flanking movement against the enemy dreamed up by Grant's engineer Cyrus Comstock. Comstock's plan could only have worked if the rebels had somehow failed to notice Hancock's threatening movement on the Confederates' left flank. The unmet need for intelligence on the enemy's positions and intentions was so dire that Hancock resorted to sending men up trees to gaze around in an attempt to get the lay of the land and discover any potential threats. There is a disturbing suspicion that Grant and his headquarters cohort somehow believed the enemy would not notice what the Federals were doing or hoped they would sit still while Grant made his moves. Meanwhile, the enemy duly noted Hancock's attempted flank attack, and the 2nd Corps had to be speedily and precariously withdrawn from its isolated perch across the Po. This would not be the last of Comstock's startlingly inept performances.[4]

The 2nd Corps's movement proved a far cry from a surprise for the enemy. Nor would Hancock come near being able to strike the Confederate's left flank. Comstock's maneuver saw the 2nd Corps having to cross the Po River twice, and darkness overtook the men before they could complete the crossing. While all this perilous and ultimately futile business was going on, Warren's 5th Corps was ordered, once again, to attack Laurel Hill, an assault that Comstock and Grant were sure would prevent the enemy from sending troops to confront Hancock. Though Warren made the advance, it did not succeed in distracting or deterring a watchful enemy. In the night, R. E. Lee sent General William Mahone's division to contest Hancock's continued crossing of the Po and General Henry Heth's division to attack Hancock's left flank. While hasty plans had to be drawn up to extricate the 2nd Corps from its hazardous position, the 5th Corps was ordered to probe the enemy in their front in Grant's never-ending search for a weak place in their line. Grant was often overly confident that when he attacked one place on the rebels' line, the resulting shift of troops in response would leave a vulnerable place elsewhere. The results of the probes Warren was ordered to make on the morning of May 10 provided ample proof that the Confederates still manned the defenses at Laurel Hill in force, at the cost of another few hundred 5th Corps casualties. Warren and the other corps commanders would soon be more than familiar with this use of reconnaissance in force as Grant and company's habitual response when they lacked information and their plans went awry. As historian David Jordan comments, Comstock's sending the 2nd Corps across the Po, twice, had been "an ill-planned, ill-advised operation, and it was endangered by Grant's lack of knowledge of his opponents' movements."[5]

Meanwhile, it's always interesting to consider what Charles Dana, Edwin Stanton's observer at Grant's headquarters, was reporting to the administration, for while one must always make allowances for Dana's unfettered biases, his missives are often a window into the gossip circulating at Grant's headquarters. A report from Dana to Stanton rather lets the cat out of the bag regarding Comstock's bad judgment in instigating the 2nd Corps's Po River expedition, when Dana repeats Comstock's own assessment that the ground Hancock fought to gain across the Po proved worthless, since every position surrounding the 2nd Corps was strongly held by the enemy in force. As Roebling pointed out, it had also delayed Hancock for many hours from effectively confronting the enemy where doing so would have proven useful. Dana also made the startling confession that Grant had no idea whether Lee's whole army was at Spotsylvania or if some part of it had slipped off somewhere else—another unsolved mystery courtesy of the missing Federal cavalry. Speaking of the cavalry, Dana also reported that Sheridan had seen nothing of the Confederate cavalry he was supposed to be fighting, and neither Sheridan nor Grant had any idea where J. E. B. Stuart might be.

Unbelievably, though the 2nd Corps's Po River venture had failed miserably, Grant and Comstock weren't done yet. After withdrawing Hancock's corps before it was annihilated, they were already hatching a plan for yet another attack. Reports from the front seemed to have no effect upon Grant's plans. If they contained news he didn't want to hear, he didn't hear it. Grant reasoned that the enemy's response to the Federals' fumbling activities on the Confederate left had surely weakened other places along their line, and, despite Warren's reports, Grant was certain that one such weak place

General William Mahone.
National Archives and Records Administration.

was in front of the 5th Corps at Laurel Hill. So he ordered preparations for yet another frontal assault to be made along Warren's front by the 5th and 2nd Corps after they had returned from their adventure across the Po. But Roebling's and others' scouting efforts had revealed that the enemy had not yet fully dug in in front of the sector that was the 2nd Corps's intended position, and Warren assumed that the longer they waited for Hancock's difficult extrication of his corps from across the Po, the less likely the assault was to succeed. Permission was granted for the attack to take place before the entire 2nd Corps arrived, and Roebling was sent to accompany and help position its first arrivals, Generals John Gibbon's and Francis Barlow's divisions, for their approach to the rebel entrenchments. Though a Confederate account described Warren's attack as a fierce assault, it failed nonetheless. Roebling estimated the Federal losses at two thousand, adding that he doubted the enemy had lost two hundred.[6]

General Horatio Wright.
Library of Congress.

Dana also took the opportunity to savage General Warren regarding the 5th Corps's May 10 assault, stating, "I witnessed it in Warren's front, where it was executed with the caution and absence of comprehensive *ensemble* which seem to characterize that officer." Smearing Warren was no doubt another attempt by Dana to assist his friend, General Wilson, in his quest to gain command of the 5th Corps. He also took a shot at the soldiers of the Army of the Potomac in general, commenting, "Of course, great numbers of men who are lying around in the woods will soon return to their commands, but many of these are worthless for fighting purposes." (Dana, by the way, begged off serving himself in the army because of his bad eyesight. Or was it his bone spurs?) A great number of 5th Corps soldiers were indeed "lying around": the dead and dying from the repeated assaults at Laurel Hill. Since the Army of the Potomac had crossed the Rapidan on May 4, an estimated 27,621 of its soldiers had been killed, wounded, or captured, 11,982 of them from Warren's 5th Corps.[7]

The scenario of that day's action would play out again and again during the Overland Campaign. Based on inadequate and often unheeded information about the enemy's positions and strengths, Grant maintained an ironclad belief that Lee would respond to any incursion he made by stripping his defenses in some other sector. Grant would subsequently hurl frontal assaults against still fully manned fortifications, nor, when these attacks failed, did the lieutenant general learn from experience. Grant seemed unable to abandon or modify the tactic. While I am averse to trying to psychoanalyze historical figures, the word "perseveration" does come to mind. It refers to the behavior of repeating an action again and again, regardless of the outcome, in response to a particular stimulus. Ironically, while Grant and Meade concentrated their attention on Hancock's maneuvers and Warren's futile assault on the Federal right, General Ambrose Burnside, on the extreme Federal left, had inadvertently marched his corps around the rebel right flank and was nearing Spotsylvania Court House. Here was the golden opportunity Grant had been waiting for, but as he was unaware of the advantage Burnside had gained, it slipped through Grant's fingers, when he ordered the 9th Corps to withdraw and regain its connection to the 6th Corps. The great unmet need for cavalry reconnaissance was never more critical.[8]

On May 10, a partially successful attack by twelve regiments under the command of Colonel Emory Upton led the new commander of the 6th Corps, Horatio Wright, to suggest that another attack would bring further success. This brought Grant's engineer, Colonel Comstock, to the Union left to choose the place where a grand assault could be made on the enemy's lines on May 12. Pouring rain hampered visibility, and Comstock became lost and wandered off all the way to the far left where Burnside's corps was positioned. It was therefore near dark when Comstock and the 2nd Corps officers accompanying him approached the site of Upton's previous attack, the Mule Shoe, a bulge or salient in the enemy line. Regardless of the lack of visibility, this spot was chosen for Hancock's assault early the next morning, May 12. It was a promising location in that one could approach through woods to within a few hundred feet of the enemy's line, a far different situation from the open fields other corps had to cross to reach the rebel entrenchments. Leaving only pickets behind at its former position on the far Federal right, the 2nd Corps was withdrawn and shifted to the left for the next morning's assault. Hancock would be taking up a position on the 6th Corps's left, which would support the 2nd Corps's assault by demonstrating against another portion of the salient. Burnside and Warren got the unenviable orders to be ready both to assault the enemy fortifications on their respective fronts and to send some

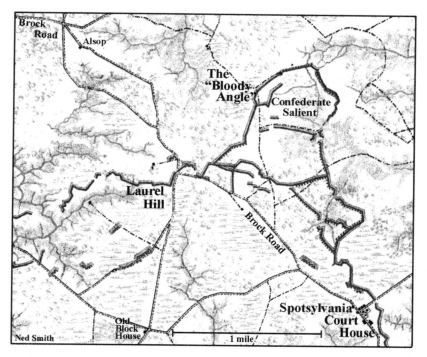

Confederate defenses at Spotsylvania, May 10.
Adapted from Plate XCVI, OR Atlas and sketch map by Jed Hotchkiss, 2nd Corps,
Army of Northern Virginia; Library of Congress.

portion of their corps to support the 2nd and 6th Corps' assaults, all the while keeping their own sectors secure. Being ready either to make an assault or to withdraw at a moment's notice posed challenges for Warren and Burnside that anyone can appreciate.[9]

The 2nd Corps had already withdrawn from the Federal right when Roebling led Colonel John Howard Kitching's brigade of heavy artillerymen to replace Hancock's pickets. Though it was near dawn when Roebling arrived, he found that Hancock's pickets had already withdrawn, and it was broad daylight before he was able to get the artillerymen in place with much skirmishing going on along the line.

While the May 12 attack at the Mule Shoe, or Bloody Angle (as it became known), will always be considered a 2nd Corps fight, here's what was expected of Warren and the 5th Corps on that day: At 6:30 a.m., Meade sent a circular stating that each division commander, when ordered, should send in a strong skirmish line followed by a main line of battle "to draw an initial volley from the enemy." After receiving this fire, they were to charge the enemy's works. Roebling remarked,

> Peremptory and reiterated orders came from Gen. Meade for us to attack along our whole line; skirmishing was going on as usual and we had no evidence that the enemy was weakened in our front. The attack was made by us at 8.15 a.m. and quickly repulsed as was anticipated; it was the 4th or 5th unsuccessful assault made by our men [at Laurel Hill], and it is not a matter of surprise that they had lost all spirit for that kind of work; many of them positively refused to go forward as their previous experience had taught them that to do so was certain death on *that* front.[10]

At this point, constructive communications between Meade, who had just moved his headquarters farther away from the front, and Warren, who reported his men could advance no further, broke down completely. Warren's assaults were intended to prevent Lee from moving soldiers from Warren's sector to assist in his defense at the Mule Shoe, but Grant also believed that Lee had already removed troops from Warren's front. When directed to launch additional attacks, Warren made it perfectly clear that the enemy's earthworks on his front were still fully manned, but Meade nonetheless became furious, seeing Warren's reports as delaying or, perhaps, questioning his orders. His adjutant, General Humphreys, who (unlike Meade) had actually seen Warren's front, forwarded Meade's peremptory order to attack immediately but added this message to his friend: "Dear Warren, Don't hesitate to attack with the bayonet. Meade has assumed the responsibility, and will take the consequences. Your friend, A. A. Humphreys." In Humphreys's mind at least, Meade taking full responsibility for launching the 5th Corps on yet another assault on Laurel Hill somehow absolved Warren of any culpability for sending his men to their deaths for little or no apparent gain. But Warren apparently did not feel exempt from blame, for he would be giving orders to again assault the very same works that, as Humphreys acknowledged, headquarters had previously deemed impregnable.[11]

Warren was again in the position of having to ignore his own and his division commanders' judgment and order his soldiers to make an attack he and his subordinates knew would be a costly failure. Exchanges between Warren and Meade became more strident and discordant, but when Meade told Grant that Warren seemed reluctant to attack, matters came to a head. Orders came from Meade instructing Warren to attack at all hazards, and if his assault was repulsed, Warren was to draw in his right and forward his troops as rapidly as possible to Wright and Hancock. Warren attacked, his terse message to his division commanders being "Do it." One of the enemy's brigade commanders described the Yankees coming across the clearing beautifully in two lines of battle until the Confederate volleys and a battery opened on them. The lines disintegrated, and the survivors broke and ran. The rebel earthworks were manned by the divisions of General Charles Field's Texans and General Joseph Kershaw's South Carolinians, who described Warren's attacks as "two violent assaults" but also reported that they were "easily repulsed with great loss to the enemy." Of the four corps of the Army of the Potomac, the 5th Corps sustained two thousand casualties, or one-third of the Federal total of six thousand for May 12, high numbers for a corps that supposedly did nothing more than hold its place in line while Hancock assaulted the Bloody Angle.[12]

After yet another failed attack on Laurel Hill, Meade then ordered General Humphreys to attend to the shortening of Warren's line and forward 5th Corps troops to the Army of the Potomac's left. As Spotsylvania historian Bill Matter points out, this order was tantamount to the replacement of Warren by Humphreys as 5th Corps commander. Grant had advised Meade, "If Warren fails to attack promptly, send Humphreys to command his corps, and relieve him." Humphreys, when he arrived on Warren's front, promptly called off any further attacks. Though Warren was not officially relieved, Meade and Grant's message to him was crystal clear: they were uninterested in receiving his reports on conditions on his front, nor did they want to hear his suggestions or excuses. The taking of troops from Warren to send to the left was occasioned by the resistance the enemy made to the demonstration by Wright's 6th Corps in support of the 2nd Corps's assault. A nervous Wright was quick to call on the 5th Corps for support, heedless that the latter was already stretched thin covering its own and Hancock's former position. So while Wright called for and got reinforcements from Warren's 5th Corps, when they arrived at the 6th Corps position, instead of having them join or support his battle line, Wright withdrew his own men and had the 5th Corps men replace them at the 6th Corps front. A disgusted Roebling would observe that when General Joseph Bartlett's brigade, which had been sent to assist, received an enemy attack, contrary to Wright's dire alarms, it had "amounted to nothing." A nervous General Wright had called, unnecessarily, for reinforcements from the thoroughly engaged 2nd and 5th Corps. Though Meade that same day had accepted Wright's assessment that the enemy was too strong for him to make an assault and later accepted Humphreys's decision not to attack, he would accept no such judgments from Warren. It had to be a bitter pill for a man who had once held Meade's entire trust. Though the underreporting of casualties muddies the waters, one official Federal report estimated the losses as 4,733 killed, wounded, or missing, though others, as previously mentioned, tallied the losses as much higher, at six thousand casualties for May 12.[13]

Though there was little to celebrate on Warren's front this day, when the news of Hancock's costly but seemingly successful attack at the Mule Shoe, now being called the Bloody Angle, reached the men of the 5th Corps, it was greeted with jubilation, and cheers were given for every one of the twenty pieces of artillery Hancock had captured. While the fight at the Bloody Angle will always be considered a 2nd Corps fight, let it not be forgotten that the 5th and 9th Corps also paid a high price, with attacks on their own fronts and when they reinforced Wright's 6th Corps. Warren and Burnside, told that they had to be ready on May 12 to assault or withdraw, had had to prepare to meet both these incompatible eventualities, orders that would give any conscientious commander a headache. This, in conjunction with the high command's refusal to believe reports from those on the ground that the works they faced were still fully manned and defended by artillery, had to be more than a little discouraging, not to say maddening. As for sending soldiers onto an open field to establish whether sufficient enemy remained to kill them all before they had reached the enemy works, it was akin to sending sheep across a minefield. Warren, on the morning of May 12, was then called upon to send his 4th Division, under the command of Lysander Cutler, to Hancock. Cutler took Peter Lyle's brigade of the 2nd Division along as well. As Roebling reported, when Cutler arrived everything on Hancock's front was, to put it mildly, very much disorganized. Roebling noted, "It soon became apparent that we [the Federals] would do well if we held the captured line and carried off the guns; the enemy still held on firmly opposite the left of the 6th and on the right of the 2d. At 6 p.m. the enemy made an attempt to regain their line, but were repulsed. The firing on the part of Cutler's men continued most of the night. Gen. Rice received his mortal wound; our principal losses were from artillery fire."[14]

While failing to report his casualty numbers for this day, Grant, in his dispatches to Washington, DC, tried to minimize actual losses by asserting he didn't lose entire units like the enemy had. He also declared, again, that Lee's Army of Northern Virginia was disintegrating, having reached its "last ditch." Grant's dispatch to Henry Halleck on May 12 at 6 p.m. reads, "The eighth day of battle closes, leaving between 3,000 and 4,000 prisoners in our hands for the days work, including 2 general officers and over 30 pieces of artillery. The enemy are obstinate and seem to have found the last ditch. We have lost no organization, not even that of a company, while we have destroyed and captured one division (Johnson's), one brigade (Dole's) and one regiment entire of the enemy."[15]

Hancock and his 2nd Corps, on May 12, had given Grant, Meade, and the administration in Washington the victory they'd been wanting. All the appearances of victory were present, as the enemy had been forced to abandon his salient and was pushed to his second line of defense. Many prisoners were captured, as were thirty of the Confederates' colors and an impressive number of their artillery. The fight that became known as the Bloody Angle cost an estimated six thousand Federal casualties, losses conveniently not mentioned in Grant's reports to Washington. General Meade's desire to please the lieutenant general seemed, at this point, to know no bounds. When he wrote to his wife of the great victory on May 12, Meade also commented, "Our losses have been frightful; I do not like to estimate them." Yet, when Grant commented to Meade several days later that he regretted their heavy losses, now amounting to more than thirty-three thousand for the campaign, Meade replied, "We can't do these little tricks without loss." He was apparently under the impression that his willingness to agree with and take up all Grant's wants and suggestions would reap rewards, for on May 13 he was informed that Grant had recommended both him and William T. Sherman for promotion to major general in the regular army. Grant said that he would not like to see one promoted before the other, but that was just what happened: both Sherman and Sheridan would be appointed major generals before Meade. Stanton suggested that Meade should not be promoted until he took Richmond. Grant concurred.[16]

After the fight at the Bloody Angle, General Grant's patron in Congress, Representative Elihu Washburne, carried a letter from the lieutenant general to Washington, DC, in which Grant enthusiastically reported to Halleck,

We have now ended the 6th day of fighting. The result up to this time is much in our favor. But our losses have been heavy as well as those of the enemy. We have lost to this time eleven general officers killed, wounded and missing, and probably twenty thousand men. I think the loss of the enemy must be greater—we have taken over four thousand prisoners in battle, while he has taken from us but few except a few stragglers. I am now sending back to Belle Plain all my wagons for a fresh supply of provisions and ammunition, and propose to fight it out on this line if it takes all summer.

It would indeed take all summer (and the next fall, winter, and spring as well), with Roebling's fate irrevocably linked to that of General Warren and the men of the 5th Corps. However difficult the campaign had been to date, they had many hard and challenging days ahead. Roebling described the 5th Corps's position on the rainy night of May 12, holding the Army of the Potomac's extreme right flank with only Samuel Crawford's division and the green heavy artillerymen. A dark night of rain had turned the country around the 5th Corps headquarters in an old sawmill northeast of Laurel Hill into a sea of mud. Roebling remarked that there was great apprehension as to what would happen if the enemy attacked Crawford; as he observed, "The cavalry being all gone, there was nothing to give us any warning on our right flank." When Crawford's skirmish line pushed out the morning of May 13, the men found that the enemy was still in their front "in full force"—if anything, they were stronger than the day before. Warren and the 5th Corps anxiously awaited the return of Griffin's and Cutler's divisions, which had been sent to bolster the 2nd and 6th Corps's positions. It is perhaps just as well that Robert E. Lee had much to distract him from the precarious condition of the Federal right flank. The terrible battle fought at the Bloody Angle had resulted in his having to secure his new line at the base of the salient. But Lee had also received news that day that Sheridan had finally found J. E. B. Stuart, and the commander of the Confederates' cavalry had been killed in the fight at Yellow Tavern.[17]

23

The Fighting at Spotsylvania Continues

THE EXTREME RIGHT FLANK OF THE ARMY OF THE POTOMAC ON THE morning of May 12 was being guarded by one division of the 5th Corps, that of the often unreliable General Samuel Crawford. All other divisions had been sent to support the assaults by the 2nd and 6th Corps the previous day. Gouverneur Warren also had at his disposal on his right flank the inexperienced heavy artillerymen, an unknown quantity should they be called upon in an emergency. After a thankfully quiet night, it was with considerable relief that Warren greeted the return of Charles Griffin's division, which had been sent to support the attacks on the Bloody Angle but had not been needed or engaged. Lysander Cutler's division soon followed Griffin back to the 5th Corps's fold, though the 6th Corps was once again calling for assistance, causing Peter Lyle's brigade to be sent to General Wright. News also came from General Hancock's front that, while he had maintained control of much of the Mule Shoe, the rebels were successfully defending the line they had fallen back to at the base of the salient.[1]

In the early evening, as rain began to fall again, Warren was ordered to be ready to withdraw and move to the left, and at 10 p.m. Griffin's division moved out. Washington Roebling's report reveals the difficulties of what they were being asked to do: "we were expected to march all night, get into position on the left of [Ambrose] Burnside's [Corps] in an unknown country, in the midst of an Egyptian darkness, up to our knees in the mud, and assault the enemy's position which we had never seen, at 4 o'clock in the morning, in conjunction with the 9th Corps, who had been whipped the day before, and felt in fine spirits for such work."

Roebling said that the route of the march was across a field and down a narrow muddy road that led to the shallow Ny River. After the troops had waded across the Ny, there was no road, and they were sent across more fields and through woods where, thankfully, a track had been cut. Adding to the 5th Corps woes, "a dense fog began to settle, so that not even the numerous fires that had been built to guide the column could be seen." As exhausted men began to straggle, Roebling was sent ahead to locate General Burnside, but neither he nor his second in command, General John G. Parke, seemed able to offer Roebling any guidance. Finally, one of Burnside's brigade commanders, Colonel Elisha Marshall, directed Roebling and the 5th Corps to their position on the 9th Corps's left flank.[2]

The night move had not gone well; getting lost and the exhaustion of marching all night had taken a toll. Roebling described, as day dawned, how "the only troops on hand were 1,200 fagged out men of Griffin's Div. And it was fully 7 o'clock before Gen. Cutler got 1,300 of his men together." George Meade confided to U. S. Grant that the condition of the men made it doubtful they could do anything that day, but when Warren expressed the same opinion, Meade ordered him to deploy for an assault, though later notifying him that the order was suspended. Here was found a skirmish line of dismounted cavalrymen holding entrenchments previously occupied by Burnside, and Warren's tired men took their places. No rest for the weary, for the enemy soon came calling to see who had moved into the neighborhood. Skirmishing commenced, and it became light enough to see the enemy's lengthy entrenchments near Spotsylvania Court House. It also became apparent that the enemy's artillery position on a high hill near the Jett House would make the 5th Corps's position near the Beverly House untenable. General Griffin had spotted the advantages of the Jett House position and sent a few hundred of General Romeyn Ayres's regulars to take the hill. They successfully drove off the enemy's cavalry, which had held the position, but soon relinquished the hill to Emory Upton's Federals, sent by General Meade. Before Upton was established, a large contingent of Confederates from General A. P. Hill's corps took back the hill, while Generals Meade and Wright, who had been watching nearby, came perilously close to being captured. The 6th Corps was ordered to retake the hill, but failing that, General Ayres's soldiers eventually regained the position that evening.[3]

Meade was grateful for Warren's assistance in securing the Jett House hill with the additional benefit of giving him and General Wright time to escape enemy capture. But the good feeling would not last. When Burnside expressed worry that he was about to be attacked, Meade ordered Warren to attack the well-manned fortifications on his front if the enemy assaulted Burnside. Warren's suggestion that it might be just as well to assist Burnside directly rather than making a frontal attack on the enemy's earthworks annoyed Meade, who let the order stand. The men of the 5th Corps stood under arms from 5 p.m. to 9 p.m.; then they spent the night lying on their arms, until the order was finally rescinded. More rain on May 13 through 17 brought additional actions to a halt, and muddy roads meant rations and forage for the 5th Corps were in short supply. When Warren was finally able to bring up his supply wagons, Meade insisted that he advance his pickets, which was apt to bring on a shelling from the enemy. Although Roebling had been sent with the unenviable job of bringing Meade a sketch and an explanation of Warren's actions, his attempt to get food and forage to his men, the disgruntled Army of the Potomac commander nonetheless reported Warren's delay to Grant, who responded that his suggestion of an advance was just a matter of wanting to know the state of affairs on Warren's front. Luckily for Roebling, a visit by Comstock to the 5th Corps front confirmed that an assault there would gain nothing but Federal casualties, and Warren was thereby spared another costly advance. Warren's engineers, meanwhile, were occupied with building roads, including one that would give access to the Jett House without the need to cross the Ny River. Roads and platforms were also constructed for Warren's artillery, some capable of enfilading the enemy's line. Warren would have need of good positions for his guns, for on the night of May 17, while the 5th Corps held the army's entire front, the 2nd, 6th, and 9th Corps shifted to the Federals' right in preparation for yet another assault at the Angle on May 18. As Roebling described it, the Army of the Potomac was going to "see if they could find the Rebels anapping," but, he added, "they had at least one eye open and were protected by acres of impenetrable slashing; the expedition was unsuccessful." Roebling's flippant assessment aside, the Federal assault at the Bloody Angle that day was a grim affair, with the enemy ready and waiting for the Unionists, who were attempting to maneuver over a battlefield still covered with the dead from the fighting on May 12.[4]

At daylight on May 18, Roebling took Warren's Maryland Brigade and a contingent of Colonel John Kitching's heavy artillerymen to once again establish a Federal picket line at the Jett House, which General Wright had relinquished. The position was once again returned to the 6th Corps's care. Roebling then established Kitching's men and a battery on the Federal right, across the Ny near the Harris House. They were joined there by Robert Tyler's contingent of heavy artillerymen. Around 5 p.m., heavy firing was heard at the Harris Farm, and Roebling went to see what the matter was. Roebling found Kitching and his battery heavily engaged and General Tyler forming up to bring his reserve force up on Kitching's right. The enemy had set a Federal wagon train and its cavalry escort on the run, with many riders and driverless wagons flying by, closely followed by rebel skirmishers. Roebling was impressed by Tyler's advance, which, he stated, was made in "fine style, two ranks deep." The rebel assault was plainly being made in force, the Federals taking prisoners from General John B. Gordon's brigade and General Jubal A. Early's division of Richard Ewell's corps. Roebling returned to 5th Corps headquarters to bring up the Maryland Brigade, and Crawford's division was summoned to come to their aid.[5]

When Roebling returned to Kitching and Tyler, he found the heavy artillerymen still holding their own, though many wounded were being brought to the rear. He observed,

> Tyler's command had never been in action before, but were well-drilled; the fighting was done as if on parade, and loss correspondingly heavy; the idea of fighting under cover seemed unknown. The whole line, perfectly dressed stood unprotected in an open field, and fired as if on drill, scores of men falling all the time; then yards in their rear was a fence in a little raised bank which would have given them very good cover and enabled them to do the same execution; I think however that this unbroken front of Heavys, with new muskets and uniforms, taking the Rebel fire without flinching scared back the rebels as much as the musketry fire. A thick cloud of powder smoke hung over everything, especially in the ravine between the two lines and I am sure that many of our men were killed by our own fire. Gen. [Henry] Hunt and I myself were fired at in that way. The whole affair reflected great credit upon the Heavy Artillery, and the honors belong exclusively to them, and the Maryland Brigade.

Roebling estimated the Federal loss on May 19 at thirteen hundred killed and wounded. So while given a harsh baptism by fire, the artillerymen had proved to themselves and to their Army of the Potomac comrades that they were a force to be reckoned with.[6]

As the Maryland Brigade went into action this day, it happened that the 1st Maryland Veteran Regiment, consisting of the men who had reenlisted, was coming down the road from Fredericksburg on its return from furlough. Finding the enemy across the road, they pitched in, without waiting for orders, driving him off and effecting a junction with their comrades in the Maryland Brigade. The Marylanders took up a position on the right of the 1st Maine Heavies, who were making a stand near the Alsop Farm. The 1st Maine's casualties were typical for all the heavy artillerymen this day. The Maine men, who were experiencing combat for the first time, lost four hundred of their members, standing shoulder to shoulder in the open field. Around this time, General David Birney's large division arrived, though, Roebling's account clearly states, it did not become engaged before darkness fell and the fighting was over. This did not prevent General Grant from crediting Birney's division with saving the day on the Federal right. The enemy returned to its own lines, disappointed in its hopes of acquiring a Federal wagon train and threatening the Unionist right flank. The heavy artillerymen, new infantrymen in the making, and the Marylanders had done a good day's work. But Roebling estimated that the Federal dead outnumbered the enemy's four to one. The next day he was sent out to assist with the withdrawal of the heavy artillerymen and Birney's division, and his reconnaissance a mile out along the enemy's path of withdrawal showed that only a few rebel stragglers remained on the 5th Corps's right.[7]

The men of the 5th Corps and the Army of the Potomac could only have been glad to hear they would be leaving the battlefield at Spotsylvania. They were leaving behind eighteen thousand of their comrades, many of them unburied on fields now in rebel hands. Confederate losses were estimated at nine thousand, though half that number were prisoners taken on May 12 at the Bloody Angle. Illustrating the amount of ammunition fired at Spotsylvania, Confederate ordnance officers who "mined" the battlefield collected 122,000 pounds of lead, which would be recast into balls and fired at the Federals before the Overland Campaign was over. In considering General Warren's experiences at Spotsylvania, one of his biographers, Emerson Taylor, writes that he was "a man of special gifts and temperament, a scientific soldier, he takes part in a rat fight. Again and again he is compelled to order frontal attacks against entrenchments, which could succeed only at ruinous cost, when, as he is perfectly aware, sounder tactical methods would accomplish better results."

Taylor goes on to say that the effects of the carnage, as well as the knowledge that he had lost the confidence of his commanders, had a negative effect upon Warren. He likely realized that in order to succeed in Grant's armies, one had to do what one was told immediately without question or comment, and without regard for the consequences to one's men. Grant continued to report to Washington that the enemy was "whipped" and that the men of the Army of the Potomac were "in the best of spirits and feel greatest confidence in ultimate success." By contrast, Henry Halleck was sending Grant advice on how to deal with the prevalence of straggling and desertion, suggesting that Grant should hold drumhead courts-martial and execute the miscreants by way of example.[8]

Massaponax Church, General Grant leaning over a map held by
General Meade.
Library of Congress.

As the Army of the Potomac prepared to leave Spotsylvania on May 20, Roebling directed General David A. Russell's 1st Division of the 6th Corps to its position to relieve Birney's division on the extreme right, where it had defended the Army of the Potomac's flank overnight. That morning, orders had been issued to the army for an ultimate change of base to the White House, and the 2nd Corps was the first to depart. Russell's men preceded the 5th Corps, with Crawford, Kitching, and the artillery following. Griffin's and Cutler's divisions moved away from the front together, when the enemy came out of his entrenchment in an aggressive pursuit of Cutler. Hidden from enemy view, Russell's division, which had lingered behind, laid a neat trap for the pursuing rebels that stopped them in their tracks. It was hoped that by a rapid movement, the Army of the Potomac could place itself across R. E. Lee's line of communication and between the Army of Northern Virginia and Richmond. During its rapid march to the east, the 5th Corps encountered

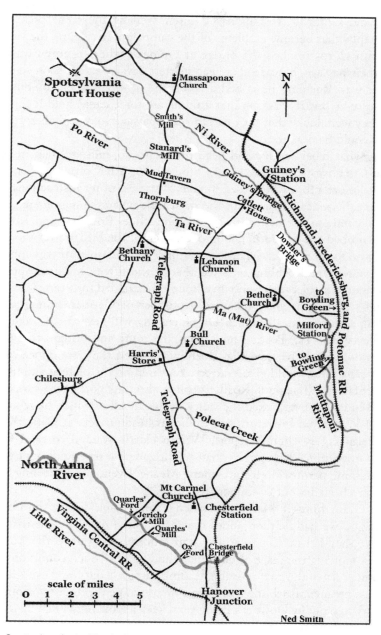

Spotsylvania to North Anna.
Adapted from Plate LXXXI, OR Atlas.

Meade and Grant at Massaponax Church, viewing the scene preserved in photographs that became emblems of the campaign. By 5 p.m., the vanguard of the 5th Corps reached the bridge at Guinea's, where enemy cavalry disputed their passage, but Meade's headquarters cavalry escort soon sent them on their way. Roebling described a landscape of swamps, cut by dikes that could serve as breastworks, so that a moderate force could hold it for a long time. They were lucky that they had forced a passage so quickly before such a defense could be organized.[9]

But what rebel cavalry had been unable to do, rain and bad maps did, for the latter two stumbling blocks brought the 5th Corps to a temporary stop. Unsure at a fork which road to take, Warren sent for instructions; in the meantime, he sent Crawford out the right fork, where he met enemy cavalry videttes a mile and a half out. At the same time, Roebling and Kitching's brigade probed the left fork, taking possession of the bridge over the Ta and pushing on to try to reach Madison's Ordinary (if possible). It was apparently a hard march, for Roebling reported that of the fifteen hundred apparently tender-footed artillerymen, only five hundred straggled into camp that night. Kitching's men apparently included a number of German immigrants, for Roebling commented, "So much Dutch cursing will never be heard again in the valley of the Ta." Posting men along the route and bridges that the 5th Corps would likely be traveling, Roebling realized the importance of these positions, for they would give Warren a foothold on the plateau and its major thoroughfare, the Telegraph Road. Roebling also took note of the surrounding wooded hills that overlooked the valley of the Ta, all of which he reported to General Warren on his return to 5th Corps headquarters at Catlett's house. Upon receiving Roebling's report, Warren clearly wanted to send Cutler's division to reinforce Kitching's exhausted brigade but dared not do it without first obtaining permission from General Meade. Eventually, Roebling led one of Cutler's brigades out to support Kitching.[10]

As Grant himself would acknowledge years later, during the Overland Campaign, "we had neither guides nor maps to tell us where the roads were or where they led to. Engineer and staff officers were put to the dangerous duty of supplying the place of both maps and guides." Such conditions found Roebling at dawn the next morning leading a brigade out to relieve Kitching's tired, hungry men. Roebling had been able to scrape together two companies of cavalry to scout by Downer's Bridge and keep a look out. When he went out to check on his cavalry vidette at Lebanon Church, two hundred yards from the church he found an enemy wagon train and ambulances moving rapidly south, apparently unguarded by any troops. Roebling watched the continuous stream of wagons for nearly half an hour, while the vidette told him how he been hearing the wagons rumbling all night. Despite his best efforts, Roebling was unable to get the cavalry's commander, Lieutenant Colonel Edmund Pope, to attack the train. Roebling sent a dispatch to A. A. Humphreys at 6 a.m. on May 22, 1864: "I have just returned from the road leading to Nancy Wright's, on the Telegraph road, and was at a point half a mile from the Telegraph road. A rebel wagon train was passing south on the Telegraph road and had been passing since daylight. Our cavalry under Lieutenant-Colonel Pope are out there, and can capture it, I think, if they try. General Warren being asleep I send this in my own name."

Roebling would later lament, "Tried to get Lt. Col Pope to make a dash on the wagon train but he would not do it. Here was a chance to capture the whole of Lee's wagon train; never was the want of cavalry more painfully felt. Such opportunities are only presented once in a campaign and should not be lost."[11]

While this unfortunate drama played out at Lebanon Church, Grant was beginning to have second thoughts about the situation in which he had placed the corps of the Army of the Potomac. He had allowed them to become widely separated—some even say that he had purposely isolated Hancock's 2nd Corps in hopes of luring Lee to forsake his entrenchments and come out to attack the lone Federal corps. But by May 22, this had not happened, nor was Grant so confident that this had been a good idea, and orders were given that would bring the corps within three or four miles of one another. By the time the 5th Corps was allowed to advance, there were only two roads upon which the four corps of the Army of the Potomac could travel. Grant naively suggested that by using farm and plantation roads and impressing local guides, they could probably find a road for each corps. Unfortunately, the Federals were relying on maps so bad that they showed roads that did not exist, while neglecting to show the ones that did. The men of the 5th Corps were stopping at houses to ask for directions as they tried to navigate this landscape of swamps, drainage ditches, and streams. Nonetheless, with hard marching, Warren was running only an hour behind schedule to reach his goal for the night, Harris's Store. But Grant's attack of caution had cost the Army of the Potomac, for Lee's rear guard was estimated now to be several hours ahead. Warren, again by hard marching, was able to catch up with it. Though Griffin's 3rd Brigade failed in their attempt to capture the enemy's horse artillery, left to delay the Federal advance, they at least managed to send the rebel horsemen on their way. But by the time Warren reached Harris's Store, the Army of Northern Virginia had arrived at Hanover Station in force. All indications were that more hard fighting was in the Army of the Potomac's future.[12]

While the constant movements and the severity of the campaign had seriously disrupted the stream of daily letters between Roebling and Emily Warren, Washington did finally find time to drop a reassuring letter to his anxious sweetheart. His take on how things were going is of interest when compared with Grant's glowing reports. Once again, the accuracy of the reported Army of the Potomac's losses is called into question, for Roebling writes that as of May 15, the 5th Corps had less than half the number of men with which it had started the campaign. As for the spirits and expectations of the combatants, Roebling wrote, "Uncle Robert Lee isn't licked yet by a long shot and if we are not mighty careful he will beat us yet. I think we have done very well to avoid that fate so far. Our fighting so far has been very severe & every one is played out, including your humble servant." He told Emily that her brother, "G. K. [Warren,] has a heavy disgust on." Several day later, he described to Emily the 5th Corps's experience at Spotsylvania of "still pegging away at the same old place, and our prospects have not improved one bit. We are laughing ourselves sick over the glorious news contained in the Yankee papers; It is so comical to read about great victories when none existed; if you heard the shelling that is going on now around our ears you wouldn't think that the rebs have given up; the shells whistle along like flocks of wild geese at the rate of 30 per minute."

While Washington generally tempered the news he sent Emily out of consideration for her concern for her two brothers and her fiancé at the front, on this occasion he reported that a shell had landed in their headquarters and, thankfully, not burst. He also wrote that General Warren was enthusiastically taking possession of it to add to his collection of "shells of the battlefields."

Emily's reply apparently expressed much apprehension for her dear ones, for Washington's next letter attempted to reassure her. He reminded her that any bad news would travel to her much more quickly than the good. Thus, Roebling suggested, "when you hear nothing just hope for the best." Roebling described how things stood as the Federals left Spotsylvania: "Our matters here are at a deadlock; unless the rebs commit some great error they will hold us in check until kingdom come; Neither of our commanding Generals seem to be smart enough to do anything beyond mediocrity. Everyone knows that if Lee were to come out of his entrenchments we could whip him, but Bob Lee is a little too smart for us. Well we can afford to wait, we have plenty to eat and the country is very fine around here—we feel very dirty, haven't changed clothes for three weeks, because we can't get at our wagons."

These 5th Corps's wagons were the very ones rescued by the heavy artillerymen, and Roebling was full of praise for these untrained soldiers who fought off the veterans of Ewell's corps.[13]

North Anna, Totopotomoy, and Cold Harbor

THE PASSAGE FROM SPOTSYLVANIA TO THE NORTH ANNA SAW WASHING-ton Roebling constantly in the saddle. As he told his worrying Emmie, from dawn until the wee hours of the night, there was little or no time for writing the letters that consoled her. He had, in fact, during this movement experienced a three-day stretch of no sleep at all, while he was trying to locate roads and river crossings and find the rebels before they found him. Writing just after the 5th Corps had been the only corps to make it across the North Anna, and having successfully fought off a substantial enemy assault, a tired Washington told Emily that they believed they had finally caught the Army of Northern Virginia out of a good defensive position and could finally force R. E. Lee to retreat back into the defenses of Richmond. Reminding Emily that he would be celebrating his twenty-seventh birthday in a few days, Washington asked her to bake him a cake and not to worry so but instead try to be of good cheer.[1]

Despite Roebling's optimism, U. S. Grant's attack of caution on May 22 had rather defeated the purpose of his intended movements, for the time taken to regroup the Army of the Potomac's corps before their next collision with the Army of Northern Virginia at the North Anna had allowed Lee not only to avoid an open-field confrontation with Grant but also to place his army in another deceptively strong defensive position. As the 5th Corps attempted to find a road to and a crossing for the North Anna River near Mt. Carmel Church, it bumped into Hancock's 2nd Corps cavalry escort, commanded by General Alfred Torbert. Informing Gouverneur Warren that he was on the road the 2nd Corps expected to travel, Torbert inadvertently did the 5th Corps a good turn. Abandoning the road for Winfield Hancock's

Jericho Mills pontoon bridge.
Library of Congress.

use, Warren and his staff began searching for an alternate route and a crossing further up the river. Roebling struck the river and saw places of crossing, but all showed the presence of the enemy as well. Meanwhile, it was said that there was a crossing at a place called Jericho Mills, but where was that? Warren soon found a guide, an elderly black man who had not been on that road for fifty-three years but thought he could remember. Blessed with a good memory, the old man led the 5th Corps another 2.5 miles to Jericho Mills. There was no bridge there—merely a tow boat ferry above a dam—nor was there an appreciable enemy presence. The river was fordable, if you didn't mind wading in waist-high water, and General Joseph Bartlett's 3rd Brigade of Charles Griffin's 1st division did just that.[2]

The whistling of enemy locomotives in the distance only strengthened Warren's resolve to reach the other side of the North Anna. Though completely out of touch with Army of the Potomac headquarters and without support, Warren took the initiative to cross the river. While Roebling was sent back to

Mt. Carmel Church to guide Horatio Wright's 6th Corps to the Jericho Mills crossing, a pontoon bridge was installed at the ford, but before the 6th Corps could be brought up, A. P. Hill's corps launched an attack on the newly arrived Unionists. Lysander Cutler's division broke under the enemy onslaught, but Griffin's division and the heavies held their ground. A well-placed Federal battery brought the rebel breakthrough to a halt, sending Hill back to the Virginia Central Railroad line he had been tasked with protecting. Warren's fight at the North Anna was heard four miles away at Army of the Potomac headquarters, and even Charles Dana enthused to his Washington administrators about the enemy attack Warren had "triumphantly repulsed." George Meade sent congratulations to Warren, but his benevolent mood was roughly terminated there at the North Anna when Dana read aloud a telegram from W. T. Sherman to Grant. According to Meade's aide, Theodore Lyman, "Sherman therein told Grant that the Army of the West [Sherman's army], having fought, could now afford to maneuver, and that, if his [Grant's] inspiration could make the Army of the Potomac do its share, success would crown our efforts." Meade took this, understandably, as an insult both to himself and to his army.[3]

In the coming days, the Army of the Potomac confronted Lee's well-defended position at the North Anna, and though Lee was said to be ailing, he once again brought Grant's army to a standstill. On May 24, Roebling scouted in advance of the 5th Corps's lines far out on the Army of the Potomac right near Noel's Station, where Warren reported that "good" cavalry would be of much assistance. Was it a coincidence that this day also saw the return of Philip Sheridan's cavalry and that the commander's wildly exaggerated report of his triumphs, written two years later, makes an accurate consideration of the cavalry's accomplishments quite difficult? According to Sheridan, he experienced "constant success and the almost total annihilation of the Rebel Cavalry. We marched when and where we pleased; were always the attacking party, and always successful." Sheridan also essentially reported to Meade that he could have taken Richmond if he had wanted to. One can't help but wonder why he didn't! Whatever Phil Sheridan had accomplished, one must consider the steep price tag paid by the Army of the Potomac in the number of lives and battles lost due to the woeful lack of cavalry reconnaissance and screening. In the ensuing stalemate at the North Anna, one of the few real accomplishments for the Army of the Potomac was the destruction of a few miles of the enemy's railroad, but Roebling commented that "a good working party would repair it again in 10 days."[4]

On May 24 the awkward command structure in which Ambrose Burnside's independent command reported to Grant was corrected, and the 9th

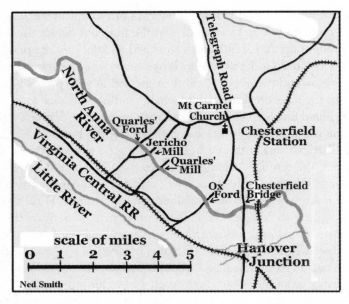

North Anna.
Adapted from Plate LXXXI, OR Atlas.

Corps became part of the Army of the Potomac. On the 5th Corps's left, Roebling assisted—one might say, tried to oversee—Samuel Crawford's division's attempt to clear the way for Burnside's 9th Corps to cross the river at Ox Ford. Roebling reported that that ford was a poor one, which, combined with stubborn resistance from a well-placed enemy, prevented Burnside's crossing. When Grant was finally convinced that Lee had no intention of retreating into the Richmond defenses, on May 26 his orders again set the 5th Corps into motion, and once again the rains came. That dark night they trudged through mud, crossing the North Anna at Quarles' Mill and heading for Hanovertown on the Pamunkey. The rainy night was followed by a hot and dry day with water scarce and reliable roads heading in the right direction even scarcer. The tired soldiers halted several miles from the Mangohick Church. Early the next morning Roebling began a thorough reconnaissance of the area in order to push through to the corps's next position, with orders to deploy with its left resting on the road from Harris's Store to Linney's and its right on a little run west of Bockenbrough's. With a mile of line to defend on the Army of the Potomac's left flank, Warren was stretched necessarily very thin and was forced to plug a hole at his center with unsupported artillery.

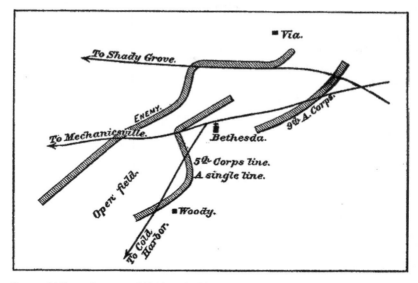

General Warren's map of Bethesda Church, accompanying his report of June 3, 1864.
OR 36, III, 536.

Roebling noted in his report for May 28 that when Sheridan's cavalry were engaged that day beyond Harris's Store, the 2nd Corps on the 5th Corps's right was called upon to send a brigade to Sheridan's assistance at Haw's Shop. It seems this day Sheridan was neither marching when and where he pleased nor always succeeding, thanks to his encounter with some of the enemy cavalry he had previously "annihilated."[5]

Scouting for roads and bridges and avoiding unexpected collisions with the enemy were not the only dangerous occupations Roebling was performing. Thinking back over the passage from the North Anna to the Totopotomoy, Washington wrote a flippant letter to "My dear old woman," telling Emily that he had also been struck by lightning and fallen down a well, though he was none the worse for it. "We are certainly traveling about at the most astonishing rate—Wherever we chance to drop down the people express the most unbounded surprise at our appearance, it seems to them as if we fall from the skies." In this letter, headed "Patrick Henry's farm, Hanover Co. Virginia, 4 a.m. May 29, 1864," Washington admired the surrounding countryside as a great improvement over where they had been, for he found fine estates encased in bowers of roses. As for the Army of the Potomac's progress, he commented that they were now only seventeen miles from Richmond, adding, "The joke of it is the Johnnies thought we were retreating and I dare say they were a little surprised to find us after them so soon." The coming days would see Roebling acting as courier and scout between Warren, Burnside, and Hancock, attempting to coordinate their movements and positions.[6]

On the morning of May 29, instead of providing the Army of the Potomac with much-needed information about roads, rivers, and Confederate positions, Sheridan's cavalry retired from the front to recover from their ordeal at Haw's Shop. Therefore, the infantry was ordered to make a reconnaissance in force of the various roads on the Army of the Potomac's front. General David Gregg kindly notified Warren that his cavalry pickets had been ordered to withdraw; yet headquarters assured Warren that Federal cavalry would protect his left flank. Sent out to find Sheridan's troopers, Roebling was unable to locate one nearer than four miles away, causing Warren to send out one of his brigades to guard his left flank. Warren also requested that Burnside's 9th Corps be brought up to plug the sizable gap between the 5th Corps's right flank and the left of the 2nd Corps. When Griffin's 1st Division made it across the river and began driving the enemy, the scene was reminiscent of the Federal' advance at North Anna, for Hancock's corps had been unable to dislodge the enemy in order to cross over. Only the 5th Corps had managed to make it across the Totopotomoy, once again making it the only corps with a force on the same side of the river as the enemy. The 9th Corps did try to come up between the 5th Corps and the 2nd, but confusion reigned. General Burnside complained bitterly that every time he caught up with Griffin's line, Griffin advanced, leaving him behind. Meade scolded Warren for not keeping Burnside, who incidentally also had orders to advance, apprised of his movements.[7]

Reports of enemy movement in force toward the 5th Corps's position on the left flank of the Army of the Potomac, as well as the appearance of rebel cavalry on his left, had kept Warren on the alert. He felt it necessary to warn the brigade commander he sent to protect his left flank not to rely on the Federal cavalry, for once again Roebling could find none of Sheridan's troopers closer than four miles away, far enough to allow real trouble to slip through unheeded and unimpeded. Despite Warren's concerns for the left flank of the army, he and the other corps commanders were ordered to once again advance his whole line along his front to feel for the enemy. Roebling reported that a black man had told him that the enemy was at Shady Grove Church, and when Griffin advanced, he found this to be true, with Richard Ewell's corps entrenched and waiting for him, and Roebling described a swampy ravine that would have to be crossed before any assault could be made on the well-placed enemy. But the sounds of a confrontation on Warren's left flank and rear were increasing, for Confederate general Robert Rodes's division from Jubal Early's corps was attacking on Warren's left near Bethesda Church and overwhelming Crawford's brigade left there to protect the vulnerable flank. Pursued by the triumphant rebels, a well-placed Federal battery finally checked the enemy, pulling Crawford's force from the brink of disaster. General Warren's arrival on the scene enabled a successful defense against Rodes's further attempts to pass the Federal left flank and gain its rear, but Warren longed to bring Griffin's division from his right as insurance against the enemy's designs on the Army of the Potomac's left flank.[8]

Shortly after 3 p.m. on May 30, Warren reported the enemy's attack to Meade's headquarters and requested that Burnside relieve Griffin's division on the 5th Corps's right to allow the latter to join in the defense of the Federal left. Roebling was sent to urge Burnside's relief of Griffin's troops, first having to convince the 9th Corps commander that Warren had requested that he replace Griffin on the 5th Corps's right, not send a contingent to the 5th Corps's left. To further complicate matters, initially Warren's request was inexplicably denied, Meade asserting that the front Griffin's division was covering would be too long a line for Burnside's 9th Corps to occupy. Nor was Meade willing to release Burnside from acting as reserve for the army, though it is hard to know what he was saving the 9th Corps for, if not for the sort of emergency occurring on his army's left flank. The uproar on the Federal left could be heard clearly at Meade's headquarters, but the only assistance provided to the 5th Corps this day was Meade's order for Hancock's 2nd Corps to make an assault on their own front, an operation that did nothing to relieve the immediate threats with which Warren was coping. Roebling reported that by 10 p.m. the enemy had been driven from the battlefield on Warren's left, leaving many dead and wounded behind. Confederate commanders squabbled among themselves, with Early asserting that if Richard Anderson had attacked Griffin on his front while he attacked Warren's left flank and rear, they could have destroyed the 5th Corps. Luckily for Warren and the Army of the Potomac, Anderson had not come out of his entrenchments to assault Griffin and thereby make good on Early's idea. Burnside did eventually relieve Griffin's division on Warren's right flank some seventeen hours after Warren's initial request. As for the cavalry that were supposed to be guarding the Army of the Potomac's left flank that day, Sheridan reported that he had driven the rebel cavalry to Cold Harbor in a "very handsome affair, and that he had had his troopers connected to the 5th Corps left the entire day." Since the rebels' cavalry and an entire division had moved

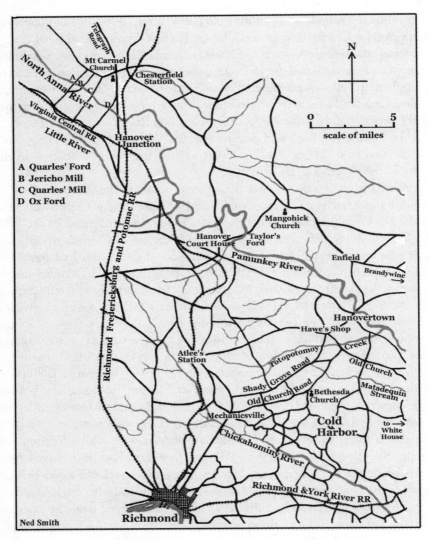

Totopotomoy to Cold Harbor.
Adapted from Plate LXXXI, OR Atlas.

unobstructed around Warren's left flank to make an attack, another way of looking at it was that Sheridan lied.[9]

Roebling spent the next day in the saddle reconnoitering and found that the enemy had established a new line 1.5 miles from Bethesda Church. Roebling was luckier, or perhaps more careful, than two of new division commander General Henry Lockwood's staff members, who were both captured while scouting on their front. Roebling reported that the 6th Corps would be moving that night to the Federal left, to a place called Cold Harbor. The 5th Corps would be remaining where it was, except its line had to be well extended. When Roebling went the next morning to watch the enemy's movements, he witnessed the rebels moving double-quick toward Cold Harbor, their flankers directly in front of the 5th Corps's skirmish line. When Roebling reported this to Meade, Meade sent him back to Warren with orders to attack immediately. When Warren launched an attack by two divisions across an open field, the enemy responded with devastating effect with an entrenched rifled battery. The 6th Corps, by June 1, was now somewhere to the 5th Corps's left, some five miles away at Cold Harbor, and Roebling was sent with the Maryland Brigade to try to find General Wright's right flank. The intent was to keep an eye on the gap that would be expected to be filled by General William Smith's 18th Corps, newly transferred from Butler's army at Bermuda Hundred. Delays caused by Grant's staff misdirecting Smith were increasing apprehension that the enemy might already be between Warren and the 6th Corps.[10]

In an attempt to discover where the right flank of Baldy Smith's 18th Corps might be, Roebling was sent to scout the 5th Corps's left. Moving cautiously, he found no enemy until he reached a place with the innocuous name of "Woody's," which showed signs of recent enemy occupation. Mr. Woody told Roebling that a division of Anderson's corps had left a bare ten minutes previously. Roebling, on next encountering the aggressive Emory Upton of the 2nd Corps, suggested that he might want to pursue the newly departing enemy. When Roebling reached 6th Corps headquarters around 1 p.m. on June 1, he found General Wright with the newly arrived General Smith, who had actually arrived at White House landing at midday on the previous day. Smith had served with Grant in the West and was anxious to please him. He therefore started out with ten thousand of his sixteen thousand men who had landed so far and, in a decision that would later have serious repercussions, before his ammunition trains had arrived. But Smith's try for a speedy arrival at the Army of the Potomac front met with failure when Grant's staff misdirected the 18th Corps commander, sending him miles out of his way to a destination a considerable distance from the confrontation brewing at Cold Harbor. And though Grant had reassured Smith that the route he was traveling had been secured, it was overheard at headquarters that Grant would like nothing better than for Lee to strike at Smith's isolated corps. It was not beyond question that the enemy would take such an opportunity, for a Confederate spy had reported the 18th Corps's impending arrival to Lee, the rebel operative having heard the news from the overly garrulous General George Armstrong Custer.[11]

The orders that brought the 6th and 18th Corps to Cold Harbor were prompted by Sheridan's cavalry's having taken possession of the valuable crossroads at that location. Sheridan had then, unfortunately, chosen to abandon it, but Army of the Potomac headquarters insisted he regain the intersection. Sheridan found himself contesting with the six brigades of General Robert Hoke's division, also newly arrived from Bermuda Hundred, for Lee was, as was Grant, receiving fresh reinforcements. While Sheridan struggled to regain possession of Cold Harbor, James Wilson's cavalry were assigned to guard the Army of the Potomac's right flank. He had also been tasked with destroying several railroad bridges on the South Anna but sent word to Meade that his orders had been changed to only protecting the army's flank. Meade sent word that Wilson's orders had indeed *not* been changed and that he was to screen the army's flank *and* destroy the bridges. At this point Wilson declared that he could not, for he had no powder or slow matches to complete the demolition. Once supplied with the needed materials, Wilson managed to destroy two railroad spans, but he was discovered by rebel cavalry, and one of his brigades was cut to pieces. Once again cut off from his army, Wilson didn't return to the army until June 3, when he complained to Meade that the entire cavalry corps should have been detailed to destroy the bridges, not just his division.[12]

Beyond the misdirection of Smith, almost nothing had gone right with the Army of the Potomac's movement to Cold Harbor. With confidence that Sheridan would regain control of Cold Harbor, Wright's 6th Corps had been ordered to march fifteen miles on the night of May 31 to June 1 and reach Cold Harbor by dawn to support Sheridan—another unrealistic timetable for a movement in the dark over unknown roads. Headquarters was unhappy with Wright, who didn't arrive until 9 a.m., well after Sheridan had fought off another attack. But much as he had on the first day at Spotsylvania, when the infantry showed up, Sheridan packed up and rode off, leaving Wright to fight alone on an unknown field. Believing Sheridan was on his way to attack Lee's flank and rear, headquarters would learn the next day that he had done nothing of the kind since "his orders hadn't reached him in time," and when the orders did arrive, he had already dispersed his troops. Dana nonetheless reported to Washington that if only Wright had arrived on time that day, he and Sheridan would have destroyed Lee's army. Roebling, meanwhile, spent many dangerous hours trying to find the elusive flanks of the 6th and 18th Corps.[13]

After Sheridan departed Cold Harbor, Wright felt his isolation and, though encouraged by headquarters to attack, delayed until Smith arrived. The conversation at the 6th Corps headquarters between Generals Smith and Wright, to which Roebling was privy, must have been an interesting one, for, on finally arriving at the front, Smith had realized that his orders would be nearly impossible to fulfill. He had been tasked with forming a line between the 6th Corps at Cold Harbor and the 5th Corps on the Totopotomoy, a line so long and thin that Smith felt he would then be unable to attack. It was a dilemma that Warren and the 5th Corps already knew too well. At this point, Anderson's corps was entrenched on Smith's front, while Wright was facing the somewhat lesser threat of Hoke's division and Fitzhugh Lee's cavalry. But Wright still called upon and received support from Smith. The first attack at Cold Harbor on June 1, despite moments that seemed to promise success, resulted in a terrible slaughter of the attacking Federals netting insignificant or transient gains, with even the dauntless Upton describing the day's assault as "murderous."[14]

While the soldiers of the 6th and 18th Corps met their fates at Cold Harbor, the 2nd, 5th, and 9th Corps remained on the Totopotomoy, digging in and trying to strengthen their positions. Warren's line was stretched thin, extending from Bethesda Church for five miles toward Cold Harbor to reach out for the right flank of the 18th or perhaps the 6th Corps in their unknown locations. Warren hoped the intervening swamps would deter the rebels from taking advantage of a number of gaps in his line, or at least slow them down. But that was not all the 5th Corps commander had to be concerned about, for while Roebling was off with the Maryland Brigade in another attempt to find Wright and Smith's positions at Cold Harbor, the 2nd, 5th, and 9th Corps began receiving orders to press up against the enemy and report his numbers and activities. Warren, no doubt hoping the enemy would not notice the fragility of his line or that he had no reserve to call upon, was understandably put out, for the enemy was moving quite securely through his own entrenchments, defenses that had previously been deemed too strong to attack. Then, too, it was plain that when he attacked, the rebels would need only turn to their left and blaze away at their attackers. Warren nonetheless sent Cutler's and Henry Lockwood's divisions across the open swampy landscape, where, as soon as the rebels spotted the Federal advance, they opened with a devastating fire from a rifled battery in an entrenched position. Warren would later report that they had in fact attracted the enemy's attention, for the moving infantry stopped momentarily and turned to the left to shoot at the Yankees. No more was accomplished than the capture of the enemy's advanced rifle pits and more Federal casualties.[15]

On the 5th Corps's left, Roebling led an advance on the enemy's defenses. After placing the Maryland Brigade in a strong position, he moved forward with a skirmish line half a mile, when the enemy opened with batteries and musketry on both their flanks. The line disintegrated, and when the men returned to their starting point, Roebling found that the Maryland Brigade, unnerved by the greeting their skirmish line had received, was gone. When it was acknowledged that the enemy was not pursuing, Roebling was able to bring some of the Marylanders back and patch together a line that remained at the front overnight. Roebling then encountered General Lockwood's division, quite lost but still intending to find the 18th Corps's right flank. The men had no idea where they were, but, to their credit, they were moving toward the sound of the guns. Roebling took it upon himself to add Lockwood's division to the left of the Marylanders' line. It was now dark, and Roebling intended to report back to Warren. Lest too little be made of the difficult conditions around the 5th Corps's position, Roebling told that the horse of the orderly who had been acting as his guide back to headquarters that dark and rainy night had drowned in one of the swamps. And the rains continued to come down to add to the misery. Washington somehow managed to write a note to Emily, at its end telling her, "I am very tired my darling—would like to rest, oh so much; if I once commence there will be no end to my resting, we all feel so."[16]

Apparently sadly out of touch with what his soldiers were enduring, Meade wrote to his wife during this period, "Indeed we are pretty much engaged all the time, from early in the morning till late at night. I don't believe the military history of the world can afford a parallel to the protracted and severe fighting which this army has sustained for the last thirty days. You would suppose, with all this severe fighting, our severe losses, constant marches, many in the night, that the physical powers of the men would be exhausted. I have no doubt in time it will tell on them, but as yet they show no evidences of it."[17]

Another sort of casualty this day was the hapless Lockwood, who, after his division's futile assault on the 5th Corps's front, had been sent off to the left to attempt to connect with Smith's right flank. While Roebling reported finding

Lockwood and his division with no idea where they were, he also pointed out that Smith's flank was a good mile and a half from and well behind where it was expected to be. It was the last mistake Henry Lockwood would make as a division commander, and he was sent packing. But Grant and Meade apparently also needed someone to blame for the failure of the 6th and 18th Corps to accomplish something of significance that day at Cold Harbor. Ever a source of malicious gossip at Grant's headquarters, Edwin Stanton's eyes and ears at the front, Charles Dana, reported to Washington that Meade and Grant were "intensely disgusted" by Warren's failures that day. Dana's comments suggest that Meade was willing to join the efforts to throw Warren to the wolves. It is unlikely that Meade realized that the wolves, in this case, were "Grant's Men," for many in Grant's inner circle fancied themselves likely candidates to replace not only Warren but also Meade. Dana also claimed that Meade had said a radical change must be made, no matter how unpleasant it might be to make it. Dana added that he doubted Meade would actually resort to such an extreme remedy.[18]

Warren, relying heavily on Roebling's reports from his reconnaissance in force and skirmishing on the 5th Corps's left, reported to Army of the Potomac headquarters throughout the day of his efforts to comply with Meade's orders despite considerable adversity. But the lieutenant general, at the time and later, would point the finger of blame for the day's disappointments at Warren and Warren alone. In his memoirs, Grant declared, "Warren was ordered to attack him [Anderson] vigorously in his flank. Warren fired his artillery at the enemy; but lost so much time in making ready that the enemy got by, and at three o'clock he reported the enemy was strongly entrenched in his front, and besides his lines were so long that he had no mass of troops to move with. He [Warren] seemed to have forgotten that lines in rear of an army hold themselves while their defenders are fighting in their front." While disparaging the attack Warren's 5th Corps made this day, the lieutenant general was apparently unaware or had forgotten that General Hancock also experienced considerable delay in obeying orders for his advance, with Hancock reporting that it was his opinion that the 2nd Corps's assault would fail. It did.[19]

The days that became known as the Battle of Cold Harbor would add to a growing list of cruel encounters in the brutal campaign between Lee's Army of Northern Virginia and Meade's Army of the Potomac during the spring of 1864. The 5th Corps would play a difficult, dangerous, and often denigrated role in the conflict. Washington Roebling would be called upon, again and again, to find the enemy before the enemy found the Army of the Potomac.

25

Cold Harbor

THE 2ND CORPS HAD MADE A FORCED MARCH ON THE NIGHT OF JUNE 1–2 with the intention of arriving at dawn in Cold Harbor in time to join the 6th and 18th Corps in their frontal assault on the rebel fortifications. But one of George Meade's aides, attempting a shortcut, took Winfield Hancock's corps on a road too narrow for its artillery, delaying its arrival until well past daybreak in an exhausted condition. The grand assault was thus postponed until evening, and then until early the following morning. General Meade no doubt found the delay embarrassing, which perhaps contributed to the Army of the Potomac commander's obstinate aggression when the attack was finally made.[1]

Meanwhile, after days of intense and costly frustration for the 5th Corps, Gouverneur Warren's strung-out corps and Ambrose Burnside's 9th Corps on its right were attempting to cope with a large force of rebels on their respective fronts. As Roebling noted, he found that Warren's line was some four miles long, extending from the Shady Grove Road to a mile shy of Woody's. It was still a single line, though Warren had tried to create a few reserves on the right to deal with emergencies, and emergencies were on the way. The enemy's presence was heaviest on the 5th Corps's right, where Jubal Early's corps had been reinforced by Henry Heth's division. Though Warren explained that the rebels were proving annoyingly aggressive, the 5th Corps was nonetheless ordered to move to the left and shorten its line to three miles, while the 9th Corps would retire altogether and mass on the 5th Corps's right rear. Warren was told that he would be responsible for protecting the army's right flank and must also be ready to make an attack on his front as well. Burnside, on his withdrawal from the army's extreme right, was expected to mass behind Warren as support and reserve. Notwithstanding the objections of both commanders, the order stood. When the 9th Corps began its withdrawal during a

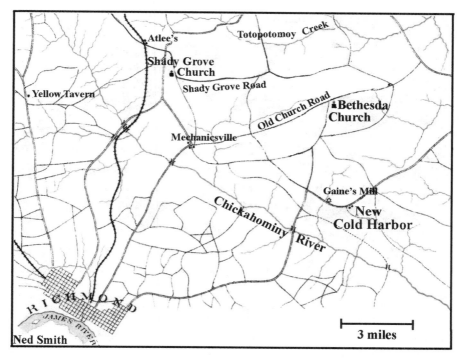

Area of Cold Harbor.
Adapted from Plate LXXXI, 3 OR Atlas.

heavy thunderstorm, the enemy sent a battle line against Burnside, capturing the 9th Corps's skirmishers. The rebels then turned their attention to the 5th Corps, driving down between its skirmish line and its main line. They cut off four hundred or so of Warren's skirmishers, who would spend the rest of the war in Confederate prison camps.[2]

The enemy wasn't finished with the 5th Corps yet. When rebels threatened the right of Warren's main line, they were met by a strong defense from Charles Griffin's division, which then counterattacked, driving them back. This action would prove another case of U. S. Grant either not knowing or forgetting what had happened that day, for in his memoirs he again expressed great anger toward Warren, accusing him of failing to counterattack after the enemy's assault on the 5th Corps. Was Grant not told at the time that Griffin, though his line was overstretched trying to maintain contact between the 9th and 5th Corps, had nonetheless successfully repelled the enemy's assault and launched a counterattack that drove Robert Rodes's division all the way back to the Shady Grove Road? It is true that the enemy had cut the telegraph wires between the 5th Corps headquarters and Meade, but Warren had kept headquarters apprised of the assault on his line and Griffin's counterattack by courier. Meade's response, when it finally came, was that Warren had to be prepared to attack on his front at 4:30 a.m. the next morning, June 3.[3]

Burnside's corps returned to the 5th Corps's right, taking shelter behind breastworks previously held by the 5th Corps. Before night fell, Roebling went out to the right of the 9th Corps to see how far the enemy's left extended, with some surprising results: "I went within 50 yds. of the road leading from Mrs. Via's to the Shady Grove road where I could see the end of the rebel line in the Shady Grove road, busy firing at Griffin. There was a chance here for Robert Potter's Div. [9th Corps] to have got into the rear of the rebel line which might have resulted in the capture of Richard Ewell's Corps before night." One of Potter's staff officers, escorted by Roebling to the spot, agreed with him, but when Roebling took his case to Generals Potter and Burnside, they "took no notice." While fighting continued on the 5th Corps's right, around 8 p.m. Warren sent Roebling to General Meade to describe in person the inviting situation he had discovered on the Confederate left flank. When Roebling arrived at Meade's headquarters around 11 p.m., he was carrying Warren's message urging the Army of the Potomac commander to come himself to the Federal right the next morning and take command of the situation. Roebling recorded, "This he [Meade] refused at once, saying that at 3 a.m. he had ordered his coffee, at 4 he was going to mount with his staff, and at 6 he would smash the rebel army at Coal [sic] Harbor."[4]

Regarding the proposition that Warren be given temporary authority over the 9th Corps in order to allow the two corps to attack the rebel flank, Meade was somewhat more amenable, but he nonetheless sent Roebling to Grant. When Roebling explained the situation,

> the Lt. Gen. did not have much to say one way or another; he did not think it proper to put Gen. Warren over Gen. Burnside; he gave me a note to Gen. Meade, the contents of which I did not learn. However he [Gen. Meade] dictated a note to Gen. Warren to the effect that he and Gen. Burnside should cooperate, that they should be good boys and not quarrel, that they should attack the enemy at precisely 1800 seconds after 4 o'clock, and that if the enemy gave way at all we should at once follow him closing in to the left and south; in as much as the enemy was due North of us this latter injunction was a manifest impossibility.

ing the Army of the Potomac across the James in the coming days and paying
little attention to what Meade and the Army of the Potomac were doing at
Cold Harbor. Meade claimed to have had "immediate and entire command
on the field all day," and his chagrin at having had to cancel the assault the
previous day left him determined to ensure that no man could question his
willingness to attack. That Meade ordered his soldiers to attack, and then to
attack again, leads one to believe that he was a man very much haunted by the
storms of criticism he had endured when he had previously refused to fight
when the enemy clearly held the advantage. Such painful reflections and a
sense of vindication are quite clearly evident in the letters he wrote to his wife
on the days after the battle.

> I feel satisfaction in knowing that my record is clear, and that the results
> of this campaign are the clearest indications I could wish of my sound
> judgment, both at Williamsport and Mine Run. In every instance that
> we have attacked the enemy in an intrenched position we have failed,
> except in the case of Hancock's attack at Spottsylvania, which was a
> surprise discreditable to the enemy. So likewise, whenever the enemy has
> attacked us in position, he has been repulsed. I think that Grant has had
> his eyes opened, and is willing to admit now that Virginia and [R. E.]
> Lee's army is not Tennessee and [Braxton] Bragg's army. Whether the
> people will ever realize this fact remains to be seen.

To add to the horror of this battle that saw seven thousand Union casualties,
the wounded would lie on the field beside their dead comrades for three days.
Grant refused to ask Lee for a truce on the field in order to bring them in
because that would be tantamount to admitting he had lost the fight. So when

General Grant at his Cold Harbor
headquarters.
Library of Congress.

Grant finally agreed to do so three days later, most of his wounded were dead. Regarding the June 3 attacks, there are stories that some of the men of the 2nd, 6th, and 18th Corps did not fight with vigor. There are even stories that some of the men refused to advance at all. But Confederate accounts offer a different view. Lieutenant Colonel Charles Venable of Lee's staff later wrote of the Federal assault, "The dead and dying lay in front of the Confederate lines in triangles, of which the apexes were the bravest men who came nearest to the breastworks under the withering, deadly fire."[6]

On June 3, while Smith, Wright, and Hancock made their ill-fated attacks on the rebel left and center, Warren's line, now drawn further left, was confronting a mere two miles of the enemy's front. The 5th Corps was still drawn out in a single line but unable to stretch far enough to connect with the 18th Corps. Prisoners taken showed that Warren was confronting elements of Richard Anderson's and Ewell's corps, while Burnside's 9th Corps, on the 5th Corps's right and rear, was capturing soldiers from A. P. Hill's corps. On

General Meade at his Cold Harbor headquarters.
Library of Congress.

being ordered to assault on his front, Warren sent Griffin's 1st Division on two assaults that morning in cooperation with two divisions of Burnside's corps. Warren, meanwhile, had to simultaneously fight off a wave of attackers the enemy had sent against the 5th Corps's right center. With the telegraph between the 5th Corps and Army of the Potomac headquarters still down, Warren sent a courier to Meade to alert him to the rebel attack on the army's right and to ask for reinforcement. Two hours later, the answer came, even as Warren was receiving another attack: there would be no reinforcement, and Warren was still expected to move three-quarters of a mile further to his left and support Smith's attack at Cold Harbor. At 6 p.m., Griffin alone made another attack on Heth's entrenched division. Every assault Griffin had made that day had ended in a bloody repulse of his 1st Division.[7]

Despite the 5th Corps's arduous day on June 3, neither Warren nor Roebling had forgotten about the rebel left flank in midair, and Roebling was still working to inform Burnside and encourage him to attack. When Roebling discovered James Wilson's cavalry escorting a contingent of previously

275

wounded soldiers returning to the front, he tried to convince Wilson to support the 9th Corps attack on Heth's right and rear. As the time for the attack approached—literally as Burnside's skirmishers were moving forward—orders came from Meade's headquarters canceling the assault. Agonizing over this lost opportunity, Roebling would declare, "It was countermanded for some unknown reason, perhaps because there was a prospect of success." That night, General Early reported to Lee's headquarters that his left flank was very much exposed, and he was given permission to withdraw. Thus the fighting for the day was over. Despite being on the sidelines of June 3's main event at Cold Harbor, the 5th and 9th Corps added their own sixteen hundred killed and wounded to that day's terrible toll. Theodore Lyman, Meade's aide, would comment regarding Warren at this time, "Some people say he [Warren] is a selfish man, but he is certainly the most tenderhearted of our commanders. Almost all officers grow soon callous in the service; not unfeeling, only accustomed, and unaffected by the suffering they see. But Warren feels it a great deal, and that and the responsibility, and many things of course not going to suit him, all tend to make him haggard." Lyman also remembered Warren saying, "For thirty days now, it has been one funeral procession past me; and it is too much." By contrast, Meade, in his letter to his wife on June 4, expressed a rather callous indifference and considerable miscalculation in his observations on the fighting of the previous day, June 3. Acknowledging that it had ended without any decided results, Meade made the puzzlingly and wildly inaccurate suggestion that the losses were about equal on both sides, "ours roughly estimated at seven thousand five hundred in all." He added, "The enemy, as usual, were strongly fortified, and we have pretty well entrenched ourselves. How long this game is to be played it is impossible to tell; but in the long run, we ought to succeed, because it is in our power more promptly to fill the gaps in men and material which this constant fighting produces."[8]

On the morning of June 4, Roebling was sent out to discover what was happening on the enemy's left flank, and he discovered the rebels had withdrawn from Burnside's front and Warren's right, though they had not gone very far. Roebling found them massed in force just west of the Shady Grove Road, and Meade suspected Lee might be forming for another attack on his army's right flank. But that didn't deter Meade from ordering movements for the next day for both Warren's and Burnside's corps that would result in Burnside taking up the protection of the army's right flank, with the 5th Corps to take up a position in reserve, an assignment unique for it in this sanguinary campaign. The 9th Corps was to withdraw from its front during the day in preparation for moving into Warren's position. As

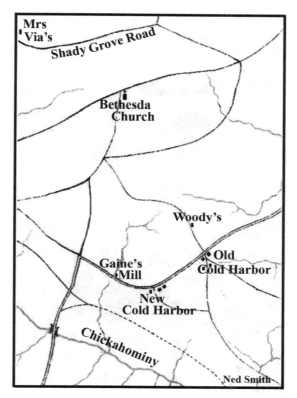

Cold Harbor detail.
Adapted from Plate LXXXI, 3 OR Atlas.

Burnside completed his withdrawal, the 5th Corps alone held the Army of the Potomac's right flank; nonetheless, orders arrived late that evening for the 5th Corps to push up to the enemy as close as possible. Roebling commented, "No preparations had been made for it, and as it could not be accomplished without well digested arrangements there was nothing done for that night." The same circular drawn up for this movement also ordered Philip Sheridan to keep cavalry out on both of the army's flanks.[9]

As Warren prepared to obey orders for his own withdrawal the next day, no cavalry could be found closer than two miles from the 5th Corps's right flank. Though Wilson had let the 5th Corps down again and again with dire consequences, Warren wrote calmly to him, "I understand from headquarters Army of the Potomac that you are to watch my right flank and give me notice of any efforts to turn it. Your nearest pickets are 2 miles off from my flank. On May 30 I was told that the cavalry would guard my flank, and they did not, so that enemy attacked me from where they [Federal cavalry] should have been. If your instructions do not require you to connect with me, then I am misinformed by high authority." In a relatively respectful manner, Wilson responded to Army of the Potomac headquarters regarding Warren's concerns, and despite its being broad daylight, Wilson offered excuses regarding the difficulties of maintaining communications at night. Then, too, the line he was guarding was too long, and he had not been kept apprised of the location of the 5th Corps's right flank. General A. A. Humphreys, Meade's chief of staff, wasn't buying it and informed Wilson that Warren's right flank had been at Bethesda Church for days. If Wilson's reply to Meade offered up relatively polite excuses, his answer to Warren was decidedly cheekier: "My instructions are to cover the right flank of the army from the incursions of the enemy. This duty requires me to watch a line at least 4 miles in length. I don't understand that I am to place my command in your front, or to dispose it specially to take care of your flank." Wilson added that he had had no idea Warren was on the Army of the Potomac's right flank and that the infantry "should not rely too much upon me for close connections, since I have so much country not only to watch but to guard from attacks of cavalry." Wilson closed by suggesting Warren try to get General Alfred Torbert's division somewhere near Cold Harbor to come over.[10]

Army of the Potomac headquarters forwarded both Warren's and Meade's messages to Sheridan, and if Wilson's reply to Warren was surly, it was nothing compared to Sheridan's response to Meade, for Sheridan wrote, "General Wilson reports the connections with General Warren complete since some time last night, and the reason why the connection was broken was the withdrawal of some army corps without any notification to the cavalry. Infantry commanders are very quick to give the alarm when their flanks are uncovered, but manifest inexcusable stupidity about the safety of cavalry flanks." Sheridan again felt quite free to express utter disregard for his orders, displaying complete confidence that he would pay no penalty for his disobedience or insubordination.[11]

Generals Sheridan and Wilson could not make their animosity or unwillingness to act in good faith with the 5th Corps clearer. This would have additional serious repercussions for the men of the 5th Corps and the Army of the Potomac in the weeks ahead.

26

The 5th Corps Screens
Grant's Move to the James

I<small>N PREPARATION FOR PREVIOUS ORDERS, WASHINGTON ROEBLING HAD</small>
spent the morning of June 4 reconnoitering on the corps's left, but when he
returned to Gouverneur Warren's headquarters at midday, everything had
changed. The 5th Corps would be withdrawing during the night to Leary's,
north of Cold Harbor; by this movement it would abandon all ground north
and west of the Matadequin and take up a strictly defensive line behind Allen's
Mill Pond and the stream running into it. In the afternoon, Warren sent
skirmishers a short way out the Shady Grove Road, where they encountered
enemy cavalry and discovered that the rebels had reoccupied their old line.
Meanwhile, Roebling investigated the road upon which they would travel that
night and saw to what necessary repairs the limited time allowed. At sundown,
Romeyn Ayres's brigade made a demonstration on Warren's front, designed
to deceive and distract the enemy from the withdrawal of Samuel Crawford's
division, and then Lysander Cutler's, with Charles Griffin's division bringing
up the rear. The night was very dark and the road muddy, and straggling meant
it was almost dawn before Griffin left Bethesda Church. By daylight on June
6, the 5th Corps was encamped around Leary's, and the 9th Corps, formerly
to the right of Warren, was now the Army of the Potomac's right flank.[1]

The weather was warm and the location dusty, but for once the officers
and the men were away from the pressures of the front. Unavoidably filthy
and lousy since they'd been unable to bathe or change clothing since crossing the Rapidan, they were looking forward to this opportunity to bring up
their trains with their promise of clean clothes. Though George Meade was
unavailable, Warren and A. A. Humphreys decided to give it a try, but when
Meade returned to army headquarters, permission was denied, and the wagons

were sent away. It seems that Ambrose Burnside, now defender of the Army of the Potomac's right flank, was uneasy and calling on Warren for assistance. Roebling, sent to ascertain what was happening, reported that he couldn't see where the 9th Corps needed any assistance, for, as Warren tried to point out, Burnside's right and rear were protected by an impenetrable swamp and the narrow, easily defendable Allen's Mill Dam. Jubal Early did try to find a way to get at the 9th Corps but failed, as Warren had said he would. But Meade insisted that Warren's corps be held in readiness for the enemy breakthrough that never came, Crawford's and Ayres's divisions remaining under arms all day. A frustrated Warren commented, "To be always ready is to be never ready, for men cannot stand with belts, knapsacks, &c, on all the time without becoming broken down." One wonders whether Meade's recalcitrance this day was also sparked by U. S. Grant, once again, responding to another bout of Philip Sheridan's disobedience and insubordination toward Meade by sending Sheridan off on another independent cavalry mission, this time to destroy rebel railroads and meet General David Hunter's ill-fated expedition.[2]

Warren took this time of relative calm to reorganize the command structure of the corps. General Charles Griffin remained in command of the 1st Division, Joseph Bartlett and Jacob Sweitzer commanding two of his brigades, and a new 1st Brigade was created for Colonel Joshua Chamberlain to command. With the unexpected departure of Henry Lockwood, Romeyn Ayres would command the 2nd Division, consisting of his Maryland Brigade and John Kitching's heavy artillery brigade. A disgruntled Cutler commanding the 4th Division was left with two brigades when some of his men were given to Chamberlain's new brigade. There would be precious little rest for two of the divisions, Griffin's and Cutler's, for orders arrived on the night of June 6 that they were to take up a position to the left of the 2nd Corps on the Chickahominy. The enemy was driven across the river at Sumner's Bridge and at a railroad bridge, where Cutler's left connected with the cavalry, while Griffin's right connected with David Birney's division of the 2nd Corps. While it was believed that the sparse force confronting Griffin at Sumner's was made up of Richmond clerks, the enemy brought its formidable railroad monitor up to the bridge at Cutler's position, the gun a rifled thirty-two pounder that caused some little excitement when it commenced firing. It was speculated that the three-hundred-pound shells being thrown at them had been taken from the Federals at Plymouth, North Carolina. Though the monitor provided an occasional thrill, pulling picket duty at the crossing proved tedious, so Griffin's and Cutler's camps, a mile from the river, gave the men of their divisions some moments of respite.[3]

On June 8, Generals Meade and Grant with General Warren spent some time studying a map spread out on the grass under an apple tree, a surprising development, considering the disdain the lieutenant general and the Army of the Potomac commander had so recently displayed toward Warren. But the upcoming movement would entail a very special assignment for Warren and the 5th Corps. Grant was planning the withdrawal of the Army of the Potomac from Cold Harbor and preparing to execute a daring passage across the Chickahominy and the James Rivers with a goal to attack and capture Petersburg. While the 2nd, 6th, and 9th Corps began their trek toward the James, it would be Warren's task to screen them and to confront the Army of Northern Virginia. With Sheridan having ridden off the previous day with the entire cavalry force except for General James H. Wilson's division, Wilson would be providing the 5th Corps's only support, a fact that could hardly have given Warren much comfort. In a further display of comrade-like activity, Warren and Meade and their staffs made a two-mile pilgrimage to Edmund Ruffin's estate, Roseneath, which Wilson had appropriated for his headquarters. After reviewing a brigade of the U.S. Colored Troops, on their return to Army of the Potomac headquarters, Roebling witnessed General Meade drumming out of the army one Edward Crapsey, a *Philadelphia Enquirer* reporter who had erroneously reported that at the Wilderness Meade had urged Grant to retreat back across the Rapidan instead of seeking further battles with Lee. The story was picked up by other newspapers, and a furious Meade sent Crapsey riding backward on a mule through the encampment with a placard round his neck reading, "Liar, etc."[4]

As Roebling commented, with the planning of their next movement, maps of the lower Chickahominy were much in demand, but, for the most part, they all had to settle for what they could learn from some thorough and considerably risky scouting. Roebling rode down to the Chickahominy on the morning of June 10 and found all quiet both at Cold Harbor and on the Army of the Potomac's left, where he found Cutler's pickets at the railroad bridge exchanging papers and trading tobacco with the rebels. On June 11, Ayres's and Crawford's divisions were brought down to a position within striking distance of crossing over the Chickahominy that night. Roebling wrote, "Great care was taken that our movement should not become known to the enemy; pickets were placed all around to keep Federal stragglers in camp and unwanted strangers out." Roebling learned from deserters from A. P. Hill's corps that there was no enemy force south of White Oak Swamp to their knowledge. After dark on the night of June 12, the 5th Corps would cross the Chickahominy at the Long Bridge with orders to move out as far as Quaker

Road or until stopped by the enemy. The 2nd Corps would follow the 5th Corps, while the 6th and 9th Corps crossed lower down at Jones Bridge. Baldy Smith's 18th Corps would be returning to the Army of the James by water. It became Roebling's job to find the roads on which the 5th Corps could approach the Chickahominy unobserved. Roebling judged the crossing at Long Bridge to be a crossing easily held should the enemy choose to do so, so Roebling found another crossing below Long Bridge where the Federals could cross and "uncover" Long Bridge from behind should it prove necessary.[5]

As Meade prepared the Army of the Potomac for departure from Cold Harbor, though he had consistently defended Grant in his letters home to his skeptical wife, he was beginning to express disillusionment: "Now, to tell the truth, the latter [Grant] has greatly disappointed me, and since this campaign I really begin to think I am something of a general." Undoubtedly Meade was much upset regarding the widespread publication of Crapsey's fabrication that he had urged Grant to retreat back across the Rapidan instead of pressing on after R. E. Lee and the Army of Northern Virginia. But Meade was also beginning to doubt Grant's veracity regarding his reports to Washington. While Meade was unsurprised that the press gave Grant full credit for all that the Army of the Potomac did, he also noticed that his name was never mentioned in Edwin Stanton's communications. He was somewhat placated to learn that Assistant Secretary Charles Dana was the one sending daily telegrams to Stanton and that the lieutenant general never communicated directly with the secretary of war, only with General Henry Halleck.[6]

The upcoming move of the Army of the Potomac away from Cold Harbor meant it was time for Roebling to be scouting the enemy and learning all he could about the streams, rivers, bridges, and fords the Federals would be needing. Some information was gleaned by a visit to the picket post at Long Bridge, where the Yankees and their rebel counterparts often chatted. Roebling reiterated his concern that Long Bridge would be a bad place to force a crossing, since Confederate cavalry were there in force and the approach to the bridge was a narrow neck of land with swamp on either side. Warren therefore suggested that Federal cavalry could cross unimpeded below, and then come up and clear away opposition at Long Bridge for the infantry's crossing. But Roebling's reconnaissance rides by necessity soon extended well beyond Long Bridge, and the vital information he brought to Generals Warren and Meade helped formulate the plan to bring the Army of the Potomac unobserved to the James River.[7]

At 5:30 p.m. on June 12, Generals Grant and Meade reached Warren's headquarters at Moody's as the corps prepared to start for Long Bridge. The pontoon trains had already been sent, the men repairing the road as they advanced. On reaching the bridge, Warren's advance found Wilson and his cavalry just arriving, and since the troopers were charged with establishing a bridgehead across the stream, the men of the 5th Corps settled down to wait. After skirmishing and attempting to find the alternative ford across the river, Wilson finally made it across the Chickahominy, and at 10 p.m. the installation of the pontoon bridge finally commenced. Roebling's report of this night's activities, as written here, is a far cry from what Wilson had to say about this night. Wilson's late crossing substantially delayed the passage of the 5th Corps, and it is unknown whether any displeasure was expressed, officially or otherwise, by Warren. Wilson tells quite another tale, one of an out-of-control General Warren allegedly cursing furiously at one of Wilson's young aides, who returned to Wilson's headquarters in tears. While Roebling mentions no such conflict in his report for this day, Wilson's account, infused with considerable drama in his memoirs, was a cooked-up scenario sure to arouse Grant's anger, for, as Wilson well knew, Grant had a deep aversion to profanity. Nor did Grant at this point care much for Warren, who complained far too often about his favorites, Sheridan and Wilson. Wilson would write that Grant responded to his story of Warren's abusive treatment of the young aide with, "Well I'll take care of Warren anyhow." While Grant's statement regarding his intention to "take care of Warren" does not bode well for the 5th Corps commander, this ominous declaration may be nothing more than another James Wilson fiction, one of many. But with Wilson's known ambition for corps command and his reputation for smearing his rivals, one must exercise caution when considering the version Wilson wrote many years later. Yet Wilson's description of Grant's supposed reaction to Wilson's account and growing dislike for Warren seem all too probable, given the fate Warren would suffer in the future at the hands of Grant and Sheridan.[8]

As obstruction in the road caused further delay, it was nearly daybreak on June 13 before the cavalry got across the Chickahominy and on their way. The 5th Corps followed, and though the movement had already turned out to be hardly as secretive as contemplated, the infantry's vanguard reached its goal, the plateau two miles beyond the crossing, by sunrise. Crawford's division formed a battle line, while Wilson's cavalry pushed on, driving rebel cavalry they encountered beyond New Market cross roads. The infantry and a battery soon came up to dig in and defend the intersection, while the cavalry drove the enemy across White Oak Swamp. Warren's other divisions deployed on the plateau in support of Crawford, taking care to secure nearby river crossings, and a lively artillery duel ensued between the 5th Corps and an alert enemy. While the rest of the Army of the Potomac was withdrawing and heading for the James River, for one full day Warren's lone 5th Corps would entertain the enemy and hopefully baffle Lee and his Army of Northern Virginia as to U. S. Grant's intentions for the coming days. Roebling witnessed at one point on this day Wilson's cavalry racing back to the Federal line, running past Crawford's infantry line to safety. The pursuing rebels did not attack but dug in, in plain sight, to remind the 5th Corps they were there.[9]

When Warren's job of screening the Army of the Potomac and protecting it from rebel attack was done, he would need to make a strategic and speedy withdrawal. The available maps were, once again, woefully inaccurate, especially regarding the environs of the White Oak Swamp, so at noon Roebling and Warren's headquarters escort were sent out to determine the best roads to St. Mary's Church, the 5th Corps's escape route and path to follow to rejoin its army. Roebling soon found a road that would lead them to safety and didn't interfere with the movements of the Army of the Potomac's other three corps. As darkness fell, the 5th Corps successfully withdrew, and though Wilson's cavalry were supposed to have acted as the expedition's rear guard, he and his troopers pushed their way through to the advance of the retreating infantrymen. The 5th Corps reached relative safety at St. Mary's Church around midnight and went into bivouac, chiefly because Wilson's cavalry refused to move out of the road. When shots were heard, the exhausted foot soldiers, believing they were under attack, formed a battle line, much to the merriment of the cavalrymen. They thought it a great joke to throw cartridges into their camp fire and startle the plodding column into deploying for defense. It is unlikely that any of the 5th Corps's weary men found it amusing.[10]

With Wilson's cavalry finally out of the way the next morning, the 5th Corps started for Charles City Court House and, upon arriving at noon on June 14, occupied the earthworks that Winfield Hancock's soldiers had thrown up the day before. It is interesting to contemplate that so little was known of the enemy that the 2nd Corps found it expedient to dig in wherever it bivouacked. On the 5th Corps's arrival nearer the James, Roebling was startled to find that the pontoon bridge was not yet ready, nor could he find anyone who knew of a road leading from Charles City to the James. With the bridge unavailable, General Hancock started crossing his corps over the river on ferry boats, a process that continued the next day, for it is said that crossing the infantry corps by boat took four times as long as it would have by the pontoon bridge, which was ultimately used chiefly by artillery, trains, and the cavalry. The pontoon bridge across the James was something of an engineering marvel, being two thousand feet long and standing in eighty-five feet of water in places.[11]

The Road to Petersburg

EVEN AS THE ARMY OF THE POTOMAC HAD BEEN FUTILELY ASSAULTING the rebel fortifications at Cold Harbor at the beginning of June 1864, elements of General Benjamin Butler's Army of the James planned an attempt to raid Petersburg and destroy its railroads that came to naught. While U. S. Grant had concerns about Butler's lack of military training and experience, as well as doubts about his judgment, it is ironic that he chose to send General William Smith to him, for Smith was a man notorious for his lack of cooperation with his superiors. Grant also sent another West Point–trained commander, Quincy Gillmore (USMA 1849), to provide advice and guidance to Butler and his army. Neither Gillmore nor Smith would serve General Butler particularly well. Gillmore, though he had clamored for command of the early June assault on Petersburg, when given the opportunity, failed utterly to bring off an attack on the barely defended city. While the fortifications protecting the railroad hub of Petersburg were formidable, much of those earthworks lay empty of defenders, for the city's commander, General P. T. Beauregard, had nowhere near enough troops to man his miles of fortifications. Gillmore had at his disposal his own 10th Corps, General Edward Hinks's U.S. Colored Troops (USCT) division, and the cavalry division of General August Kautz (USMA 1852).[1]

It is interesting to remember the mission Lieutenant General Grant initially gave to General Butler and his Army of the James at the beginning of their campaign, timed to coincide with the Army of the Potomac's crossing of the Rapidan. Butler was to, first and foremost, establish a base in the Bermuda Hundred–City Point area where the James and Appomattox Rivers met. Once he had secured a base of operations, he was to make a try for Richmond; failing that, he was to establish a hold on the James in preparation for Grant's bringing the Army of the Potomac to join him. However, Grant was unable to

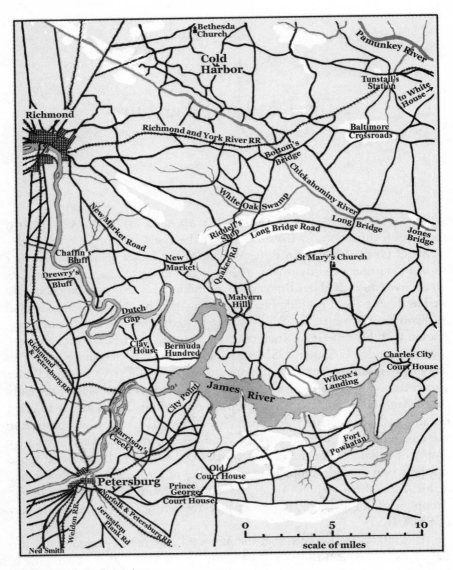

Cold Harbor to Petersburg.
Adapted from "Field of War around Richmond & Petersburg"; Library of Congress.

General Quincy Gillmore.
Library of Congress.

complete his part of the plan, taking more than five weeks instead of his estimated ten days to get to Richmond. While Butler failed to "take" Richmond,
surprisingly, he was given no orders to try to take the important railroad hub
at Petersburg, and when Butler got the news of Grant's supposed great victory
at the Wilderness, he figured he needn't worry about hurrying to act on his
own when Grant and the Army of the Potomac would soon arrive. While an
army of enthusiastic Butler bashers likes to recite the story of Butler getting
himself bottled up at Bermuda Hundred, it is all too easy to forget that Butler
at least completed the first part of his mission quite well, that of establishing
a base of operations for Grant and the Army of the Potomac. In the end, the
"minders" Grant had set to assist Butler quite glaringly failed, for the hesitant
Gillmore and Smith both rather inexplicably did not seize a number of very
real opportunities to capture Petersburg.[2]

As for the first Federal attempt on Petersburg, after Smith's 18th Corps
was sent to the Army of the Potomac at Cold Harbor, Butler was holding

Bermuda Hundred with just the 10th Corps, Hinks's USCT, and Kautz's cavalry, but he nonetheless planned a raid upon Petersburg on June 9 in hopes of destroying its railroads. Butler assigned command of the infantry assault to General Edward Hinks, but when General Quincy Gillmore got wind of the expedition, he asked for and got command of it. Gillmore had a force of forty-five hundred infantry to assault the left portion of the Confederates' poorly manned earthworks on the Dimmock Line, while General August Kautz and his thirteen hundred cavalrymen would detour past the long line of fortifications to the enemy's right flank at the Jerusalem Plank Road and await Gillmore's assault to make their own attack. The troopers skirmished with fewer than two hundred of the ragtag civilian defenders who had gathered at Rives Salient, but Kautz would wait in vain for the infantry's attack. With one delay after another, Gillmore's infantrymen finally approached the one part of the Dimmock Line where the "old men and boys" of Petersburg, as well as patients from the hospitals and prisoners from the jail, were manning the Confederate fortifications. Upon consideration, and without notifying Kautz, Gillmore decided to cancel the infantry's attack and took his soldiers back to Bermuda Hundred. It is known that Hinks clamored for his men to be allowed to attack this day, and many believe that, had Butler's raid been made as planned, led by General Hinks as Butler intended, it would have succeeded. While Gillmore's raid was never intended to capture and hold Petersburg, the destruction of vital enemy railroads would undoubtedly have benefited both Smith's and the Army of the Potomac's upcoming investment of Petersburg. As it was, only when Baldy Smith and the 18th Corps began arriving back with the Army of the James did Smith learn that it would be his turn to "take Petersburg." The 18th Corps had been marched from Cold Harbor to White House, where it embarked by boat for Bermuda Hundred, having priority over all other corps and traffic. Fresh from the horrors of the Cold Harbor front, Smith did not learn until he arrived at Bermuda Hundred that that he would be attacking the Dimmock Line the very next day.[3]

While Gouverneur Warren and the 5th Corps were completing their mission to screen and safeguard the Army of the Potomac's passage across the James, things were going less well for Philip Sheridan and his cavalry. Their mission was to destroy enemy railroads and unite at Charlottesville with General David Hunter's raid in the Shenandoah Valley. But Sheridan got no further than Trevilian Station, where he was confronted on July 11 by Wade Hampton's and Fitzhugh Lee's Confederate cavalry divisions. At first, victory seemed within Sheridan's grasp, but by the next day, Hampton and Lee had Sheridan on the run. In fact, General George Armstrong Custer got

General August Kautz.
Library of Congress.

himself into such a tight spot at Trevilian Station that one historian called it a dress rehearsal for the Little Big Horn. Sheridan abandoned any thought of trying to get to Charlottesville, blithely leaving Hunter to his fate, and in the following days, as Sheridan tried to get back to the Army of the Potomac, his every step was dogged by enemy cavalry. Nearing the Army of the Potomac, Sheridan, much to his disgust, was asked to accompany a long train of supply wagons, but the enemy was still snapping at his heels. Sheridan's solution was to task General David Gregg's division with guarding the train, while Sheridan and the rest of the cavalry corps rode on to army headquarters unmolested. With Gregg's division outnumbered by five rebel brigades to his two, Gregg lost heavily and came near being captured en masse. During the eleven days that the bulk of the Federal cavalry had been gone, leaving the Army of the Potomac in General James H. Wilson's incapable hands, Sheridan had accomplished nothing. He had once again deprived the Army of the

General Edward Hinks.
https://web.archive.org/web/20071108090345/
http://www.generalsandbrevets.com/ngh/hinks.htm.

Potomac of much-needed reconnaissance and screening as it moved through enemy territory with faulty maps. This also meant that time and time again, Washington Roebling risked his own life to gain the information vital to the 5th Corps's safe passage.[4]

To return to the James River, on June 15 General Hancock completed ferrying the 2nd Corps across on boats, as the 9th and 5th Corps awaited their turns. Grant had come down to admire his remarkable pontoon bridge, and one of George Meade's aide's reported that the lieutenant general was overheard saying that "all effect of the battle of Cold Harbor seemed to have disappeared," adding, with a smile, "I think it is pretty well to get across a great river, and come up here and attack Lee in his rear before he is ready for us." Meade, while he directed Hancock to be ready to march to Petersburg, also alerted him to Grant's order that on reaching the other side of the James, he was to await the delivery of rations. But by 10:30 a.m. on June 15, the rations

General P. T. Beauregard.
Library of Congress.

still had not arrived, and Hancock chose to leave without them. Grant would claim in his memoirs that he had informed both Meade and Hancock that the 2nd Corps was expected to support Smith's assault on distant Petersburg that day, but Grant also acknowledges his own order for Hancock to receive rations after crossing the James and before leaving the river. But the confusion did not end there. Around noon on June 15, Grant had also tried to change Hancock's orders, informing him that the elusive rations were instead to be sent to Hancock's supposed goal for the day, a position on Harrison's Creek at Petersburg. Never mind that said position would turn out to be well within the enemy's lines.[5]

One suspects that, while Grant played the cards of his battleplans very close to his chest, much of the breakdown in the planning for the Army of the Potomac's movements that day can also be laid at General Cyrus Comstock's door. Grant's engineering officer had chosen the crossing point for the Army of the Potomac on the James and was instrumental in choosing the corps's routes to Petersburg and their positions on arrival. On June 15, as Smith was advancing to assault Petersburg and Hancock and the 2nd Corps, as ordered, were waiting at the James for their rations, Comstock and Charles Dana rode in advance of the 2nd Corps toward Petersburg and got lost on the way. While it was not the first time Comstock had gotten lost while on an important mission (see his reconnaissance for the 2nd Corps's point of attack at the Bloody Angle at Spotsylvania), it was a particularly embarrassing blunder, for Comstock further stirred the pot of confusion by sending a dispatch to Grant saying that he and Dana, traveling by horseback, couldn't understand why they hadn't caught up with Hancock's men marching toward Petersburg. That Comstock and Dana had taken a wrong road likely explains all, but there is no explanation for why orders were given to the 2nd Corps misdirecting them to Harrison Creek within the enemy line, thereby lengthening their march and delaying their arrival at Petersburg by several hours.[6]

There were reasons why Hancock, Meade, and others in the Army of the Potomac began receiving unexpected urgent messages to hie to Petersburg without delay. When Baldy Smith had arrived back at City Point with the 18th Corps, he was told, apparently much to his surprise, that he would be attacking Petersburg the next day, a directive that would unnerve many a corps commander, but perhaps more so one who had just experienced the sort of confusion and carnage Smith had at Cold Harbor. Perhaps a statement that Grant made regarding one of his command-style habits explains much. Grant declared, "I never held a council of war in my life. I always made up my mind to act, and the first that even my staff knew of any movement was when I wrote it out in rough and gave it to be copied off." In this case, and perhaps in others, Grant's reticence might be the major reason why a quite magnificent move by the Army of the Potomac ended in costly failure at Petersburg. But Grant may have thought it unnecessary to tell Meade and the corps commanders of the Army of the Potomac about his plans for another reason. It seems that the lieutenant general was dead certain that his man, Baldy Smith, would capture Petersburg on June 15 and wouldn't need help from Meade and the easterners. Grant's correspondence regarding Smith's assault and the days that followed it makes clear that he was in denial that Smith had failed. Years later, Grant would write, "I believed then, and still believe, that Petersburg could have been easily captured at that time."[7]

A much-relieved Roebling reported on June 15 that the 5th Corps would have an easier time getting down to the river than the 2nd Corps had had. He found that, with much labor, good roads had been laid down through a cypress swamp. Roebling and the 5th Corps waited impatiently for their turn to cross the river. The 2nd Corps was still crossing, and the 9th Corps would go next. No one in the Army of the Potomac knew that General Smith was making an assault on Petersburg that day.

There is no question that things were going badly wrong with Smith's attack. He had at his disposal his own 18th Corps, Hinks's USCT, and Kautz's cavalry, which would once again be sent to penetrate the far right of the enemy's fortifications. Something about the Dimmock Line seemingly mesmerized the West Point–trained engineers whom Grant had picked for the job, for Smith, much as Gillmore had been, was apparently quite intimidated by the rebel fortification. That Smith also chose to attack one of the few sections of the enemy works that was manned, though sparsely, left him repeating the hapless Gillmore's unfortunate assessment of how daunting it was to make an attack on the Dimmock Line. After a lengthy reconnaissance, Smith's assault did not begin until late in the afternoon, allowing plenty of time for Beauregard to gather together a limited force to defend the city. Hinks's black soldiers, attacking to the left of Smith's assault, were sent by their resourceful general to pierce the Dimmock Line at a weak spot and come in behind the defenders. It was a just criticism of Captain Charles Dimmock's design that all his deterrents, the earthworks and batteries, for the most part faced the front. If the attackers could get behind the Confederate works, the rebels would become, for all practical purposes, defenseless. Despite its late start, Smith's assault captured a mile of Petersburg's fortifications with eight of its batteries. But inexplicably, with the city apparently lying helpless at his feet, Smith stopped. When he finally learned that Hancock was supposed to come to his support, he decided to await the arrival of the 2nd Corps before making any further advance.[8]

After a mind-boggling confusion of orders and misdirection, the first elements of Hancock's 2nd Corps did not arrive at Petersburg until last light on June 15. On his arrival, the ailing Hancock knew nothing of the battlefield he was facing, and Smith was disinclined to make any further attack that night. While Hancock received word from Grant that rebel reinforcements were beginning to come to Petersburg's defense, he nonetheless tasked Hancock with being ready to receive the rations that had already caused so much trouble and delay for the tired and surely hungry men of the 2nd Corps. Grant, meanwhile, began sending urgent messages for Meade to rush the remaining Army of the Potomac corps to Petersburg. In the aftermath of the Battle of Petersburg, when the blame was seemingly laid upon some failure of the 2nd Corps to come to Smith's aid, Grant placated the angry Hancock but told him the inquiry he was demanding was unnecessary. Grant would nonetheless state in his memoirs that, had Hancock received his orders promptly, Petersburg would have fallen. Grant neglected to say just who was at fault for Hancock not receiving those crucial orders.[9]

As Grant's plans for Smith to take Petersburg had begun to unravel, he was forced to address the problems he had created by his own failure to tell either Hancock, whose corps would be the first of the Army of the Potomac to make its way to Petersburg, or Meade, that army's commander, that Smith was making an attack on June 15. Grant's confidence that Smith would easily take Petersburg apparently started to waver, for he began to send dispatches of increasing urgency for the Army of the Potomac to make haste to get to Petersburg and for General Meade to come and take command of the assault to be made by the 18th Corps and the newly arrived 2nd. Grant then, in an astounding abdication of responsibility, left the front and went to his headquarters eight miles away at City Point. Behind him he left the ailing Hancock with the geographically challenged Comstock to assist in preparing for the assault. Though Grant had already told Washington, DC, that Smith's assault was succeeding, as the truth of the matter became all too apparent in the days that followed, it seems almost as if Grant lost interest in Petersburg altogether. In late June, Meade confessed that he had no idea what Grant's plans were for the Army of the Potomac. In the months to come, it would also seem that Grant's prime interest in the investment of Petersburg was the Army of the Potomac's ability not to capture that city but to keep much of R. E. Lee's Army of Northern Virginia pinned down there to prevent its being sent to reinforce opposition to William T. Sherman's and Sheridan's operations elsewhere.[10]

On the evening of June 15, the 9th Corps crossed the James on steam ferryboats, and at daybreak on June 16 Charles Griffin's and Lysander Cutler's divisions of the 5th Corps began crossing on boats departing from Wilcox Landing, while Samuel Crawford's and Romeyn Ayres's divisions of the 5th Corps departed from nearby Southard's Landing. By 1 p.m. Warren's infantry was across the river, while his artillery and train were crossing the pontoon bridge. By 2 p.m., the 5th Corps was on the road, and a hot and dusty road it was, with no potable water along the way. Inexplicably, shortly after Warren left the river, he received a dispatch from Grant to the effect that Petersburg had been captured, but the ongoing clamor of heavy firing ahead of them on their march told the men that the fight was not over. Warren was met by Kautz's cavalry near Prince George Court House and received a timely warning that saved him from a premature collision with the enemy. Kautz warned that if Warren took the route already taken by Ambrose Burnside's 9th

Corps to Petersburg as planned, their march would undoubtedly be delayed by rebel interference. As a result, the 5th Corps marched instead through Sycamore Church and Prince George Court House. By the time it had reached Sycamore Church, Grant was urging Warren to come to Petersburg with all possible speed.[11]

Not until midnight on the night of June 16–17 did the 5th Corps arrive safely near Petersburg. When Kautz's cavalry were ordered to return to Butler's Army of the James, Roebling was reluctant to see them go. They had provided the 5th Corps with effective scouting and screening, which the infantry corps was sadly unaccustomed to. Though little could be seen at the front in the darkness, Warren spent the night examining what he could of the situation. Roebling reported seeing "the works captured by Baldy Smith and the niggers," commenting that he thought the Confederate works were formidable but unconnected and held primarily by artillery. Warren met with Meade, Hancock, and Burnside, the latter preparing for the attack he would make before daybreak. While Burnside's assault succeeded in carrying a part of the enemy's line that day, capturing prisoners and guns, he would find it much harder to hold onto all the positions he had gained. The men of the 5th Corps, done in by their night march, were allowed to rest that day. There would be more than enough for them to do in the days to come. The Avery House, a landmark much mentioned on this battlefield, would be taken by the Federals but regrettably given up for lack of troops to hold it. When the Confederates reoccupied it, they installed a squad of sharpshooters that would make the 5th Corps's movements a misery in the coming days. Though Warren had much to think about on June 17 to prepare for the fighting he knew was coming, he wrote to his wife, Emily, that he hadn't forgotten this day was their first wedding anniversary.[12]

Federal pressure on June 16 had been sufficient to force a portion of the enemy's main defensive line to fall back. The rebels threw up a new line, which would become known as the Hagood Line. Roebling went forward to observe it from Burnside's position on the morning of June 17 and described the enemy's new position as "a low breastwork with two guns behind the Avery house, enfilading the plain in front. There were two more four gun batteries, the one farthest north being in the open field in front of their line; this last mentioned battery was only worked at intervals during the day, our own artillery fire keeping it silent most of the time. The enemy did not show a very heavy force behind their lines, although they may have had a heavy body concealed in the thick pine woods." Around noon on June 17, Crawford's and Griffin's divisions were brought up and formed behind the 9th Corps, with the 5th Corps's divisions stopping near the line captured from the enemy by Burnside the previous night. Roebling spent most of the morning reconnoitering and found that Burnside's position "commanded" Hagood's newly constructed line, which had no abatis, and since the ground behind it was open, no reinforcement could be sent in without being subject to Federal artillery fire. Toward noon, Cutler's division, with the Maryland Brigade from Ayres's division on hand to assist him, was brought up and joined a mix of 9th and 2nd Corps troops skirmishing with the enemy. Cutler's men were deployed east of the Avery House, which was still in enemy hands, and Roebling would later lament that they did not take the house when it was lightly defended by rebel sharpshooters.[13]

The Battle of Petersburg would be one of lost opportunities. While P. T. Beauregard tried in vain to convince Robert E. Lee that the Army of the Potomac had come to Petersburg, the Dimmock Line was barely manned with inexperienced civilians; much of its miles of fortification lay virtually empty of men. But that undefended state was not realized or found out, let alone fully exploited, by Smith on June 15. The door to Petersburg lay open to U. S. Grant, but General Lee was about to slam it shut. Major Washington Roebling's, General Warren's, and the 5th Corps's role in the Battle of Petersburg was about to begin in earnest.

28

The Battle of Petersburg

EARLY ON JUNE 17, AFTER WASHINGTON ROEBLING HAD LED LYSANDER
Cutler's division to a position east of the enemy-held Avery House, he then,
accompanied by the horsemen of the Warren's headquarters escort, began to
scout on the Army of the Potomac's left. He moved down the Norfolk Pike
beyond Wells's to a railroad platform, and then down a woods road leading
past Sturtevant's Mill, before striking the Jerusalem Plank Road at Mrs.
Temple's. He went up that road as far as the Jones House, later writing, "A
lot of the enemy's cavalry was posted across the road here and I did not go
any further." Undoubtedly by questioning locals, Roebling was able to report
that it was James D. Dearing's cavalry and that the Jerusalem Plank Road
was patrolled twice daily by roughly seventy of Dearing's troopers. When
Roebling returned to Gouverneur Warren's headquarters at 4 p.m., Ambrose
Burnside's 9th Corps was preparing for another assault, though it was almost
dark before the attack got under way at 7 p.m. Burnside succeeded, after heavy
fighting, in capturing a part of the enemy's position, but as his left was forced
back, his line soon rested at right angles across the Confederate line, and an
enemy battery enfiladed the Federal line, doing great damage. Although it
was now fully dark, Samuel Crawford's division of the 5th Corps was ordered
into the fight.[1]

Roebling remarked that it was never understood or explained why, instead
of leading his division straight in on flat ground, Crawford wandered into
nearby ravines. As a result, he became disoriented and was quite delayed
in coming to the 9th Corps's assistance. It would not be the last time that
General Crawford got lost. But in the way that the incompetent sometimes
accidentally do something right, when Crawford's division finally arrived at
the scene of the fighting, it captured sixty rebels and an Alabama regiment's
battle flag from one of George Pickett's divisions. Crawford's men then

Avery House, which became Warren's headquarters.
Library of Congress.

became hopelessly mixed in with the 9th Corps, and presently everybody fell back so that no part of the enemy line captured by the Unionists that night was retained. Meanwhile, the Confederate prisoners taken admitted that their force was presently very small but asserted that reinforcements were on the way, and it turned out they were right about that. Not until the night of June 17–18 did R. E. Lee finally commit the Army of Northern Virginia to Petersburg's defense, but it was the 5th Corps's and the Army of the Potomac's misfortune that, whereas on previous days much of the Confederate works stood empty, the assaults made on June 18 would find the Federals attacking enemy defenses fully manned by Lee's veterans. Firing was kept up all through the night, and Roebling reported that "toward midnight the enemy were seen to burn a gun carriage in the field in front of their line." Roebling correctly noted that it looked like the enemy was preparing to retire again.[2]

Orders were issued during the night of June 17–18 that the 5th Corps would be making an attack with the 9th and 2nd Corps at 4 a.m. the next morning, June 18. Since Meade's headquarters was unaware of the enemy's withdrawal from the Hagood Line, the Army of the Potomac advanced as scheduled, expecting to quickly encounter the enemy. Roebling described Cutler's advance at daylight, a fog covering the men's movement, but the enemy had abandoned the Avery House and also its line beyond the edge of the woods. Roebling told of finding one startled old Confederate asleep in the Avery House. "He stated that there was a line of battle there when he fell asleep in the middle of the night." Roebling soon reported to General Warren that the enemy had entrenched a new line along the ridge on the opposite side of the ravine where the Norfolk and Petersburg Railroad entered Petersburg. Warren forwarded this information and news that Cutler's and part of Crawford's skirmishers had driven the rebels over the railroad. Meanwhile, reports began coming in from other Federal commands that the enemy had also evacuated the line in their fronts, retreating to the new line that would be known as the Harris Line. Roebling soon brought orders to Cutler to advance, keeping his left on the Norfolk Road, since near the Avery House the road appeared to run nearly due west. As soon as Cutler appeared west of the Avery House, the rebels opened from a rifled battery on a crest. An entrenched line was also visible there, with men standing on the parapet, and when the Maryland Brigade, on Cutler's right, tried to advance across an open field, the enemy's artillery fire encouraged them to edge off to the left under the cover of woods. Roebling further reported the "planting [of] two rifled batteries in position to answer the enemy."[3]

After discovering that the enemy had fallen back, when Cutler tried to continue his advance, he found that his whole line would have to get across the Norfolk and Petersburg Railroad, which was in a deep cut turning to the right. A bridge that would have helped them cross was still in flames, destroyed by the enemy. It took some time for Cutler's line to dislodge enemy skirmishers on the other side of the cut and finally make their way across. Reforming on the other side, Cutler's division continued to push the rebel skirmishers back. Roebling says that Jacob Sweitzer's brigade and Crawford's skirmishers now advanced over the open field with Crawford's division on the right of the Norfolk Turnpike and Sweitzer's on the left. With no bridge to take them across the deep cut, they went up the railroad cut, though Roebling commented that it was easier to get the soldiers into the cut than it was to get them out. Roebling noted that Romeyn Ayres's division minus the Maryland Brigade, which was on loan to Cutler, moved off behind Cutler's division, advancing along the old line of captured fortifications (Dimmock Line batteries 20–24). With half his troops on either side of the old fortification, Ayres faced to the west, protecting the 5th Corps's and the Army of the Potomac's left flank. It took no time for the enemy to spot Ayres, who came under heavy artillery fire at Rives Salient, where, as Roebling described, the rebels' newest line, the Harris Line, which was frantically prepared during the wee hours of June 18, joined onto the original fortification of the Dimmock

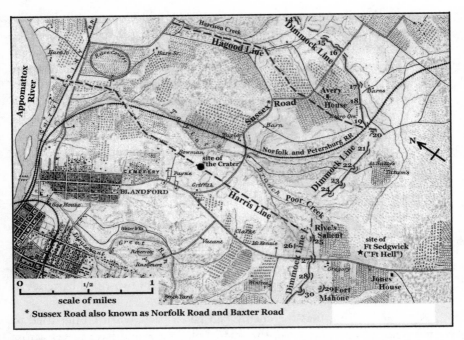

Petersburg, eastern front.
From Plate XL, 1 OR Atlas.

Line at Confederate Battery 25 opposite Ayres's 10 a.m. position. Roebling's report states that while the Confederate battery at Rives was doing "considerable execution" against Ayres's division, the sharpshooters from that position were plying their trade against Cutler's right. Over the course of the day, the fierce fire from both Rives Salient and a nearby detached fortification, Fort Mahone, encouraged Cutler and Ayres to move back and to their left to get out of the withering enemy fire.[4]

With his plan for a dawn attack upended by the withdrawal of the enemy's line, by midmorning, a thoroughly frustrated Meade gave orders to prepare for a simultaneous attack along the entire Army of the Potomac line at noon. Those units on the 5th Corps's left, Ayres's and Cutler's divisions and the 1st and 3rd Brigades of Griffin, had a long distance to advance—in some cases a mile and a half, every inch of it contested by the enemy. George Meade directed that the entire Federal line make the noon assault "at all hazards," causing Roebling to comment, "No matter whether we understood the ground or not or were prepared anyhow." Roebling related that "every energy was bent toward accomplishing that," but the ground they had to traverse presented many obstacles, and the enemy's sharpshooters were keeping him from reconnoitering properly. Roebling also acknowledged that the curve and deep cut of the railroad had caused considerable trouble for Crawford's division and Sweitzer's brigade, which had both remained over on Burnside's left. Various ravines and swampy areas that formed the head of Poor Creek left an inevitable gap between Sweitzer's and Griffin's other brigades. Joshua Chamberlain's 1st Brigade eventually took up a position in front of Rives Salient with Joseph Bartlett's 3rd Brigade in reserve, while Cutler's and Ayres's divisions were on the 5th Corps's extreme left. Roebling pointed out that the ground was such that one division commander could not tell how any other divisions were "getting on." He reported to Warren around 1 p.m. from the 5th Corps's extreme left that Ayres was close in to the enemy's main line, but both Cutler and Ayres had edged to the Federal left over the course of day, drawing back from the fierce enemy artillery fire from Rives Salient and its nearby battery in Fort Mahone.[5]

In a great confusion of times and expectations, Roebling at noon on June 18 had handed General Cutler an order to attack. Cutler claimed not only that the paper Roebling handed him was blank but also that Colonel Chamberlain and his 1st Brigade, which had just had a long fight to a position in front of Rives Salient, believed they were to attack the crest where Cutler was posted. Someone was thoroughly confused, but it was not Chamberlain. If Cutler is any indication of how things were going on the 5th Corps's left, it's no surprise that Warren missed Meade's noon deadline; not until 1 p.m. could he report that his left was finally in hand before the enemy and he was ready to make an assault. Warren nonetheless suggested to Meade that they make the general assault at 3 p.m. Meade agreed, though likely with gritted teeth and bulging eyes. It was left to Chamberlain's brigade to make the assault on Rives Salient at 3 p.m., with Cutler, to Chamberlain's left and rear, advancing shortly after. The distant Sweitzer, still acting on Crawford's left, did not make an assault until 6 p.m., while Ayres, on the extreme left, found the enemy fire so concentrated that he could not advance at all, though he would later make the last costly advance of the day. Roebling reported the outcome of the advance made by General Cutler's division: "The result was a repulse with a loss of say 1600 men killed and wounded. The nearest approach to carrying the enemy's line was in Griffin's front; some of the men were shot there within 20 feet." It is undoubtedly the men of Joshua Chamberlain (Griffin's 1st Brigade), with their 3 p.m. assault, who came nearest to reaching the enemy fortification at Rives Salient, despite being under heavy fire from both Rives Salient and

General Lysander Cutler.
Library of Congress.

Fort Mahone on their left. Roebling noted that the rest of the Army of the Potomac's assaults on June 18 had been even less successful than those of the 5th Corps.[6]

Roebling reported of Cutler's advance that only five hundred men of that division got beyond Poor Creek on their front, and they were feared lost until they were able to make their way back in the dark of night. Roebling suggested that Crawford's division and Sweitzer's brigade, separated from the rest of the 5th Corps by the swampy terrain of Poor Creek, had an easier assault on the enemy's line on June 18 because the ground they advanced over was steeper, and the enemy fired over them. It is also worth remembering that Sweitzer and Crawford were attacking the rebels' brand-new line, the Harris Line, which consisted of whatever the enemy had been able to throw together since 1 a.m. on the morning of June 18. Roebling said that after the 3 p.m. assault, an attempt at straightening the 5th Corps lines was made for the purpose of making another attack, but the idea was abandoned. The night of June 18 saw the survivors of the day's assaults coming back to their lines, and

General Romeyn Ayres.
Library of Congress.

Roebling reported that batteries were brought up to Cutler's position, though Cutler's division and Chamberlain's brigade were pulled back to straighten the 5th Corps line. During the night of June 18–19, the 5th Corps was able to bring in most of its dead and wounded, and while Bartlett's brigade, which had remained in reserve that afternoon, relieved troops on Griffin's front. The next day found General Warren taking the Avery House as his headquarters, and Roebling also reported that up on Burnside's front, the enemy's sharp-shooters were very active. He related that nowhere on the eastern bank of the railroad cut was it was safe to show oneself, so though there was no actual fighting, the 5th Corps lost three hundred or so of its men on June 19.[7]

On June 19, a downhearted Roebling wrote to his Emily, "We are still wearily fighting along day by day; nothing has been achieved by us that would ensure any lasting substantial success. It is the same old story every day, kill—kill—kill." Washington commented that Emily wouldn't think him despondent if she could hear her brother, General Warren, talk about the war. The sentiments Warren expressed earlier that month are perhaps a window to the horror that both he and Roebling felt at the slaughter they were witness-ing. Warren said, "To-day I saw a man burying a comrade, and, within half an hour, he himself was brought in and buried beside him. The men need some rest." Roebling also often tempted fate with his rides along the Federal front, as he told Emily: "My old Nancy was pegged yesterday; I hope the beast will get better; why didn't you give her a portion of your heart, it might have saved her," a sentimental tribute to the imagined powers of guardianship bestowed by Emily's love.[8]

A few days after the bloodletting of June 18, Generals Meade and Warren had a heated argument. It was witnessed by Warren's inept division commander and Meade's old friend, General Crawford, and apparently was also overheard by much of the staff at the 5th Corps headquarters. Warren reputedly told Meade that "he was no creature of his" and, as he later told his wife, that he would not allow himself to be made anyone's scapegoat. There is no question that Meade's temper had been on the boil during the day of June 18, and Warren's inability to reach the enemy's main line as soon as Meade wanted had no doubt caused the latter no end of frustration that day. Meade seemingly refused to acknowledge that Warren had made a sufficient effort, given that his corps had had to traverse more than a mile and a half over ravines and railroad cuts, with every inch under heavy fire from the enemy's skirmishers and batteries. It wasn't, in this case, even a matter of jockeying for position or taking time for deployment; he simply had to first fight his way forward in order to get his men close enough to assault the enemy's main line. Delay for Meade's attack had been inescapable from the earliest part of the day, given the enemy's withdrawal to its new Harris Line. And evidence was coming in that Lee was providing substantial reinforcement for P. T. Beauregard's beleaguered force at Petersburg, where empty fortifications were now filling with the Army of Northern Virginia's seasoned veterans. But then the talk around U. S. Grant's headquarters was that the Army of the Potomac hadn't fought very well at Petersburg. Edwin Stanton's man, Charles Dana, who hadn't witnessed the assaults since he had spent the day sick at Grant's headquarters at City Point, nonetheless sent Cyrus Comstock's assessment to Washington that the fighting "hadn't been equal to our previous fighting owing to the heavy loss in superior officers." Without missing a beat, Dana also reported that from June 16 to June 18, the Army of the Potomac had lost about seven thousand men, although that number would soon be set higher at ninety-five hundred.[9]

After the argument between Meade and Warren, the other rumor going around headquarters and the army's camps was that Meade had given Warren an ultimatum. It was said that he had demanded Warren ask to be relieved or he would press charges against him. Based on no more than a rumor, Dana sent this hot gossip to Washington, and though it was untrue, Warren nonetheless heard from Baldy Smith, ever the one to stir things up, that it was common talk at Grant's headquarters. Weeks later, Warren discovered it was being published in a Pennsylvania newspaper and asked Meade for an explanation. Meade replied that while he hadn't said as much to Warren, he had considered relieving him and had spoken to General Grant about it. Claiming that he had been considerably hurt by his loud argument with Warren, Meade said that he didn't wish to harm him and supposed that the circumstances that had caused the grievance would not be repeated. Meade nonetheless declared that if harmony and cooperation were left wanting, "a separation is inevitable." Warren would write to his wife at the end of July that he did not think it possible that he and Meade would ever be on a friendly basis again, nor did he have confidence that his chief would act with patience and judgment. Months of conflict still lay ahead for Warren; his aide, Washington Roebling; and the soldiers of the Army of the Potomac.[10]

29

Roebling's Redoubt and the
Exploding of Burnside's Mine

BY JUNE 20, THE ARMY OF THE POTOMAC WAS BEGINNING TO FEEL TOWARD its left. Washington Roebling reported that Romeyn Ayres's pickets on the army's extreme left flank advanced a little so that they overlooked the Jerusalem Plank Road. During the night, most of General Charles Griffin's division withdrew, while Lysander Cutler's division and Jacob Sweitzer's brigade stretched to cover the gap made with as few men as possible in order to free up men for another movement. Roebling commented that twenty-five hundred men per mile was considered sufficient to hold a line. The rest of Griffin's division was subsequently brought around to the left, massing near the Chever House. General David Birney, commanding the 2nd Corps while Winfield Hancock was disabled by his Gettysburg wound, sent his chief of staff, Lieutenant Colonel C. H. Morgan, an old friend of Roebling's and Gouverneur Warren's from their 2nd Corps days, to look over the ground to the 5th Corps's left where Birney would be advancing the next day. Warren had reassured General Birney that the valuable services of his scout Roebling would be made available to him. On June 21, Birney moved his corps across the Plank Road near the Williams House, the future site of Fort Davis. When Meade noticed that Griffin had not moved as fast as the commanding general had wanted, Roebling told, "Genl. Meade rode past Griffin's Hd Qrs at the Chever house and made a fuss because his Div. was massed there yet; they [Griffin's brigades] accordingly moved up at once without much opposition to the edge of the timber overlooking the field south of the rebel line." Griffin's left lay on the Plank Road at a spot that would be the future site of Fort Sedgwick. Its ever-expanding works, first known as Roebling's Redoubt since he helped design and build it, would soon become the most famous fortification on the field, dubbed Fort Hell for the ferocity of the exchanges with its rebel counterpart across the way, called Fort Damnation. When rushed forward by George Meade, Griffin was forced to move without his artillery, but he nonetheless kept his right connected with Ayres while maintaining one brigade in reserve at the Chever House. Griffin had his men dig in on Joseph Bartlett's and William S. Tilton's fronts, and Roebling noted a gap on the Plank Road between Griffin's left and the 2nd Corps's right, but it was the gap that was to develop between the 2nd Corps's left and the approaching 6th Corps that would lead to disaster.[1]

On June 22, the 6th Corps was ordered to come up on the 2nd Corps's left, and when it didn't come up as quickly as he wanted, Meade once again became impatient and ordered the 2nd Corps to advance for an assault without waiting for General Horatio Wright. When Birney's 2nd Corps began to press forward toward the open country south of the enemy's lines on the afternoon of June 20, it received a sharp attack on its left flank by General William Mahone's division. Roebling described the attack as "so sudden and vigorous that before [Birney's division commander, John] Gibbon had time to change his front the enemy had doubled up almost two brigades taking 2300 prisoners and 4 guns" from a Federal battery, as well as several stands of colors. One can almost hear General Griffin muttering, "Haste makes waste." Mahone then retired back to his works as quickly as he had come. Griffin and his troops had seen Mahone come and go, and Griffin apparently remarked that if he'd been allowed enough time to bring up one or two batteries, the disaster that befell the 2nd Corps would never have happened. Otherwise Griffin could only send his reserve brigade to assist Gibbon, though it was not called upon. The next day Cutler's division in particular had much to endure from the enemy's artillery fire, and although the Federals had as many as twenty-eight pieces in position to play upon the rebels, they were unable to silence the Confederate artillery. Roebling commented that the rebel guns "seemed to be located in a depression of the ground formed by the head of the ravine of the Poo[r Creek] so that our direct fire from Ayres's and Cutler's fronts could do them no harm." As the 2nd Corps's historian described Mahone's attack, "Nothing but the extraordinary quickness and precision of the Confederate movements on this occasion would have made such a result possible. The second Corps had been defeated almost without being engaged." Meade and the Army of the Potomac would eventually learn that they would pay dearly for giving rebel general Mahone any opportunities, for he would turn Federal mistakes into mayhem.[2]

Others apparently saw Roebling as unmoved and unemotional regarding the chaos and danger in which he moved, but his letter to Emily on the day after the 2nd Corps's disaster on the Federal left tells a different story. Roebling confessed to her what, apparently, he confessed to no other:

> Last night was an anxious one again for your poor cuss; I wish I had it in my power to maintain that utter indifference to surrounding events that other people seem to have; but if anything goes wrong it worries me exceedingly even if it don't concern me personally; people talk about getting used to fighting and to battles, but I don't see it in that light, and the more experience I have the worse it gets; I believe if I stay any longer than next winter my hair will all turn grey; if it were black it would I expect.

Roebling's anxieties had been provoked by the fact that apparently no lesson had been learned at Army of the Potomac headquarters after the calamity of June 22 when Meade had rushed the 2nd Corps forward. The very next day Meade urged the 6th Corps to advance to a position on the left of the battered 2nd Corps, where Wright, too, was attacked by Mahone. Wright lost six hundred men, despite both Griffin and Ayres contributing brigades to support the 2nd and 6th Corps. While telling Emily about the sad fate of the 2nd Corps the previous day, Roebling added,

> They must put fresh steam on the man factories up North; the demand down here for killing purposes is far ahead of the supply; Thank God however for this consolation that when the last man is killed the war will be over. This war you know differs from all previous wars in having no object to fight for; it can't be finished until all the men on the one side or the other are killed; both sides are trying to do that as fast as they can because it would be a pity to spin this affair out for 2 or 3 years longer. Civil wars have always been the most horrible & cruel during all times past, and they must of necessity be more bloody because the two sides being of the same nation are more evenly matched and greater efforts are therefore necessary to produce any results; I will bet that when this war is once over there will not be another one for a hundred years to come, not if I can help it anyhow.

What a despondent Roebling could not say to others, he said to Emily. Despite his anguish and anxiety, he would be out scouting and leading men to the front again and again in the coming days. But Roebling was far from thinking of his activities as heroic, and while expressing his admiration for the

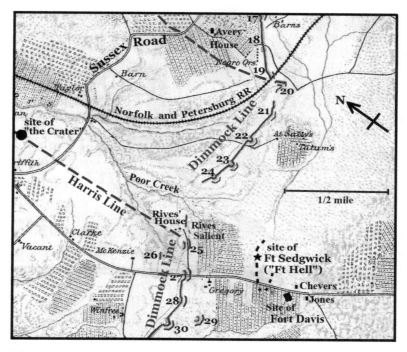

After the Battle of Petersburg.
From Plate XL, 1 OR Atlas.

foot soldiers in the battle lines, he also realized there was a limit to what they could endure: "The biggest heroes in this war are the privates in the line—the man with the musket. When I think sometimes what those men all do & endure day after day, with their lives constantly in danger, I can't but wonder that there should be men who are such fools, I can't call them anything else. And that is just the trouble we are laboring under now—the fools have all been killed and the rest think it is about played out to stand up and get shot." While he could pour his heart out to Emily, he could also find refuge in his imaginings of their future together. On a much lighter and more hopeful note, he wrote, "There are so many subjects about which I want to commence writing to you more fully before long, if it wasn't for this infernal fighting all the time; as long as it lasts it seems foolish for me to touch on them. About all I can foresee at present is that some fine morning next winter I will have to jump out of a dirty shirt into a clean one and run up to Cold Spring and get married the next day. All these matters would then have to be settled

309

afterwards." Until the day when they would be reunited, Roebling was often found consulting his pocket watch, with its reassuring photograph of Emily within.[3]

Not until June 24 was Samuel Crawford's division relieved his position in support of Ambrose Burnside's 9th Corps, with which it had been since June 17. When Crawford was finally allowed to return to the 5th Corps, Roebling reported that he was then sent out to relieve Gibbon's division of the 2nd Corps on Griffin's left. As Crawford took up a position with his right eventually resting on the Jerusalem Plank Road, he remarked to Roebling that Gibbon's men were very much demoralized. General Meade, several days after the Army of the Potomac's failure to take Petersburg, suggested that as his army had been fighting and marching for forty-nine days straight, perhaps it was time for a rest for the sake of morale. Meade may have left that a bit late. Though the incessant forced marches were, for the most part, over, there was little to cheer up a Federal soldier that June 1864. The heat under the intense Virginia sun was appalling enough, but a constant musketry and artillery fire was kept up day and night. Though there were no fights to speak of, the 5th Corps was nonetheless losing between thirty and seventy men a day in late June and early July. Time was spent strengthening the earthworks and placing abatis along the corps's entire front. Despite the Army of the Potomac's grim situation, Roebling made the effort to write a lighthearted letter to his Emily, relating the good news that they had hit the jackpot by finding a cook who had originally served on a French packet. Saying that they had enjoyed a lobster salad, Washington related that the fellow "knows how to make a great many dishes out of very few articles and give them some relish at the same time." Other than the impossibility of getting Emily's daily letters at the front, the only cloud on his horizon, Roebling reported, was the dwindling supply of the Sanitary Commission's chocolate, but he also related that they had received the less than good news of William T. Sherman's Atlanta endeavors, courtesy of Confederates, noting that "the Johnnies of course are jubilant and sent us yesterday evening's Petersburg Express containing the news."[4]

While the 2nd and 6th Corps had suffered at the hands of General Mahone, James H. Wilson's cavalry, supported by General August Kautz's division, some five thousand horsemen under Wilson's command, headed out on an expedition from June 22 to July 1 intending to distract the Confederates and destroy enemy railroads. Instead, when the rebel cavalry got hold of him, as Roebling commented, Wilson came near being "gobbled up" in a fight with rebel cavalry. During Wilson's wild retreat back to the Army of the Potomac, he discovered the hard way that, contrary to his belief that Philip Sheridan had control of Reams Station, the enemy occupied it, dashing his best hope for a safe haven. So Sheridan, in aborting his mission after his defeat at Trevilian Station, not only let down David Hunter but also had a serious impact on Wilson's expedition. To compound his callous lack of concern for the fates of others, when called upon, Sheridan ignored orders to go to Wilson's rescue, and a 6th Corps division was sent out to help what was left of Wilson's division limp in. Wilson had lost fifteen hundred men, his trains, and all twelve of his guns. But in case he wasn't sufficiently embarrassed, the Richmond newspapers printed stories of plunder, such as wine and silver, being found in his abandoned headquarters trains. When Meade asked Wilson about it, U. S. Grant and Wilson became angry that the subject was even brought up, and Meade let it drop.[5]

Despite the bad feelings that existed between himself and Meade, Warren found it impossible to remain silent after the punishment General Mahone had dealt out to the Federal 2nd and 6th Corps. Though Warren was often mistakenly portrayed as or maliciously accused by his rivals of being a commander who always delayed and demurred when asked to attack, Warren made a bold suggestion on June 23—that the Army of the Potomac abandon its present confrontation of Petersburg and direct its efforts to destroying the enemy's lifelines, the railroads coming into the city. By moving Meade's entire force west to the Weldon Railroad, he believed, they could force R. E. Lee to leave his defenses. Though Meade sent back a skeptical reply, he forwarded Warren's suggestion on to Grant, but nothing came of it. Warren admitted that his plan had risks but argued that "with our unparalleled losses and exhausting efforts we can scarcely say we are much nearer destroying Lee's army than when we were on the Rapidan." Warren expressed his discouragement in a letter to his wife, Emily, citing the Federal losses since crossing the Rapidan, a devastating seventy thousand men. Lamenting that they still lacked generalship, Warren declared that with each frontal assault on enemy entrenchment, he lost confidence in Meade, adding bitterly, "And then disregarding the useless slaughter of thousands of noblest soldiers the country grows jubilant, and watches the smoke wreathes from Grant's cigar as if they saw therefrom a way to propitiate a God."[6]

With some relief, one finds that Roebling had cheered up to some extent, considering a letter he wrote to Emily on July 1. Roebling, who had become known in the army for the lack of buttons on his coat and the disgraceful condition of his pants, reported, "I am strutting around today arrayed in a new pair of pants the gift of your kind brother G. K. He also offered me a pair of boots but I couldn't get in them; my feet you know are very large—almost as large as yours; never mind Darling I am ready to kiss your toe any day as punishment for this heresy."[7]

One wonders, however, whether Roebling was able to maintain his apparent good mood for many days, for on July 3, after the enemy had had several weeks to strengthen the fortifications that the Army of the Potomac had been unable to take on June 18, Grant asked Meade, "Do you think it possible, by a bold and decisive attack, to break through the enemy's center, say in General Warren's front somewhere?" Meade responded that he would consult with Warren and Burnside. A distrustful Warren replied, "I would rather the opinion of some one independent of me should decide the question, as circumstances in the past leave me without much strength in declining any proposed attack whatever." Warren would further request that competent staff officers be sent to his front "so that the opinion can rest on mere military grounds and not hereafter be a question of individual willingness, ability, or boldness." Later, a touchy Warren strenuously objected when Meade wrongly stated to General Grant, "Major-General Warren does not deem any [offensive operations] practicable in his front," adding, "My opinion was that it was not advisable to do it by assault, not that I could not carry on 'any offensive operations' in my front."[8]

In early July, attempts to get around the enemy's right flank by both the 2nd and the 6th Corps had again failed, and when a survey was made regarding the advisability of another general Federal assault against the enemy's lines, no general was in favor. Roebling recorded, "By this time the project of Gen. Burnside to dig a mine under the advance position which Gen. Griffin had taken possession of in the charge of the 18th began to attract some attention; it had been somewhat ridiculed heretofore." Referring to Burnside's tunnel as "the only resource left in the way of making offensive movements against the enemy," Roebling added,

> To take full advantage of the successful explosion of the mine it would be necessary to mass all the available force of the Army there, consisting of the 2nd and 6th Corps, then on our left, and holding a position of no importance. It was determined that we should hold the flank of the Army by two or three detached redoubts of large dimensions, able to take care of themselves if the enemy should break in between them. Before these were located the sense of the community was once more taken upon the advisability of a general assault against the lines, but the report of every general was unfavorable.[9]

Roebling recorded that on July 4, Meade's chief engineer, Major James Duane, and the officer Grant had put in charge of the siege operations at Petersburg, General Henry Hunt, were out on the 5th Corps's front selecting sites for guns to assist in and support Burnside's assault. Their goal was to find a good location for batteries and counterbatteries that would sweep the ground behind the enemy's lines on Burnside's front and prevent the rebels from reinforcing their lines. The site for Fort Sedgwick/Fort Hell was also chosen, as Roebling reported, for its ability to control the whole of the open country near the enemy's lines toward the Weldon Railroad. Though the railroad was much coveted by the Federals, General Meade objected, for reasons Roebling didn't explain, to having the site for the redoubt acted upon. Regardless, the lines for Fort Sedgwick were marked out by a rifle pit after

General Henry Hunt and Chief Engineer, Army of the Potomac, James Duane.
Library of Congress.

dark. Duane's and Hunt's proposals prompted what was, sadly, a rare flash of optimism from Roebling, who commented on July 4, "There is a prospect that we may be in Petersburg by the 4th of Sept. Some sensible orders were given yesterday which will ultimately lead to an advantageous result."[10]

By July 6, Warren had notified General Griffin about the upcoming construction of the fortification that was first known as Roebling's Redoubt:

> The general lines of the redoubt on your left have been marked out by a rifle-pit as near to the enemy's works as it was desirable to put them. I wish an earth-work with a strong profile made at that point and that you should give your earnest effort to have it made promptly and thoroughly. Major Roebling, of my staff, fully understands my views, and will under you, if it suits you, take charge of the construction of the work. The men in that vicinity should prepare themselves with abundant shelter in the rear in case the enemy opens fire upon this point, which is very close to their batteries.

There seems little question that the building of the redoubt, which Roebling would be supervising, would draw the attention of the enemy and its guns at Fort Mahone/Fort Damnation. With large details of soldiers from Griffin's division and from the 2nd Corps, work on the redoubt progressed rapidly. Historian Earl Hess writes, "The fort consisted of eighteen embrasured gun emplacements and a smaller redan to its right for four guns. The Engineer Battalion did much of the detailed work at Fort Sedgwick, including numerous traverses held up by gabion revetments. The Federals enclosed the gorge with a stockade, placed abatis in front, and slashed timber in front of the work." Captain G. H. Mendell, commander of the Battalion of Engineers, offered further description of Major Roebling's fort, saying that during the second week of work, excavations for two magazines, twelve feet by six feet, were being dug. Meanwhile, the 2nd Corps's workmen dug a covered way from near the Avery House to Fort Sedgwick that was twelve feet wide and four feet deep, with enough logs and dirt banked on the sides to provide eight feet of cover. Remarkably, Fort Sedgwick was almost ready after only three weeks of intense labor. By the time three redoubts, Forts Sedgwick, Davis, and Prescott, were ready for occupation on the Army of the Potomac's left, Warren was confident that they would safeguard the army's flank and leave the greater part of the 5th Corps free for an advance on Lee's lifeline, the Weldon Railroad. Before the fortifications were finished, however, the 6th Corps was sent away from the Army of the Potomac to help defend the capital against

Jubal Early's raid. On July 9, the 2nd Corps and Crawford's division filled the gap left by the 6th Corps's departure, and Roebling recalled that there was a feeling of unease, with the troops under orders to be ready to move at a moment's notice.[11]

As Meade contemplated matters of offense and defense at Petersburg, he referred rather wistfully in a letter home early that July to it's being the first anniversary of the Battle of Gettysburg. While all eyes were turning toward yet another of Lee's "invasions" of the North, General Early's raid into the Shenandoah Valley, Meade suggested that, as the war went on, perhaps the results of his victory in Pennsylvania would be appreciated. He went on to ask his wife, "Have you ever thought that since the first week after Gettysburg, now more than a year, I have never been alluded to in public journals except to abuse and villify [sic] me? And why this is I have never been able to imagine." Meade took considerable interest in the threat Early was posing to the nation's capital, commenting, "This is a bold stroke of Lee's to endeavor to procure the withdrawal of this army from its menacing attitude and to prevent the sending of reinforcements to Grant. The manoeuvre thus far has been successful, as not only has the 6th Corps been sent away, but the Nineteenth Corps (twenty thousand strong), which was to reinforce us, has been diverted to Washington." But Meade was watching developments for another reason: there were rumors that he would be sent to take charge of the defense of Washington, meaning that he would once again have an independent command, one without Grant looking over his shoulder every day. Then, too, other rumors would have left Meade believing that his position at the head of the Army of the Potomac would never be secure, for his friend, Winfield Hancock, had warned that reliable sources were saying he himself was meant to replace Meade as the army's commander. A visit to the army that summer by Senator Morton S. Wilkenson of Minnesota, who had attacked Meade severely in a speech in the Senate the previous winter, was not the only reminder for Meade of just how many political enemies he had. A fresh attack in the newspapers blamed him for following Grant's orders to expel several journalists from the army.[12]

By July 12, with two of the forts fully manned and Fort Sedgwick nearly finished, the 2nd Corps was able to move away from the Federal left, leaving only one of its brigades behind on picket. On this day, Roebling noted, "Col. Davis, 39th Massachusetts was killed today in the large redoubt [Fort Warren] by a shell bursting under the chair he was sitting on." Fort Warren was renamed Fort Davis in his memory. Work continued on the redoubts, with timber being cut on each side of the Plank Road, while General David Gregg's cavalry division and General Edward Ferrero's U.S. Colored Troops protected the Army of the Potomac's left flank near the Jerusalem Plank Road. The next day, Roebling rode out around Ferrero's line, selecting the ground for a new picket line, continuing along Thomas Smyth's brigade of the 2nd Corps until he came around to Crawford's front. Ferrero's soldiers would man the new picket line in his front, and Crawford would replace the 2nd Corps brigade on the picket line. Still work continued on the redoubts, with Fort Sedgwick almost ready to receive its guns. The Army of the Potomac was settling into a routine of life in the trenches and redoubts at the front, where one day could be much like the next. Any unusual event that broke the routine was noted, such as on July 15, when a shell from one of the 9th Corps batteries caused an explosion in a rebel battery opposite.[13]

As the work on the various batteries was being completed, the captain of the Battalion of Engineers, G. H. Mendell, described the battery that Major Roebling was constructing on General Griffin's left, in which "embrasures were cut out of the revetment and partially revetted with gabions, and the excavations for two magazines 12 by 6 were well advanced." Most batteries were completed, the few exceptions being a few nearest the site of Burnside's mine. Although the coming of rebel deserters into the 5th Corps lines had become a regular event, the night of July 17 was notable for the number who arrived after dark, saying that an attack would be made on the Federal lines before daybreak. As a result, the 5th Corps's lines were manned all night, but nothing came of it. Otherwise, most nights were occupied by work parties, some one thousand to fifteen hundred men, continuing to labor on the redoubts and batteries, including the two heavy mortar batteries. As work continued, the batteries began taking over defensive measures so that the need for infantry was materially lessened. With temperatures soaring and men dropping from heat exhaustion, on July 20 Hancock's 2nd Corps was withdrawn to be sent across the James to challenge the enemy at Deep Bottom. While the 2nd Corps sweltered on its unsuccessful expedition, all the while the Pennsylvania miners of the 9th Corps, who were digging the tunnel for the mine on Burnside's front, continued to bore quietly away, advancing ever closer to the Confederate line. The tedious routine was broken when rebel cavalry appeared on the 5th Corps's left flank, the incursion inspired, Roebling believed, by the enemy's investigation of the suspicious departure of Hancock's 2nd Corps from the Army of the Potomac's front lines. In these days of prodigious labor on the redoubts but otherwise relative quiet for the 5th Corps, Roebling related his only personal excitement: "That foolish little stallion of mine fell down today causing me to describe a somersault over his head but I was up long before he was & had to kick him to make him get up."[14]

July 28 and 29 were days of busy preparation, for on June 30 Burnside's mine would be exploded, and Roebling reported that some of the 5th Corps's preparations were not completed until that morning. The night of July 29 was spent getting the eight- and ten-inch mortars in position and putting shells and powder into their magazines. The night before the explosion, Roebling went down to view the arrangements at the tunnel and was clearly not impressed by what he saw.

> One single narrow and crooked covered way led to the ground near the mouth of the mine, where the charging column formed previous to the assault; the space here was very limited and entirely inadequate for assembling a large body of men for making a rush. The greater part of this covered way was exposed to the enemy's fire, especially where it descended and emerged from the railroad cut; Owing to the *place d'armes* being so small, the progress of the column coming down the covered way would necessarily be very slow, leaving them exposed to the enemy's fire so much longer.

Before daylight on July 30, General Ayres's division was massed in the railroad cut, ready to go in after all Burnside's men had advanced. In addition, the 9th Corps was supported by Edward Ord's 18th Corps and also by the 2nd Corps, which had come back from Deep Bottom. Roebling commented that almost the entire army was therefore at hand.[15]

Owing to a defect in the fuse, the explosion did not go off at 4 a.m. as scheduled, and several intrepid volunteers went back into the mine to repair the break. Roebling told of that fateful morning:

> The charge I think was 8,000 pounds [of black powder]; depth of ground 25'. As no one present had ever seen that much powder exploded at once, the most extravagant expectations were indulged in as to the effect. When it did take place everyone was disappointed. There was a solid column of smoke, flame and dirt, say 200' wide and 200' high, visible for perhaps 15 seconds, then everything subsided and a heavy cloud of black smoke floated off. The whole mass of earth had settled down again into the hole, of course thoroughly shaken up and with everything on top turned upside down or partially buried; there was a small crater in the center of the mine. The charge of powder had not been sufficient to throw the earth far, and no damage at all was done to the enemy's lines immediately adjacent to the mine. The location of the mine was also

short of the proper point, as the enemy's covered way remained intact behind the edge of the crater.[16]

Immediately after the explosion, the Federals opened upon the area surrounding the crater with fifty-two field guns, sixteen heavy mortars, eleven coehorns, and twenty rifled 32s. Though Roebling was clearly reporting only what he could see from Burnside's headquarters, supplemented with a large amount of overheard speculation, he related,

> I went over to Gen. Burnside's Hd Qrs. to ascertain how he was getting along and how soon he would need our cooperation. His men had been lying for several hours waiting for the explosion, and were pretty well scared when it did take place; moreover for weeks previous their minds had been wrought up about it. The result was that for half an hour the men refused to go forward, and the most favorable opportunity was lost for taking advantage of the surprise. The plan had been that our troops should march right through the opening caused by the explosion, and mass on the crest beyond, overlooking the town, instead of rolling up the enemy line right and left by the flank. [General James] Ledlie's Div. stopped in the crater instead of going any further, glad to find shelter from the musketry fire the enemy was pouring in from each flank; the men were so disorganized when they got up there after running the gauntlet for 150 yds. that nothing could be done with them. After this one Div. was out of the way the colored troops rushed up and piled in on top of the white Div. lying in the crater; this only added to the confusion; some efforts were made to go farther which only ended in the men plunging headlong into the covered way beyond; one gun of the enemy's played into this mass at short range; our guns could not silence this piece owing to the obstructions caused by a grove of trees in the 9th Corps front which had not been cut down the night previous.[17]

Roebling's report for this day of the Battle of the Crater was written several months after the event, and it conveys much of the initial confusion, brief hope, and gradual devastating loss and disappointment of that day. He acknowledged that the artillery fire from Warren's front had been effective, though apparently it was not enough, while the works he and the Army of the Potomac troops had labored over for weeks were barely tested by fire from the enemy.

The batteries on our own 5th Corps front had completely silenced the enemy's artillery, and the musketry which at first sprang up soon subsided. Our mortar practice which at first was very poor owing to defective powder grew better, and caused several explosions in the salient at which it was principally directed. Some people were rather disappointed that the enemy did not fire more, so as to bring into play for at least a few hours that immense covered way which our army had been constructing for at least a month or longer. By this time, 6 a.m., our men had put up some flags on the crater, which became visible as the smoke ceased and our unnecessary cannonading slackened. It appeared then to us lookers on that we had at any rate effected a permanent lodgment there, if nothing more.[18]

When General Crawford reported that the enemy was leaving his front, General Meade ordered that he at once make an assault. Orders were also sent to General Warren that Crawford should make a demonstration against the enemy lines with a brigade or two. Roebling recorded, with some evidence of contempt, that Crawford "did not think even this was practicable and so nothing was done." Crawford's decision not to attack perhaps inspired some of the criticism directed at Warren after the fact. But it is also likely that Warren's later testimony before the court of inquiry regarding the failure at the crater did not sit well with Meade. While Warren suggested that he had been ready and waiting to obey orders from Burnside, which never came, he also declared that "some one should have been present to have directed my command as well as General Burnside's and General Ord's, some one person." Though Warren did not state that this one person should have been Meade, perhaps it was implied. Warren biographer David Jordan, who surprisingly often sides with Meade against the supposedly recalcitrant Warren, in this case provides ample evidence that Meade's subsequent testimony about Warren's responsibilities on the day of the Battle of the Crater was inaccurate and unjust. Meade's farcical description of what had been expected of Warren that day likely inspired Grant's later laying blame for the failure of the assault at the crater not upon Burnside, or Meade, or himself but upon Warren. Meanwhile, if there is any doubt about Grant's animosity toward General Warren and his continued intent to blacken Warren's reputation, consider this: On a world tour in the 1870s after his presidency, Grant declared to reporter John Russell Young regarding General Warren and the Battle of the Crater, "Instead of obeying—and knowing that the power which was guiding him would guide the others—he would hesitate and inquire, and want to debate. It was this quality which led to our disaster at the mine explosion before Petersburg. If Warren had obeyed orders we would have broken Lee's army in two and taken Petersburg." Young's book, which Grant read and approved, was published in 1879, several years before Warren's death.[19]

The reality of the 5th Corps infantry's role at the Battle of the Crater, as it became known, was that Roebling continued to wait upon Burnside for his orders to Warren to join the attack—orders that never came. Roebling therefore recorded the grim realities of the disastrous assault from his viewpoint at 9th Corps's headquarters:

> At 8 a.m. The niggers still held the crater, that one gun firing into them all the time. Gen. Ord attempted one or two assaults on the enemy's lines to the right of the mine, but they failed altogether. Gen. Ayres was now directed to examine the ground and approaches on the left of the mine for the purpose of making an attack on the enemy lines there and if possible capture that piece of the enemy. After the examination was made, and while Gen. Meade's approval was still awaited, a sudden stampede occurred among the colored troops at the crater; a black swarm of men was seen rushing for our lines, and presently everyone saw that it was all over for that day.[20]

Roebling continued with what was likely the sentiment of many: dismay at having to stand by and watch the results of the grand plan of the mine turn into a disaster. "A column of the enemy's reinforcements which had been moving in a covered way were now seen and shelled by our batteries causing half of them to turn back, but the rest went to the mine, and then a slaughter commenced which lasted pretty much all day. Most of the white troops were captured and the niggers were pretty much all killed before night." Roebling added the horrific final observation that "spectators amused themselves with looking at the crater and seeing the rebs hunt niggers and shoot them. Every little while some fellow would run the gauntlet and get back to our line, but many were shot on the way back."

While Grant himself had been on the field at one point during the morning, he saw very little of what was going on. Roebling, with the benefit of his own observations, and no doubt some hindsight as well, suggested, "One great drawback to the success of the affair was our [Federal] artillery fire which opened as soon as the mine exploded, covering the whole field with a pall of smoke and frightening our men more than the rebel fire did, especially as a great many of our shells burst short; most frequently from the battery near the Avery House." Two days passed before the Unionists sent out a flag of truce so that they could bury their dead. Roebling commented, "The wounded had all died by this time from thirst and the intense heat. Musketry firing was still kept up at the mine, night and day."[21]

While Roebling and the 5th Corps had been building the fortifications to guard the Army of the Potomac's left flank, they were also constructed to free up troops who could serve elsewhere, including, of course, providing support for Burnside's assault after the exploding of the mine. With a disturbing observation on where he thought the primary blame initially lay for the failure at the Battle of the Crater, Roebling wrote to Emily on July 30, the day of the doomed assault,

> This has been a sad sad day for us—the work and expectations of almost 2 months have been blasted by both powder and by the niggers giving way in the assault after the mine exploded. The first temporary success had elated every one so much that we already imagined ourselves in Petersburg, but 15 minutes changed it all and plunged every one into a feeling of despair almost of ever accomplishing anything; few officers can be found this evening who have not drowned their sorrows in the flowing bowl—the greater the expectations formed, the greater the revulsion in feeling when they are not realized. The 30th of the month is one of our usual killing days; we managed to kill about 1,500 head this time on our side.[22]

After the Battle of the Crater, Roebling and the men of his corps and his army could only go back to grim routine, continue to strengthen their fortifications, and endure the seemingly aimless shifting of troops.

30

Digging in and Maneuvering at Petersburg and a Strike at the Weldon Railroad

WHEN WASHINGTON ROEBLING PAID A VISIT TO FORT HELL IN EARLY August, one of the battery officers reported suspicious sounds in one of the magazines, much like the striking of a pickaxe underground. The Unionists were apparently not the only ones who could tunnel toward the enemy. Both Roebling and Gouverneur Warren came to listen, and though they weren't positively convinced that the source of the noise was excavating rebels, precautions were taken. "Three pits were sunk in the ditch down to the water line, and two galleries were driven toward the enemy for a distance of 20 feet. These were intended chiefly as listening places, beside answering as the commencement of a countermine." Roebling later concluded that, since nothing came of it, the sounds were likely an illusion or coming from their own lines. Meanwhile, work was kept up each hot August night on the Federal lines and works, with the enemy doing the same.[1]

Roebling was still scouting, reporting that the enemy was working on his rear line on the Jerusalem Plank Road and building forts along the Weldon Railroad by the lead works. Rebel deserters, Roebling reported, were frequent, and information from reconnaissance and prisoners revealed that General Joseph Kershaw's division had reputedly gone north. Warren made a proposal to headquarters to capture the enemy picket line on the Jerusalem Plank Road, but it was "not acceded to." That rebel activities on that road merited some attention became evident when the enemy began shelling the U.S. Colored Troops' camp with a rifled thirty-two-pounder from a position on its line there.[2]

Roebling duly recorded the terrible explosion at City Point on August 9, believed to have been caused by careless handling of ammunition on a barge at the docks. Conspiracy theories abound as to the cause of the blast, with a Confederate agent taking credit for the explosion. Roebling also acknowledged that a committee investigating the failure of the Federal mine "was also going full blast creating considerable stir." City Point was a beehive of activity with ships coming and going, but it was also where U. S. Grant made his headquarters. It was apparently quite comfortable and safe, explosions aside, as Grant demonstrated by having his family there. It also was also extravagantly well supplied, as the biographer of Ely Parker, Grant's military secretary, describes: "The new location, high on a bluff overlooking the junction of the Appomattox and the James rivers, was amply supplied by riverboats, so that Parker could boast of having ice cream and cakes at every meal. These headquarters, away from the battlefield, were a relief to the staff, and their memories of City Point were pleasant ones." The troops in the trenches at Petersburg that summer were undoubtedly storing up less pleasant memories. Roebling reported that the demands of heavy work details building the fortifications and bombproof shelters were "causing much dissatisfaction."[3]

While disappointed at being shut out of command of the department confronting Jubal Early, George Meade was much aggrieved when he heard that, contrary to Grant's assurances, William T. Sherman, Winfield Hancock, and Philip Sheridan had all been promoted, while Meade still had not. When Meade confronted him, Grant admitted that the omission was his doing, in that he had asked for the immediate appointment of the others but not for Meade. Meade later recounted Grant's explanation: "if Sherman and myself had been appointed on the same day, I would rank him, and he wished Sherman to rank me." Grant assured Meade that he still had great confidence in him and would see that Meade eventually was promoted. But the lieutenant general went on to give a convoluted explanation for why he thought it necessary for Sheridan to be promoted before Meade. Killing two birds with one dubious stone, Grant tried to explain away not only Meade's lack of promotion but also his broken promise to put Meade in command of Sheridan's Middle Division. When Meade asked the lieutenant general when he would be given, as promised, command of the Middle Division presently commanded by Sheridan, Grant stated he would have appointed Meade earlier but could not. Grant explained that since Sheridan had been forced to fall back from the enemy, if Grant replaced him with Meade at that point, it would be construed as Sheridan having done something wrong. Better to disappoint Meade than to cast any possible aspersions upon the unassailable Sheridan.[4]

Roebling expressed his own disappointment at news reaching the Army of the Potomac of the panicked reaction to Early's raid that summer. Roebling observed, "The rebel raid now going on in Maryland & Pennsylvania gives some strong examples of the cowardly nature of the people; they are almost ready to sacrifice the last woman to save their own hides; in contrast with this the conduct of the Southern people appears many times truly noble as exemplified for instance in the defense of Petersburg; old men with silver locks lay dead in the trenches side by side with mere boys of 13 or 14; it almost makes one sorry to have fight against people who show such devotion for their homes & their country."[5]

While the drama of Meade's disappointed ambitions was playing out at Army of the Potomac headquarters in August, the 2nd Corps, with David Gregg's cavalry division and elements of the 10th Corps, engaged in the Second Battle of Deep Bottom (August 13–20). Based on Grant's belief that R. E. Lee was sending three divisions of infantry and one of cavalry to go to Early in the valley, the lieutenant general was determined to save his favorites, Sheridan and Sherman (on his march through the South), from facing a reinforced enemy. Hancock's return to the north bank of the James was in many ways a replay of the less than successful expedition he had made in July, with one major difference. While the cavalry and artillery went by land, Hancock's infantry force was boarded at City Point onto oceangoing steamers to attempt to deceive the enemy into believing that they were being sent to bolster the defense of Washington. But the effort turned into a fiasco, for not only did the enemy fail to buy the deception, but a justly cautious Hancock also found on investigating that the docks where his force was expected to disembark were in great disrepair, nor could the deep-draft ships carrying his troops come near enough to the shore to land his troops. Delay after delay plagued Hancock's expedition, and a coinciding heat wave left many of his men prostrated with heat exhaustion, some to the point of convulsions and death. It was a sad fate for the expedition's foot soldiers, who believed they were about to make a sea voyage to the capital, only to discover that their secret destination was, once again, Deep Bottom. The price tag for Hancock's second expedition there was 2,786 killed, wounded, or captured. Meanwhile, back at Petersburg, Roebling commented, "The state of affairs here in the army is very peculiar now—only two Corps of the old Army of the Potomac are here now and with neither of its commanders is Genl. Meade on speaking terms. This is harmony with a vengeance."[6]

Hancock's expedition was not the only one designed to keep Lee's forces pinned to Petersburg. General Warren's 5th Corps was withdrawn from the Army of the Potomac's left front and prepared for an expedition to destroy the tracks of the Confederate lifeline, the Weldon Railroad, and, as Roebling stated, to act as a reconnaissance in force. Accompanied by Colonel Sam

Spear's cavalry, on August 17 Roebling headed out to find the best road for the 5th Corps's movement the next day. He and the troopers rode out around the Federal pickets on a road past Williams's house and returned on the road from Temple's house, finding that to be the most advantageous route. At 4 a.m. the 5th Corps set out for Globe Tavern, roughly four miles south of Petersburg, where the railroad crossed the Halifax Road. Roebling's belief, likely reflecting that of General Warren, was that whatever portion of the tracks it captured and destroyed, the 5th Corps wasn't really expected to keep a permanent hold on its acquisitions. Warren's expedition would be a reconnaissance in force, gathering much-needed information about the rebel right flank and rear. Roebling qualified his impressions regarding the goals of Warren's expedition by adding that Lieutenant General Grant expected more from Warren than did Meade. But then Grant's expectations rested upon his erroneous belief that the ever-aggressive General Mahone and his division would remain north of the James confronting Hancock. Grant was wrong.[7]

Following the roads chosen by Roebling, moving past Temple's and Gurley's houses, Charles Griffin's division was in the lead when it was deployed from column into line of battle, his skirmish line driving in the enemy's videttes. By 9 a.m., Griffin was at the railroad by the Yellow House, and destruction of the tracks began. While Roebling and fellow topographical engineer Captain Emmor B. Cope went out to the right to investigate small roads through the woods, around one hundred of Spear's troopers pressed forward up the railroad, soon to be followed by Romeyn Ayres's division. While Ayres formed a line across the railroad at the Blick House, the Federal troopers crossed a field to the Flower House, driving enemy cavalry before them and disappearing down the Halifax and Vaughan Roads, where little was seen of them for the rest of the day. Muddy fields slowed the arrival of the other divisions, while the weather—intermittent squalls alternating with periods of intense sun—left many with heatstroke. Therefore Ayres was on his own when he formed a battle line with General Joseph Hayes's brigade on the right, the Maryland Brigade on the left, and the 15th New York heavy artillerymen in reserve and began to advance down the railroad. Roebling reports that the enemy opened with two rifled guns from the White House with a clean sweep of the track and the Halifax Road. When Ayres's skirmishers pressed forward, they found a field full of ripe corn, an unknown number of the enemy concealed within, while rebel skirmishers were reported in the woods to Ayres's right.[8]

When Samuel Crawford's division finally came up on Ayres's right, the two divisions began an advance, one met by a simultaneous advance by the enemy on Ayres's left, where the Maryland Brigade had been positioned to protect General Hayes's exposed left flank. Roebling was on the spot and reported, "I was at this point a few minutes before it happened, and noticed that the flankers on the left of the Md. Brig. were not far enough out in that direction, not far enough to give warning at any rate. The result was that in a few minutes the Md. Brig gave way compelling the left of Hayes' line to fall back, and stopping the advance on our right. At least 200 of the Marylanders were taken prisoners." Those soldiers of the Maryland Brigade who escaped capture fell back upon their reserve, the 15th New York Heavy Artillery, and an admiring Roebling observed of the New Yorkers, "They stood their ground nobly, pouring rapid volleys into the enemy, checking them at once and driving them speedily back to the shelter of their cornfield. They kept up this firing for half an hour after the enemy had left, and only with difficulty was their martial ardor abated."[9]

By dark, Ayres and Crawford, after laboring through tangled underbrush and woods that limited visibility to twenty feet ahead, had penetrated to the edge of a very large field, beyond which the enemy's main line near Fort Mahone (Fort Damnation) was visible. Though cavalry videttes were maintaining a connection between the 5th Corps's extreme right and the 9th Corps on the Petersburg front, General Edward Bragg's 1st Brigade of Lysander Cutler's division of the 5th Corps was sent for to come up to protect Crawford's exposed right flank. Roebling was disturbed to find when he rode out before dark on Crawford's right that yet another field of corn on Crawford's front prevented the pickets he had posted from seeing anything. Roebling also expressed wonderment that no one had thought to put anyone up a tree to keep an eye on the situation, for, according to Roebling's estimate, the Federals had already encountered at least one division, or roughly six thousand men, of the enemy's infantry on that day, August 18. Prior to the movement, Meade had made clear to Warren that, since Meade had no reserve, Warren was on his own for his expedition to the Weldon Railroad. But Meade relented within the first twenty-four hours, for as the first day closed, the 5th Corps was notified that divisions from the 9th Corps would be sent to them the next day. Gersham Mott's division from the 2nd Corps returned to the Petersburg line to release three divisions of the 9th Corps to support Warren.[10]

Roebling wrote of the start of August 19, "There had been considerable rain in the night making the ground very sloppy and slippery; in the morning it was misty and foggy with frequent showers of rain preventing any extensive view. Matters were tolerably quiet at first." Bragg's brigade came up and was ordered to connect with Crawford's right and with the 9th Corps's left near the Williams House, halfway between it and the Aiken House. At least part of

General Edward S. Bragg.
Library of Congress.

Bragg's line would be in woods with a maze of unknown roads somewhere in the vicinity of the Strong House and Fort Davis. Roebling encountered Captain William H. Paine, who was bringing the 9th Corps reinforcements sent by Meade and who wanted Roebling's instruction on where to position them. Roebling advised Paine to mass them in a position in a field within supporting distance of Bragg, but on his way back, he found the 9th Corps positioned a full three-quarters of a mile to the rear of the position he had indicated, nor had the position of Bragg's picket line been changed as Roebling had recommended, an unremitting rain no doubt having repressed a timely obedience to orders. Roebling, returning to headquarters to report, was sent out again by Warren to see that his orders were being carried out. Locating Crawford, Roebling took him to the place where Warren wanted his picket line, but Crawford demurred, wanting General Bragg on his right to take care of it.[11]

Roebling, honest raconteur that he was, then confessed that he himself spent the next hour and a half lost in the woods and its byroads, finally finding and adjusting General Bragg's picket line. Though Captain Cope had been sent to guide Bragg's brigade to its position on Crawford's right, Roebling recorded,

> About 1½ [1:30 p.m.] I found a little man in a blue overcoat wandering in the woods all alone. He asked me who I was, and I told him, he then stated that he was completely lost, and wanted me to show him where he was, which I did, and he went off. Before he was out of sight an orderly came along; I asked him who that little man was, and much to my surprise, he told me it was Gen. Bragg, whom I did not know personally. I gave him [General Bragg] his instructions at once, and he was glad to have my assistance. I found he had been working at random all the morning without a compass, had lost his horse and his orderly, and was completely played out.

Roebling related that General Bragg, upon finding his headquarters, prepared to send another one of his regiments, the 6th Wisconsin, out on his picket line, while Roebling rode out on Bragg's line to find the 7th Wisconsin strongly posted. When he returned to Bragg's headquarters, he received a rather surreal invitation from a grateful Bragg that he couldn't refuse. Everything being pretty quiet,

> General Bragg's dinner was ready and we sat down to eat something before posting the men. We were just finishing when a couple of shots were heard in the direction of the 7th Wis.[consin,] where I had just been. We did not think anything of them at the time; 3 or 4 minutes afterward more shots were fired and presently a small volley, which told us what was the matter. The 6th Wis.[consin] was immediately sent for, and had quite a little fight in that field, holding the enemy for some little time, long enough to have given Lyle and Coulter [commanding brigades in Crawford's division] a chance to make proper preparations.[12]

After reporting to 5th Corps headquarters that a concerted attack was being made upon Crawford, Ayres, and William S. Tilton's brigade, Roebling raced to bring up the 9th Corps. He wrote, "Owing to their [9th Corps] being so far back from the place where they were needed, some 20 minutes were consumed before Willcox's Div. was in line and ready to advance; their left rested on Tilton's right, for a start. I did not find any Brig. Genls. about, and put the Div. [Willcox's] in line myself, with the aid of Lt. Fisher of Willcox's staff." It was not a moment too soon, for when Willcox's line was ready to advance, now joined by Potter's division of the 9th Corps, a rebel line of battle began emerging from the woods, with firing commencing at once. The Federal line advanced slowly. Though Crawford's division was badly rattled, apparently by friendly fire from its own artillery, the rebel attackers were driven from the field and some distance into the woods. But Roebling was hardly satisfied, for he believed that if the 9th Corps line hadn't halted and refused to follow the enemy into the woods, fewer Unionists would have been captured by the retreating rebels. Then, too, he was lamenting that the 9th Corps had not

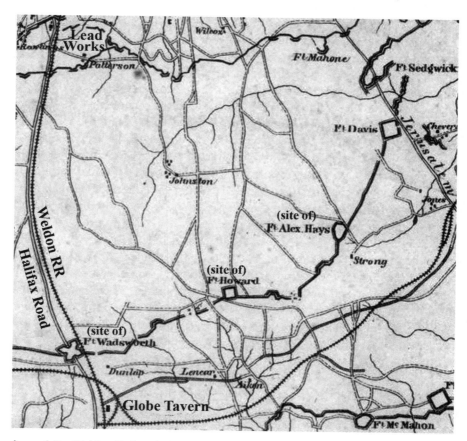

Area of the Weldon Railroad.
Adapted from "Entrenched Lines in the Immediate Front of Petersburg," Major N. Michler (Library of Congress).

taken up the position he had indicated in the morning and, too far to the rear, had taken too much time to come forward. These delays were also responsible for the misfortune of Peter Lyle's brigade of Ayres's division, which captured a whole brigade of Confederates but, unsupported, had been unable to bring them off the field. Roebling felt that but for these balks and blunders, they would not have incurred such loss. When Warren appeared on the field, he was able to accomplish what a lowly major, Washington Roebling himself, could not: get Willcox's line into the woods to pursue the rebels, "with the happiest effect, prisoners being taken in considerable quantities."[13]

Warren was not the only one to receive reinforcements that day, for when Confederate cavalry commander General James D. Dearing reported the Yankees' activities, P. T. Beauregard sent General Henry Heth with two brigades, which had joined the attack on Ayres's division. Though the hapless Maryland Brigade was again driven back, Ayres was able to regroup and drive the enemy in turn. But the greater danger came when General Lee, informed of the threat to the Weldon Railroad, sent the more potent force of General William Mahone's division, three brigades strong, and Fitzhugh Lee's cavalry from Deep Bottom back to Petersburg. On his arrival, Mahone, with his intimate knowledge of all the local roads, was able to pass by Crawford's right flank, break through Bragg's skirmish line, and make a devastating attack on Bragg's and Crawford's rear. General Warren himself, rallying his broken troops, brought them forward to regain the ground they had temporarily lost, taking many prisoners and two of the enemy's flags. But Warren was aware that his position was still less than secure, and it had been a terrible day for the 5th Corps, with casualties of 382 killed and wounded and 2,518 missing, the vast majority of the latter from Crawford's division. The rebels' losses had also been severe, and by nightfall they had withdrawn. Roebling, accompanied by the horsemen of the headquarters escort, was sent out to find them. When Roebling found the enemy's position, he thought it would be possible to drive rebels completely off the field, but when he put the case to the 9th Corps's General Potter, who was nearby, Roebling recounted, Potter "did not seem inclined to believe it, and at any rate took no steps to push the rebs." Yet Roebling concluded with faint praise that "the 9th Corps fought quite well as far as it went."[14]

The costly trials and tribulations of the day aside, Roebling closed his account of August 19 on a high note: "The night closed finding us still in secure possession of the Weldon R.R. and one Div. almost unengaged yet. We were still good for another fight. The roads were horribly muddy, impeding the movements of supply trains and artillery." But to Meade's surprise, and thanks to General Warren and the 5th Corps's determination, it was fully realized now that they would hold on to the Weldon Railroad at all hazards. The tenacious General Warren was all too familiar with the dangers of fighting, as it so often seemed, on ground of the enemy's choosing. Warren therefore chose to escape the woods and web of local roads favoring the rebels, and on August 20 he drew his lines back a mile to more easily defended open ground, with the added benefit of being able to bring the 5th Corps's artillery into play. Warren's soldiers began to dig in. As for the 5th Corps, it was reported to Meade, "We have lost in numbers, but not in morale." The fight for the Weldon Railroad was far from over.[15]

Hanging On to the Weldon Railroad

IN THEIR NEW POSITIONS, THE 5TH AND 9TH CORPS PREPARED FOR THE attack they knew was imminent. They didn't need the reports coming in all day on August 20 to tell them that the enemy's troops were moving in their direction. Washington Roebling acknowledged that orders had been sent out to the 9th Corps for parties of twenty to thirty men to investigate the situation on their front, but to his knowledge, the orders had not been acted upon. But Roebling also reported, "I started out myself, but met a party of Johnnies before I went out a hundred yards." With trouble like that in the offing, Roebling was glad to see a brigade of David Gregg's cavalry join them that day. Roebling was sent to bring up another 9th Corps brigade to position it on Robert Potter's right and remain to help the men establish their picket line. Continuing his scouting, Roebling was able to assure Gouverneur Warren that afternoon that the 9th's men had a "picket-line that holds that house in the corn-field and are intrenching themselves on a very good line." But he also informed his commander that the rebels were not where they had been, and the 5th Corps spent the night of August 20 digging in and strengthening its line.[1]

On the morning of August 21, thirty enemy guns opened on Warren's lines, before General A. P. Hill and his corps, with part of Robert Hoke's division and Confederate cavalry, attacked at 10 a.m. The enemy was repulsed all along Warren's line, but another assault was made, this time by the ever-aggressive General William Mahone. Attacking on Warren's left flank, Mahone's force was broken by the 5th Corps's artillery before the rebels came within range of the Federal muskets. An exception was the brigade of General Johnson Hagood, which, upon reaching the works held by General Lysander Cutler's division, went, as Roebling described it, from the frying pan into the fire. Hagood's men, on nearing Cutler's line, came unexpectedly under the full fire of Charles Griffin's division upon their flank. When the rebels were nearly surrounded and had stopped firing, the Yankees stopped firing too and "holloed to them to come in," which many of them did. The rest of the Confederates, meanwhile, were believed to have surrendered, and Captain Daly of Cutler's staff left the works and went down with a dozen men to bring in the prisoners. But when Daly went to seize a flag from Hagood's hands, the Confederate officers began firing. With Cutler's men mixed in with Hagood's, the Federal defenders in their works were unable to fire, and some of the enemy escaped. Nonetheless, Cutler gathered in six rebel battle flags and 517 prisoners, many of them from Hagood's brigade. In yet another example of the high cost of attacking an entrenched enemy, this instance in the Federals' favor, the Confederates were said to have lost three thousand, while the Federals lost three hundred.[2]

Many gave Warren sincere praise for refusing to relinquish his ever-stronger hold on the Weldon Railroad and acknowledged the result of his expedition as the first real extension of the Federal line since June. Though Warren's breaking of the enemy's rail line at Globe Tavern did not completely halt the flow of supplies over that line, it forced the rebels to load provisions on wagons and, detouring around the intruding Yankees, haul their material beyond the thirty-mile gap in the railroad that Warren had created. General R. E. Lee also had to immediately cut the rations of his troops in half. But the only communication from George Meade to the commander of the 5th Corps was a forwarded message from U. S. Grant, who, although he acknowledged that he was not on the field, thought Warren should have done more. Grant urged him to leave his works and pursue the enemy into Petersburg, to which Warren replied, politely but firmly, that such a move would force him to attack the enemy in *their* entrenchments, with the added risk of exposing Warren's own flanks; Meade suggested that by leaving his works and advancing on the rebels, he would force the enemy to watch *their* flanks. Meade acknowledged that with the constant rain on August 21, the roads had become impassable, making Warren's batteries immovable. Warren pointed out that if he left his works, he'd also have to leave his guns behind and would lose the advantage of his highly effective artillery. As for Grant's comments, Warren replied, "I have fought against the army opposed to me to know pretty well what to do here on the field." After darkness had fallen, Meade examined Warren's front and reported to Grant that an offensive movement on Warren's front was "impracticable." Stating that Warren was confident he could fight off any enemy assault, Meade added, ever mindful of Grant's view of things, that, should the rebels attack the 5th Corps again, he had ordered Warren to "follow up their repulse." Meade's order was clear: if the enemy attacked and was repulsed, Warren was to leave his earthworks and artillery and "pitch in" to the enemy as the lieutenant general desired.[3]

Meade wrote to his wife of the 5th Corps's fight, "We have had some pretty hard fighting to secure our lodgment on the Weldon Railroad." With a heavy dollop of sarcasm, he added, "Grant and Warren are the heroes of the affair. I must confess I do not envy either of them their laurels, although in the Weldon Railroad affair Grant was sixteen miles away, and knew nothing but what was reported to him by myself." If Meade was disgruntled, it is no wonder that a discouraged Warren declared to his wife that he had "no confidence in Genl Grant's abilities to use an army," then stated, "We cannot afford to prove the incapacity of our commanders at such cost of men and means. So I do hope that I am mistaken in my estimate of his ability."[4]

With General Hancock seemingly unable to keep R. E. Lee's forces at Deep Bottom, his corps was brought back to Petersburg and immediately assigned to continue the destruction of the Weldon Railroad. Though exhausted, the men of the 2nd Corps, supported by Gregg's cavalry, were ordered out to begin their work. But General Lee was still not ready to relinquish the railroad and had sent most of three brigades of A. P. Hill's corps—Richard Anderson's brigade of James Longstreet's corps and two divisions of Wade Hampton's cavalry, some ten thousand combatants—to confront Hancock. While Warren had constructed formidable works to protect his position, Hancock's force on August 25 was in the slight entrenchments at Reams Station, works that had been "hastily thrown up by troops sent to Wilson's relief in June." While Meade gave Hancock permission to withdraw, Hancock reported that, although he wished to join Warren, he had become too closely engaged with the enemy to do so. Meade's apprehension that the enemy would drive down between Hancock and Warren proved fully justified, and Warren reported at 8:15 p.m. to Meade's headquarters that Major Roebling had just reported in from the front that the enemy had got between Hancock and Warren just before dark. While Warren's position remained secure, Hancock's 2nd Corps was driven from Reams Station, losing 610 men killed and wounded, among them a disproportionately large number of officers. He also lost 1,762 missing and nine guns. Hill reported capturing twelve stands of Hancock's colors, nine guns, 2,150 prisoners, and 3,100 stands of small arms.[5]

Let us consider the assessment of General Charles Wainwright, chief of artillery of the 5th Corps, regarding the accomplishments of General Warren's 5th Corps in this advance upon the Weldon Railroad and the subsequent movement of Hancock's 2nd Corps against that same objective. General

Wainwright, formerly of the disbanded 1st Corps, was no friend of Warren's; he was in fact highly critical of him and deeply resented Warren's authority over his artillery. Yet a few days after Warren's and Hancock's respective fights that August, on reading accounts in the New York newspapers, Wainwright expressed his astonishment that Hancock's debacle at Reams was being reported as almost a Union victory. Wainwright exclaimed, "Twice as much is made in the paper of this [Hancock's] fight as of ours [5th Corps's] of the 21st, for which there are two good reasons. First, Hancock keeps a reporter and seeks newspaper reputation, while Warren does neither; and second, Hancock's fight needs bolstering, our does not. Somehow that fight of ours seems to be very little talked of, though it was really one of the most brilliant and perfect affairs of the whole campaign."[6]

Warren's 5th Corps spent the last days of August continuing the destruction of the Weldon Railroad, which Roebling declared would be done right this time, without hope of repair. Washington lamented, "My felt hat is in a most shocking state, full of holes, so are my nice pants. In a campaign of a week I always manage to ruin one suit of clothes completely. However, it will soon be considered patriotic to be clothed in rags." Telling that the "Johnnies" were quiet for the moment, Washington was looking forward to getting out of Warren's present headquarters, a house "infested with cockroaches & bats." Roebling would also be startled from his sleep when two rats ran over him, a situation he remedied by stopping up their hole. Meanwhile, Washington and Emily continued to discuss their plan for him to resign at the end of the year and for them to be married sometime in the winter of 1864–1865. Roebling conjectured pessimistically, "Ten years is the least limit put down now for the duration of the war; fine prospect is it not; anyone that proposes to remain in the service until the end of the war may as well make up his mind to devote his whole life to it. I am beginning to feel that unless I get out of it very soon I shall be unfit for anything else and will have to stick to it as a matter of necessity." Roebling signed this letter of August 26, "Your discontented Wash." It is hard to know what most disturbed him: two days without a letter from Emily, the bats and cockroaches, or the idea that he likely would not see out the war with the 5th Corps and the Army of the Potomac. His letter of the next day perhaps provides the answer. Saying that the 2nd Corps had just been "pretty well smashed up," he informed Emily of mutual friends who had been killed or were missing. Washington added, "This business of getting killed is a mere question of time; it will happen to us all sooner or later if the war keeps on." Roebling does not leave us guessing as to where he placed the responsibility for the stalemates the Federals were facing. On August 28,

Roebling commented in a letter to Emily, "'Useless' Grant came to pay us a visit today, staying but a short time however; he expressed himself satisfied; but we don't exactly see things in the light he does."[7]

During the 5th Corps's occupation of the Weldon Railroad and hiatus from fighting, Roebling took the opportunity to write to his Emily every day. On August 28 he told her that his friend Chief of Staff Francis Walker, who'd been counted among the 2nd Corp's missing, was being reported in the Petersburg newspaper as having safely arrived "at the Calaboose" in that city. Roebling commented, "If the rebs swallow all his stories they will surely give up in despair." He told a grimmer tale of a friend who had just had his leg amputated and was unlikely to survive. Roebling took advantage of the lull to get himself a new hat and sew up the rent in his pants, "so I am once more respectable looking." Much to this writer's relief, the headquarters staff took a break from harassing their black servants to give their attention to a tame pigeon, which, unwilling to put up with the guff of the bored young officers, was said to be a "rascal who bites like a fury." Washington would later ask Emily whether she knew that pigeons roosted standing on one leg, which was why they were pigeon-toed. Meanwhile, the servants had not escaped all unpleasantness, for Roebling also wrote, "Our French cook and the bandy legged nigger waiter Jim have had a fight; Frenchy hit Jim on the head with a coffeepot and Jim flattened Frenchy's nose." Roebling also mentioned that "two strange dogs have ingratiated themselves here, one knows how to shake hands, the other how to eat meat; both have fleas."[8]

Ever ready to tease, Roebling wrote to Emily that on the first of September a whole Southern family, a mother with children of all ages, came through the 5th Corps's lines determined to make their way north. He told Emily one of the tribe was "Miss Annie, a pretty fair maid of 18 summers with nice curls, upon seeing her I had to pull out my watch at once and look at your picture so as to counteract the effects. The boys had slipped through the lines some nights before and told us that their mother was waiting a chance to come in; so the Gen. [Warren] had determined that I should go out with a party and bring them in. Fortunately she came in [on her own] this morning and I was saved from becoming a Don Quixote." In the unlikely event that Emily should have any doubts about his constancy, Washington closed by saying, "Good night my darling, I wish I could lie nestling in your arms tonight in place of a hard old floor and buffalo robe—I remain, love, as ever Your naughty Wash." Emily apparently needed some warm reassurance and cheering up, for she had been having nightmares about the exploits of her risk-taking sweetheart.[9]

Lieutenant Colonel Francis A. Walker.
Jason G. Gauthier, "Captured! The Civil War Experience
of Superintendent of the Census Francis Amasa
Walker," U.S. Census Bureau, https://www.census.gov/
history/pdf/fawalker-captured7-25-16.pdf.

Reporting quite a break in their tedium on September 6, a cold drizzly day, Washington wrote to Emily that upon sitting down to write to her, "Just as I was commencing a little explosion scared us out of our boots; it was so cold today that we made a fire in the grate, some johnny must have left some cartridges under the ashes or something else because the whole contents of the fireplace jumped into the room all at once, so they did, the cinders burning lots of holes in our blanket." If the cold snap had been prompting Roebling to daydream about a chilly fall leading to a winter that promised to bring him release from his duties in the army and reunion with his Emily, that fire had given him a sudden and unwelcome call back to reality. But things were so quiet on the Army of the Potomac's front that General Meade had taken leave, something very rare since he had taken command of that army. The days dragged for Roebling and the men of the 5th Corps, and by

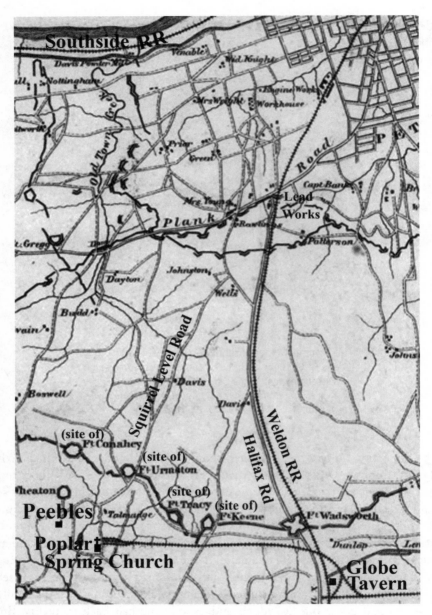

Area of Peebles Farm and Poplar Springs Church to Southside Railroad.
Adapted from "Entrenched Lines in the Immediate Front of Petersburg,"
Major N. Michler (Library of Congress).

mid-September he commented, "It is nearly a month now since we have come to this place. . . . [W]e are beginning to feel that it will soon be time to have another fight, and we certainly don't have far to go to get one." Meanwhile, he teased Emily to be sure to electioneer against "Little Mac," the Democrats' presidential candidate, former Army of the Potomac commander George B. McClellan, in the coming campaign.[10]

While one might think the 5th Corps would relish this time of inactivity, that was hardly the case. Washington told Emily that writing to her every night was one of the few things he had to look forward to. He said, "This is getting to be a great place to go on benders; yet I can't blame anyone. This dreary monotonous life is perfectly soul killing; it is the same routine day after day, and the most endless resources for killing time are finally exhausted." But while there were no movements, there was always the matter of staying vigilant near an aggressive enemy, and on September 15 Roebling accompanied a large body of infantry and Federal cavalry on a reconnaissance in force. Still plagued by inaccurate maps, Henry Baxter's brigade of the 5th Corps pushed out toward Poplar Springs Church and Peebles Farm, with the enemy reportedly building fortifications at the latter. Baxter was complimentary of Roebling in his dispatches, remarking that "with his knowledge of the roads and localities, together with his energy and promptness of action, [he] rendered valuable service." And on the night of September 20, Roebling was out posting a picket line, returning to headquarters at 10 p.m. to have his dinner and to write his letter to Emily. He commented, "While the news regarding [Philip] Sheridan's activities in the valley seemed good, I shall wait for details before I make up my mind to be right glad." He also asked Emily to find out who "Syphax" was, since they had discovered that it was a Confederate nickname for Grant. It was not a compliment. Washington finished his letter while a band played a Virginia reel outside headquarters, and it took his mind back to meeting his Emily at the 2nd Corps Ball in the spring of that year. How much had happened to them both in those event-filled months.[11]

At the end of September, Roebling started to think they would not likely remain where they were much longer, though he quipped, "There is a small fight coming off in a day or two from which we will probably be let off because we were such good boys the last time; if such turns out to be the case it will be the first." Noting that General Grant had paid them a visit, Roebling undoubtedly realized that something was up, for he fretted that both of his horses were lame, and he hardly knew what to do since he couldn't afford to buy another one. He conjectured, "If we keep on at this rate trying to get around Petersburg we will probably get through with it by this time next year and then the Rebs will probably retire in good order across the Appomattox, quietly laughing in their sleeves but still holding onto Petersburg." In the first week of October, General Meade had moved his headquarters nearby to the Aiken House, and Roebling was relieved to report that Meade's demeanor was more neighborly and friendlier than previously. While Meade's improved attitude might be attributed to his having just returned from a very rare visit home, one also wonders whether his growing suspicion that Grant was no friend of his made him wish to regain his lost friendship with Warren. Another group of incoming Federals, black soldiers of the U.S. Colored Troops who moved into position on the 5th Corps's left, had Roebling expressing his dissatisfaction. He declared that they could expect "a constant series of alarms as long as they are there." He added disparagingly, "They claim to be as good as white men because they say they are fighting for the same cause." Roebling's opinions offer a disturbing glimpse of what were, perhaps, common attitudes and biases of the time. His discounting of the black soldiers' fighting for the same cause as justification for their being considered equals offers no apparent consideration of the fact that the cause the black soldiers were fighting for was *their* freedom, likely providing ample incentive for their willingness to embrace the Unionists' war goals. Then, too, as Roebling well knew from his direct observation of that dark day at the Battle of the Crater, the black soldiers faced much harsher treatment at the hands of the Confederates than their white counterparts.[12]

Roebling was back scouting the area and reported finding what he called a "marl pit" in the woods, full of water and said to contain the bones of mastodons and mammoths. He commented that such had been found at the Davis House on the Squirrel Level Road, but Roebling feared the bones had likely been destroyed by the cannonading of the combatants there. Still lacking any definite word of an upcoming move, Roebling related, "Our family of kittens is gradually emerging from the cellar and becoming sociable; they will be a great acquisition to our stock of amusement which was never so low as it is now. People don't know what to talk about any more; the war is too hackneyed to be discussed, the last battle is forgotten in a few days, and that there will be another one before long is taken as a matter of course and therefor not thought of; politics are tabooed and as regards sweethearts and wives, men like to keep thoughts concerning them to themselves."[13]

That October, Washington's mother, Johanna Roebling, though only forty-seven years old, became dangerously ill, and he was allowed to go home and somehow managed to see his Emily briefly. His father, John Roebling,

General John G. Parke.
Library of Congress.

who had been away, as he often was, building a bridge in Cincinnati, also arrived at their Trenton home. It was likely a strained reunion, for his father, upon arriving, sent away the physician who had been treating Johanna and replaced him with a "hydrop." John adhered fanatically to various unorthodox theories of hydropathy, including cold baths, steam baths, and douches, as well as severely restrictive diets, none of which was likely to comfort his ailing wife or improve her condition. In the weeks to come, his father asked for Washington's assurance that he would leave the army at the end of December and come serve as his assistant engineer in building the bridge at Cincinnati. This raised the subject of whether Washington would bring his new wife west to what Washington knew, from his previous experiences working with his father, would be an arduous existence. Though Washington warned Emily that he would be working very long hours and living in spartan conditions, Emily made her intention to go with him abundantly clear.[14]

While Roebling was away from the army, General Warren had also taken leave, and when Warren returned to 5th Corps headquarters, General Meade commented to him that he might just as well have stayed away four or five days longer. Roebling commented, "That was a mighty mean thing to tell a man *after* his return." By October 26, though suffering from a heavy cold, Roebling was back in the saddle before daybreak, "for the long expected fight for the hoped for acquisition of the Southside R.R." was being contemplated. Feeling sentimental, and perhaps a bit vulnerable, Washington told Emily he would not send back her photograph as he had promised. "I look upon it as a sort of talisman and therefore can't part with it in time of danger." He added that with the inevitable losses the 5th Corps would incur before the upcoming election, "a good many votes for Lincoln will be spoiled during the operation."[15]

The First Battle of Hatcher's Run
and the Hicksford Raid

WHEN ROEBLING WAS ONCE AGAIN SETTLED INTO HIS QUARTERS, HE made friends with another of the local inhabitants. This time it was a little lizard that he described as "the cutest little cuss you ever saw, he will crawl all over you without being scared." Washington was somewhat dismayed when his new friend jumped out the window, for, he confessed, that it was lonely there, as his roommate, Captain Emmor B. Cope, was away. Washington commented that though Cope was "the most taciturn of men, still he was company." But by October 26, Washington had plenty to occupy his mind.[1]

Prior to the October 27 movement against the enemy's railroads, General Gouverneur Warren's assignment for Roebling was to search for what turned out to be largely nonexistent roads. Roebling's scouting was limited by the close proximity of the Federal cavalry's picket line to the Unionists' main line. Every mile he moved beyond his own pickets made being killed or captured by the enemy that much more likely, so a full investigation of what few roads existed through a tangle of woods and wandering streams proved particularly hazardous. General Grant not only ignored his own chief engineer, John G. Barnard, who advised against this undermanned venture into unknown, unmapped territory, but also concocted yet another plan to extend the Federal line on both of its flanks simultaneously. Elements of Benjamin Butler's Army of the James would demonstrate against the enemy north of the James, while the 2nd Corps, with the support of the 5th and 9th Corps, would attempt to extend the Army of the Potomac's left. There were no roads running in the direction in which Warren would be making his advance, but he would nonetheless be expected to support and operate between the 9th and 2nd Corps and maintain contact with both Winfield Hancock's and John G.

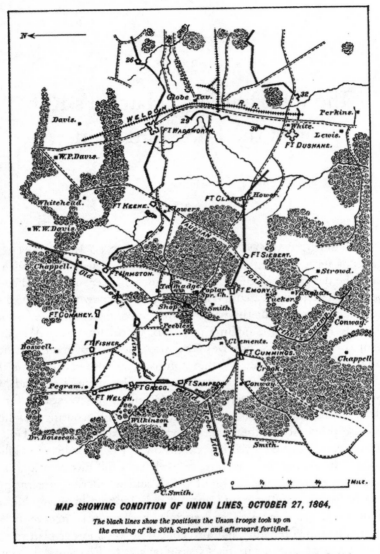

MAP SHOWING CONDITION OF UNION LINES, OCTOBER 27, 1864,

*The black lines show the positions the Union troops took up on
the evening of the 30th September and afterward fortified.*

General Warren's "Map Showing Condition of Union Lines, October
27, 1864."
OR 42, I, 449.

Parke's flanks. There wasn't much chance of the Federals' getting successfully around the enemy's right flank, for the great length of the Confederates' fortified line would, by necessity, take the Federals making the attempt to a position dangerously isolated from their rest of their army. When Warren issued orders for a 5:30 a.m. advance on October 27, Grant soon changed that to 4 a.m., disregarding Warren's previous observations that marching in the dark always seemed to end up in confusion and delay. Roebling's scouting report influenced the first part of the 5th's early-morning advance, but the corps was soon obliged to try to "hunt up a road to Hatcher's Run." In listing the troops at his command, Warren reported that the vast majority of Charles Griffin's 1st Division were new, untrained recruits, a situation only slightly less pervasive in his other two divisions.[2]

Less than an hour into Warren's advance, it began to rain, and he acknowledged that, with that and it still being dark, connections between his brigades were being lost. When it finally grew light at 5:30 a.m., Warren continued to push ahead, all the while trying to maintain his hold upon the left flank of Parke's 9th Corps. There being no roads except ones running north-south, Warren began to build one through the woods going west for half a mile, when the vanguard of Griffin's division met rebel resistance and drove them into strongly held enemy breastworks with abatis and slashing. Warren then received word that General Parke would not be able to advance and George Meade desired him to cross Hatcher's Run and communicate with General Hancock. While Warren sent word to Hancock, he also sent Roebling with Warren's headquarters escort, the 4th Pennsylvania Cavalry, to scout to the left for the enemy, while Warren himself reconnoitered on his front. When Warren returned from examining his lines, he found both Grant and Meade at his headquarters, and Roebling came in reporting that Griffin had advanced to Hatcher's Run. Warren was instructed to go to Hancock's support and, upon their connecting with the 2nd Corps, have General Griffin attack the enemy's flank on his front.[3]

Unfortunately, the division nearest Hancock's was Samuel Crawford's, and after strengthening it with a brigade from Romeyn Ayres and a twelve-pounder battery, Warren accompanied Crawford's advance toward Hatcher's Run and Hancock. Beyond Crawford's proclivity for getting lost and often failing to carry out his orders, his division faced a real challenge, an area of tangled woods full of meandering creeks, or "runs," one looking much like another as Crawford sought to find Hatcher's Run. As the men struggled through underbrush and timber the enemy had felled, sound was their only guide, so Warren sent orders for General Griffin to begin shelling the enemy to give Crawford an opportunity to march to the sound of the guns. But the seemingly inevitable became the reality as large numbers of Crawford's men and ultimately whole regiments became lost in the woods. An exasperated Warren ordered Crawford to get his men in order and advance, while in turn Warren left to find and consult with Generals Meade and Hancock. Upon reaching them, he found that the enemy had come between Crawford and Hancock's 2nd Corps and had attacked Hancock "with great violence." Meanwhile, when Crawford finally reached Hatcher's Run, he also found the enemy waiting to dispute his crossing, and Warren and Meade, apparently agreeing that Crawford's initial engagement with the enemy would prevent him from reaching Hancock in time, ordered General Ayres to go to the 2nd Corps's assistance. Ayres reached Hancock when darkness was falling and the fighting was trailing off. As described below, the enemy confronting Crawford did not stay in his front, but Crawford let this golden opportunity to cross Hatcher's Run before the enemy was reinforced slip through his incapable fingers.[4]

When General Grant questioned why Crawford had not come to Hancock's defense on October 27, Meade came to his friend's defense, describing the woods he'd had to move through as "worse than the Wilderness." Warren would later offer a more lukewarm exoneration of Crawford in his report for that day, a sort of "not for want of trying" defense that described the conditions that had caused Crawford's delay. But Roebling, who had had the unenviable task of carrying dispatches from Warren to Crawford and back, was less forgiving in his report and told a very different story regarding Crawford. When he found Crawford, who had finally brought his division to the banks of Hatcher's Run, the men were inexplicably halted, though the rebels they had previously been engaged with had abandoned their breastworks on Crawford's front. Roebling wrote, "I then went to General Crawford and asked him why he had halted at the very moment when he had victory in his grasp. He replied that he had positive orders from General Warren not to advance another step." One of Crawford's captains came up and "begged hard" to be allowed to cross the creek with fifty men and clear out the line of breastworks. "Permission was refused." Crawford, never one to recognize an opportunity or take a risk, presented the 5th Corps with yet another missed opportunity. After Crawford's refusal to consider crossing Hatcher's Run and take over the enemy's abandoned works, Roebling rode hard to find Warren. After explaining the situation, he set off with "positive orders" for Crawford to cross Hatcher's Run, but by the time he returned, the rebels had penetrated between Hancock and Crawford, and with the enemy showing up on Crawford's flank and in his rear, it was too late to advance and claim victory, instead of defeat, for the Army of the Potomac at the First Battle of Hatcher's Run.[5]

As for Crawford's getting lost in the woods earlier on October 27, to be fair, many soldiers got lost that day, including those of the enemy. Roebling, while returning to headquarters that afternoon, had this encounter: "When I got back to the Crow house voices shouted out of the pines, 'Stop that man on horseback.' They turned out to be eight rebels under charge of two of our men who had lost their way. I brought them in. These men of ours had been taken prisoners by the rebels in the first place, but not one of the whole party knew where they were, so they had made up their minds to follow the first man who knew where anywhere was."[6]

When darkness drew the fighting on October 27 to a close, the Army of the Potomac and its opponents spent a miserable night in the pouring rain. When Hancock drew back his lines at daybreak on October 28, Warren ordered Crawford to do the same; then he sent Roebling out to Crawford's line for the unenviable task of collecting all Crawford's stray soldiers from the woods and bringing them in. Roebling also went out onto Hancock's battlefield of the previous day and found it devoid of the enemy, though rebel cavalry pickets were visible in the distance. That morning, the 2nd, 5th, and 9th Corps began their withdrawal, with Warren leaving the field with 269 rebel prisoners and the knowledge that they had accomplished little beyond inflicting heavy losses upon the enemy but at a considerable loss of their own.[7]

Of this fight, known as the Battle of Boydton Plank Road or the First Battle of Hatcher's Run, Roebling would say after their return from the front on October 29,

> We are back again, tired and played out as usual after a fight—The result upon the whole has been unsatisfactory notwithstanding that the Lt. Gen. was present in person to direct operations. We have taken a large number of prisoners more by accident than by fighting. Tonight however the whole army is back in its old camp and we are no nearer being in Petersburg than we were; I rather fancy that "Useless" Grant is in a brown study tonight what to do next. I met with no mishap, one bullet intended for me went through my orderly's heart killing him instantly. Several of our staff lost their way & were captured, and then recaptured, the rebs losing their way likewise. Do you imagine it was a pretty mixed up affair.

Several days after the expedition, Washington would tell Emily that, as he was writing up his reports, "the chief digs [dignitaries] are hunting around for some scapegoat to bear the blame, with very poor success so far; the papers will howl, and we expect lots of fun reading the accounts; the amount of it is that both sides ran away from each other during the night as has so often happened before now. This business of fighting is pretty much a matter of brag." The Hatcher's Run expedition cost the Federals 1,758 men, while the Confederates suffered a loss of 1,300. During this movement, Roebling had a near miss from an exploding enemy shell, and, as he mentioned, while he was searching for one of his own skirmish lines, the sudden appearance of a squad of rebels ended with his orderly being killed. And a road Roebling had previously scouted down in search of a way to Hatcher's Run saw a fellow scout captured by the enemy. How many more of these fights could Washington Roebling take part in before he became one of the 5th Corps's casualties?[8]

The month of November was taken up with Roebling writing out his long and detailed report of the Overland Campaign, but on November 3 his mind was much occupied with thoughts of his and Emily's upcoming reunion, only forty-five days off. He declared, "If only that were absolutely certain how glad and happy I would feel." With their wedding planned for mid-January in the new year, it's not hard to realize what Washington feared might get in the way, for on November 5 Roebling wrote to Emily, "We expect Father Lee will be apt to give us a turn about election day & interfere with the voting, but we are ready for him." After the election, Roebling wrote, "Hurrah for old Abe; we have already heard that he is elected through the telegraph." Roebling plainly fretted that there might be another battle before he departed from the army, writing on November 11 that there might still be "time for two more busts before winter." Another advance on Hatcher's Run was considered for November 20, but days of rain caused it to be called off.[9]

Sad news arrived at 5th Corps headquarters for Washington Roebling from Charles Swan, his father's factory foreman in Trenton, for on November 22 his mother, Johanna Roebling, had died. General Warren saw to it that Roebling had a leave of ten days to go home, where his siblings all gathered for the funeral. He took advantage of his time at home to go to Philadelphia with his sister Elvira and his brother Ferdie to buy things necessary for his January wedding. On the night before Roebling left his home in Trenton, he, Ferdie, and Charles Swan drowned their sorrows with three bottles of wine. Yet, when Washington returned to the army in early December, he confessed to Emily that he was "almost tempted to exclaim 'home again,'" saying that the army "seems so much like home to me after being away for nearly 2 weeks." But he also said that word had gone out that the 5th Corps was about to leave its winter camp. In the course of a day or two, the 6th Corps, returning from the Shenandoah Valley, would be relieving Warren's corps,

Yellow House/Globe Tavern.
Library of Congress.

which would "move back in reserve, ready to go wherever wanted." Roebling said that "being in reserve always means the direct opposite," and they expected they were about to see action again. While trying to concentrate on their January plans, Washington nonetheless warned Emily that he supposed he would "get away by Christmas or New Years at farthest, although there will be quite a little campaign between now & then." As for the tenuous nature of their plans, he said that at least it sounded like Emily's brothers, General Warren and Robert, would in all probability be able to come to their wedding.[10]

Emily and Washington rightly feared that the war could still rob them of their reunion, and as the 6th Corps relieved the 5th Corps, there was for Warren's soldiers the additional aggravation of having to leave the winter quarters they had worked to make as comfortable as possible under the circumstances. Roebling had to relinquish his comfortable billet in the Yellow House at Globe Tavern, the headquarters for General Warren and his corps. One suspects Washington of a sort of well-meant evasion in his letter to Emily on the night before Warren's December 7 advance for yet another assault on the Weldon Railroad, a movement that involved some twenty-two thousand infantrymen, cavalry, and artillerymen. Claiming that he had inadvertently fallen asleep before writing to her, Washington declared that his missive would therefore be a short one. While he admitted to being tired out from being all day in the saddle, he omitted mentioning that this arduous duty had entailed scouting for the next day's routes. Washington made the dubious statement to Emily that he had no idea where they might be sent. He even speculated that, with news that William T. Sherman was approaching the seacoast at Savannah, perhaps the 5th Corps might be sent to join him, a prospect Washington declared he did not relish. Given that the expedition would begin the next day, December 7, at 6 a.m. and be led by Warren, it is hard to imagine that Roebling, as an aide, scout, and courier at 5th Corps headquarters, was unaware of the corps's orders.[11]

His reticence may be explained by the fact that Emily was feeling the strain of the last days of their separation, making Washington loath to tell her that he would once again be in harm's way. He likely tried to spare her at least a few days of worry before the newspapers or her brothers made her aware that the 5th Corps was on the move. But Washington did share an all too plain indication of his own anxieties. He told Emily of a disturbing nightmare, in which he was in the clutches of a homicidal maniac who was trying to kill him with a poker, an odious dream that he felt would "stick with him for many a day to come." Considering Roebling's years of hard service, in which he had seen and experienced enough to fuel anyone's nightmares, a maniac with a poker is rather a surprising scenario for his subconscious to serve up, but it nonetheless offers some indication of his own unease and apprehension. The expedition that the 5th Corps was about to embark upon would be another arduous test of Warren's capacity to command and of Roebling's and the corps's ability and willingness, despite extremes of winter weather and the enemy's desire to stop them, to get the job done. Roebling would be undertaking the journey as Colonel Roebling, a grateful Warren acknowledging his aide's faithful service from Gettysburg to the Battle of Petersburg and beyond. Warren was leading some twenty-two thousand men on this expedition, a movement that would take him miles from the Army of the Potomac, leaving his forces dangerously isolated in the presence of an enemy desperate to preserve what was left of the railroads that were its supply lifelines.[12]

Though few among the South's politicians or the commanders of the Confederate armies would admit it publicly, the Confederacy was facing its final days. Warren's previous interruption of the northern end of the Weldon Railroad and obstruction of the steady stream of food and supplies from the plantations of the Carolinas was the beginning of the end. With the tracks of the Weldon Railroad destroyed from Petersburg to Rowanty Creek, just north of Stony Creek, the rebels had to bypass the break in the Weldon Railroad by loading supplies onto wagon trains at Stony Creek Station and hauling them to Petersburg by way of the Boydton Plank Road. Warren's December raid was

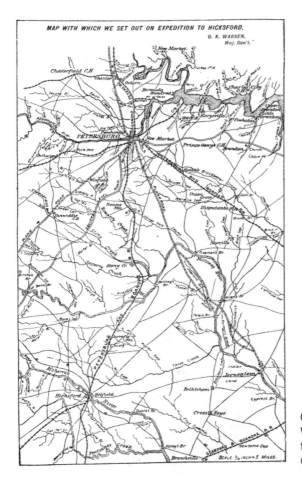

General Warren's "Map with Which We Set Out on Expedition to Hicksford." OR 42, I, 448.

meant to put a stop to the wagon trains and destroy the remaining portion of the Weldon Railroad upon which the Petersburg defenders were depending. With the fall of Petersburg would come the fall of Richmond.[13]

General Warren's expedition included his own 5th Corps, Gersham Mott's division of the 2nd Corps, David Gregg's division of cavalry, four batteries of field artillery, and three companies of engineers and their 250-foot pontoon bridge. The weather, for once, was clear and mild, the roads good, and the passage of the Federals became marked with discarded great coats and blankets, which many a marching infantryman would have cause to regret. General Warren, despite bridges destroyed by the enemy, managed to get his entire force across the Nottoway River early on December 8. When the 5th

Corps struck the Weldon Railroad just south of the Nottoway, from 6 p.m. until midnight, the destruction of the tracks leading toward Jarretts Station was carried out by moonlight. Gregg's cavalry took care of resistance offered by the rebel cavalry, driving them across the Meherin River. On reaching Hicksford, Warren found the enemy had a considerable force ensconced in three forts with batteries and rifle pits, and upon personally examining the site, Warren also took into account that his men had accomplished their mission and used up their rations. His corps was now thirty miles away from the Army of the Potomac, and with signs of more bad weather threatening, Warren turned back toward Petersburg. The 5th Corps put in a few more hours of destroying the Weldon Railroad, making a long line of railroad-tie bonfires that lit the increasingly stormy night. The 5th Corps and its supporters left behind seventeen to eighteen miles of ruined tracks that would not be fully repaired until the last month of the war. They were joined on their return by a sizable throng of fugitive slaves from the plantations the expedition passed.[14]

As the 5th Corps began its return, sleet made the Federals' all-night trek a freezing misery, and roads became a mire. The days and nights of the march

General Wade Hampton.
Library of Congress.

would be remembered for the extremes of weather, and also for the discovery by a number of Unionist soldiers that the locals had not only hens and pigs but also barrels of applejack hidden on their properties, and soon canteens were filled with the potent brew. Though it may have had a temporary "warming" effect on the soldiers, it made a bit of a shambles of the expeditions' intended forced march back to safety. This unfortunate state of affairs had another, more sinister outcome, for it seems that Yankee stragglers, not a few of them under the influence, were turning up dead, and when one unfortunate was reportedly found with his throat cut, things turned ugly. Outraged Federal troops, fueled by rumors of additional atrocities, burned buildings that had been spared on the expedition's way south and destroyed the town of Sussex Court House. When Warren came upon this destructive mayhem, he and other officers put an end to it.[15]

Gregg's cavalry did double duty as Warren's expedition turned toward home, for while some of his troopers were sent on ahead to stop the continued harassment by Wade Hampton's cavalry, others were acting as rear guard to deal with the rebels from Hicksford who tried to follow the retreating Federals. There was no sign of A. P. Hill's corps, which had been sent out to stop Warren, for apparently Hill was convinced that the Federals would make for the Southside Railroad after their destruction of the Weldon. Hill's force was sent on a trajectory mistakenly thought to promise a confrontation with Warren. General Meade, apparently none too comfortable with this midwinter advance Grant had demanded and apprehensive that the rebels would catch up with Warren in his isolated position, sent Potter's division of the 9th Corps to a position on the Nottoway to support Warren. As Warren approached the river on December 11, he sent Colonel Roebling ahead to report back to Warren with the position and readiness of Potter's force. But once Warren was confident they would regain safety before the enemy caught up with them, he sent word for Potter to head back to Petersburg. When Warren's expedition reached the Federal lines, Roebling's work was far from done. He would lead the men sent out on Ayres's picket line to their designated position between the Halifax Road and the Jerusalem Plank Road. For Roebling, another expedition had been not only successfully completed but also survived. Arriving back at Petersburg, far from daunted by his arduous days and nights of what became known as the Hicksford Raid, Warren included in his report suggestions for another expedition to complete the destruction of the enemy's supply lines.[16]

Once back safely from the Hicksford Raid, in his December 14 letter Washington spoke freely about it, telling Emily that the headquarters mess was well supplied with ducks and geese captured on the expedition. When it looked like Washington's scouting and courier days were finally over, he wrote that he was planning to leave the army in a week and to go to Trenton, where he would wait for acceptance of his resignation. Yet he was unable to feel entirely free from worry, commenting, "I hope now that we won't go on any more moves between now and the 20th; but as I have stood it for 3 ½ yrs I guess I can endure it for a week longer." In what would be his last letter from the front, Washington reminded "Emmie" that, along with other soldiers of the 5th Corps, he still missed his comfortable winter quarters in the Yellow House at Globe Tavern. He was instead spending his last days in the army in a tent in an open field, which he and his tentmate, Cope, were trying to make livable, installing bunks, a table, and a fireplace. He also said that their tent was decorated with maps stolen from Sussex Court House, though he insisted that they had been very moderate in their thieving, despite the chance to steal choice books. Roebling and Cope, however, had succumbed and taken just one, titled *Advice to Married People*, which he and Cope were "reading with great gusto."[17]

Praise be, for this prospective bridegroom, Washington Roebling, had just written the last of his many letters to Emily from the army. Having no faith that the war would be over any time soon, after three and a half years of hard service, Washington kept his promise to Emily and to his father and tendered his resignation. While Roebling, like General Warren, believed the war must go on and on, if he had imagined that it would be over in four short months, would he have stayed on? And if he had stayed, would he have survived? Warren and the 5th Corps's capture and destruction of the Weldon Railroad made possible the battles that would see Robert E. Lee withdraw from Petersburg and lead to his eventual surrender at Appomattox. Yet Warren's fights are often not even mentioned in the timelines of Federal battles during the last year of the war. Scant credit is given him or his stout-hearted aide and scout, Washington A. Roebling, but Warren, Roebling, and the men of the 5th Corps, though the sacrifices made and price paid were terrible, could look back with pride on what they had accomplished. In those last days of December 1864, Washington Roebling embraced his good luck, rejoicing that, despite the many risks he had taken, he had beaten the odds. He was on his way home to prepare for his wedding to Emily. Their life together would be happy, inspiring, tragic, and, in many ways, the stuff their dreams were made of.[18]

Epilogue

WASHINGTON AND EMILY ROEBLING

One would like to ascribe to the young lovers, Washington and Emily Warren Roebling, a fairytale marriage and life lived happily ever after. And in some ways, it was. After their wedding, the couple went to Europe, where (when Washington wasn't studying other engineers' ideas on bridge and caisson design) they toured England and the Continent. The ever-adventurous Emily, though knowing she was pregnant, journeyed on, with the result that she delivered their son, named John after Washington's father, while visiting the

Washington and Emily Roebling.
Rutgers University Library, Roebling Collection.

Roebling family's city of origin, Mühlhausen, Germany. When they returned from their foreign travels, Washington was to act as his father's second in command on what would be the engineering project of the century: the Brooklyn Bridge, which would span the East River, linking the bustling boroughs of Manhattan and Brooklyn. John Roebling, famous for his bridges and wealthy from the productions of his "wire rope" factory in Trenton, New Jersey, was giving his son a legacy the son of any immigrant could envy. But as the building of the bridge began, with all its complex engineering and construction details to be seen to, the story started to turn dark for the young couple.

John Roebling, the engineer, was possessed of a great and inventive mind, but as a husband and father, he was, as described by his son, Washington, an abject failure. John had met and married his immigrant wife in the town he helped found when he came to America: Saxonburg, Pennsylvania. Washington described his father as ashamed of his wife, who had far less education than her engineer husband and spoke little or no English. But many of the trials in the Roebling family circle came from John's obsession with hydropathy, a belief in the curative powers of water in the form of baths, cold and hot, douches, and steam baths. No other medical practitioners or practices were allowed in the Roebling house. Combined with John's adoption of numerous bizarre diets and restriction of the family to an impossibly small budget, Washington's childhood was often a misery of cold and hunger. But nothing left Washington with more horrifying memories than the many beatings his father administered to him. Yet it was Washington who, when John Roebling's foot was crushed on the building site of the Brooklyn Bridge, nursed his father as best he could, though John refused to see any doctors and insisted upon employing his own water cures. Tetanus set in, and John Roebling died a horrible death, as witnessed by Washington. Despite his tumultuous childhood, Washington still held his obstinate father in considerable esteem, as demonstrated by the name of his first and only child, John A. Roebling II.

There were those who would have denied young Roebling, after the death of his father, the right to take over as chief engineer of the bridge, despite his being an exceptionally intelligent and innovative engineer with bridge experience in his own right. But no one understood his father's ideas and plans as Washington did, and no one knew as much about building the underwater caissons so necessary for this bridge's construction. Then, too, though John Roebling had refused to listen to any design advice that Washington might offer, he had disagreed with elements of his father's plan and now implemented his own ideas.

As Roebling showed during the war when he scouted for the 5th Corps, he was determined to allow no man to go where he dared not go himself. The building of the bridge, with its groundbreaking use of deep-water caissons, as well as the great heights of the structure itself, made for hazardous work. While testing the limits to which a healthy man could tolerate working in the artificial atmosphere of the caissons, Roebling was struck with a severe case of the bends, or caisson disease. It came near to killing him and left him an invalid, often utterly helpless physically, for an entire decade of his life. Though he was often barely able to speak and could not write, his mind and his drive to go on remained strong. What a loyal helpmate the intelligent Emily Roebling would prove, and how grateful she and Washington must have been for her quick mind and the education that her brother, Gouverneur Warren, had seen she received, one unusual for a woman of her time. But Emily also made it her business to study the terminology and understand the principles of engineering, as she carried her husband's orders to the crews building the bridge, which he could no longer personally supervise onsite.

Washington slowly recovered his health and, after the completion of the bridge in 1883, led a rather reclusive life in Trenton, New Jersey. His passion was collecting rare rocks and minerals, which led to a vast collection that was eventually willed to the Smithsonian and now forms an important part of its mineral and gem collection. He also wrote a biography of his father, which often veered into Washington's remembrances of his own wartime experiences. Given that other accounts he wrote after the war of the battles he had witnessed have disappeared, the John Roebling biography and Roebling's wartime correspondence and reports are our best sources for revisiting his experiences.

Washington and Emily enjoyed a prosperous life in the last years of the nineteenth century, but fate again dealt the couple an unfortunate hand. In 1903, Washington took Emily Roebling's death from stomach cancer hard, and so he was as surprised as many others when, five years later in 1908, he met and married Cornelia Witsell Farrow, a young widow from South Carolina who was said to have brightened his previously melancholy days. While he continued to benefit substantially from the earnings of the Roebling factories, his brothers and their children directed the company, and Washington had little responsibility, until, at the age of eighty-four, following the younger Roeblings' deaths, he had to take over the helm of the vast company. The Roebling enterprises benefited from the Roeblings' innovative and engineering genius, as well as from their being in the right place at the right time. The new, stronger "wire rope" was needed not only for suspension bridges but

This painting by Carolus-Duran shows Emily in the court dress she wore to the coronation of Tsar Nicholas II.
The Brooklyn Museum.

also for the elevators that made skyscrapers possible, as well as for cables for steamships, underwater communications, and eventually the nation's airplanes.

Washington Roebling maintained an extensive, affectionate correspondence with his son, John A. Roebling II, whose ill health kept him in sunnier climes than New Jersey. It is said that Washington himself seldom experienced a day free of pain. He lived out his days in his Trenton mansion with his wife, Cornelia, and a stray Airedale he had named Billy Sunday after a famous red-haired evangelist of the time. Roebling, who refused to ride in automobiles, was a familiar figure on the Trenton streetcars, which, although it was not an official stop, would pick Roebling up in front of his home along with Billy, supposedly the only dog allowed to ride for free on the Trenton cars.

Washington Roebling in later
years. In this painting by
Theobald Chartran, the famous
bridge can be seen through
the window.
The Brooklyn Museum.

Washington Roebling, after a life packed with an unimaginable number of remarkable and hair-raising experiences, reached the age of eighty-nine before he died in 1926. He is buried next to his first love, Emily Warren Roebling, in the cemetery of her hometown, Cold Spring, New York.

While the iconic, world-famous Brooklyn Bridge is quite enough of a legacy for any man and woman to have left behind them, the sacrifices of Washington and Emily Roebling leave with us another gift that may prove an even more valuable and admirable benefaction for our chaotic day and age. In a time in which the advocates of Ayn Rand's and like philosophies seem to dominate our social and political spectrum, with all their resultant greed and selfishness, Washington Roebling's demonstrated commitment—one he risked his own life for—never to send a man where he dared not go himself is worth embracing. It comes wonderfully near to that far older dictate: do unto others as you would have them do unto you. Would that we could all, for the sake of ourselves and all others, build such bridges for humanity.

Much has been written about Washington and Emily Roebling, for the most part well focused on the inspiring challenges posed by the design and construction of the Brooklyn Bridge, still considered one of the most important engineering feats of all time. Best known is David McCullough's best-selling *The Bridge*, which, even though its title proclaims its central theme, nevertheless gives a dozen or so pages to consideration of Washington's Civil War service. Other works, such as Clifford Zink's *The Roebling Legacy*, focus primarily on the industrial powerhouse founded by the patriarch, John A. Roebling, one that made the entire family very wealthy but, with life such as it is, did not always ensure happiness. It is easy to say that Washington Roebling faced the many challenges his life threw at him with admirable courage and extraordinary determination.

GOUVERNEUR K. WARREN

After Washington Roebling's resignation, General Warren likely felt a considerable loss with the departure of his reliable aide, scout, and courier. And Roebling, following news of his commander, his corps, and the Army of the Potomac from afar, could only have been deeply unhappy at the fate that befell his brother-in-law. Roebling had been with the army during its fall advances and the December 1864 Hicksford Raid by Warren and the 5th Corps. They were movements that put the Army of the Potomac in a position for the spring offensive intended to result in the entrapment of Lee's Army of Northern Virginia, followed by the fall of Petersburg and Richmond and the beginning of the end for the Confederacy.

After Sheridan's victory in the Shenandoah Valley, General Grant had given him orders to ride south and join Sherman's army, but Sheridan instead brought his force to Petersburg to be in on what was likely to be the final push. Far from being chastised, Sheridan was given the starring role: command of the cavalry strike force in an assault on the rebel right flank. The 5th, 2nd, 6th, and 9th Corps were thereby relegated to supporting rolls in Sheridan's flanking movement.

Sheridan would prove himself unequal to the task of assaulting the rebel right, and, far from entrapping or driving the enemy, he was punished by George Pickett's infantry and the rebel cavalry and found himself and his troopers under threat and penned up at Dinwiddie Court House. In urgent need of assistance, Sheridan called upon Warren and the 5th Corps to pull his fat out of the fire he had created. When Warren and the 5th Corps joined Sheridan's cavalry at Five Forks, the day was eventually won by Warren's infantry. Despite Warren having saved him from ignominious defeat, Sheridan not only took credit for the Union victory at Five Forks but also falsely accused Warren of purposely delaying the infantry attack and being absent from the front during the battle, serious and painful charges for a conscientious officer such as Warren. With the authority General Grant had given him over both cavalry and infantry, Sheridan removed Warren from command of the 5th Corps. Though he had control of both his cavalry and much of the infantry of the Army of the Potomac in the following days, Sheridan allowed Lee and the Army of Northern Virginia to slip out of Petersburg. Days of confusion followed, largely the result of Grant's and Sheridan's determination that supposedly Sheridan and his cavalry, not the Army of the Potomac, would strike the final, telling blow. Roebling expressed his feelings of deep frustration, and likely not a little guilt, when he commented that if only he had been there at Five Forks, perhaps he could have somehow prevented the injustice done to his former commander and now brother-in-law, General Gouverneur Warren.

Roebling's scouting and service as courier could very well have been of great assistance to Warren that day at Five Forks. Any delay in the attack Sheridan had ordered the 5th Corps to make was in large part caused by the erroneous reports the cavalry supplied to Warren. As a result, Romeyn Ayres's division found the enemy where he was not expected, while the men of Charles Griffin's division, realizing they'd been led astray by Sheridan's faulty intelligence, had to take it upon themselves to change course and march to the sound of the guns. But not the ever-bumbling General Samuel Wylie Crawford, who heedlessly continued to lead his division away from the enemy's main position. While Crawford concentrated on skirmishing with General Thomas Munford's Confederate cavalry, General Warren chased down and succeeded in turning the errant division toward the rest of the 5th Corps's assault on the rebels' earthworks. After Warren and the 5th Corps, including Crawford's division, had won the battle for Sheridan, then, and only then, did Sheridan accuse Warren of not being in the fight, and, with the authority Lieutenant General Grant had given him, he removed Warren from command and sent him from the battlefield. In his effort to understand what happened, Roebling would later write of Sheridan, "Sheridan's hatred of Warren dates back to the night march from the Wilderness to Spotsylvania when Sheridan's cavalry got in the way and prevented the 5th Corps from reaching Spotsylvania in time. Warren complained of him at Hdqrtrs and Sheridan never forgot it." Apparently Grant never forgot it either.

All Warren's requests for an investigation regarding his removal from command at Five Forks were denied, and when Sheridan's self-justifying report on the battle was published just after the war, Warren wrote his own account of the hours leading up to the battle and the details of the fight itself. Warren remained in the regular army, serving as an engineer with the rank of major, while Sheridan rose to the top of command under the continuing influence of General in Chief, then President Grant's ever-embracing patronage. Sheridan himself eventually became general in chief of the U.S. Army and ultimately rose to the rank of lieutenant general. Combined with the unlikelihood that any soldier or politician beholden to Grant would support Warren's cause, Warren could also, on a major's pay, little afford the great expense of hiring legal assistance. Washington's wife, Gouverneur Warren's sister Emily, would, with her own money and when her reluctant brother allowed, advance him funds when needed. Warren was denied a hearing for years by Grant and his protégés, W. T. Sherman and then Sheridan himself, both of whom would follow Grant as generals in chief of the U.S. Army.

There would be no hearing for Warren until an administration not beholden to Grant and his minions came to power in Washington. The findings of that court of inquiry, after lengthy hearings, absolved Warren of most of Sheridan's accusations, but Warren died in 1882 before the findings were released. Though Warren had continued in the regular army, having returned to his duties as an engineering officer, he left instructions that he not be buried in uniform or with any trappings of his military service, a sad ending for a soldier who gave so much and had such an impact on the Union's prosecution of the Civil War. But there were those who refused to let General Warren's outstanding service be forgotten, nor would they let the destruction of Warren's military career be the final word. In 1888, a statue of Warren was placed on Little Round Top at Gettysburg with an inscription that reads in part, "Led to this spot by his military sagacity, on July 2, 1863, General Gouverneur Kemble Warren, then Chief Engineer of the Army of the Potomac, detected Gen. Hood's flanking movement, and by promptly assuming the responsibility of ordering troops to this place, saved the key of the Union position." Erected by the members of one of Warren's first commands, the 5th New York Duryee Zouaves, it is a touching memorial spoiled only by the presence nearby of a larger-than-life monument to Major General Samuel Wylie Crawford, commemorating his false claim of being the savior of Little Round Top on the second day of the Battle of Gettysburg. It was erected on Crawford Avenue at the base of Little Round Top in 1888, the same year as the Warren statue.

But at least the influential Samuel Wylie Crawford, who would inexplicably be awarded the rank of major general in the regular army for his near disastrous role at Five Forks, did not get to fulfill his postwar plan for today's carefully preserved summit of Little Round Top at Gettysburg. Crawford,

Colonel Washington Roebling on Little Round Top, Gettysburg, beside the statue of General Gouverneur K. Warren.
Schuyler, *The Roeblings.*

insistent that he and his command at the time, the Pennsylvania Reserve Brigade, were the heroes of the second day, wanted to level the top of the hill where Strong Vincent, Stephen Weed, Patrick O'Rorke, Charles Hazlett, and so many others had died, in order to build a museum dedicated to Crawford and his Pennsylvanians. This would have obliterated the place where Vincent's brigade, including Joshua Chamberlain and his stalwart 20th Maine, fought to prevent the enemy from crushing the vulnerable Federal left flank. Luckily, there are sometimes limits set on the ambitions of men like Crawford, and Little Round Top has been preserved much as it was on that day in July 1863, a monument to all the men who fought and died there. Though Grant, Sheridan, and the witless Crawford would have denied Warren the credit he was due for his role in extending the encirclement of Petersburg and the eventual Federal victory at Five Forks, Gettysburg will forever remain a monument to his ability and tenacity. This public remembrance undoubtedly proved a balm for Washington Roebling and his painful regret that he had not been by his chief's side in the final days of the war, as he had been with him at Little Round Top.

Recommended reading regarding General Warren includes Warren's *An Account of the Operations of the Fifth Army Corps at the Battle of Five Forks.*

Also see Joshua L. Chamberlain's *Passing of the Armies*. Chamberlain, one of Warren's brigade commanders in 1864 and 1865, wrote of the days just before and during Five Forks and the injustice done to General Warren and the 5th Corps. Also see the Sheridan epilogue within for other examples of Grant's near irrational preference for and defense of Sheridan and his war record. For information regarding Grant's dislike and distrust of General Warren, see my *Command Conflicts in Grant's Overland Campaign*, which reveals how General James H. Wilson and others skillfully stoked the fires of Grant's animosity toward Warren for the purposes of furthering their own ambitions. There were those who hoped to see Sheridan and Wilson displace Meade and Warren as commanders of the Army of the Potomac. As it was, by the end of the war, though Meade still nominally commanded the soon-to-be-disbanded Army of the Potomac, not one of the corps commanders who started out in the spring of 1864 with that army on Lieutenant General Grant's Overland Campaign remained in command when the war ended a year later.

GEORGE GORDON MEADE

A case could be made that Grant, a mediocre military man, had his head turned by the praise and adulation he received from his staff and friends, further augmented by his eventually being hailed as the "savior" of the Union. One could also say that General George Gordon Meade, the commander who took on Lee at Gettysburg and won, ended up having *his* head turned in a quite lamentably different way. Meade assumed command of the Army of the Potomac a few days before the three-day bloodletting at Gettysburg, which ended in victory against an enemy commander who had seemed invincible. Meade received not praise but his administration's criticism and scorn. Jealous, vengeful, and ambitious men, like Henry Halleck, Daniel Sickles, Joseph Hooker, Daniel Butterfield, and their supporters, including members of the influential Joint Committee on the Conduct of the War, saw to it that Meade received no thanks from a grateful nation such as would be bestowed upon U. S. Grant. Grant would reap the rewards of the victories he claimed in the west, eventually being awarded the rank of lieutenant general and command of all the U.S. armies, while Meade would have to be satisfied with his having retained any command at all.

When considering the largely manufactured controversies regarding Meade's leadership during the aftermath of the Battle of Gettysburg, perhaps it is wise to consider the testimony of intelligent and experienced soldiers like General Meade, General A. A. Humphreys, General Gouverneur Warren, and General Henry Hunt, as well as the subject of this book, Washington

Roebling. These eyewitnesses testified to the difficulties of the Army of the Potomac's pursuit of the still dangerous Army of Northern Virginia. Such men as these, after inspecting Lee's defenses at Williamsport, declared that an attack such as Halleck and the administration demanded would have resulted in a bloodbath that rivaled Fredericksburg, and with the same result: nothing but outrageous casualties. But at the time, such testimony was ignored, and vitriolic criticism continued to be heaped upon Meade, questioning everything from his intelligence to his patriotism, his courage to his sanity. Such hostility and censure undoubtedly left its mark, but George Meade, for better or for worse, soldiered on.

In the aftermath of Gettysburg, while Halleck and the administration were still hounding Meade to hurry up and get at the wily Lee, whatever the cost, they also took from him a considerable portion of his army. First, soldiers were sent to deal with the New York Draft Riots, and as additional troops were lost as their terms of enlistment expired, several thousand more were detached from the Army of the Potomac for an expedition to South Carolina. Yet Meade developed and submitted plans to Washington for a more promising approach from which to launch an attack upon Lee than his present position allowed. Although his plans were remarkably similar to those Lieutenant General Grant would put into action the next year, Meade's plans were rejected outright. Adding insult to injury, Halleck and the administration, in response to Lee sending James Longstreet's corps west, removed Meade's 11th and 12th Corps from Army of the Potomac and sent them to U. S. Grant. Lee promptly attempted to take advantage of Meade's shrinking troop numbers and disadvantageous position. Ironically, the result was a rare bright spot in the Federals' autumn of angst, a small victory by General G. K. Warren, commanding the 2nd Corps during Winfield Hancock's absence. General Warren arranged a brilliant rearguard action at Bristoe Station, which delivered an embarrassing and costly loss for Lee and the Army of Northern Virginia. But although the fight at Bristoe Station had given Lee an unexpectedly severe check, it was not the open-field battle Meade and the administration most desired.

Halleck's insistence that Meade and the Army of the Potomac launch their attack from where they were resulted in yet another disappointing advance at Mine Run in late 1863. Meade once again bore the brunt of the administration's criticism, and while he placed most of the blame where it belonged, upon the head of General William French, who inexplicably held up a promising advance, Meade also decided that General Warren, his former trusted advisor, shared responsibility. Washington Roebling had been the

General Meade.
Library of Congress.

unfortunate who carried Warren's message to Meade that he had called off the assault, and he bore firsthand witness to Meade's extreme dismay at the news. Meade was unwilling to overlook Warren cancelling an attack without his express permission, despite agreeing that it would have gained nothing but severe casualties. So while Meade's report blamed General French, it also included criticism of Warren. One could make the case that the beleaguered Meade showed remarkably little loyalty to General Warren, his right-hand man at Gettysburg and man of the hour at Bristoe Station. As a result, General Warren had to quickly get used to being a trusted advisor no more, with the result that the two men's relationship would never be the same.

It is of interest, however, that despite this breach between Meade and Warren, and despite often being on the receiving end of Meade's sharp tongue and criticism, Roebling still retained respect for and confidence in Meade as a commander (if not an ally). And in the upcoming shakeup in the command structure of the Army of the Potomac before the Overland Campaign, Meade still retained enough confidence in Warren to give him the much-coveted command of a corps. Upon the return of Hancock to the 2nd Corps, General Warren received command of the 5th Corps. Although Meade retained command of the Army of the Potomac in the spring of 1864, Grant's decision to accompany that army resulted in a command structure remembered for its awkwardness and dysfunction. Meade was grateful that Grant had allowed him to retain his command and wished to please the lieutenant general, who, while looking over Meade's shoulder, was far from silent. Then, too, Meade's memories of his inability to attack Lee at Mine Run and the anger he felt at Warren cancelling an assault were all too fresh. As a result, within twenty-four hours of the beginning of Grant's Overland Campaign, there was conflict between Warren, Meade, and Grant. Although Meade may have had little opportunity or inclination to disagree, he nonetheless seemingly joined with Grant and his tribe to heap undeserved blame upon Warren and the 5th Corps. The Wilderness was the first of a number of instances in which Meade displayed little loyalty to Warren and his corps, when there was plenty of blame to go around for mistakes and derelictions by all the participants in the Overland Campaign.

Yet Grant and his cronies had little appreciation for Meade's adherence to their views on the inadequacies of the Army of the Potomac. One of Grant's entourage, former journalist Charles Dana, was most famous for having helped foment the "On to Richmond" frenzy that urged the Union army into a disastrously premature battle with the rebels at First Bull Run. But Dana then became an assistant secretary of war and acted as Stanton's man at the front out west, where he became a Grant supporter extraordinaire. Not only did Dana see Grant as a future candidate for president, but he also had high hopes that one of his numerous ambitious cronies might soon replace General Meade as commander of the Army of the Potomac. During the Overland Campaign, Dana's report to Stanton regarding Meade, which was forwarded to Abraham Lincoln, stated, "No man, no matter what his business or his service, approached him without being insulted in one way or another, and his own staff officers did not dare to speak to him unless first spoken to, for fear of either sneers or curses." No one could surpass former journalist Dana in his ability to blacken someone's name.

Beyond the many broken promises Grant made to Meade regarding promotion or assignment to an independent command, perhaps the saddest chapter of what Meade endured as Grant's subordinate came in the last days of the war in the aftermath of Five Forks. In a moment perhaps of empathy excited too little and too late, Meade apparently asked Grant to reconsider Sheridan's sudden and unwarranted removal of Warren from command of the 5th Corps. But since that could be construed as calling Sheridan's judgment into question, something Grant would never tolerate, Meade's request was ignored. But there's more: Grant allowed Sheridan, despite the mess he had gotten himself and his cavalry into at Dinwiddie Court House prior to the Battle of Five Forks, to assume overall command of the last confrontations with the Army of Northern Virginia before it abandoned Petersburg. In the days after Five Forks, not only were the various infantry corps of the Army of the Potomac acting under Sheridan's confused and ineffective orders, but even that army's commander, General Meade, had to apply to Sheridan to know his intentions and what orders he was giving to Meade's soldiers. Sheridan made an astonishing mess of it, allowing Lee and the Army of Northern Virginia to slip away from Petersburg, with a complicit Grant vacillating between terrible worry that the enemy might gang up on Sheridan and a desire to ensure that the commander to receive laurels for finally bringing Lee to bay would be Sheridan. Once again, Sheridan would need assistance from the Army of the Potomac, though its contribution was largely ignored.

After the disbanding of the Army of the Potomac, Meade served as a commander in various locations in the South. While still somewhat confident he would receive the recognition and advancement that Grant had assured him he deserved, the final betrayal came when Grant assumed the presidency. The day after his inauguration, Grant appointed General Sherman head of the army and, bypassing Meade and Halleck, gave a lieutenant generalcy to Sheridan.

Meade never wrote his memoirs or courted fame for his war service. He was plagued with bouts of pneumonia, the residual effects of his severe wounding early in the war. He died in the fall of 1872 at the age of fifty-seven and was buried beneath a modest gravestone in Laurel Hill Cemetery in Philadelphia.

In the years after the war, Roebling reflected on George Gordon Meade, comparing him to other less able commanders he had served under. He proclaimed, "How different was Meade at Gettysburg! The qualities of a great commander showed in his every act!" Recalling General Hooker's sorry performance at Chancellorsville and his removal from command of the Army of the Potomac just before Gettysburg, Roebling again thought of Meade, declaring, "When I recall the incredible personal efforts put forth by General Meade, the masterly manner in which he laid his plans and carried them to a successful issue on the instant, I felt thankful that the opportunity to lose this battle [Gettysburg] was taken away from Hooker in time." Grant was less generous in his postwar assessment of General Meade. Thankfully *after* Meade's death in 1872, Grant blithely stated that if either of his two favorites, Sheridan or Sherman, had been in command at Gettysburg, Lee's army would have been destroyed. We can only hope, as did Washington Roebling, that General George Gordon Meade rests in peace.

For a consideration of Meade, Gettysburg, and its aftermath, see Isaac Rusling Pennypacker's *General Meade* and General A. A. Humphreys's *From Gettysburg to the Rapidan*. For a consideration of Warren, Roebling, and the 5th Corps, Army of the Potomac, in 1864, I recommend my own book, *Command Conflicts in Grant's Overland Campaign*. Meade's *The Life and Letters of George Gordon Meade* provides a valuable window into Meade's private thoughts during the trials and tribulations of his commands. For an eyebrow-raising account of Sheridan's performance at Five Forks and his botched pursuit of Lee afterward, see Isaac Rusling Pennypacker's *Meade* and Joshua Chamberlain's *Passing of the Armies*. Ethan S. Rafuse's *George Gordon Meade and the War in the East* is also an interesting read. Rafuse confirms that Meade did not seek or employ political allies, something Grant did or had done for him with consummate skill. Rafuse also acknowledges that General Meade was not permitted to make the approach against Lee that Grant eventually employed during the Overland Campaign (IMO rather badly and at terrible cost). However, I part ways with Rafuse in his assessment that Grant, Sheridan, and Sherman, with their embrace of Lincoln, Stanton, and Halleck's doctrine of total war, thereby deserve genius status (not the word I think of when contemplating that trio), which somewhat denigrates the role of Meade and the Army of the Potomac in winning the war. It causes me to recall Joshua Chamberlain's statement that the Army of the Potomac had been criticized for not moving enough, but never for not dying enough.

Ulysses S. Grant

It would be nice to be able to say that, after a failed military career and a series of failed ventures in civilian life, with the advent of the Civil War, Ulysses S. Grant was able to redeem himself, doing what he did best: soldiering. But, in fact, strategically applied political influence, within the army and in Washington, had propelled Grant to the top of the military heap. Having hit rock bottom in life before the war, there was a certain desperation about Grant, for along with his string of failed businesses, he had also failed as a provider for the one bright spot in his life: his wife and family. His desire to succeed where he had failed in the peacetime army and in civilian life seemingly brought out a ruthlessness that would color his performance as a commander in the Union army. In his pursuit of his own and his favorites' advancement, many other commanders, both the worthy and the unworthy, would have their careers diminished or destroyed as they were pushed aside for the benefit of Grant and his allies.

Any number of promoters made Grant's rise possible: Representative Elihu Washburne and Assistant Secretary of War Charles Dana in Washington and

General Henry Halleck in the army itself. A good many others also recognized a promising opportunity when they saw one and rode Grant's coattails to the pinnacles of the nation's political and military commands. Men like William T. Sherman, a failed commander in his own right, often supplied, in person and in his letters to Grant, highly sycophantic declarations regarding Grant's superior military prowess. Such declarations lend credence to a comment Washington Roebling offered about Lieutenant General Grant, whom he sometimes referred to in his personal correspondence as "Useless Grant." Such stroking of Grant's ego by Sherman and others caused Roebling to make this damning assessment: "Grant, swollen by the fulsome praise of his personal staff, tacitly accepted the honors belonging to other and better men." Yet any number of historians have and will insist on making statements about Grant's military "genius." They point to his plan as lieutenant general to fight the war on more than one front as if no one before had ever contemplated or attempted to do such a thing. Nor are such sympathizers apt to consider that Grant's plan to bring Robert E. Lee and the Army of Northern Virginia to battle in 1864 was much like that proposed by General George Gordon Meade the year before, the difference being that Meade was denied permission by Henry Halleck and the administration to carry it out. Then, too, in the fall of 1863, Meade's Army of the Potomac was stripped of several of its corps to send west to assist Grant in his campaigns. By contrast, when Grant made his advance in 1864, his call for reinforcements led to the unprecedented stripping of Washington's garrisoned troops, with heavy artillerymen suddenly handed rifles and declared infantrymen.

Many among Grant's benefactors in the U.S. Army and in Washington had seen his potential as a candidate for president after the war's conclusion. Though the last year of the war was needlessly costly, Grant had undeniably brought the conflict to an end, and the label "Savior of the Union" was bestowed upon him as an addition to his already substantially manufactured popularity. A few of "Grant's Men," such as Adam Badeau and James Wilson, even discussed the likelihood of a military dictatorship after the war, with Grant playing the role of an easily manipulated dictator. The wartime Badeau-Wilson correspondence reveals that they saw themselves, and often rightly so, as wielding considerable influence over Grant. As Badeau encouraged Wilson to hammer home his ideas and suggestions upon Grant as the assistant adjutant general, John Rawlins, was doing, he commented, "There is only one sledge at work, and that is Rawlins." Badeau also related that he and others at headquarters, such as Rawlins, Wilson, Charles Dana, and the like, would stage conversations in front of Grant until Grant brought forth their ideas as his own. While Badeau likely suffered delusions of his own grandeur, the loyalty that Grant displayed toward him and other conniving companions, more than evident in the advancements he arranged for them, lends some credence to Badeau's claims of influence. As for a military dictatorship, it is said that President Andrew Johnson feared such a possibility enough to have considered replacing the increasingly angry General in Chief Grant with General William T. Sherman, whom Johnson saw as more loyal and reliable.

After the war, Grant was initially obedient to President Johnson's orders, such as his demand that Grant appear with him in public at political events, including on his "swing around circle," a three-week, two-thousand-mile campaign in outspoken promotion of his pro-Southern policies. The embarrassment Grant suffered at being seen to endorse Johnson's policies, it is said, sent him to seek solace, as he had in the past, in an alcoholic binge. But Grant also cooperated with Johnson when he "suspended" Secretary of War Edwin Stanton. When Johnson asked Grant to serve as interim secretary of war as well as general in chief of the army, Grant agreed. But when Johnson announced his intention to replace General Philip Sheridan, Grant's favorite, as commander

Ulysses S. Grant.
Library of Congress.

at New Orleans, Grant rebelled, and his supporters' presidential plans for him began to come to the surface.

As it was, a few years after the war, Grant was easily elected, and some of his benefactors did quite well, while others were disappointed. On the day of his inauguration, Grant made William T. Sherman general of the army and appointed Philip Sheridan lieutenant general, jumping over an expectant General Gordon Meade and shocked General Henry Halleck. But Grant also appointed his wartime chief of staff, John Rawlins, as secretary of war, and when Rawlins insisted that all army orders be under his, not Sherman's, control, he became, for all practical purposes, head of the country's army. The Sherman-Grant relationship never entirely recovered from the resulting rift, though when the consumptive Rawlins died, Sherman, at Grant's request, served briefly as interim secretary of war.

Adam Badeau, the former theater critic who became Grant's military secretary in the last year of the war, was a short, slouching, nearsighted little red-haired man once described by Grant as looking like a "bent ha-penny." Badeau, who bragged about his influence over Grant, used it to advocate for his intimate friend General James H. Wilson, who also spent considerable time with Grant, often blackening the reputations of those Wilson saw as rivals or enemies. While most of the benefits Wilson received occurred during the war, Grant, as president, saw that Badeau was rewarded with diplomatic posts in Europe and Cuba. Grant also relied heavily upon Badeau's unreliable material while writing his own memoirs. A comparison of Grant's memoirs with Badeau's often inaccurate and biased 1881 *Military History of Ulysses S. Grant* indicates that Grant drew heavily upon Badeau's work. In fact, in later years, when Badeau fell on hard times after Grant's death, he unsuccessfully tried to sue the former president's widow, Julia Dent Grant, for a portion of the profits from Grant's book, claiming that he had, for the most part, written it. Badeau was also compelled to sign a note in his last years acknowledging that he owed his onetime friend, the actor Edwin Booth, some $10,000.

It is worth considering how it is that so many works, from those of his contemporaries to those being written today, give such fulsome praise to Grant and "Grant's Men," while seemingly reserving any and all criticism for those whom the lieutenant general and his cronies pushed aside. Red flags should be raised and caution exercised whenever one encounters works that rely chiefly or solely, as they do all too frequently, upon Grant's and his favored underlings' accounts. The defensive spin that Grant and others have put upon much of the history of the Civil War in the west, of the Overland Campaign, and of the final months of the war should be balanced with a consideration of the many other available primary sources and witnesses. General Sheridan's reports of his campaigns report nothing but victory, and if any wobbles were mentioned, the fault lay at someone else's door. Grant ally William Sherman would describe his own campaigning as "never checked—always victorious; so rapid in motion—so eager to strike; it deserved its name of the 'Whip-lash,' swung from one flank to the other, as danger called, night or day, sunshine or storm." No false modesty there, folks. It leaves one wishing one could remind General Sherman of Shiloh and Chattanooga, but alas. Some didn't receive quite the gratitude, by way of advancement, from Grant that they felt was their due. Elihu Washburne had expected to be appointed as President Grant's secretary of state. Grant allowed him to occupy that seat for only a few days before his first choice for the position took over. For his unfailing, if shady, advocacy of Grant during the war, Charles Dana had expected the lucrative appointment of collector of the Port of New York. When he didn't receive it, Dana, who had returned to journalism, made it his business to vilify President Grant in the press, questioning his intelligence and his honesty. Dana had a field day considering the rampant corruption in Grant's administration. James H. Wilson, a master of political intrigue but a soldier of very limited ability, may also have felt slighted. Among the many stories he fabricated about perceived competitors or enemies, he told of Grant going to pieces at the Battle of the Wilderness, throwing himself upon his camp bed and sobbing. Wilson, who was not there, cited as his source the supposed testimony of his friend, John Rawlins, who, by the time Wilson spread this story, was long dead.

For further reading about Grant during the Civil War, I recommend my own work, *Command Conflicts in Grant's Overland Campaign*, as well as Carswell McClellan's *The Personal Memoirs and Military History of U. S. Grant versus the Record of the Army of the Potomac* and General Andrew Humphreys's *The Virginia Campaign of 1864 and 1865*. I also recommend Frank Varney's *General Grant and the Rewriting of History* and John Marsalek's *Commander of All Lincoln's Armies: A Life of General Henry W. Halleck*. For a statistical comparison of the war in the west with the war in the east, James McPherson's *The Mighty Scourge* is worthy of consideration. Meanwhile, no other historian knew U. S. Grant as well as John Y. Simon, editor of *The Papers of Ulysses S. Grant*, whose meticulous annotation resulted in more than thirty volumes. They are an invaluable resource in considering the life and legends regarding U. S. Grant. I cannot recommend Ron Chernow's lengthy new biography, for while the author gathers a myriad of anecdotal details, he does not have the depth of knowledge to make sense of them. The result is a great many unfortunate and misleading statements, such as that the heavy artillerymen provided as reinforcements to Grant during his Overland Campaign had been part of Grant's plan to ensure that there would be "no more shirkers or laggards." Those heavy artillery regiments had in fact been held in Washington by the administration with stubborn tenacity for the protection of the capital, and Chernow might have considered their record once they reached Grant's front. For instance, one of those regiments, the 1st Maine Heavy Artillery, had the highest casualties (two-thirds of the regiment killed and wounded in a single battle) of any in the war, making Chernow's damning description of skulking Washington garrison troops as unfortunate as it is inaccurate. One must ascribe to Chernow's unfamiliarity with his subject his reference to the soldiers of the Army of the Potomac as lacking in confidence until Grant came on the scene and seeing themselves as "virgin troops" outclassed by southern opponents, an exceedingly odd way of referring to the bloodied, yet victorious, army that held the field after the Battle of Gettysburg. Then, too, the Army of the Potomac had lost fifty-five thousand of its soldiers during Grant's ill-directed, blood-soaked Overland Campaign. Or, as General Joshua Chamberlain, commander in the 5th Corps, once pointed out, while that army had over the years been criticized for not moving enough, no one ever accused its men of not dying enough.

Philip Sheridan

In the epilogue for my book chronicling the 5th Corps's role in the 1864 Overland Campaign, *Command Conflicts in Grant's Overland Campaign*, I describe the relationship between U. S. Grant and Philip Sheridan as more like an infatuation than a friendship. Grant again and again displayed unconditional approval of Sheridan despite the latter's behavior or performance, even when he demonstrated outright disobedience or defiance of his benefactor. For instance, Grant's orders went unheeded when Sheridan was initially reluctant to confront Jubal Early's raid in the Shenandoah Valley in 1864. Sheridan also refused, after his eventual successful completion of his Valley Campaign, to go with his force as ordered to Sherman's assistance. Instead, he brought himself and his command back to Petersburg, where *he* wanted to be. The material I considered for my book *Command Conflicts* convinced me that Sheridan's only loyalty was to himself, and the research for this work on Washington Roebling, which took me beyond the scope and time frame of the Overland Campaign, only strengthened that conviction. Further evidence also presented itself regarding Grant's boundless, though undeserved, admiration for Sheridan. It provided more puzzling evidence of Grant's willingness to overlook all Sheridan's many faults and failures in his insistent effort to see this diminutive, mendacious specimen of a general as the infallible genius he was not.

As it was for many others, Grant's first impression of Sheridan was a negative one. He found a work party standing in the rain waiting in vain when Sheridan failed to come to command the detail. When Grant complained to his superior, Henry Halleck, about Sheridan's negligence, there were no repercussions, for Sheridan was acting as personal quartermaster for Halleck's well-stocked mess table. But before long Grant himself succumbed to Sheridan's charms. Grant would dismiss all Sheridan's indiscretions, including one of his first and foremost ones, which should have been a career breaker: Sheridan's attacks with a bayonet and his fists upon an upperclassman at West Point that saw him suspended instead of being tossed out. It is indicative of Grant's feelings toward the belligerent Sheridan that he would complain of even that lenient treatment as unfair to "poor Sheridan." Then, too, standards that others were held to seemingly didn't apply to Phil Sheridan; witness the flight from the Chickamauga battlefield that ended others' careers but not his.

When Grant became lieutenant general in 1864, he brought Phil Sheridan east and, despite the latter's scant cavalry experience (previously only ninety days leading warriors in the saddle), Grant had him appointed commander of the Army of the Potomac's horsemen, more than ten thousand troopers. Experienced Army of the Potomac cavalry commanders were pushed aside to make room for Sheridan and two other Grant appointees with little or no cavalry experience, James H. Wilson and Alfred Archimedes Torbert. Perhaps most puzzling is Grant's tolerance of Sheridan's insubordination toward General George Meade at the Wilderness and Spotsylvania and his failure to carry out his orders, resulting in the loss of many lives and an unnecessary crushing defeat for the Federals. Far from punishing him, Grant awarded the cavalry commander the independent command Sheridan desired, along with permission to ride away with the Army of the Potomac's entire cavalry force, leaving that army in the perilous position of moving blindly through enemy territory.

Meade was not the only one who learned that it was futile or perhaps fatal to one's career to criticize Phil Sheridan to U. S. Grant. Washington Roebling attributed Sheridan's hatred for General Warren to the May 1864 movement of the 5th Corps from the Wilderness to Spotsylvania, when Warren complained that Sheridan had failed utterly to clear and protect the marching route of the 5th Corps. In the spring of 1865, with Grant's blessing, Sheridan committed one of the most vengeful acts of the war, removing General Warren from command of the 5th Corps after the Battle of Five Forks. General Sheridan took full credit for winning that battle, which would have been lost if

Sheridan on a hunting trip with
President Chester A. Arthur.
Library of Congress.

it hadn't been for General Warren and the 5th Corps. For years, Grant refused to permit an investigation of this injustice toward Warren.

Examples of Grant's fierce determination to protect his favorite abound, another occurring after the end of the war when his relationship with President Andrew Johnson was proving tumultuous. Grant at first reluctantly cooperated with the president, appearing with him at political events, and Grant even agreed to serve as interim secretary of war when Johnson removed Stanton from office. But when Johnson criticized Sheridan and moved to replace him in his command of New Orleans, it was the last straw for Grant, and his cooperation with Johnson ceased. Grant's reaction to anyone who challenged his favorite remained consistent.

After the war, Sheridan, perhaps more than any other, reaped the rewards of being one of "Grant's Men." On the day of his inauguration as president, Grant, passing over senior generals Halleck and Meade, promoted Sheridan to the rank of lieutenant general, whereupon he requested permission to go to Europe as an observer of the Franco-Prussian War. On his return he declared that there was nothing to be learned from the Prussians and certainly not the French. But Sheridan had given *his* advice to his Prussian hosts, whom he thought neither aggressive nor destructive enough. He advised them to leave "more burning villages" in order that after the war the French would have nothing except their eyes, with which to weep. In 1883, Sheridan succeeded Sherman as commanding general of the U.S. Army, the post he filled during much of the subjugation of the Indians in the west. But America's accolades for Sheridan, who died young, were not yet complete, for as he lay on his deathbed, Congress acted to reinstate the rank of general of the army that had lapsed on Sherman's retirement and granted it to Sheridan so that he might join Washington, Grant, and Sherman in holding that honor. Having overindulged in the many good things of life, Sheridan died on August 5, 1888, at fifty-seven years of age and was buried at Arlington.

General George Crook, who served with Sheridan in the Shenandoah Valley, later clashed with him over Sheridan's harsh Indian policies. Sheridan insisted upon the use of futile military force to subdue the Indians rather than allowing Crook to right the wrongs that were causing the problems in the first place and negotiate with the warring tribes. General Crook left this scathing assessment of Sheridan shortly after the death of his former commander, whom he accused of taking credit for his and other commanders' victories during the Civil War:

> After examining the grounds and the position of the troops after twenty five years which have elapsed and in the light of subsequent events, it renders General Sheridan's claims and his subsequent actions in allowing the general public to remain under the impressions regarding his part in these battles [Fisher's Hill and Cedar Creek], when he knew they were fiction, all the more contemptible. The adulation heaped on him by a grateful nation, for his supposed genius turned his head, which, added to his natural disposition, caused him to bloat his little carcass with debauchery and dissipation, which carried him off prematurely.

For additional information about Sheridan's performance as cavalry commander with the Army of the Potomac, I recommend my own work, *Command Conflicts in Grant's Overland Campaign*, Edward Steere's *Wilderness Campaign*, and William Matter's *If It Takes All Summer*, as well as Carswell McClellan's *Notes on the Personal Memoirs of P. H. Sheridan* and *The Personal*

Memoirs and Military History of U. S. Grant versus the Record of the Army of the Potomac. As McClellan commented, "For a quarter of a century past, all criticism, or argument, or narration, tending to support, or defend, the reputations of the veterans of the Virginia battlefields [Army of the Potomac], as against statements, or implications, or claims, made by, or on behalf of Generals Grant and Sheridan, has been met by clamorous charges of jealousy." McClellan concluded, "General Sheridan's Memoirs are interesting commentary upon this line of argument." Cavalry historian Eric Wittenberg's *Little Phil* offers another window into Sheridan's performance during the Civil War, providing additional evidence of Sheridan's mendacious nature. As Wittenberg points out, Sheridan lost most of the battles he fought with the Army of the Potomac's cavalry under his command. Too many histories have relied too heavily upon Grant's and Sheridan's often self-serving accounts and reports, the latter written in many cases well after the events. With the advantages of hindsight and heavy dollops of self-promotion, such sources have depicted and implied qualities of leadership that, in my opinion, Sheridan does not deserve. For an eyewitness account of the days leading up to and during the Battle of Five Forks, as well as its aftermath, consider Joshua Chamberlain's *Passing of the Armies* and Gouverneur Warren's own account, *An Account of the Operations of the Fifth Army Corps at the Battle of Five Forks.*

While a consideration of Philip Sheridan's career after the Civil War was entirely beyond the scope of this work, I recommend Paul Hutton's *Phil Sheridan and His Army* for a detailed look at Sheridan's conduct during Reconstruction and his command of the U.S. Army during the Indian Wars. The country's subjugation and, in some cases, genocidal policy toward Native Americans is offered up in detail by Hutton. Sheridan's postwar military service provides further examples of his apparent continuing belief that the rules, let alone the laws, just didn't apply to him. Sheridan sent U.S. military raiding parties under his command in the South and West across the international border into Mexico, and was poised to violate our border with Canada as well, in his desire to pursue fleeing Indians. While my research has shed light on occasions of Sheridan's untruthfulness and unreliability during the Overland Campaign and beyond, historian Hutton (p. 336) offers examples of Sheridan lying about atrocities committed by his troops against Native Americans.

Notes

Introduction

1. Washington A. Roebling (hereafter WAR) to Raymond Arnot, Esq., August 31, 1922, in Washington A. Roebling, Letterbook, Roebling Collection, Brooklyn Historical Society (hereafter WAR LB).
2. Rutgers University Library, Special Collections, Roebling Collection (hereafter Rutgers Roebling Collection), MS Box 9, folders 16–17.

Chapter 1: Gone for a Soldier

1. Washington Roebling, "Life of John A. Roebling, C.A.," transcription, Rutgers Roebling Collection, MS Box 10, folders 23–36 (hereafter JAR bio transcription), 212–13; E. R. Knorr to WAR, May 27, 1861, WAR LB, 54. The depth of his father's patriotic fervor can also be judged by the $100,000 loan that the usually parsimonious John made to the cash-strapped federal government.
2. JAR bio transcription, 212–13; George A. Hussey, *History of the Ninth Regiment New York State Militia* (New York: Veterans of the Regiment, 1889), 36–39, 59. For details of Company K's passage to Washington, DC, and swearing in versus the 9th New York's swearing in in New York, see Graham Matthew, *The Ninth Regiment New York Volunteers (Hawkins Zouaves)* (New York: E. P. Coby, 1900), 50–54. While Hussey's *History of the Ninth Regiment* seemingly implies that the entire 9th New York Regiment rushed to Washington's defense, regimental histories, including Hussey's, show that this was clearly not the case, for it didn't leave New York City until the first week of June. So it becomes apparent that Company K went to the capital and was installed at Camp Cameron, an artillery training camp, in May 1861, well before the main body of the 9th departed New York on June 5–6, 1861. The 9th, minus its Company K, received a tumultuous send-off before sailing to Fortress Monroe. It seems likely that only their absence could have caused the fledging artillerymen to neglect mentioning the parade down Broadway, the flag presentations, and the rapturous cheering crowds.
3. WAR to J. E. Boos, Albany, New York, June 19, 1921, Rutgers Roebling Collection, MS Box 12, folder 4; WAR LB, 68; Hussey, *History of the Ninth Regiment*, 36–39, 58. See Washington Roebling, *Washington Roebling's Father: A Memoir of John A. Roebling*, ed. Donald Sayenga (Reston, VA: American Society of Civil Engineers, 2009). WAR Service

Record, Muster Roll, National Archives (hereafter NA); Hamilton Schuyler, *The Roeblings: A Century of Engineers Bridge-Builders and Industrialists* (Princeton, NJ: Princeton University Press, 1931), 172. Company K traveled to Washington under the command of Captain Thomas B. Bunting, though Bunting, according to William Henry Turner's correspondence, was dismissed as incompetent. His replacement was one of the company's lieutenants, the highly regarded Walter M. Bramhall. Artillery Notebook, Roebling Collection, Rensselaer Institute Archives and Special Collections. Washington Roebling, at his father's insistence, entered Rensselaer in Troy, New York, at the tender age of seventeen. While proud of its Brooklyn Bridge alumnus, Rensselaer likely winces at the descriptions he left behind of his experiences there. He was highly critical of its policy of having all classes in lecture form in combination with a severe regimen that kept the students hard at their studies from dawn to dark. As Roebling pointed out, the grinding nature of the course of studies whittled his Class of 1857 from its starting number of sixty-five aspiring engineers down to twelve by the time he graduated. The source of this information, Schuyler's 1931 work, benefited greatly from the anecdotes and materials that the Roeblings' descendants provided personally to him, though one must exercise the usual caution when depending upon a family's oral history.

4. "William Henry Turner, 6th N.Y. Independent Battery," Staten Island Soldiers: Civil War Letters from the Letter Box of William Taylor, https://civilwarcorrespondence.wordpress.com/william-henry-turner. Turner's letters confirm that Company K started out with only two guns—James rifles according to this site's annotation without citation—as opposed to six guns initially attributed to them by other sources. Craig Swain, author of *To the Sound of the Guns* (https://markerhunter.wordpress.com), suggests that the description of the guns as old indicates that they may have been 1840s castings later converted to James rifles. As for unserviceable, likely they had been used and abused before they fell into Company K's hands. Finally Company K acquired six pieces and became a full mounted battery used with the infantry; it was later equipped as a horse or flying battery, acting with the cavalry. John Hennessy, *First Battle of Manassas: An End to Innocence, July 18–21, 1861* (Mechanicsburg, PA: Stackpole, 2015), 2–7.

5. Official Record of the Union and Confederate Navies (hereafter OR), 2:680, 685, 689, 691–698, 701–703, 709. With the withdrawal of the regulars that had been in his command, Patterson also lost what perhaps could have been the steadying hand of their regulars' cavalry commander, Major George Thomas, the man who would become the general known as the Rock of Chickamauga. Hussey, *History of the Ninth Regiment*, 58–59; Frederick Phisterer, *New York in the War of the Rebellion*, 3rd ed. (Albany: Lyon Co., 1912), 2:1574; WAR LB, 57.

6. Jonathan A. Noyalas, "Martinsburg during the Civil War," *Encyclopedia Virginia*, last modified October 27, 2015, https://www.encyclopediavirginia.org/Martinsburg_Virginia_During_the_Civil_War#start_entry. Martinsburg would change hands thirty-seven times during the war; OR 2, 157–59, 163–64, 658–60. Before leaving Martinsburg, Patterson was told that the enemy had been reinforced and numbered twenty-six thousand, with twenty-four rifled guns of large caliber. Steve A. Hawks, "Timeline of the Department of Pennsylvania 1861," *Civil War in the East*, http://civilwarintheeast.com/us-armies/dept-pennsylvania. The rebels had destroyed the B&O Railroad tracks to Harpers Ferry along with forty-eight trains. "Locomotive and Tender Thrown from the Rail Road Bridge at Harpers Ferry by the Secessionists," *Encyclopedia Virginia*, https://www.encyclopediavirginia.org/

media_player?mets_filename=evm00001906mets.xml, citing the testimony of an eyewitness, puts the number of engines destroyed at fifty. A sketch of the wrecked bridge and locomotive is included.

7. WAR LB, 57; OR 2, 473; "Patterson's Defence," *New York Times*, July 26, 1861; OR 2, 166, 175–76, 178–79, 680, 693–96, 717, 725, 729–30, 732–34. Lieutenant General Scott sent several spies, including William Johnston and the team under Captain John Newton, to spy on the enemy in the area around Harpers Ferry and inform Patterson. It is likely that they were responsible for wildly inflating enemy strength, and Patterson openly expressed his doubts to Scott about the reliability of the spies' reports. Despite John Newton's dubious performance as a scout, by the fall of 1861, he was brevetted a brigadier general of volunteers. Another source of information came from rebel deserters who claimed that Johnston's force at Harpers Ferry numbered twenty-five thousand, some fifteen thousand more than he actually had. General Patterson's description of his predicament while in command of the Federal force confronting Johnston and Lieutenant General Scott's response make most interesting reading.

CHAPTER 2: FOR WANT OF A WAGON . . .

1. WAR LB, 57, 59; Richard N. Griffin, ed. *Three Years a Soldier: The Diary and Newspaper Correspondence of Private George Perkins, Sixth New York Independent Battery, 1861–1864* (Knoxville: University of Tennessee Press, 2006). Private George Perkins's diary tells a long tale of deprivation, in which grown men were often expected to exist on hardtack and coffee and, if they were lucky, intermittently, a piece of salt pork. When the men of the 9th received beefsteak on July 4, they reported that it was the first real meal they had had in a very long time. OR 2, 162–63, 654–55.

2. WAR LB, 57, 60.

3. Randall Kennedy, *Nigger: The Strange Career of a Troublesome Word* (New York: Pantheon Books, 2002).

4. WAR LB, 57–58.

5. WAR LB, 58–59; OR 2, 162–66, 170.

6. OR 2, 166–71, 175; WAR LB, 60; Jack Zinn, *The Battle of Rich Mountain* (Parsons, WV: McClain Printing, 1971). Zinn's detailed chronicle of Rich Mountain could be used as a primer for how a commander can take undue credit for his subordinates' labors and accomplishments.

7. JAR bio transcription, 215. The quotation "The wicked flee when no man pursueth" is from Proverbs 28:1. McClellan commanded Military Division of the Potomac (July 25–August 15, 1861) and Army and Department of the Potomac (August 15, 1861–November 9, 1862) and was commander in chief, USA (November 5, 1861–March 11, 1862). Robert Patterson's *A Narrative of the Campaign of the Valley of the Shenandoah in 1861* (Philadelphia: John Campbell, 1865) argues compellingly that Scott and McDowell made Patterson a convenient scapegoat.

8. WAR LB, 59.

9. WAR LB, 60–61; OR 2, 166–67; "The Modern Battle of Bunker Hill," *New York Times*, July 15, 1861, http://www.nytimes.com/1861/07/18/news/the-modern-battle-of-bunker-hill.html. A body of Confederate cavalry had offered some small resistance upon the Federals' entry to Bunker Hill, with one rebel killed and five taken prisoner. WAR LB, 165. In an

indication of the attitude WAR and John A. Roebling (hereafter JAR) held toward religion, WAR was baptized by the postmaster "in the absence of a clerical gentleman. I think it made no difference in my life, neither do I know whether my father did it by way of derision or as an ecclesiastical experiment." Roebling also said that his father, John Roebling, liked nothing better than an argument on religion, including cornering some hapless minister and tearing strips out of him if he didn't agree with the senior Roebling's opinions. JAR bio transcription, 73, 252.

10. WAR LB, 61–63; J. Albert Monroe, "The Rhode Island Artillery at the First Battle of Bull Run," *Personal Narratives of the Battles of the Rebellion Being Papers Read before the Rhode Island Soldiers and Sailors Historical Society* No. 2 (Providence: Sidney S. Rider, December 1, 1875), 5; Gary J. Schreckengost, "The Artillery Fight at the First Battle of Bull Run," *Field Artillery Journal*, July 2001, http://vcwsg.com/PDF%20Files/The%20Artillery%20 Battle%20At%20The%20First%20Battle%20Of%20Bull%20Run.pdf.

11. WAR LB, 63–64; Schreckengost, "Artillery Fight," paragraphs 15–16, 22, 27–39; Monroe, "Rhode Island Artillery," 5. 1st Rhode Island Artillery historian Monroe gives a somewhat different and more modest version of the batteries' performance, telling how their first action at Bull Run, in a tight spot at Matthew's Hill, saw the novice artillerymen admittedly firing as fast as they could without regard for whether they hit anything. However, he goes on to say that they later took his one remaining gun to a position between Griffin's and Ricketts's batteries at the very moment when they were hit by a rebel attack. The Federal gunners were ordered to hold their fire at the approach of an enemy mistaken for friendly reinforcement. With their gun still harnessed to its team of horses, the Rhode Islanders were able to withdraw, unlike the West Pointers, whose horses lay dead. The commander of the West Point Battery, aka Battery D, 5th U.S. Regular Artillery, Charles Griffin (USMA 1847), went on to have a distinguished career in the war, eventually commanding the 5th Corps, Army of the Potomac. He would no doubt have taken exception to the Rhode Islanders' disparaging remarks, as would have Adelbert Ames (USMA Class of 1861), the West Point Battery's 2nd lieutenant, who was severely wounded at First Bull Run and awarded the Medal of Honor for his service there. Another of Griffin's lieutenants, 2nd Lieutenant Charles Hazlett (USMA 1861), would go down in artillery history, dying as he did by the guns of the West Point Battery on Little Round Top at Gettysburg. Many consider McDowell's placement of Griffin's and Ricketts's batteries confronting Henry's Hill the fatal blunder of the battle.

12. WAR LB, 61–62.

13. WAR LB, 63–65. Roebling took enough interest in the bridge to investigate its remains; he was able to identify the Bellman foundry as the original manufacturer of the iron in the structure. See "Locomotive and Tender Thrown from the Rail Road Bridge." In June 1861, retreating Confederates destroyed the bridge at Harpers Ferry. A *Harper's Weekly* artist, Alfred Wordsworth Thompson, drew a picture of the destroyed bridge and locomotive. Thompson reported that the rebels destroyed no less than fifty locomotives on the B&O line at Martinsburg and other points.

CHAPTER 3: SEEING THE ELEPHANT

1. WAR LB, 65–67; JAR bio transcription, 169, 215. Hydropathy was the treatment of illness with water, taken either internally or externally, with often extreme measures such as cold

or steam baths. John Roebling additionally imposed bizarre diets upon his family, severely limiting what and how much they could eat.

2. New York State Military Museum (NYSMM); JAR bio transcription, 214–15; OR 2, 765–67; Phisterer, *New York in the War of the Rebellion*; WAR Service Record, NA.

3. JAR bio transcription, 215; Blaine Lamb, *The Extraordinary Life of Charles Pomeroy Stone* (Yardley, PA: Westholme, 2016), 118–23. McClellan commanded Military Division of the Potomac (July 25–August 15, 1861); "Eddie Lincoln," Abraham Lincoln Research Site, http://rogerjnorton.com/Lincoln67.html. Edward Baker Lincoln, born 1846, died of diphtheria or TB at three years of age, a loss that permanently scarred his parents.

4. Lamb, *Extraordinary Life*, 121–23; "Disaster at Ball's Bluff, 21 October 1861," National Museum of the United States Army, July 17, 2014, https://armyhistory.org/disaster-at-balls-bluff-21-october-1861; James A. Morgan III, "The Accidental Battle of Ball's Bluff," American Battlefield Trust, fall 2011, https://www.battlefields.org/learn/articles/accidental-battle-balls-bluff; WAR LB, 119.

5. Lamb, *Extraordinary Life*, 124–29, 135; Caspar Crowninshield, "A Ball's Bluff Letter," *Civil War Monitor*, October 20, 2017, https://www.civilwarmonitor.com/blog/a-balls-bluff-letter, 1. Captain Crowninshield of the 20th Massachusetts, in a letter written shortly after Ball's Bluff, averred that his colonel, William Lee, had sent notice of their confrontation with the enemy and remained on Ball's Bluff because of instructions not to withdraw until ordered to do so by General Stone.

6. Lamb, *Extraordinary Life*, 126–27; Crowninshield, "A Ball's Bluff Letter," 3, 6; "Disaster at Ball's Bluff," 3; Roebling Ball's Bluff account, Rutgers Roebling Collection, Box 11, folder 56. Harrison's Island was three miles long but only 350 yards wide. Only five hundred feet of river lay between it and the Virginia shore, with Ball's Bluff's imposing one-hundred-foot cliff overlooking it.

7. Roebling Ball's Bluff account, 142–78; Lamb, *Extraordinary Life*, 121, 132–36, 140–41, 143–58.

8. Roebling Ball's Bluff account; Lamb, *Extraordinary Life*, 132–33, 139–40, 150.

9. WAR Military History, Rutgers Roebling Collection, MS Box 9, folders 21–24; Roebling Ball's Bluff account, 142–78; Lamb, *Extraordinary Life*, 142–78; JAR bio transcription, 215, records on October 21, 1861, that Union loss was 49 killed, 158 wounded, 714 missing and captured.

CHAPTER 4: DUELING WITH THE REBELS

1. Harrison A. Trexler, *The Confederate Ironclad "Virginia" ("Merrimac")* (Chicago: University of Chicago Press, 1938), 2, 5. As for the guns in the rebel battery opposing the Federals at Budd's Ferry, all of the *Merrimac*'s forty guns had been removed some time before she was scuttled when Federals abandoned their Gosport base. Since the rechristened ship *Virginia* only carried ten guns, the others were more than likely distributed elsewhere as needed. JAR bio transcription, 217–28. When Shipping Point was later abandoned by the rebels, they found a Whitworth shot on the former Confederate surgeon's mantelpiece with a label saying that the Yankees had hit his house with it. "12 pdr. Whitworth Breechloading Rifle," CivilWarWiki, http://civilwarwiki.net/wiki/12_pdr._Whitworth_Breechloading_Rifle. The Whitworth was a rare gun during the Civil War, and those few that existed were mostly in rebel hands. Their accuracy was remarkable, but their unique ammunition made them difficult and expensive to keep supplied. There were similar problems with the Confederates'

Blakelys. Griffin, *Three Years a Soldier*, 16–17, 31, 346. The axletrees of the Whitworths' gun carriages bore the inscription "Presented to the United States of America by her loyal citizens abroad." As for the artillery company's other guns, Perkins recorded that during their passage from Poolesville to Budd's Ferry in early December, the 6th New York encamped at Washington, DC, long enough to trade in their James rifles for six bronze Hotchkiss field guns. WAR LB, 77.

2. Griffin, *Three Years a Soldier*, 3–9, 16–18, 21; JAR bio transcription, 218; WAR LB, 68–70.
3. WAR LB, 71–72.
4. WAR LB, 71, 76–77. Roebling's "cake would have been dough" comment alludes to Shakespeare's *Taming of the Shrew*, Act 5, Scene 1; in this case, he is wryly pointing out that the souvenir hunters would have suffered quite a disappointment if the second incoming shell had exploded. Griffin, *Three Years a Soldier*, 22.
5. WAR LB, 73–82; Griffin, *Three Years a Soldier*, 19, 21, 24, 27, 33, 346–47; Roebling would meet the outspoken Wainwright again in 1864 when he served as chief of the 5th Corps's artillery during the Overland Campaign. Though ambitious, Washington apparently also had strong feelings about whom he wanted to serve with and where, for he declined when his state's governor offered him a commission as major in the 10th New Jersey Volunteers. Interestingly, he felt the need to describe to his father at great length why he had refused the promotion.

CHAPTER 5: AFTER AN UNEXPECTED NAVAL ADVENTURE, THE 6TH NEW YORK BATTERY JOINS MCCLELLAN ON THE PENINSULA

1. WAR LB, 83–85. Sickles, in the days before he left for Washington, had conducted a reconnaissance, and from Roebling's description, you'd swear his returning 1,500-man force was made up of that many thieves, for every man was loaded down with spoils, which, though mostly livestock and horses, also included a grandfather clock one fellow carried on his back. Griffin, *Three Years a Soldier*, 38–40. Thomas Keneally, *American Scoundrel: The Life of the Notorious Civil War General Dan Sickles* (New York: Anchor Books, 2002), 159–200. As for Sickles's past notoriety, he had ducked a murder charge by pleading insanity for killing his wife's lover.
2. JAR bio transcription, 219; Trexler, "*Virginia*," 46–48, 54–55, 57–58, 64–65, 83–84. It was later proved that, beyond the difficulties of getting past batteries and the steam-powered rams brought in to confront her, the *Virginia* was particularly unseaworthy and, ironically, posed no threat to Washington or anywhere else, for she wasn't going anywhere. However, that didn't stop Confederate politicians from hoping that she'd be able to do just that, with New York City as the number one target after Washington. Confederate secretary of the navy Stephen Mallory fantasized that "peace would immediately follow."
3. WAR LB, 83–88; Griffin, *Three Years a Soldier*, 39–40; Trexler, "*Virginia*," 48–49. As Secretary of War Stanton panicked over the exaggerated threat he saw posed by the *Virginia*, he more or less put a bounty on the rebel ironclad, asking Cornelius Vanderbilt "what sum [he would] contract to destroy the Merrimac or prevent her from coming out of Norfolk." "Vanderbilt," Naval History and Heritage Command, October 21, 2015, https://www.history.navy.mil/research/histories/ship-histories/danfs/v/vanderbilt.html. His ship, the *Vanderbilt*, originally built as a transatlantic passenger and mail steamer, was offered to the army by her owner, Commodore Cornelius Vanderbilt, in early 1862 and transferred to the navy

on March 24, 1862. While the plan had been to refit her as a ram to confront the rebel ironclad *Virginia*, she apparently had not been outfitted for that purpose at the time of the *Virginia*'s appearance at Hampton Roads on April 11, 1861, and, it seems, made no effort to engage the *Virginia* or the Confederate ships that accompanied her.

4. JAR bio transcription, 231; WAR LB, 86–90; Griffin, *Three Years a Soldier*, 40–41; "USS Naugatuck (1862)," ibiblio, https://www.ibiblio.org/hyperwar/OnlineLibrary/photos/sh-usn/usnsh-n/naugatck.htm.

5. Trexler, *"Virginia,"* 61–62. The ship's captured by the rebel ship *Jamestown* were the brigs *Marcus* and *Saboah* and the schooner *Catherine T. Dix*, along with thirteen of the ships' crews. WAR LB, 86–90; OR 7, 219–25. Roebling, many times in his later years, would tell about his witnessing of this "2nd battle of the Monitor and the Merrimac," despite the *Monitor*'s failure to engage. It is not surprising that Roebling and his fellow artillerymen were, to put it mildly, seriously startled to find themselves trapped in the middle of a dramatic confrontation with an enemy of such feared repute as the *Virginia* and came away from that experience feeling that they had witnessed a battle and an important slice of history. Trexler, *"Virginia,"* 43, 46, 48–51, 58–60, 84–85, 87. Trexler comes to the same conclusion as Roebling that the *Virginia* was able to paralyze the Union advance on the peninsula, suggesting that the *Virginia* was rather the terror weapon of its time. "All the Federal correspondence and all the Federal activities in the subsequent two months [of the *Virginia*'s emergence from Norfolk] or until the *Virginia* was destroyed by her own crew, prove that the Union Navy lived during that time in a state of chronic fear." Trexler goes on to say, "In addition to these fears and humiliations the projected 'grand advance' of the army of Potomac was all but ruined before it was initiated." Secretary of War Stanton's reaction to appearance of the *Virginia* was one of panic, predicting the doom of the Federal navy, the capital, and northern ports. McClellan wired the commanders of six northern harbors to prepare to defend themselves against the Confederate ironclad. But at least there seems to be little doubt that McClellan's plans and the security of his force on the peninsula depended on the U.S. Navy, so a threat to them in the immediate area of the Unionist's advance was a threat to McClellan's campaign. Finally, Roebling was hardly the only one disappointed as a result of the almost, but not quite, second meeting of the *Merrimac* and the *Monitor*. Northern newspapers, especially those averse to Lincoln's administration, had a field day reporting the capture of three Federal ships under the very noses of the Federal navy.

6. WAR LB, 89–91, 93; Griffin, *Three Years a Soldier*, 42–43; JAR bio transcription, 220.

7. WAR LB, 92–97; JAR bio transcription, 220–22. WAR was apparently distressed with what he saw regarding the life expectancy of the gun crews on the front line, for after he was transferred away from the 6th New York Battery, he commented in later life that the transfer had perhaps saved his life, a startling reflection considering the excess of dangerous situations he put himself into as a topographical engineer in the next years of the war.

8. Rutgers Roebling Collection, MS Box 9, folders 21–24; JAR bio transcription, 220–22; Phisterer, *New York in the War of the Rebellion*, 2:1574–1575.

9. JAR bio transcription, 221–22; OR 5, 617–19. The letter from Lieutenant Colonel Barton S. Alexander to General John Gross Barnard, chief engineer of the Army of the Potomac, October 13, 1861, recommended the use of suspension bridges, suggesting that they go to John Roebling in Trenton for wire rope and the men who knew how to use it.

CHAPTER 6: LIEUTENANT ROEBLING, BRIDGE BUILDER AND SOLE GUARDIAN TO ONE HUNDRED CONTRABAND

1. OR 12, III, 293. On May 30, 1862, Quartermaster General Meigs notified General McDowell that Lieutenant Washington Roebling had been assigned to him to build a bridge across the Shenandoah and repair a bridge at Front Royal. Roebling was to confer with "Col. McCallum"; this should read "Col. [George Washington] McCullum." JAR bio transcription, 222–23. Washington Roebling, Report to General M. C. Meigs, Rutgers MS Box 11, folder 58 (hereafter WAR Report to Meigs); David C. Houston (USMA 1856). WAR recorded that the Chatham bridge led from the foot of Fredericksburg's Commerce Street to an island and then to the northern shore immediately below the Lacy House, covering 1,028 feet.

2. JAR bio transcription, 223–24; General Rufus King (USMA 1833). As his epileptic fits became more frequent, King resigned in 1863. WAR Report to Meigs; WAR LB, 98, 101. WAR found that the stone piers that remained were badly damaged, for when the rebels fired the bridge, they smeared tar on the stonework to make it burn well, causing the stone to crumble in many places.

3. JAR bio transcription, 224–25; WAR LB, 104; Fredericksburg Bridge Diary, Rutgers Roebling Collection, Civil War Materials #1. The construction corps were engineer troops consisting of two hundred or so picked mechanics from McDowell's corps. After his Fredericksburg tribulations, Roebling declared that if he ever had to build a bridge again, he must have these men "in place of being obliged to educate a parcel of damned niggers and green soldiers into it." It would be a long time, however, before Roebling was entirely free from his bridge-building worries, for the Quartermaster's Department continued to send many pressing demands for reports and inventories of materials and tools for which it wanted accounts. Meanwhile, the pay due to the extra-duty men of the 11th Indiana was turning into a bureaucratic misery. While many men less honest and persevering would probably have said "to hell with it," Roebling spent weeks and months seeing that the men who had worked for him got their due.

4. WAR Report to Meigs; JAR bio transcription, 225–26.

5. John Hennessy, *Return to Bull Run: The Campaign and Battle of Second Manassas* (New York: Simon and Schuster, 1993), 8–9, 13, 22–23, 83–84, 87–88; Benjamin Franklin Cooling, *Counter-thrust: From the Peninsula to the Antietam* (Lincoln: University of Nebraska Press, 2007), 80. Ironically, the bridge WAR was unable to start at Waterloo would be completed by rebel engineers in August during the days leading up to Battle of Second Bull Run, when flood waters trapped the force of General Jubal Early on the wrong side of the Rappahannock. JAR bio transcription, 226–27; WAR LB, 96–97. "My cake is dough again" is a line delivered by Gremio in Shakespeare's *Taming of the Shrew*. The Battle of Cedar Mountain was a confrontation between Union general Nathaniel Banks and Confederate generals Stonewall Jackson and A. P. Hill, with the outnumbered Banks coming off the worst in it. It was a turning point, with the fighting shifting from the peninsula to Pope's army in northern Virginia. WAR LB, 101–2. WAR expressed considerable disgust at how some newspapers' misleading reports were portraying Banks's fight at Cedar Mountain as a great victory. As a major clash with the enemy was becoming inevitable, Roebling expressed confidence in General Sigel, though he commented that Sigel was too "dutch" to make himself understood in a council of war, so they didn't bother to invite him. Interestingly, though there is no indication that he was ever misunderstood because of it, Roebling probably still

carried some semblance of a German accent. It was likely a carryover, for Washington had spent the first decade of his life in a German immigrant settlement founded by his family in Pennsylvania, where no English was spoken. As for the other troops at Pope's disposal, WAR saw McDowell's large corps as the most efficient and the one Pope would rely on.

6. Hennessy, *Return to Bull Run*, 3–12; JAR bio transcription, 227; WAR Report to Meigs. Military map by Captain Paine was a result of this reconnaissance.

CHAPTER 7: AIDE AND TOPOGRAPHICAL ENGINEER TO GENERAL IRVIN McDOWELL

1. WAR LB, 104–16; Fitz John Porter Papers, reel 2, Library of Congress (hereafter LoC).
2. Hennessy, *Return to Bull Run*, 24, 30; WAR LB, 105, 117; JAR bio transcription, 227.
3. Hennessy, *Return to Bull Run*, 42–45; WAR LB, 105, 117–18. Roebling would cross paths with the intrepid 5th New York Cavalry again under dramatic circumstances at the Battle of the Wilderness in 1864. See Diane Monroe Smith, *Command Conflicts in Grant's Overland Campaign* (Jefferson, NC: McFarland, 2013), 109–10.
4. WAR LB, 105; Hennessy, *Return to Bull Run*, 42–49; "First Michigan Cavalry Flag," *Seeking Michigan*, http://seekingmichigan.org/civil-war/first-michigan-cavalry-flag. By September 2, the 1st Michigan's Colonel Brodhead's luck would run out, for he received two gunshot wounds to the lungs on August 30 at the Battle of Second Bull Run. The regiment's major, likely the fellow who failed to shoot J. E. B. Stuart or his aide, Major Von Borcke, was later taken a prisoner of war. See Hennessy, *Return to Bull Run*, 45. As John Hennessy points out in his seminal work *Return to Bull Run*, Roebling likely mistook one of J. E. B. Stuart's aides, the mustachioed Heros Von Borcke, for Stuart himself. John Michael Priest, *Before Antietam: The Battle for South Mountain* (Shippensburg, PA: White Mane, 1992), 24. Roebling would hardly be the only one to make that mistake, as the similarly plumed Von Borcke was often mistaken for Stuart. Edwin C. Fishel, *The Secret War for the Union* (Boston: Houghton Mifflin, 1996), 191–94. One is tempted to announce "spoiler alert" regarding the tale of a spy from General Franz Sigel's corps who supposedly infiltrated General Lee's inner circle. It is said that Sigel's spy had brought news of Lee's impending attack to Pope well before Brodhead captured Lee's orders. It relegates Brodhead's and Roebling's expedition to no more than a convenient cover story to protect Sigel's spy.
5. WAR LB, 105–6, 117–18. Many of the details of Roebling's excursion to Louisa Court House and his brush with Stuart were found in his later claim for $130 for the horse he'd had to abandon on the reconnaissance, a substantial loss in more ways than one for the young lieutenant. All such claims had to be endorsed by the supplicant's commanding officer as witness to the event, an impossibility, as Roebling pointed out, since Colonel Brodhead had received a mortal wound in the Battle of Second Bull Run and the 1st Michigan Cavalry's second in command (likely the same major who hadn't been quick enough to do in either Stuart or Von Borcke at Verdiersville) had himself become a prisoner of war. Hennessy, *Return to Bull Run*, 48–54, 61, 466. Brodhead earned a final footnote in history after his death, when a letter he wrote accusing McDowell of treason surfaced and was widely published. The great irony of Roebling's comment that Pope's Army of Virginia had "moved for no apparent reason whatever" is that the satchels of papers that Brodhead's cavalry expedition had captured at Verdiersville contained Lee's orders for his attack on Pope. When delivered to Pope's headquarters, they provided ample incentive for Pope to move his army from their vulnerable position to one of greater strength.

6. WAR LB, 106–8; Hennessy, *Return to Bull Run*, 12, 60–61, 76–79, 85–87.
7. Cooling, *Counter-thrust*, 74–75; WAR LB, 106–8. Roebling identifies Beverly Ford as the site of the rebel cavalry's bombardment and attempted incursion on August 22. "Rappahannock Station," National Park Service, https://www.nps.gov/abpp/battles/va023.htm.
8. Cooling, *Counter-thrust*, 75; Fitz John Porter Papers, reel 2, LoC; Hennessy, *Return to Bull Run*, 63–77; WAR LB, 106–8.
9. Hennessy, *Return to Bull Run*, 68–70; Cooling, *Counter-thrust*, 75–77; WAR LB, 104,106–107, 501. The letterbook transcription mistakenly identifies Freeman's Ford as Fruman's Ford, and Roebling identifies this crossing as the site of the rebel cavalry's bombardment and attempted incursion on August 22. JAR bio transcription, 228, 299.
10. WAR LB, 108; Hennessy, *Return to Bull Run*, 12, 76–77. Soon after assuming command, General Pope sent out an order addressed to "the Officers and Soldiers of the Army of Virginia" that many officers in the eastern armies took as a mortal insult. Declaring that the western armies had never been defeated, always advanced, and never retreated, he said he didn't want to hear about "lines of retreat" or "bases of supply"—words that would come back to haunt Pope as he retreated. Fitz John Porter Papers, reel 2, LoC.
11. WAR LB, 109; Hennessy, *Return to Bull Run*, 70–71. Sulphur Springs, with its sulfur waters, like New York's Saratoga Springs, had been a popular resort for wealthy Virginians before the war. Roebling was likely unaware that much of the devastation inflicted on the area's buildings occurred during their recent use as Union hospitals. Fitz John Porter Papers, reel 2, LoC.
12. Ethan Rafuse, *McClellan's War: The Failure of Moderation in the Struggle for the Union* (Bloomington: Indiana University Press, 2005), gives a detailed and revealing consideration of the changing parameters of what was and was not acceptable when a nation finds itself at war or, as in this case, confronting an armed insurrection by its own citizens.

CHAPTER 8: THE EVENTFUL DAYS LEADING TO THE BATTLE OF SECOND BULL RUN

1. Fitz John Porter Papers, reel 2, LoC. McDowell attended the College de Troyes in France before graduating from the United States Military Academy in 1838. WAR LB, 109–10; Hennessy, *Return to Bull Run*, 141, 160–61. Roebling's assessment of Ricketts's incompetence may be harsh, for, as Hennessy points out in *Return to Bull Run*, it was unlikely that Ricketts's division of five thousand could protect three mountain passes over a six-mile front and stop Longstreet's corps of twenty-five thousand. Roebling reported that Longstreet passed through Hopewell Gap with seventeen full regiments and thirty-five guns.
2. WAR LB, 110–11; Hennessy, *Return to Bull Run*, 148–50, 168–69; Fitz John Porter Papers, reel 2, LoC. Roebling reported that King had such a violent seizure on August 22 that he was thought to be dead, but he revived. Roebling also comments, however, that King was "drunk and not epileptic on that occasion as his friends claim."
3. WAR LB, 111–12; Hennessy, *Return to Bull Run*, 198–200; Fitz John Porter Papers, reel 2, LoC; Cooling, *Counter-thrust*, 108–11.
4. Hennessy, *Return to Bull Run*, 138–51; Fitz John Porter Papers, reel 2, LoC; WAR LB, 112; Cooling, *Counter-thrust*, 112–15. When fighting commenced in earnest on Longstreet's front, artillery shells set fire to the dry grasses or the field where the Federal dead and wounded of the previous night's fighting still lay untended.
5. WAR LB, 112–13; Fitz John Porter Papers, reel 2, LoC.

6. WAR LB, 112–13; Fitz John Porter Papers, reel 2, LoC.

7. WAR LB, 112–13; Fitz John Porter Papers, reel 2, LoC; Cooling, *Counter-thrust*, 121–24, 127–28.

8. WAR LB, 114–15; Fitz John Porter Papers, reel 2, LoC; Cooling, *Counter-thrust*, 127–34.

9. OR 12, I, 268–69. Roebling's testimony before the McDowell court of inquiry in February 1862 supported McDowell's version of the controversial meeting on the battlefield between him and General Robert Milroy. But Roebling expressed disgust for the thorough coaching he received from McDowell regarding his responses to questions already agreed upon by the court. WAR LB, 114–15; Fitz John Porter Papers, reel 2, LoC; Hennessy, *Return to Bull Run*, 417–18. See Cooling, *Counter-thrust*, 139–41, for a consideration of the condition of the Army of Northern Virginia after the Battle of Second Bull Run. It seems that regardless of the exhaustion of the rebel force, its leader, Robert E. Lee, seemingly had further proof of his men's invincibility.

10. WAR LB, 115–16. Roebling refers to General William B. Franklin here.

11. Hennessy, *Return to Bull Run*, 92–115, 119–20.

12. JAR bio transcription, 228–29. King Belshazzar of Babylon holds a celebratory feast using the sacred chalices of the defeated enemy. God takes exception to this action and writes upon the wall that Belshazzar's reign will soon end (Daniel 5). Hennessy, *Return to Bull Run*, 111, 198–99. Though Stuart and his cavalry had joined Jackson's march, they were not, as Roebling implies here, the force that captured Manassas Junction, though they certainly got to enjoy the spoils.

13. JAR bio transcription, 236.

14. JAR bio transcription, 229; Cooling, *Counter-thrust*, 136. The Confederates sustained 8,350 casualties at Second Bull Run.

15. JAR bio transcription, 230; Hennessy, *Return to Bull Run*, 441. Joshua Chamberlain, *Passing of the Armies* (New York: Bantam Books, 1993), xvii. Chamberlain, in this history of the 5th Corps in the last days of the war, wrote regarding the belief among its men that they had been discriminated against because of their loyalty to Porter: "It may not be improper to state here that there was a manifest prejudice against the Fifth Corps at Government Headquarters,—particularly Stanton's,—on account of the supposed attachment for McClellan and Porter among its members. This was believed to be the reason why no promotion to the rank of General Officers was made in this Corps for a long time, unless secured by political influence. Brigades and even divisions were in many cases commanded by colonels of State regiments." Chamberlain's book is a chronicle intended to set the record straight regarding the role played by the 5th Corps at Five Forks and the injustice done to General G. K. Warren and the 5th Corps at the hands of Generals U. S. Grant and Philip Sheridan. Roebling not only admired Warren but also would count his commander as his brother-in-law when Roebling married Emily Warren, General Warren's sister, in 1865.

CHAPTER 9: WITH HOOKER'S ASSAULT AT SOUTH MOUNTAIN

1. Hennessy, *Return to Bull Run*, 436–37, 440–46; OR 12, II, 82–83.

2. Cooling, *Counter-thrust*, 147–52; Hennessy, *Return to Bull Run*, 446–55; Rafuse, *McClellan's War*, 266–74. Stevens was so highly regarded that it was said he was being considered as the next commander of the Army of the Potomac.

3. Cooling, *Counter-thrust*, 154–56; Rafuse, *McClellan's War*, 273–75, 279, 288. McClellan's "new" Army of the Potomac consisted of the former 1st, 2nd, and 3rd Corps of Pope's

Army of Virginia, the 2nd, 3rd, 5th, and 6th Corps of the "old" Army of the Potomac, the troops that had served with Burnside in North Carolina and at Second Bull Run, now designated the 9th Corps, and the Kanawha Division from western Virginia. Added to this mix was a flood of green, untrained recruits who had responded to Lincoln's July 2 call for three hundred thousand men. "MGen Fitz John Porter's Official Report," Antietam on the Web, http://antietam.aotw.org/exhibit.php?exhibit_id=136. Though McClellan was able to assist General Fitz John Porter in retaining command of the 5th Corps, its divisions were scattered, with Porter and one division initially retained in Washington, DC, to protect the capital. On September 11, McClellan asked for and received permission to order Porter and his corps to join McClellan in the Maryland Campaign.

4. JAR bio transcription, 231, 234; McPherson, *Battle Cry of Freedom* (New York: Ballantine Books, 1989), 537; Rafuse, *McClellan's War*, 274–75, 279, 285–91, 294. Fishel, *Secret War*, 215, 237. Fishel makes the case that, despite the desperate need to discover the enemy's positions, Pinkerton, as he had during McClellan's Peninsula Campaign, didn't bother to actively scout for the enemy. Instead, he and his team of seven operatives depended on largely unreliable interrogations of deserters, stragglers, and other prisoners. Pinkerton later reported to President Lincoln that Lee's army had numbered 140,000, which goes a long way to show how wrong Pinkerton could be. Nor did Pinkerton (or anyone else, for that matter) know for a certainty how the garrison at Harpers Ferry was faring, communications having become uncertain. Priest, *Before Antietam*, 82, 216. Twenty of the regiments in McClellan's Army of the Potomac had been in the service less than two months. The death of General Jesse Reno, shot by one of his own men while reconnoitering on his front, offers a poignant example of how things could go wrong with insufficiently trained troops. James McPherson, *Crossroads of Freedom: Antietam* (Oxford: Oxford University Press, 2002), 107; John David Hoptak, *The Battle of South Mountain* (Charleston, SC: History Press, 2011), 8–9, 18–19, 20–24. Hoptak presents the argument that Lee, in fact, had closer to seventy thousand men at his disposal, but his argument in defense of this estimate, that not even a commander as audacious as Lee would have attempted his Maryland Campaign with only fifty thousand, is not very convincing.

5. Priest, *Before Antietam*, 66, 68, 80–81, 83; Rafuse, *McClellan's War*, 279, 282–85, 295, 298. Though McClellan was undoubtedly too quick to believe inflated numbers for his opponents, the "intelligence" he received during this period was abysmal. Lee's army was reported to be on its way to Baltimore or heading into Pennsylvania to raid York, Lancaster, and Philadelphia. Despite this dizzying array of threatened targets, McClellan held to his belief that Lee intended to advance into Maryland. Meanwhile, Pleasonton, McClellan's cavalry commander, who should have been his commander's eyes and ears, joined in on the chorus of misinformation by reporting that Lee had one hundred thousand men north of the Potomac. Fishel, *Secret War*, 216–18, 221. On September 10, when Lincoln inquired how things were going, McClellan replied that the estimate of the rebel force ranged from 80,000 to 150,000, making for quite a startlingly vague estimate of Lee's troop numbers, and one with serious consequences. As historian Fishel comments, "Confederate strength had been doubled simply by the replacing of Pope with McClellan." Though it would be easy to place all blame on Pinkerton's faulty performance, Fishel believes that McClellan himself doubled and tripled the number of enemy he faced because that was his own mind-set. However, Governor Curtin of Pennsylvania wins the prize for panicky misinformation. On September 12, Curtin reported that the enemy had 190,000 in Maryland and 250,000 more in Virginia, the latter preparing to seize Harpers Ferry in preparation for invading Pennsylvania. Overriding Hooker's protests,

Curtin requested and was granted the services of Hooker's most reliable division commander, General John Reynolds, who was sent to take command of the Pennsylvania militia's response to impending invasion. Luckily for Hooker, the more than competent General George Gordon Meade was available to replace Reynolds as commander of the 3rd Division.

6. Priest, *Before Antietam*, 86, 89, 100, 102, 126–28. Priest paints a very negative picture of cavalry commander Stuart wining and dining during these days, while Colonel Thomas Munford's troopers shouldered the very heavy burden of providing a screen for the Army of Northern Virginia. Rafuse, *McClellan's War*, 281. Jacob Dolson Cox, *Military Reminiscences of the Civil War* (New York: Charles Scribner's Sons, 1900), 1:291–93. In his memoir, General Jacob Cox, who commanded the 9th Corps after General Reno's death, accuses Hooker of taking credit for Cox's and Burnside's accomplishments at South Mountain. Cox cites Burnside: "General Hooker should remember that I had to order him four separate times to move his command into action, and that I had to myself order his leading division (Meade's) to start before he would go." OR 19, I, 422. Cox also accuses Hooker of slander and further insubordination toward Burnside following the Battle of Fredericksburg.

7. Priest, *Before Antietam*, 108–10, 112–13, 127–28.

8. Priest, *Before Antietam*, 127–31. D. H. Hill's division was acting as the rear guard of the Army of Northern Virginia.

9. Priest, *Before Antietam*, 220–25.

10. Priest, *Before Antietam*, 225–47; Hoptak, *Battle of South Mountain*, 90–109.

11. Priest, *Before Antietam*, 250–63; Hoptak, *Battle of South Mountain*, 110–15.

12. Hoptak, *Battle of South Mountain*, 115–18.

13. JAR bio transcription, 231; Hoptak, *Battle of South Mountain*, 111.

14. Priest, *Before Antietam*, 258–63; Rafuse, *McClellan's War*, 297; McPherson, *Crossroads of Freedom*, 110.

CHAPTER 10: WITH HOOKER AT ANTIETAM

1. Rafuse, *McClellan's War*, 299–301; JAR bio transcription, 231–32.

2. Rafuse, *McClellan's War*, 302–3; Cox, *Reminiscences*, 297–98. General Cox, while admitting that the 9th Corps did not march on the morning of September 15, says that was because they had to bury their dead and hadn't gotten orders to move until noon of that day. Though Burnside has been accused of delaying all the corps that piled up behind him, Cox insists that Porter's 5th Corps was blocking the way.

3. JAR bio transcription, 231; WAR LB, 496; Rafuse, *McClellan's War*, 304–5, 307–9; Cooling, *Counter-thrust*, 223–26. Though Cooling suggests that McClellan's failure to make an earlier assault on the enemy was due to his desire to know more regarding the enemy's strength and the location of fords and bridges, evidence shows that Hooker's staff had clearly supplied the commanding general with quite accurate information.

4. Rafuse, *McClellan's War*, 310–13; Cooling, *Counter-thrust*, 225–26, 233; Stephen W. Sears, "'The Roar and Rattle': McClellan's Missed Opportunities at Antietam," HistoryNet, April 26, 2010, http://www.historynet.com/the-roar-and-rattle-mcclellans-missed-opportunities-at-antietam.htm; JAR bio transcription, 231–32. Historian Sears commented, "He [McClellan] neither issued a battle plan to his lieutenants nor called them into council to explain his intentions; he commanded that day entirely by circumstance."

5. Rafuse, *McClellan's War*, 310–13; Cooling, *Counter-thrust*, 226, 233–41; Sears, "The Roar and Rattle"; JAR bio transcription, 231–32.

6. British naval historian Tony Harrison's "From the Orlop Deck—the Naval Surgeon," Historical Maritime Society, https://sites.google.com/site/historicalmaritimesociety//about-us/the-orlop, recommends W. Turnbull's 1806 *The Naval Surgeon*, 257, and Sir Gilbert Blane's 1789 *Observations on the Diseases of Seamen*, 575, for relevant case histories.

7. Rafuse, *McClellan's War*, 304, 310–13; JAR bio transcription, 231; Cooling, *Counter-thrust*, 230–31, 246–48; Cox, *Reminiscences*, 307–11. To add to the confusion, General Jacob Cox, who had taken command of the 9th Corps at South Mountain upon Reno's death and while Burnside was serving as wing commander, says that at Antietam he had command of the 9th Corps. Cox claims that Burnside declined to return to lead the 9th Corps, leaving Cox in command, for Burnside, despite the 1st Corps's being on the extreme right of the Army of the Potomac while the 9th Corps was on the extreme left, still apparently felt he was in command of, or would soon again be in command of, one of the army's wings. It was Cox's understanding that while Hooker attacked alone on the Federal right, the 9th would create a diversion on the left, but when and how? Cox also questions whether Hooker had actually been given command over Mansfield's 12th Corps, insisting that Sumner, if anyone, should have had overall command of that part of the field. Cox relates that both Burnside and Sumner felt slighted by McClellan's orders.

8. Cooling, *Counter-thrust*, 216–25, 234–37; Sears, "The Roar and Rattle"; JAR bio transcription, 231; Rafuse, *McClellan's War*, 308–14. See "Dr. Howard and Hooker's Foot," Behind Antietam on the Web, http://behind.aotw.org/2010/02/13/dr-howard-and-hookers-foot, for a consideration of Hooker's wound at Antietam. Cox, *Reminiscences*, 332. Exacerbating the confusion over whether Burnside understood his orders and if he failed to fulfill those orders was the confusion caused by General Jacob Cox's statements regarding just who was in command of the 9th Corps. Cox had taken command of the 9th Corps at South Mountain when Reno was killed and Burnside was commanding the Army of the Potomac wing, Cox insisted that he retained command of the 9th Corps at Antietam on Burnside's orders. Even though the 9th and 1st Corps were now on opposite flanks of their army, Burnside, according to Cox, either refused to accept he was no longer in command of a wing consisting of the 9th Corps and Hooker's 1st Corps, as was the case at South Mountain, or expected he would soon be called upon once again to command a wing. Burnside's report (OR 19, I, 418) confirms that he felt Hooker's September 15 removal from being subject to Burnside as his wing commander was temporary. It also seemingly confirms that General Cox remained in command of the 9th Corps, which Burnside bafflingly describes as the "only part of my command then with me." There also is no indication in the meager correspondence (OR 19, II, 359–60) or in Burnside's report that he had orders to do anything other than place batteries with infantry support on the east side of the stream on September 16.

9. Cooling, *Counter-thrust*, 234–37; Rafuse, *McClellan's War*, 313–14.

10. OR 19, I, 213–19; Rafuse, *McClellan's War*, 314–19; Cooling, *Counter-thrust*, 237–41; Cox, *Reminiscences*, 333, 336–45; OR 19, I, 419–21.

11. JAR bio transcription, 233–34. According to Merriam-Webster, marplots ruin or frustrate a plan by meddling. Cooling, *Counter-thrust*, 242–44.

12. Rafuse, *McClellan's War*, 322, 325–27; Cooling, *Counter-thrust*, 246–50; JAR bio transcription, 233–34. Roebling's biography of his father, John Roebling, abounds with stories of the "water treatments" his father subjected the family to in lieu of more traditional medical treatment. Ironically, after the war, when John Roebling's foot was crushed in an accident at the Brooklyn Bridge site, he refused all treatment except for water baths, and Washington had the painful duty of nursing him in the subsequent days as John suffered and died from tetanus.

CHAPTER 11: A BRIDGE FOR MCCLELLAN AT HARPERS FERRY

1. OR 19, I, 10; Dennis Frye, *Harpers Ferry under Fire: A Border Town in the American Civil War* (Virginia Beach, VA: Donning Publishing, 2012), 109–13. General McClellan, determined to make Harpers Ferry his base of operations, wrote to general-in-chief Henry Halleck that a "permanent and reliable" bridge was needed across the Shenandoah and that Washington Roebling could build it upon existing piers in three or four weeks at a cost of $5,000. Why spend such an amount on a bridge that could not be moved or might be used or destroyed by the enemy? Because regular trestle and pontoon bridges could not withstand the frequent flooding of the area's rivers. See Frye for details of the many bridges destroyed during the war by the Potomac's and Shenandoah's frequent "freshets." Roebling's suspension bridge could be built high above the ravaging floods. JAR bio transcription, 234; Rafuse, *McClellan's War*, 334, 336–38, 346; OR 19, II, 342–43, 354–55, 360. On September 24, fifteen thousand copies of the Emancipation Proclamation were mailed to military commanders: "On the first day of January in the year of our Lord, one thousand eight hundred and sixty-three, all persons held as slaves within any state, or designated part of a state, the people whereof shall then be in rebellion against the United states, shall be then, thenceforward, and forever free."

2. Cooling, *Counter-thrust*, 276–77, 281–89. McClellan's Army of the Potomac at this time was more than 133,000 "present for duty" and 80,000 in garrison protecting Washington. Lee's Army of Northern Virginia had 68,000 in the field. Rafuse, *McClellan's War*, 346–52; Ted Alexander, "Stuart's Chambersburg Raid," Essential Civil War Curriculum, http://essential-civilwarcurriculum.com/stuarts-chambersburg-raid.html; Rafuse, *McClellan's War*, 341.

3. JAR bio transcription, 234. USMA in this context across the manuscript stands for US Military Academy. The new assignment for Major David C. Houston (USMA 1856) provides a lesson in "be careful what you wish for," for while spending the winter in the sunny south might have sounded attractive to Roebling, who would be spending the winter in the increasingly wintery environs of Harpers Ferry, Houston would end up participating in Banks's costly assaults on the formidable fortifications at Port Hudson, followed by that general's ill-fated Red River Expedition. While Roebling's future assignments would be far from easy, one could easily conclude that Houston's were no easier. "David C. Houston," Bill Thayer's Web Site, http://penelope.uchicago.edu/Thayer/E/Gazetteer/Places/America/United_States/Army/USMA/Cullums_Register/1712*.html; WAR LB, 128; WAR Report to Meigs.

4. JAR bio transcription, 234–36; WAR Report to Meigs; Ezra J. Warner, *Generals in Blue* (Baton Rouge: Louisiana State University Press, 1964), 261–62; WAR LB, 129–131; Daniel C. Toomey, *Hero at Front Royal* (Baltimore: Toomey Press, 2009), 52–53, 56–57, 63, 65, 85. In the action at Front Royal, Kenly was shot off his horse when a bullet grazed his head. Rising, dazed, he was next given a severe cut on the back of his head by the saber of a passing cavalryman. Kenly was officially exchanged on August 15, 1862, and with the aid of friendly politicians in Washington, he was promoted to the rank of brigadier general of volunteers "for gallant conduct at the battle of Front Royal." In March 1864, Kenly was sent to serve as military governor of the District of Delaware, and after the war, once again benefitting from his friends in high places, Kenly was appointed brevet major general of volunteers.

5. WAR Report to Meigs; WAR LB, 131–32.

6. JAR bio transcription, 234–36. Roebling repaired this bridge after Gettysburg, but it was destroyed completely during General Jubal Early's Valley Campaign in 1864. WAR Report to Meigs; WAR LB, 132. For examples of Roebling's attempts to satisfy the quartermaster's department's insatiable demand for paperwork, see Rutgers Roebling Collection, MS Box

12, folders 3, *f*4–5, and MS Box 11, folder 59. Not until May 16, 1863, was Roebling able to secure the funds and special leave to get pay that was due his extra-duty men.

7. OR 12, I, 268–69; JAR bio transcription, 236, 293–94; Rutgers Roebling Collection, MS Box 11, folder 57; "The McDowell Court of Inquiry," *New York Times*, February 4, 7, and 13, 1863.

8. JAR bio transcription, 293–94.

9. JAR bio transcription, 294–95.

CHAPTER 12: WITH HOOKER AT CHANCELLORSVILLE

1. WAR LB, 136–37; Stephen W. Sears, *Chancellorsville* (New York: Houghton Mifflin, 1996), 93–97, 118–19, 128–29.

2. James M. McPherson, *This Mighty Scourge* (Oxford: Oxford University Press, 2007), 120.

3. WAR to JAR, April 15, 1863, WAR LB, 103, 112, 136; Sears, *Chancellorsville*, 104–6, 126–27, 399–400. Hooker's chief of staff, Daniel Butterfield, was likely the brains behind this attempt at creating light divisions or flying columns. Butterfield took great interest and played a leading role in the supplying of Hooker's army and its transportation, and these principles were soon applied to the entire army. Hooker's apprehension regarding blabbing officers and irresponsible journalists was seemingly well founded. A Washington newspaperman published accurate numbers for Hooker's Army of the Potomac on April 17, figures gleaned from a talkative army surgeon. Luckily, Lee didn't receive that newspaper until later in the month, and then he doubted the all-too-accurate figures. As of March 31, 1863, Hooker's Army of the Potomac had 133,627 present for duty. Lee's Army of Northern Virginia had 61,500. Philip W. Parsons, *The Union Sixth Army Corps in the Chancellorsville Campaign* (Jefferson, NC: McFarland, 2006), 10–11. Lee was missing Longstreet and three of his divisions, numbering twenty thousand men, who were on detached duty on the Virginia coast, guarding against Federal raids.

4. Sears *Chancellorsville*, 100–102; Rutgers Roebling Collection, Civil War Materials #1; JAR bio transcription, 293–94.

5. JAR bio transcription, 182, 294.

6. Sears, *Chancellorsville*, 129–32; WAR Service Record, NA. For information on the Roebling family's industrial endeavors and successes, see Clifford W. Zink, *The Roebling Legacy* (Princeton, NJ: Princeton Landmark Publications, 2011).

7. JAR bio transcription, Box 10, folder 23–36, 297–98. *Beau sabreur* translates as dashing adventurer or swordsman. Sears, *Chancellorsville*, ix, 506, 550n27. Sears goes on to label Roebling's observations as aide and courier for Hooker as "Washington A. Roebling's imagined and self-serving account." Given Roebling's willingness in his accounts to tell of the number of times he became embarrassingly lost while acting as courier and scout, I find Sears's characterization of Roebling as "self-serving" and "twisted with self-importance" unjustified. Be wary of historians who find it necessary to savage a witness's character and honesty when, apparently, the witness's testimony does not agree with the historian's strongly held premises and theories. "Brevet Brigadier-General Joseph Dickinson, U.S.V.," All Biographies, http://all-biographies.com/soldiers/joseph_dickinson.htm.

8. JAR bio transcription, 295; Sears, *Chancellorsville*, 147, 150–51, 161–62, 168–71, 175–81, 202, 310.

9. JAR bio transcription, 296; Parsons, *Union Sixth Army Corps*, 21–26; "Charles Edward Cross," Find a Grave, https://www.findagrave.com/memorial/41459990/charles-edward-cross.

After graduating from Rensselaer Polytechnic Institute, Cross went on to graduate from the U.S. Military Academy, Class of 1861. Sears, *Chancellorsville*, 170. Aeronauts Lowe and Allen would make ascensions later in the day and one at night, spotting and counting the enemy's campfires and reporting to Hooker.

10. Parsons, *Union Sixth Army Corps*, 21–26; JAR bio transcription, 296; Sears, *Chancellorsville*, 191–92, 199, 201, 506, 562n7. Sears vehemently denies Roebling's account of a hungover Hooker sleeping in, claiming that on the morning in question Hooker had been up for hours riding his lines. Sears offers, as "incontrovertible" proof of Hooker's early-morning activities, a letter Hooker wrote to a correspondent named Bates (likely Samuel P. Bates) in 1877 and an entry in the diary of Dunn Brown, a Michigan surgeon. "Mr. Dunn Browne's Experiences in the Army," Internet Archive, https://archive.org/details/experiencesinar00fiskgoog. The diary entry Sears cites, again, as "incontrovertible" proof of Hooker's early-morning ride is, unfortunately, for May 2, the day after the all-important morning that Hooker failed to rise early. Sears further suggests that the cause of delay on the morning of May 1 was morning fog and Hooker's wanting to wait for additional intelligence to come in. Meanwhile, this diary does mention that those present described the atmosphere upon Hooker's arrival at the Chancellor House headquarters at 6 p.m. on the night of April 30 as celebratory and convivial. Cyrus Bacon, "A Michigan Surgeon at Chancellorsville One Hundred Years Ago," *University of Michigan Medical School Bulletin* 29, no. 6 (November–December 1963): 315–31. Sears offers this article as another bit of "incontrovertible proof" that Hooker was out and about early on May 1. The article, however, says nothing about Hooker's having been seen on May 1, in the morning or at other time during the day.

11. JAR bio transcription, 295. Roebling said that he wrote similar accounts of other battles he participated in and witnessed. Sadly, a manuscript he had hoped his son would publish after his death was not published, and its whereabouts are now unknown. Sears, *Chancellorsville*, 147, 150–52, 161–62, 165–68, 175–81, 186–87, 202–11.

12. JAR bio transcription, 295–96.

13. JAR bio transcription, 298; Sears, *Chancellorsville*, 133. Six of the eight regiments in General A. A. Humphreys's 3rd Corps division were nine-month regiments due to go home in May. Sears, *Chancellorsville*, 208. Sears attributes Hooker's change of heart to a visit by Dickinson to Slocum that day, and as for Hooker's subsequent order for Slocum to turn back, Sears apparently finds it reasonable, however strongly Slocum and a number of other corps commanders disagreed. He makes no mention of Roebling's role in bringing Slocum his unwelcome orders or of Slocum's pained reaction and outrage.

14. JAR bio transcription, 299. A good deal of confidence can be placed in the accuracy of the typewritten transcription since it is liberally adorned with Washington Roebling's handwritten notes and corrections. Sears, *Chancellorsville*, 64–66, 196–98. When the former commander of the 11th Corps left on what he felt was his demotion, Hooker refused to appoint Sigel's second in command, General Carl Schurz, instead appointing General Oliver Otis Howard (USMA 1854). The latter needed placating because Hooker had appointed General Daniel Sickles commander of the 3rd Corps over Howard's head. The men of the 11th Corps, the smallest corps in the Army of the Potomac, were not happy with their new Bible-thumping commander. Roebling had also encountered Carl Schurtz and Charles Devens, who was wounded at Chancellorsville. Massachusetts's Fort Devens was named in his honor. According to Merriam-Webster, a circumgyration is a movement in a circular course.

15. JAR bio transcription, 300. Stewart Sifakis, *Who Was Who in the Union* (New York: Facts on File, 1988). Carl Schurz was another of the refugees from the 1848 European uprisings

and active in antislavery politics. For those reasons and his appeal to the German immigrant population, Lincoln appointed Schurz brigadier general of volunteers. After the war he served one term as a U.S. senator and was President U. S. Grant's interior secretary. Sears, *Chancellorsville*, 133. It is also of interest, however, that fully half the men in General Schurz's division were seeing combat for the time at Chancellorsville.

16. JAR bio transcription, 301. Hiram Berry rose from commanding the 4th Maine to become a major general commanding a division in General Daniel Sickles's 3rd Corps; Berry was mortally wounded at Chancellorsville in the fighting that followed Jackson's flank attack.

17. JAR bio transcription, 302.

18. JAR bio transcription, 302–3; Sears, *Chancellorsville*, 336–40, 357–58, 550n27. Sears, in his book *Chancellorsville*, took offense at Roebling's wishing in retrospect that he had not saved Hooker's life. I, personally, am not surprised that Roebling indulged in one of the great "what if's" of the war. If the Army of the Potomac's generals who wished to continue the fight had been allowed to do so, and if the Federals had won, rather than lost, the Battle of Chancellorsville, would there have been a Gettysburg or the following year's Overland Campaign, and could some of the tens of thousands of lives lost in those sanguinary weeks and months have been saved?

19. JAR bio transcription, 303–4; Sears, *Chancellorsville*, 506, 550n27, 357, 420–22. As Roebling was a topographical engineer for the headquarters of the Army of the Potomac, his admitting to getting royally lost at the crucial time of the retreat from Chancellorsville makes historian Sears's judgment of his accounts as "self-serving" and "twisted with self-importance" all the more puzzling.

20. JAR bio transcription, 305–6; Sears, *Chancellorsville*, 428, 431, confirms that Hooker was one of the first to cross the river and did so when some of the pontoon bridges were being swept away while his army was still on the enemy's side of the river unable to cross. Sears also reports that there was no serious demoralization within the Army of the Potomac. But given Roebling's remembered response to the army's retreat, I think that claim is worthy of further debate and consideration.

21. JAR bio transcription, 305–7.

CHAPTER 13: ON TO GETTYSBURG WITH MEADE AND WARREN

1. JAR bio transcription, 306; Sears, *Chancellorsville*, 492, 501; Bridge Diary, Rutgers Roebling Collection, Civil War Materials #1.

2. JAR bio transcription, 307; Tom D. Crouch, *The Eagle Aloft: Two Centuries of the Balloon in America* (Washington, DC: Smithsonian Institution Press, 1983), 404–10. Thaddeus Lowe, inventor and civilian director of the aeronauts, did look and sometimes act more like a carnival barker than an inventor/aeronaut. But it was likely the bureaucratic nitpicking of the federal Quartermaster's Department, with assistance from Cyrus Comstock, that brought about the end of the Union Balloon Corps and its potential for artillery spotting, telegraphic and visual communications, and, of course, spying on the enemy. "May 4th, 1863, Roebling Report to Hooker," Hooker Papers, Huntington Library, Box XIII; Rutgers Roebling Collection, Civil War Materials #1. Around this time Washington heard rumors that General Burnside, who was commanding the Army of the Ohio, had apparently applied to the secretary of war for Roebling's services in the construction of a railroad bridge in Kentucky. The young engineer was apparently interested in the assignment, for

he made sure the secretary of war's office knew where to reach him at General Warren's headquarters.

3. John K. Winkler, *Morgan the Magnificent* (Garden City, NY: Garden City Publishing, 1930), 62.

4. Crouch, *The Eagle Aloft*, 405–9, 412–14; JAR bio transcription, 307; Rutgers Roebling Collection, Box 11, Folder 59. In June 1863, letters from Army of the Potomac headquarters questioned whether General Warren was keeping an eye on the Balloon Service and demanded to know the least number of men needed for each ascension.

5. JAR bio transcription, 307–8.

6. JAR bio transcription, 308–9, 311. A. A. Humphreys (USMA 1831) was a soldier's soldier, or, to be more specific, a commander among commanders, much respected by his fellow officers. Roebling would say of Humphreys that his "skill and tactical skill were alone worth a division."

7. JAR bio transcription, 309; David M. Jordan, *Happiness Is Not My Companion* (Bloomington: Indiana University Press, 2001), 80–83. While sitting at the banquet immediately following his wedding, Warren was handed a telegram to return to the army, and while he did manage to have a one-night honeymoon with his new bride at Willard's Hotel in Washington, by June 20 he was heading back to his duties. Meanwhile, Warren had described his new aide, Washington Roebling, to his wife as "a splendid young man rich and talented and accomplished." Warren to WAR, June 24, 1863, Rutgers Roebling Collection, MS Box 11, Folder 50; WAR LB, 138–39. There are some difficulties with the time line of Warren's trip to Baltimore to marry and WAR's Philadelphia and Trenton visit. WAR sets Warren's wedding as having taken place on June 27, while Jordan's biography puts the date at June 17. The June 27 date makes more sense, given the orders issued to Roebling. But Jordan places Warren at Harpers Ferry with Hooker on June 27.

8. JAR bio transcription, 309–10; WAR LB, 139–40; Harry W. Pfanz, *Gettysburg: The Second Day* (Chapel Hill: University of North Carolina Press, 1987), 14. Brigadier General Daniel Butterfield, a former executive at the American Express Company before the war, rose quickly through the ranks of commanding volunteers, likely because of considerable political influence and his willing efficiency in dealing with the more boring chores at headquarters. Disgruntled by Meade having replaced Hooker as commander of the Army of the Potomac, Butterfield would be the source of much misinformation regarding Meade's conduct of the battle at Gettysburg. Jordon, *Happiness*, 87.

9. JAR bio transcription, 311; Jordan, *Happiness*, 89; Pfanz, *Gettysburg*, 38–39, 46–48.

10. Pfanz, *Gettysburg*, 82; Jordan, *Happiness*, 90; JAR bio transcription, 311–12. WAR states that Humphreys saved the 3rd Corps from total destruction.

11. JAR bio transcription, 311–12.

CHAPTER 14: LITTLE ROUND TOP AND PICKETT'S CHARGE

1. JAR bio transcription, 313–14. Roebling explains that "peppering was one of Meade's favorite terms for scattered musketry fire." He also commented that these were Meade's exact words, sending Warren and Roebling to see what was going on at Little Round Top. OR 27, I, 202; Oliver Willcox Norton, *The Attack and Defense of Little Round Top: Gettysburg, July 2, 1863* (Gettysburg, PA: Stan Clark Military Books, 1992), 308–9. Warren, suspecting that a body of rebels was using nearby woods to pass unnoticed around the Federals' left flank, requested that a shot from a nearby battery be sent into the area. When the shot whistled toward the enemy, they turned as one to watch it, and the sun gleaming off their rifle barrels

and bayonets revealed the presence of their large force. Pfanz, *Gettysburg*, 206, 506. Gettysburg historian Pfanz comments, "Warren's story seems somewhat romantic, but there is no reason to doubt his truthfulness in the matter." Henry Hunt, "The Second Day at Gettysburg," in *Battles and Leaders*, ed. R. U. Johnson (New York: Century Company, 1887–1888), 3:307, meanwhile, confirms Smith's battery's position above Devil's Den on July 2.

2. JAR bio transcription, 313–14; Norton, *Attack*, 330–31; Jordan, *Happiness*, 33. Warren taught mathematics at West Point from August 1859 until April 24, 1861, when he was elected lieutenant colonel of a New York regiment, the Duryee Zouaves. Though the army at first refused permission for Warren to leave the regular army to accept a command in a volunteer regiment, by May 7 Warren had his leave of absence permitting him to go to war with his new regiment. At the end of May 1861, when Colonel Abram Duryee was promoted to general rank, Warren took command of the regiment. Pfanz, *Gettysburg*, 223–28, 240. Lieutenant Hazlett (USMA 1861), a survivor of Battery D, 5th U.S. Artillery's fight at Bull Run, was kneeling over the mortally wounded General Stephen H. Weed (USMA 1854) when he was killed by an enemy sharpshooter in Devil's Den. Roy P. Stonesifer, "The Little Round Top Controversy: Gouverneur Warren, Strong Vincent, and George Sykes," *Pennsylvania History: A Journal of Mid-Atlantic Studies* 35, no. 3 (July 1968): 225–30, https://www.jstor.org/stable/27771702?newaccount=true&read-now=1. "Morale," Wikipedia, https://en.wikipedia.org/wiki/Morale. Roebling's reference to "moral effect" here either is tongue in cheek or refers to the military application of the term, as defined by one of the most highly regarded military theorists of the nineteenth century: "Clausewitz stresses the importance of morale and will for both the soldier and the commander. The soldier's first requirement is moral and physical *courage*, both the acceptance of responsibility and the suppression of *fear*."

3. Norton, *Attack*, 330.

4. JAR bio transcription, 314; Diane Monroe Smith, *Fanny and Joshua* (Hanover, NH: University Press of New England, 2013), 140, 145–46, 149, 345–46. Colonel Joshua Chamberlain was, like Roebling, known for being cool under fire and able to think clearly. But there are indications, as Roebling admits here, that when the severe trials were over, Chamberlain also was subject to overtaxed nerves, in conjunction with physical illness, not to mention wounds, bringing about incapacitating exhaustion. John J. Pullen, *The Twentieth Maine* (Dayton, OH: Morningside Press, 1991), 109–13, 122–23, 129–31; Jack Welsh, MD, *Medical Histories of Union Generals* (Kent, OH: Kent State University Press, 1996), 353. The 20th Maine, in Vincent's 3rd Brigade of Barnes's division in Sykes's 5th Corps, was passing the base of Little Round Top on the way to support Sickles's 3rd Corps when Vincent was called upon to place his brigade on the Army of the Potomac's extreme left flank on Little Round Top. During the fight for the hill, Vincent was shot in the groin, and though he held on for several days, he died on July 7. The 83rd Pennsylvania Monument of Little Round Top bears a statue of Strong Vincent, and a stone marks the spot of his wounding.

5. JAR bio transcription, 315–16. In this postwar writing, Roebling was aware of Longstreet's preference to turn the Federal left. Roebling returned safely to Meade's headquarters and placed his detailed accounting of all the Federal units on the field in Butterfield's hands. When Butterfield left the Army of the Potomac several days later, he apparently took the report with him, and all requests for a copy by Roebling and later historians of the battle fell on deaf ears. Considering the many controversies that arose in the coming years over the positions held by regiments, brigades, and corps and where their monuments would be placed, Roebling's report would have been highly useful.

6. JAR bio transcription, 317–18. WAR seemingly borrowed the dramatic alliteration of "a thousand thunders" from Jesse Bowman Young's *The Battle of Gettysburg* (Dayton, OH:

Morningside Bookshop, 1976): "Silence—Then a Thousand Thunderbolts" was a chapter title in Bowman's 1913 book, which WAR had read and admired.

7. JAR bio transcription, 318–19. It seems as though the entirely irreligious Roebling may have been tempted to find proverbial God in a foxhole, as had soldiers before and after him. Roebling refers to fellow engineer Colonel William H. Paine.

8. JAR bio transcription, 319–20. Roebling witnessed the terrible losses among the artillerymen in the batteries of Lieutenant George Woodruff, 1st U.S. Artillery, and Major Alonzo Cushing, commanding the 4th U.S. Battery. Cushing is remembered for pulling the lanyard to fire his gun with his last breath; Woodruff died the next day.

9. JAR bio transcription, 320–21; Pfanz, *Gettysburg*, 61, 70; Welsh, *Medical Histories*; Warner, *Generals in Blue*. Alexander Webb (USMA 1855), or "Andy," as he was known to his many friends, was a newly minted brigadier general at Gettysburg, where he was severely wounded, shot near the groin. Webb later received the Congressional Medal of Honor for his conduct on July 2, 1863, in this action that saw 451 of his men killed or wounded. As they waited for the enemy's advance, Webb asked his men to do their duty and threatened to shoot anyone caught leaving the line of battle. He also suggested that his men shoot him if he failed to do his duty, a comment that, even in such a tense situation, must have elicited a few chuckles. Though they often served in different corps, Webb's and Roebling's paths would cross many times in the coming months.

10. JAR bio transcription, 321–22.

11. JAR bio transcription, 322–23; Welsh, *Medical Histories*, 225. Meade had been wounded at Frayser's Farm, Virginia, on June 30, 1862. He received gunshot wounds in the right forearm and a wound on the right side of his back on the crest of his ilium, where it was believed that the wound involved a kidney and the urinary tract. Recovery was slow, and although insufficiently healed, he rejoined the army in August of that year and was present at Second Bull Run, Antietam, and Fredericksburg. He was sick for three weeks with pneumonia in January 1863 and once again returned to the army before he was fully recovered. Like so many of the men and commanders of the Civil War, Meade was made of stern stuff, and it took a great deal to put him out of action. There is a diagnosis that encompasses the deadening of empathy Roebling and many veterans of combat experienced after witnessing month after month of human suffering and trauma. Compassion fatigue is defined as "the inability to react sympathetically to a crisis, disaster, etc. because of overexposure to previous crises, disasters, etc." "Compassion Fatigue," Collins, https://www.collinsdictionary.com/us/dictionary/english/compassion-fatigue.

12. JAR bio transcription, 305–6, 323–24. Suggesting that what success General Sickles achieved should be credited to his division commander, General Humphreys, Roebling credited Humphreys at Gettysburg with being primarily responsible for preventing the destruction of the 3rd Corps. Humphreys would hold the position of Army of the Potomac chief of staff throughout the Overland Campaign, up to the Battle of Petersburg. His duties included the routing of lines of march, a skill that demanded a thorough knowledge of the roads, communications, water courses, and positions of supply trains, artillery, and, of course, the enemy. It was also Humphreys's responsibility to issue the orders that would send the various divisions and corps into battle. The job, needless to say, brought him in constant contact with the engineers, such as Roebling, who were scouting and mapping the significant countryside and, as couriers, carrying dispatches, orders, and reports between the corps commanders and headquarters. Humphreys and Roebling would see much of each other in the coming months. Roebling remarked that so much of the work Humphreys did as Meade's chief of staff during Grant's 1864 Overland Campaign was "absorbed by Grant later on and passed off as his own."

CHAPTER 15: AFTER GETTYSBURG AND
THE PATH TO BRISTOE STATION

1. JAR bio transcription, 324–25; Smith, *Command Conflicts*, 67–69. Yazoo Pass was an ill-conceived attempt in the spring of 1863 by one of Grant's engineers, Colonel James H. "Harry" Wilson, whose expedition failed miserably when supporting Federal gunboats were unable to pass heavy guns set up by the rebels to stop the incursion. Wilson, as he would many times in the future, took no responsibility for his hare-brained scheme, blaming its failure on the navy. Admiral David Porter's Steele's Bayou expedition was designed to take pressure off Wilson's Yazoo Pass venture, an assault that required support from General W. T. Sherman's infantry. Boats of Porter's naval flotilla became trapped in a narrow channel when the Confederates dropped trees in front of and behind the boats. Sherman's men did manage to rescue Porter just prior to his blowing up his own boats to save them from the enemy. "Gettysburg," American Battlefield Trust, https://www.battlefields.org/learn/civil-war/battles/gettysburg. Union casualties for Gettysburg numbered 23,049 (3,155 killed, 14,529 wounded, and 5,365 captured and missing). Confederate casualties are tougher to measure, but recent studies put the number at 28,063 (3,903 killed, 18,735 wounded, and 5,425 missing and captured). "Vicksburg," American Battlefield Trust, https://www.battlefields.org/learn/civil-war/battles/vicksburg. Union casualties for the battle and siege of Vicksburg were 4,835; Confederate losses were 3,202 killed or wounded, with 29,495 who surrendered and were paroled. OR 27, III, 514. Duane Schultz, *Most Glorious Fourth* (New York: W. W. Norton, 2002), 394. Early in the morning of July 4, 1863, at Gettysburg, Lee proposed an exchange of officers taken prisoner during the battle. Meade politely refused. John F. Marszalek, *Commander of All Lincoln's Armies: A Life of General Henry W. Halleck* (Cambridge, MA: Belknap Press of Harvard University, 2004), 184.

2. Pat Leonard, "Nursing the Wounded at Gettysburg," *New York Times*, July 7, 2013, https://opinionator.blogs.nytimes.com/2013/07/07/nursing-the-wounded-at-gettysburg. An estimated fourteen thousand Federal and eight thousand Confederate wounded were being gathered up and cared for at makeshift hospitals at Gettysburg. The burial of the dead took many days. Andrew A. Humphreys, *From Gettysburg to the Rapidan* (New York: Charles Scribner's Sons, 1883), 1–4. The 6th Corps, which had seen less of the fighting at Gettysburg than other corps, was now Meade's largest, some eleven thousand strong. Colonel Reynolds is not identified but is likely one of General Sedgwick's staff officers. JAR bio transcription, 324–25; Jordan, *Happiness*, 98; Frye, *Harpers Ferry under Fire*, 135. Meade's initial plan to cross the Army of the Potomac at Harpers Ferry was foiled when General William H. French, commanding at Harpers Ferry, destroyed the bridge Meade would have used in an attempt to catch up with Lee. It would not be the only time that General French ruined Meade's plans, for in late 1863 French's failure to advance promptly during an assault doomed the Federals' Mine Run campaign to failure. OR 27, I, 606; OR 27, III, 514, 517–18. At 6:45 a.m. on July 4, the 6th Corps signal station reported the Confederate wagon trains moving away from Gettysburg accompanied by a "very heavy line of skirmishers." Meade ordered 6th Corps to assist General Warren's reconnaissance.

3. OR 27, III, 656–57; Humphreys, *Gettysburg to Rapidan*, 4–7; JAR bio transcription, 325; OR 27, I, 91–92.

4. JAR bio transcription, 325; Humphreys, *Gettysburg to Rapidan*, 4–7.

5. JAR bio transcription, 306, 325; Pfanz, *Gettysburg*, 435–37.

6. JAR bio transcription, 325–26. WAR noted that a year later, in 1864, General Early, in the midst of his invasion of the Shenandoah Valley, would destroy the bridge entirely, once and

for all. Years later, when WAR visited, he said he had difficulty finding the bridge site, so thoroughly had all traces disappeared.

7. Humphreys, *Gettysburg to Rapidan*, 10; OR 27, I, 96–97; Francis A. Walker, *History of the Second Army Corps* (New York: Charles Scribner's Sons, 1891), 313, 316; Aide de Camp documentation, Rutgers Roebling Collection, MS Box 11, Folder 62; Norton, *Attack*, 325. Francis Walker, 2nd Corps historian, describes Haskell's mounted ride along the battle line to encourage the troops during the fighting at the copse of trees during Pickett's Charge. He describes Haskell as "the bravest of the brave." Haskell was later killed at Cold Harbor in 1864 while leading a charge on enemy entrenchments. Haskell is also remembered for his book, published posthumously, *The Battle of Gettysburg*.

8. Walker, *History*, 318–19, 321; Humphreys, *Gettysburg to Rapidan*, 11; Smith, *Command Conflicts*, 79, 91–92; OR 29, II, 179–80, 186–87, 201–2, 207. As September wore on without movement, President Lincoln sent a scolding letter to Halleck questioning his unwillingness to advise Meade. Lincoln also reiterated his desire that the Army of the Potomac attack the Army of Northern Virginia, not Richmond. Jordan, *Happiness*, 103; George G. Meade, *The Life and Letters of George Gordon Meade* (New York: Scribner's Sons, 1913), 2:142–43, 150–51. Privately, Meade bemoaned the losses to his army and was candidly critical of the quality of the replacements being sent, which included men who were physically or mentally disabled or inclined to desert.

9. OR 29, I, 132–33; OR 29, II, 189.

10. Meade, *Life*, 2:148–50; Jordan, *Happiness*, 103–6, 336; WAR Military History, Rutgers Roebling Collection, MS Box 9, Folders 21–24.

11. George R. Agassiz, *Meade's Headquarters, 1863–1865: Letters of Colonel Theodore Lyman* (Boston: Atlantic Monthly Press, 1922), 23.

12. Jordan, *Happiness*, 106; Walker, *History*, 321–28; Humphreys, *Gettysburg to Rapidan*, 12–15; Meade, *Life*, 153–54; Ethan Rafuse, *George Gordon Meade and the War in the East* (Abilene, TX: McWhiney Foundation Press, 2003), 99; OR 29, II, 186–87. In mid-September, as Longstreet's men began arriving in the west, there was still some uncertainly as to whether Longstreet had in fact departed from the Army of Northern Virginia. Walker, *History*, 321–40; Humphreys, *Gettysburg to Rapidan*, 14–26.

13. Walker, *History*, 328–40; Milton Burgess, *David Gregg: Pennsylvania Cavalryman* (State College, PA: Nittany Valley Offset, 1984), 96.

14. Walker, *History*, 340–49. It was not the first time that the impetuous Henry Heth got himself into trouble. Though he had orders not to engage until the rest of Robert E. Lee's army came up, Heth pitched into the Federal cavalry that opposed him as he approached Gettysburg, thereby initiating the fighting in the ensuing three-day battle.

15. Walker, *History*, 349–56; Humphreys, *Gettysburg to Rapidan*, 27–30, 29. The 2nd Corps had in total 8,243 men present for duty, while the two 2nd Corps brigades that confronted Hill's corps numbered approximately 3,000. The return for Hill's corps reports 15,073 present for duty, while the corps following Hill, Ewell's corps, was estimated at 15,000 men. The Federal losses at Auburn and Bristoe Station were thirty officers and 403 enlisted men. Buford's and Gregg's cavalry losses were 335 officers and men killed, wounded, or captured. Jordan, *Happiness*, 108. Confederate losses at Bristoe Station were 1,360 killed and wounded, with 350 prisoners left in Federal hands. Burgess, *David Gregg*, 96. As Gregg historian Milton Burgess points out, Gregg's scouting reports alerted Meade to Lee's attempt at a flank attack, and Gregg's delaying action allowed Warren to prepare a successful fighting defense against Hill. Having the role his cavalry played left out of Meade's report must, indeed, have been galling. General David Gregg requested a court of inquiry, reinforcing his request with the assertion

that, if denied, he would consider himself relieved of duty with the Army of the Potomac. General Gregg apparently received satisfaction, for he continued to serve honorably with the Army of the Potomac, commanding that army's Cavalry Corps until the spring of 1864, when Philip P. Sheridan came east with Lieutenant General Grant and, for better or for worse (IMHO, much worse), took command of the Army of the Potomac's horsemen.

16. Meade, *Life*, 2:154; Smith, *Command Conflicts*, 93; Jordan, *Happiness*, 108.
17. OR 29, II, 346; Smith, *Command Conflicts*, 84–86. *Command Conflicts*, while chronicling the 5th Corps, Army of the Potomac, during the Overland Campaign, is prefaced with a consideration of how U. S. Grant and his supporters, including, among many, General Henry Halleck, manipulated and made short work of anyone who stood in the way of Grant's and his inner-circle cronies' rise to power.
18. Rutgers Roebling Collection, MS Box 9, folders 21–24. Within Rutgers's Roebling collection are many examples of his extensive correspondence in later years with fellow veterans and with historians researching the commanders and the battles for which Roebling could give witness.

CHAPTER 16: GENERAL FRENCH'S FAILURES DENY THE ARMY OF THE POTOMAC A FIGHT AT MINE RUN

1. Walker, *History*, 366–69; Rafuse, *Meade*, 107; Jordan, *Happiness*, 112; Humphreys, *Gettysburg to Rapidan*, 37, 42–47; Smith, *Command Conflicts*, 94–96; OR 51, I, 1125.
2. Walker, *History*, 367–69; Smith, *Command Conflicts*, 94–95.
3. Walker, *History*, 369–76; Smith, *Command Conflicts*, 96–97; Humphreys, *Gettysburg to Rapidan*, 52–63. French allowed Confederate general Edward Johnson's 5,000-man division to block the advance not only of his own 3rd Corps but also of the 6th Corps that was following him, some 32,000 Union soldiers expected and much needed on the Federal battle front that day. Meanwhile, Warren's 10,535 were trying to fend off the attentions of Early's and Rode's divisions of Ewell's corps of nearly 12,000 Confederates.
4. Humphreys, *Gettysburg to Rapidan*, 63–66; Walker, *History*, 373–78. Walker suggests that an erroneous cavalry report, which led the Federals to believe Lee might be attempting a turning movement of his own against the Federal left, delayed an earlier attempt by Warren for his assault on the rebel right. Walker commented that Federal commanders, though resolute and stubborn fighters, perhaps lacked the sort of "unflinching audacity" possessed by some of their Confederate counterparts. Martin F. Graham, *Mine Run: A Campaign of Lost Opportunities, October 21, 1863–May 1, 1864* (Lynchburg, VA: H. E. Howard, 1987), 71–75. But there was little erroneous about Federal cavalry commander David Gregg's report of enemy cavalry on the Federal left. Though it likely had nothing to do with a plan to attack the Unionist left, J. E. B. Stuart's reconnaissance carried word of the Federal buildup confronting the rebel right hours before it could be sufficiently developed. Though aware that his movement had been discovered, Warren underestimated the lengths to which the industrious rebels would go to protect themselves from his incursion.
5. Jordan, *Happiness*, 113–14; WAR to James F. Rusling, February 18, 1916, WAR LB, 412; Graham, *Mine Run*, 71–75; Smith, *Command Conflicts*, 97.
6. Smith, *Command Conflicts*, 97–98.
7. Smith, *Command Conflicts*, 98–99; Meade, *Life*, 2:157–59; Jordan, *Happiness*, 115–17; Graham, *Mine Run*, 73, 79. Meade was perhaps remembering that before he had committed to Warren's plan, one of the 6th Corps's division commanders, the ever-ambitious Horatio

Wright, had reported that while the defenses on the Confederate left were formidable, they were not impregnable. Wright's corps commander General Sedgwick disagreed, saying he saw no possibility of a successful assault on his front.

8. Smith, *Command Conflicts*, 97; Walker, *History*, 381–86; Graham, *Mine Run*, 76–77; WAR Military History, Rutgers Roebling Collection, MS Box 9, Folders 21–24; Graham, *Mine Run*, 83. Though there was no great battle, in the fighting during the Mine Run Campaign, the Army of the Potomac lost 172 men killed and more than 1,450 wounded or missing.

9. OR 29, II, 529–30; Walker, *History*, 388–90; Meade, *Life*, 2:147. In the continuing efforts to discredit Meade, Sickles and even the displaced Hooker were suggested as the real heroes of Gettysburg. The men of the Army of the Potomac were victorious, it was claimed, despite the incompetence of their commander. Humphreys, *Gettysburg to Rapidan*, 67–68.

10. Jordan, *Happiness*, 116–17.

11. Smith, *Command Conflicts*, 80–84, 99; Meade, *Life*, 160.

CHAPTER 17: UPHEAVAL IN THE ARMY OF THE POTOMAC'S COMMAND STRUCTURE IN NO WAY PREVENTS THE COURSE OF TRUE LOVE

1. Special Order No. 281, Extract 5, Rutgers Roebling Collection, MS Box 11, Folder 62; WAR to Emily, December 25, 1864, Trenton, WAR LB, 83, 416; JAR bio transcription, 212–13.

2. WAR LB, 149; Jordan, *Happiness*, 117–18.

3. Graham, *Mine Run*, 84–85; Bruce Tap, *Over Lincoln's Shoulder: The Committee on the Conduct of the War* (Lawrence: University Press of Kansas, 1998), 175–79, 182.

4. Meade, *Life*, 2:165, 185; Graham, *Mine Run*, 84–90; WAR LB, 149, 154; Jordan, *Happiness*, 118. Sykes's failure to remain in supporting distance of the 2nd Corps at Bristoe Station may have influenced his demise, while it would be hard to avoid considering French's performance at Mine Run as anything less than abysmal. Stanton based his negative opinion of Sedgwick on a complaint from General Benjamin Butler, who had launched an insufficiently organized expedition in early February and blamed its failure on Sedgwick, whom Butler accused of failing to fully cooperate and support his abortive advance. In fact, it was Butler who failed to carry through as planned, leaving elements of the 2nd Corps in jeopardy and resulting in several hundred casualties.

5. Smith, *Command Conflicts*, 36–40, 47–51, 70–71, 85; Curt Anders, *Henry Halleck's War* (Carmel: Guild Press of Indiana, 1999), 530–33; John Simon, *The Papers of Ulysses S. Grant* (Carbondale: Southern Illinois University Press, 1973), volumes 4 and 5. Halleck had once treated Grant and McClellan to the same sort of selective perfidy by telling them vastly different stories about their futures or likelihood of future success in the army. Rutgers Roebling Collection, MS Box 9, Folders 21–24.

6. OR 33, 114–18, 138. Artillery commander Colonel J. Albert Monroe reported that in the fighting at Morton Ford, Roebling had led one of his batteries to the position in which they fought. WAR LB, 150–51; Jordan, *Happiness*, 1–4. Emily Warren was from the small town of Cold Spring, New York, across the river from West Point. Ironically, Cold Spring's one claim to fame was a foundry that cast the first reliable cannons in the United States. She was one of twelve children, only six of whom survived to adulthood. Her brother Gouverneur was the oldest surviving boy and became the patriarch of the family.

7. WAR LB, 157; Roebling Pension File, NA; Agassiz, *Meade's Headquarters*, 240; Jordan, *Happiness*, 32; Erica Wagner, *Chief Engineer: Washington Roebling, the Man Who Built the Brooklyn Bridge* (New York: Bloomsbury, 2017), 116. The academy's only concessions to the fact that its students were women were courses in housekeeping and domestic economy, needlework, painting, and music.

8. WAR LB, 153; Mark Boatner III, *The Civil War Dictionary* (New York: Vintage Books, 1991), 359; "Streight's Raid," *Encyclopedia of Alabama*, http://www.encyclopediaofalabama. org/article/h-1380. Grierson's Cavalry Raid, April 17 to May 2, 1863, was an unsuccessful attempt during the Vicksburg Campaign, intended to divert attention from Grant's attacks on Vicksburg, Mississippi. Streight's Raid, conducted by Union colonel Abel D. Streight from April 19 to May 3, 1863, intended to destroy portions of the Western & Atlantic Railroad but had little effect on Union attempts to defeat the Confederate Army of Tennessee. Its principal significance lies in the legends that grew up around Confederate general Nathan Bedford Forrest's capture of Streight and his men with the aid of Emma Sansom near the present-day city of Gadsden. Meade, *Life*, 190–91. Kilpatrick's raid ended in failure and the death of Dahlgren, upon whom were allegedly found highly controversial papers reputed to be orders for Dahlgren to burn Richmond and assassinate Jefferson Davis and other Confederate officials. Called upon by Lee to testify to what part he or the federal government had played in the plot, Meade made clear that he had not authorized or approved these supposed orders.

9. Tap, *Over Lincoln's Shoulder*, 182–87; Meade, *Life*, 2:169–70, 172–81, 186–87. Grant made a very brief visit to the Army of the Potomac in mid-March 1864, and in fact Meade and Grant traveled together back to Washington, where Meade would face his second appearance before the joint committee, this time with an opportunity to bring collaborative documents. The committee members insisted they had played no part in the newspaper attacks on Meade. Meade could also take some consolation from the fact that Grant had made no mention of replacing him as commander of the Army of the Potomac. Furthermore, in a meeting with Secretary of War Stanton, Meade received reassurance that his testimony before the committee had been well received. It is hard to know how Meade managed to plan and prepare for the coming campaign when he was constantly under blistering attacks regarding his previous ones. In a preview of things to come, a pro-Grant/anti-Meade newspaper reported that, of the residences taken up by the various Federal commanders in the town of Culpeper, Grant's was eight miles nearer the enemy than Meade's.

10. Jordan, *Happiness*, 119; "Page 307: The Second Day at Gettysburg," Ohio State University, https://ehistory.osu.edu/books/battles/vol3/307. While Warren had previously testified to the joint committee that he had investigated the situation on Little Round Top on Meade's orders, later Warren wrote to a correspondent that he had suggested the reconnaissance to General Meade, who approved it. Ohio State's "ehistory" site suggests that Warren was trying to take credit for Meade's insight, but one might also interpret Warren's testimony before the committee as that of a loyal subordinate, as he well knew that Meade was under threat of losing his command. Oliver Norton, the author of the book in which Warren's October 1877 personal letter was published, did not obtain Warren's permission to do so. The letter in question was private correspondence from Warren to Little Round Top veteran Porter Farley of the 140th New York; in it Warren said that he had suggested his going to investigate Little Round Top to Meade.

11. Meade to Crawford, August 9, 1863, in Meade, *Life*, 2:142–43. Meade had a soft spot for Crawford, who had commanded one of Meade's early commands, the Pennsylvania Reserves. Meade was close enough to Crawford to be more than perfectly candid and open

when expressing his opinion of the worthlessness of the new "recruits" coming into the army after Gettysburg. Meade felt free to comment that they couldn't win the war if they didn't have men willing to fight and die.

12. WAR LB, 155–66, 170, 177–78, 182, 201; Jordan, *Happiness*, 123–24; WAR Pension Record, NA. Roebling expressed agonies of anxiety over whether his commander, General Warren, would approve of his engagement to Warren's favorite sister, Emily. Emily finally put the question to rest by writing to her brother, "Now that you have found another Emily [Emily Chase Warren] all your own, are you willing to transfer this Emily to Roebling's keeping?" He was, and, in a gesture that unmistakably expressed his positive evaluation of his young aide, when Warren was honored with the presentation of an elaborate sword from the people of his hometown, Cold Spring, New York, he had one just like it made and presented to Roebling. Roebling would also be promoted to the rank of major in May 1864. Roebling was likewise apprehensive about his father's reaction to his engagement. Much to his relief, John Roebling gave Washington his blessing and discussed his future as far as the Trenton business and bridge engineering and building were concerned.

13. Meade, *Life*, 182–83; Smith, *Command Conflicts*, 101.

CHAPTER 18: A RELATIVE CALM BEFORE THE STORM

1. Jordan, *Happiness*, 120–21; WAR LB, 159–61. The proprietors of the Virginia Hotel were a Mrs. Paine and her daughter.

2. Jordan, *Happiness*, 120–21; Edward Steere, *The Wilderness Campaign* (Harrisburg: Stackpole, 1960), 42. Meade rightly predicted that Lee would see Grant's accompaniment of the Army of the Potomac as cause to believe that it would be the focus of the campaign. See Smith, *Command Conflicts*, for an assessment of Wilson and his systematic blackening of the character of those he saw as rivals or enemies. Other commanders whom Wilson flagrantly libeled with false or damaging accusations were Generals John A. McClernand (refusal to obey Grant's orders), George Thomas (intent to insult U. S. Grant), and Warren (refusal to cooperate as ordered with Sedgwick at the Battle of Spotsylvania). In all cases, Wilson was the only "witness" to the events, even when he hadn't been there. Wilson would eventually turn on Grant, writing in his 1912 memoir that Grant had broken down and cried at the Battle of the Wilderness. Again, Wilson had not been there but claimed his source was the long-dead John Rawlins. Wilson, having been returned to his old rank of lieutenant colonel in the regular army after the war, likely felt that Grant had not adequately rewarded him. Meade, *Life*, 2:181; William H. Armstrong, *Warrior in Two Camps* (Syracuse, NY: Syracuse University Press, 1978), 96; Ely Parker to J. E. Smith, April 18, 1864, Ely S. Parker Papers, Buffalo and Erie County Historical Society, Buffalo, New York.

3. WAR LB, 164, 167. Armstrong, *Warrior in Two Camps*, 96. Grant's military secretary, Ely Parker, was even less impressed than Roebling regarding Culpeper, which he described as "an awful country—a d——d mean country," its people the "miserable spawn of humanity." Smith, *Command Conflicts* 101. Wesley Merritt had taken over command of the 1st Division of the Army of the Potomac's Cavalry Corps on the death of its commander, John Buford, the previous December. General Alfred Torbert's assignment to lead Merritt's division relegated Merritt to return to brigade command. Jack D. Welsh, *Medical Histories of Union Generals* (Kent, OH: Kent University Press, 1996), 340–41. But since Torbert was absent a great deal, suffering from both malaria and a reoccurring suppurating cyst at the base of his spine (a painful affliction for a cavalryman), Merritt often had command of the division. WAR LB,

164, 166. John J. Hennessy, "I Dread the Spring: The Army of the Potomac Prepares for the Overland Campaign," in *The Wilderness Campaign*, ed. Gary Gallagher (Chapel Hill: University of North Carolina Press, 1997), 80–81. Historian Hennessy writes that much of Culpeper County was transformed by the Army of the Potomac, whose camps, by mid-January 1864, were spread over one hundred square miles with a more than fifty-mile perimeter of pickets.

4. WAR LB, 167, 170; OR 40, I, 137. Richard Kreitner, "A Victory Parade 150 Years in the Making," *The Nation*, May 11, 2015, https://www.thenation.com/article/victory-parade-150-years-making/; Kevin M. Levin, "On the Absence of Black Soldiers in the Grand Review," *Civil War Memory*, May 20, 2015, http://cwmemory.com/2015/05/20/on-the-absence-of-black-soldiers-in-the-grand-review. Levin suggests that there was no intentional exclusion in the Grand Review, because black regiments were recruited later in the war and therefore were still on duty. It is a fact, however, that many white regiments that entered the war later were pulled away from occupation duty and replaced by their "colored" counterparts. Committee on the Conduct of the War, quoted in Robert Underwood Johnson and Clarence C. Buel, eds., *Battles and Leaders of the Civil War* (New York: Century Co., 1884), 4:548. Grant would later testify that General Burnside wanted to put his colored division in front, and the lieutenant general believed that if he had done so, it would have been a success. But while insisting that the decision had been Meade's, Grant stated, "I agreed with General Meade as to his objections to that plan. General Meade said that if we put the colored troops in front, we had only one division, and if it should prove a failure, it would then be said and very properly, that we were shoving these people ahead to get killed because we did not care anything about them. But that could not be said if we put white troops in front." Frederick Douglass, *Life and Times of Frederick Douglass* (London: Christian Age Office, 1882), 433–35. Then again, no less an advocate for the black race in America than Frederick Douglass expressed his approval of Grant's treatment of the U.S. Colored Troops.

5. WAR to Boos, Rutgers Roebling Collection, MS Box 9, folders 25–28; WAR LB, 161.

6. Meade, *Life*, 2:184–85, 191; Smith, *Command Conflicts*, 90. Grant's belittling comments regarding Meade were published in John Russell Young's *Around the World with General Grant* (New York: American News Co., 1879), which Grant had proofread and approved. Since Young's book wasn't published until 1879, one feels grateful that Meade, having already passed on in 1872, didn't have to hear Grant's disparaging remarks.

7. Jordan, *Happiness*, 120, 122, 124; WAR LB, 170, 172, 176. Roebling proclaimed photographs Warren had done at this time very good but said the "eyes are a little too fixed; they would be apt to remind you of the 2d night after the ball," apparently a night of overindulgence. Meanwhile, La Trappe is a French monastery founded by the Order of Cistercians of the Strict Observance. Ironically, the monastery is now best known for its production of a very fine ale. For a consideration of the pressures upon Meade, Warren, and their strained relationship, see chapter 4 of Smith, *Command Conflicts*. The unlucky staff member who incurred Warren's wrath is identified merely as Higby; he likely earned it by consistently winning.

8. Horace Porter, *Campaigning with Grant* (New York: Century Company, 1897), 70; John F. Marszalek, ed., *The Personal Memoirs of Ulysses S. Grant: The Complete Annotated Edition* (Cambridge, MA: Harvard University Press, 2017), 175.

9. WAR LB, 206–8.

10. WAR LB, 171, 210, 214; Agassiz, *Meade's Headquarters*, 240.

11. WAR LB, 171, 184, 210, 215; Boatner, *Civil War Dictionary*, 898. Alexander Webb (USMA 1855) commanded the 1st Brigade, 2nd Division, 2nd Corps at the start of the Overland Campaign.

Chapter 19: Into the Wilderness

1. Smith, *Command Conflicts*, 103; Hennessy, "I Dread the Spring," 75; Steere, *Wilderness Campaign*, 35. Given the swiftness of Lee's response to Meade's challenge at Mine Run the previous year, it was hoped that stepping off at midnight would give the Army of the Potomac a few more hours before the enemy could detect the movement and react. Meade, *Life*, 184–85, 192–93; John Simon, ed., *The Papers of Ulysses S. Grant* (Carbondale: Southern Illinois University Press, 1982), 10:397; U. S. Grant, *Personal Memoirs of U. S. Grant* (New York: Charles L. Webster, 1885), 2:183, 185 (hereafter *Memoirs* II).

2. Washington Roebling, "Report of the Operations of the 5th Corps, May 4 to Aug. 20, 1864," Gouverneur K. Warren Papers, New York State Library, Albany, New York, 1 (hereafter referred to as WAR Report). Roebling's report, covering the entire Overland Campaign, was written in the fall of 1864. (The original report is in the Warren Collection at the New York State Library; Rutgers has a copy with different page numbers than the original.) Steere, *Wilderness Campaign*, 44–46, 48. As early as April 28, a Confederate spy alerted General Lee that Burnside's 9th Corps was marching from Washington to join the Army of the Potomac. Simon, *Papers of Ulysses S. Grant*, 10:397; Grant, *Memoirs* II, 183, 185. Happy exceptions to haphazard histories are Steere's *The Wilderness Campaign* and William Matter's study of Spotsylvania, *If It Takes All Summer* (Chapel Hill: University of North Carolina Press, 1988), both of which offer well-researched, detailed, and balanced considerations of these complex battles. Smith, *Command Conflicts*, 105–6. *Command Conflicts in Grant's Overland Campaign* is my own assessment of the role the men and officers of the 5th Corps played in the Army of the Potomac's 1864 spring campaign. Evander M. Law, "From the Wilderness to Cold Harbor," in Johnson and Buel, *Battles and Leaders of the Civil War*, 4:118.

3. Steere, *Wilderness Campaign*, 37–40, 61, 65, 70, 80, 267–68. Concern for the Army of the Potomac's trains increased when Sheridan's cavalry rode off on the ill-conceived Hamilton's Crossing expedition, thereby abandoning the obligation to assist in their protection. Wilderness historian Steere writes, "Adoption of the plan, together with the dispositions that were made for its execution, was nothing short of a catastrophe." Adam Badeau, *Military History of Ulysses S. Grant* (New York: D. Appleton, 1885), 96–97, 112; Andrew A. Humphreys, *The Virginia Campaign of 1864 and 1865* (New York: Charles Scribner's Sons, 1883), 21–22, 53–57; Simon, *Papers of Ulysses S. Grant*, 10:397; Grant, *Memoirs* II, 183, 185. Smith, *Command Conflicts*, 105–6. *Command Conflicts in Grant's Overland Campaign* is my own assessment of the role the men and officers of the 5th Corps played in the Army of the Potomac's 1864 spring campaign.

4. WAR Report, 1–2; Steere, *Wilderness Campaign*, 48, 58. A comic character from Gilbert and Sullivan's *Mikado*, Pooh-bah, asserts that declaring something done is as good as having done it. Unfortunately, there was nothing funny about Wilson's lapses in obedience to orders and veracity.

5. WAR Report, 2; WAR LB, 214; Walker, *History*, 408–11.

6. WAR LB, 217, 505–6; Smith, *Command Conflicts*, 103–5; Steere, *Wilderness Campaign*, 95. Warren in fact issued a circular to his commanders on the night of May 4, drawing their

attention to the possibility of an attack the next day during their advance to Parker's Store, another indication that Warren had little confidence in Wilson.

7. Meade, *Life*, 2:173–92; Smith, *Command Conflicts*, 106.

8. Steere, *Wilderness Campaign*, 60, 83, 88, 262–64; Gary Gallagher, ed., *The Wilderness Campaign* (Chapel Hill: University of North Carolina Press, 1997), 117. Gallagher's book unfortunately took the same title as Steere's seminal consideration of the battle. Gallagher chalks up Wilson's dereliction to inexperience and misunderstanding, suggesting that Wilson thought he only had to take a look and then leave. But since Wilson falsely reported that he had parties out on both roads, it's clear that he understood his orders. James Harrison Wilson, *Under the Old Flag* (New York: D. Appleton, 1912), 1:379. Wilson would later try to claim he had expected, contrary to his orders, that men from the 5th Corps would relieve his troopers on the Plank Road, though he did not explain why he disobeyed orders and neglected to leave any of his men on the turnpike for the infantrymen to relieve. Steere, *Wilderness Campaign*, 49. There is ample indication, as Steere points out, that Wilson, once across the river, began moving with "extreme caution." In fact, in his first two hours after bringing his entire force across the Rapidan, Wilson advanced only two miles, calling a halt at Wilderness Tavern. That night Wilson purposely disobeyed orders to keep part of his division on the Orange Turnpike and instead gathered his entire division on the Orange Plank Road. This, and Wilson's orders to his troopers to keep their tired mounts saddled throughout the night, could lead one to believe that he was not confused but afraid.

9. Smith, *Command Conflicts*, 104–8; Steere, *Wilderness Campaign*, 39–40, 60, 63–64, 67, 69–70, 96, 262, 267–68. Sheridan would later try to blame Meade for the cavalry's wild goose chase, but responsibility clearly lay with Sheridan's own erroneous reports and his clamoring for permission to discard his orders to scout, screen, and protect the Army of the Potomac and instead be allowed to go off and supposedly engage a division of the enemy's cavalry. This resulted in sending most of the army's cavalry directly away from the encroaching enemy at this critical time. Steere offers up a revealing comparison of the performances of the Federal and Confederate cavalries at the Wilderness. While Sheridan insisted the cavalry's only job should be to fight other cavalry, Stuart managed to fight Federal cavalry and still scout, screen, and protect his army most efficiently. Meanwhile, the original plan for the 5th Corps to reach Parker's Store, then continue on and turn south on the Plank Road to reach Craig's Meeting House, was amended and curtailed, and Parker's became that day's intended destination. The advance would leave the 5th Corps still well within the confines of the Wilderness.

10. WAR Report, 2–5. In his report, Roebling consistently refers to the Chewning Farm as the Tuning Farm, a mistake no doubt caused by his reliance on the pronunciation of those he interviewed for topographical information. I've taken the liberty of correcting it to Chewning as it appears on all period maps. Steere, *Wilderness Campaign*, 37, 78, 113, 143. One must remember that there was never a bad situation that General Samuel Wiley Crawford couldn't make worse. A close friend of General Meade and commander of Meade's favored former command, the Pennsylvania Reserves, Crawford would be responsible for many of the 5th Corps's woes. This day the information he sent to headquarters misinformed his commanders regarding the Confederate corps that was coming down on the 5th Corps's unprotected left flank.

11. Steere, *Wilderness Campaign*, 102, 105; OR 36, II, 403.

12. Steere, *Wilderness Campaign*, 104, 107–8, 110–14; Smith, *Command Conflicts*, 110. It would be 3 p.m., hours after Griffin's assault, before any elements of the 6th Corps came up on Griffin's right.

13. Steere, *Wilderness Campaign*, 102–4, 113, 117, 119, 122, 125–28, 156. Rutgers Roebling Collection, Civil War Materials, Oversize Box 1.a, folder 8.a. The figure of 19,000 in Ewell's corps comes from Roebling's notes for the beginning of the campaign. Steere puts the number at 14,500. By day's end, it could hardly have been made more clear to General Warren that he was no longer Meade's trusted advisor and valued subordinate. OR 36, I, 198. Warren entered the Overland Campaign with roughly 23,000 infantry effectives in the 5th Corps, which were divided into his four divisions. WAR LB, 221, 509.
14. Roebling, "Report of the Operations of the 5th Corps, May 4 to Aug. 20, 1864," 5–7; Smith, *Command Conflicts*, 108–12; Steere, *Wilderness Campaign*, 117; WAR LB, 221–22.
15. WAR LB, 505–9.
16. WAR LB, 218, 229.
17. WAR LB, 218.
18. WAR LB, 507–8. It is interesting to consider that Roebling, in the years following the war, due to his family's highly profitable wire manufactory, became independently wealthy and beholden to no man, politically or otherwise. Unlike many of his fellow veterans, who remained in the army after the war or were dependent upon the goodwill of President Grant and his administration or U.S. Army commanders in chief Sheridan and Sherman, Roebling could speak his mind freely without fear of repercussion.
19. Steere, *Wilderness Campaign*, 259–79; Wilson, *Under the Old Flag*, 381–82. In his 1912 memoirs, Wilson, in his fanciful account for May 5, would dramatically add Hampton's two brigades and J. E. B. Stuart's whole division to the successful attack Rosser alone made upon him. Wilson also wrote that he believed that Longstreet's infantry, which had yet to arrive at the front, had also supported this horde of rebel horsemen. Lest anyone remained alive who might challenge his fictional account, regular army Wilson (USMA 1860) took a disparaging swipe at the men of his own division, letting readers know that if any mistakes had been made, they should be blamed on the volunteers in his command, who were, Wilson commented, "as nearly ready as volunteer cavalry ever is."
20. Smith, *Command Conflicts*, 86–88, 109; Wilson, *Under the Old Flag*, 384–85. Wilson not only enjoyed Grant's favor but also had firm friendships with Grant's adjutant, General John Rawlins, and Stanton's "man at the front," Charles Dana. Wilson conversed and corresponded frequently with both men. But Wilson's relationship with Grant's military secretary, Adam Badeau, is another matter. One must always consider the great difference between nineteenth-century and modern norms for expressions of affection and even love between male friends. Another difference, for example, is the not infrequent sharing of beds in the 1800s, which was indicative of nothing more than the unavailability of more private accommodations. Nora Titone, *My Thoughts Be Bloody* (New York: Free Press, 2010), 172. But Badeau was apparently unusually open for the time about his homosexuality, and his letters to Edwin Booth before the war and to James "Harry" Wilson during the war are highly suggestive of more intensely intimate relationships. Charles H. Shattuck, *The Hamlet of Edwin Booth* (Urbana: University of Illinois Press, 1969), 35. Badeau, for instance, described his relationship with "Harry" Wilson as his "bestowing his fond and tender and anxious love upon a young soldier." Far from distancing himself from the worshipful Badeau, Wilson recommended him to Grant for the position of military secretary. Adam Badeau/James H. Wilson Letters, Badeau Collection, Rare Books and Special Collections, Princeton University, July 28, August 7, September 20, October 28, 1863, and undated. While Badeau's sexual preference could be deemed, for the most part, a wholly unnecessary consideration, his apparent daily advocacy for his lover, General James Wilson, as opposed

to that for other less intimate friends, is another matter. The many worshipful letters Badeau wrote to Wilson are heavy with expressions of passion, jealousy, and possessiveness, leading a number of historians, including Grant biographer William McFeely, to speculate that they had a physically intimate relationship by any century's standards. Such a relationship may well have influenced and intensified Badeau's efforts on Wilson's behalf, for Wilson and Badeau fully intended to exploit their proximity and access to Grant, as demonstrated in a letter in which Badeau urges Wilson to increase his efforts to influence Grant. Badeau suggests that Grant "has not been hammered yet to the right heat. There is only one sledge at work, and that is Rawlins." Wilson, *Under the Old Flag*, 1:378–86.

CHAPTER 20: THE BATTLE OF THE WILDERNESS RAGES ON

1. Smith, *Command Conflicts*, 112–13; Steere, *Wilderness Campaign*, 85–87, 197–218; WAR LB, 507.
2. WAR Report, 8–9. I've taken the liberty of correcting Roebling's phonetic spelling, Tuning, to Chewning, as found on period maps. Wadsworth's 4th Division was accompanied by General Henry Baxter's 2nd Brigade of Robinson's 2nd Division. OR 36, I, 614–16. To settle some apparent disagreement or confusion regarding Wadsworth's command's movements on May 5, Warren offers a report for 4th Division prepared by its assistant adjutant general, Captain Frank Cowdrey, as substantially in agreement with Roebling's account.
3. WAR LB, 225, 231, 508; WAR Report, 9–10.
4. WAR to General G. K. Warren, March 29, 1868, Warren Papers, New York State Library, Box 24, Vol. 7C; Merlin E. Sumner, ed., *Diary of Cyrus B. Comstock* (Dayton, OH: Morningside, 1987), 245, 247–48, 251–52, 254–55. Though Comstock did do some engineering for Grant, his diary seems to show him at his happiest when he was acting as a Captain Queeg counting strawberries, hot on the trail of inaccuracies in other peoples' paperwork. He also made a fourth for Grant's nightly whist games. WAR LB, 222; Smith, *Command Conflicts*, 84–85.
5. WAR LB, 225, 227, 232–34; Smith, *Command Conflicts*, 114–15; WAR Report, 15; Walker, *History*, 430–32. General John G. Parke (USMA 1849) was Burnside's chief of staff at the Wilderness.
6. Steere, *Wilderness Campaign*, 286–93, 320, 360–62, 368, 377–86. Sheridan's suggestion that the infantry guard the army's train was hardly feasible. Apparently anyone who could hold a rifle was pressed into service at the front this day. Griffin was reinforced by 1,042 engineers of the pontoon train, and the newly arrived heavy artillery units were sent to act as Wadsworth's reserve in his assignment with the 2nd Corps. As for the cavalry, instead of remaining at a vital crossroads to protect Hancock's left, Sheridan, with his headquarters at Chancellorsville four miles away, ordered General George A. Custer to attack Longstreet's corps. Not only had the protective screen that the cavalry were supposed to provide dissolved, but, due to a lack of reconnaissance, the exact location of Sheridan's intended target, Longstreet's corps, was unknown. Custer never found Longstreet, but he did find Rosser's rebel horsemen; he barely survived the encounter, only to meet his fate at the Little Big Horn years later. Another indication of the overall performance of Sheridan's cavalry's can be found in the testimony offered by Steere's copious maps, on which Sheridan's horsemen's positions are conspicuously absent, seldom appearing anywhere near the scenes of the infantry's fighting. Sheridan repeatedly failed to provide the intelligence, support, and protection so desperately needed against Lee's sudden attacks upon the Federals' vulnerable flanks.

7. WAR LB, 226. Roebling's comments on Grant's apparent apathy about the turmoil at head-quarters contrast markedly with the account General Wilson would publish in later years. Wilson, *Under the Old Flag*, 390–91. Wilson was nowhere near Grant's headquarters but claimed to have heard from the long dead General Rawlins that Grant broke down, sobbing face down on his cot, at this turn of events. So General Warren was not the only target of Wilson's many malicious fictions, such as General Thomas's resentment of Grant and reluctance to obey orders and Wilson's best-known untruth that Jefferson Davis was captured in a dress. Wilson would concoct stories about rivals guaranteed to give rise to negative impressions in Grant's mind. But why would he wish to darken his benefactor Grant's name? It seems that a disgruntled Wilson, as one of Grant's inner circle and vocal supporters, had expected much greater future results by way of promotion and financial gain for the role he felt he had played in Grant's success. Though his performance during the Overland Campaign in no way jus-tified his aspirations, Wilson had hoped to replace Warren as commander of the 5th Corps, while another of Grant's men, Baldy Smith, was spoken of to take command of the Army of the Potomac. WAR Report, 16–17; Smith, *Command Conflicts*, 79, 84–85, 132, 190, 232n42.
8. WAR Report, 17.
9. WAR Report, 15–16; Smith, *Command Conflicts*, 115; John L. Paker, *History of the 22nd Massachusetts Infantry* (Boston: Rand Avery, 1887), 378, 411.
10. OR 36, II, 499, 503. Roebling continued to act as courier and guide as the 5th Corps remained vigilant within the smoke-filled forest and during subsequent preparations for the night's march. WAR Report, 17–18; Smith, *Command Conflicts*, 115–16, 129. A terri-ble footnote to a terrible battle occurred when, on taking control of the battlefield at the Wilderness on May 8, the rebel soldiers met Federal black soldiers for the first time. The members of the 9th Virginia rounded them up and shot them before leaving with their white prisoners.
11. WAR LB, 207, 509. Emmor Bradley Cope is best known for his map of the Gettysburg and overseeing the battlefield's preservation.
12. Smith, *Command Conflicts*, 116. "James Harrison Wilson," Bill Thayer's Web Site, http://penelope.uchicago.edu/Thayer/E/Gazetteer/Places/America/United_States/Army/USMA/Cullums_Register/1852*.html.

CHAPTER 21: FROM THE WILDERNESS TO SPOTSYLVANIA

1. Smith, *Command Conflicts*, 117–18; Matter, *If It Takes All Summer*, 4–5, 15. When Meade got his hands on the reporter who had printed the calumny that he had wanted to retreat back across the Rapidan after the Battle of the Wilderness, he had the perpetrator drummed out of the Army of the Potomac with a placard reading "Libeler of the Press" around his neck. The response further soured Meade's relations with the press, which retaliated by making lit-tle or no mention of him or his contributions for the rest of the campaign. Steere, *Wilderness Campaign*, 266. As Steere points out, Grant had relinquished the Orange and Alexandria as his supply line. "During the transit of the Wilderness and development of the turning movement against Lee's right rear, the Army of the Potomac had no fixed depot of supplies; it subsisted during this critical interim on the fifteen-day allowance of rations and forage carried by the field transport." Therefore, while it prompted his great concern with protecting the trains, this also left Grant with no choice but to advance to his next supply base.
2. Smith, *Command Conflicts*, 119–21; Morris Schaff, *The Battle of the Wilderness* (Boston: Houghton Mifflin, 1910), 338. Warren aide Schaff wrote of seeing General Grant, in his

last hours at the Wilderness, ride up to the Army of the Potomac's front at the gap in the line between Burnside and Warren and stare up at the enemy-held Chewning Plateau. It was a personal reconnaissance that came days too late, resulting tragically in missed opportunity and many lives lost.

3. Smith, *Command Conflicts*, 120–21.

4. WAR Report, 18–19; Armstrong, *Warrior in Two Camps*, 96. Smith, *Command Conflicts*, 120–22. By 8 p.m. on May 7, Sheridan was heading to his headquarters at Alrich's, some three miles from his troopers' bivouac at Todd's Tavern. Though Sheridan had previously assured Meade that he had seen that the road to Spotsylvania was free of the enemy, Sheridan would later claim that he had received no orders regarding the 5th Corps's upcoming night march down the Brock Road. Sheridan would, it seems, have us believe that even after he arrived at Alrich's, he neither found nor received any orders; this claim he apparently supposed explained away the fact that he had left his troopers at Todd's Tavern without orders or instructions of any kind. Sheridan was also seemingly unconcerned that his own earlier report that he had driven the enemy away and cleared the road in question would be easily disproved when Meade and Warren arrived to find none of Sheridan's troopers, but plenty of rebels, on the Brock Road.

5. Smith, *Command Conflicts*, 122–25; WAR Report, 20–21; Matter, *If It Takes All Summer*, 57–59, 69. Interestingly, the wandering General Wilson and his division had been given the task of protecting the Federal right during the Army of the Potomac's withdrawal on May 7 and 8. When Wilson found no enemy, he advanced all the way to Spotsylvania Court House, where he finally came to the enemy cavalry's attention. Surprisingly, Wilson did something right. He began to dig in to hang on to his position and sent a courier to Sheridan regarding his situation. Sheridan sent word for Wilson to abandon Spotsylvania and rejoin the main body of the cavalry. The Confederate cavalry that had disputed Wilson's possession of Spotsylvania, once he retired, immediately turned their attention to the 5th Corps trying to break through the rebel resistance to reach Spotsylvania.

6. WAR Report, 21–22. Though acknowledging that Robinson's wounding so early in the affair had shaken his men, Roebling would later report, "The enemy's fire was not heavy enough to justify the breaking of the men, it was chiefly owing to their being excited, somewhat scared, and hurried entirely too much." It is a curiously critical observation from Roebling in some ways, for these men of Lyle's brigade, who had had to fight their way off the Brock Road, were meeting an unknown enemy while still winded from their two-mile running charge. Abner R. Small, *The Sixteenth Maine Regiment in the War of the Rebellion* (Portland, ME: B. Thurston, 1886), 177. Colonel Peter Lyle had been commander of the 90th Pennsylvania before becoming one of Robinson's brigade commanders. Smith, *Command Conflicts*, 128–29, 233n1. Robinson Avenue at Gettysburg is named for General John Robinson, a veteran regular whose two 1st Corps brigades held off five rebel brigades there for four hours. The bullet wound Robinson received in his knee at Spotsylvania would cost him a leg, and his division had so few members left after their fight at Laurel Hill on May 8. Robinson's division would be disbanded the next day, the survivors distributed to other divisions. OR 36, I, 649–50; Jordan, *Happiness*, 142. Meade, on receiving Warren's dispatch that he had fought at least two of Longstreet's divisions, was reluctant to accept that Longstreet's corps, now Anderson's corps, was at Spotsylvania.

7. Steere, *Wilderness Campaign*, 269–79, 301; Carswell McClellan, *Notes on the Personal Memoirs of P. H. Sheridan* (Saint Paul: William Banning Jr., 1889), 18–21.

8. Smith, *Command Conflicts*, 125.

9. Smith, *Command Conflicts*, 125; Matter, *If It Takes All Summer*, 77–78, 81–82.

10. Smith, *Command Conflicts*, 126–27, 218–19; Young, *Around the World with General Grant*, 297, 300, 450, 627; John F. Marszalek, ed., *The Personal Memoirs of Ulysses S. Grant: The Complete Annotated Edition* (Cambridge, MA: Harvard University Press, 2017), 534. In the memoirs Grant wrote many years later, there is no hint that Sheridan had experienced anything but success on May 7–8: "During the 7th Sheridan had a fight with the rebel cavalry at Todd's Tavern but routed them, thus opening the way for the troops that were to go by that route at night." Though Grant was with Meade at the vanguard of the 5th Corps's column, there is no mention of him when the corps reached Todd's Tavern to find the cavalry encamped without orders and the way to Spotsylvania full of rebels.

11. Smith, *Command Conflicts*, 128–30.

CHAPTER 22: LAUREL HILL, AGAIN AND AGAIN

1. Wilson, *Under the Old Flag*, 1:395–96; Jordan, *Happiness*, 144–45; WAR Report, 21–27. It is surprising that Warren biographer David M. Jordan, though surely aware of Wilson's ongoing animosity toward Warren, accepted Wilson's story without question. Meade had, in fact, assigned command of the 6th Corps's and much of the 5th Corps's lines to Sedgwick, indicating that the only "cooperation" needed was for Warren and his men to respond to Sedgwick's orders. It is likely that this was yet another effort in Wilson and his fellow manipulators' campaign at Grant's headquarters to someday see General James "Harry" Wilson in command of Warren's 5th Corps. This appointment for Wilson would of course demand the displacement (preferably the dismissal in disgrace) of General G. K. Warren.

2. WAR Report, 26; Matter, *If It Takes All Summer*, 71–74. The men of the 6th Corps, after their all-night march, were understandably tired and hungry. But the 5th Corps, anxiously awaiting their arrival while getting hammered by the enemy at Laurel Hill, would likely have been distressed to know that the 6th Corps called a halt mid-march at 10 a.m. for breakfast and a rest.

3. WAR Report, 26–29. Jordan, *Happiness*, 145–46; Matter, *If It Takes All Summer*, 71–74, 83–95. The passage of Wright's division of the 6th Corps perhaps best illustrates the difficulties of the corps's march the night of May 7–8, with Wright taking seven hours to travel the 5.5 miles to Chancellorsville. There is speculation as to why the 6th Corps's route was altered, thereby delaying its arrival at Spotsylvania, with a possible explanation being an attempt to make it available to support both the 2nd and the 5th Corps. An interesting side note as to the severity of the hand-to-hand fighting in this combined effort by the 5th and 6th Corps late in the afternoon of May 8 is the testimony of a member of the 20th Maine of Little Round Top fame, who declared that this day's fight was the worst battle they had seen.

4. WAR Report, 27–28; Matter, *If It Takes All Summer*, 134–35; Smith, *Command Conflicts*, 134–36, 138–39. There is, for instance, evidence that it was Comstock's and General Horatio Wright's misdirection of General Gersham Mott's division that prevented much-needed support from reaching Upton's initially successful May 10 assault at the Mule Shoe. Blame was heaped upon Mott, while Comstock and Wright escaped notice.

5. Jordan, *Happiness*, 147–48. This is one of many instances in which Grant and staff greatly underestimated the amount of time it would take to move large forces over distances.

6. Smith, *Command Conflicts*, 134–35; WAR Report, 33.

7. Smith, *Command Conflicts*, 135–36; OR 36, I, 66.

8. Smith, *Command Conflicts*, 133–34.

9. Smith, *Command Conflicts*, 137–40.

10. WAR Report, 33–36; Smith, *Command Conflicts*, 135–42. Wright, on May 10 during Upton's assault, had shown an unexplained reluctance to engage the rest of his troops in support of Upton's assault; instead, blame was heaped upon 2nd Corps division commander Gersham Mott, who was peppered with conflicting orders, yet faulted for failing to support Upton's assault. Wright again displayed a serious reluctance to engage his own troops on May 12, when his constant calls for assistance, when responded to, resulted in his replacing his own troops with the reinforcements sent to him instead of augmenting his own forces on his front.

11. Smith, *Command Conflicts*, 143–45.

12. Matter, *If It Takes All Summer*, 230; J. William Jones, "Official Diary of First Corps A.M.V. While commanded by Lieutenant-General R. H. Anderson, May 7–31, 1864," *Southern Historical Society Papers* 7 (January–December 1879): 493; Smith, *Command Conflicts*, 146; OR 36, I, 68–69. The estimate of six thousand and two thousand casualties, respectively, for the Army of the Potomac and the 5th Corps on May 12 is from Dana's report to Washington. The habitual underreporting of casualties and the usual "fog of war" make it more than a little difficult to approach accuracy for losses during the Overland Campaign. When considering the number of men the 5th Corps lost on May 12, one might remember the two thousand–plus men it had already lost at Laurel Hill on May 8 to 11.

13. Matter, *If It Takes All Summer*, 213, 227–28, 232–33, 245, 254, 258; Walker, *History*, 475–76; Jordan, *Happiness*, 151–52; Smith, *Command Conflicts*, 145–46. WAR Report, 35. Keeping in mind that Grant had ordered his corps commanders to underreport their casualties, the numbers Dana sent to Washington for Federal losses on May 12 are of interest. Dana reported six thousand casualties for the four Union corps; the 5th Corps had lost two thousand. Grant, *Memoirs* II, 2:353. Several decades later, Grant was still praising Wright, who did little, while Grant continued to heap blame upon Warren, who lost two thousand men on May 12. Grant wrote that Warren "was so slow in making his depositions that his orders were frequently repeated, and with emphasis. At eleven o'clock I gave Meade written orders to relieve Warren from his command if he failed to move promptly." Grant also accused Warren of negatively affecting the impressive but transitory gains made by Hancock's 2nd Corps on May 12. Grant also belittled the 9th Corps's efforts, writing, "Burnside [whose losses were more than fifteen hundred] accomplished but little on our left of a positive nature, but negatively a great deal. He kept Lee from reinforcing his centre from that quarter. If the 5th Corps, or rather if Warren, had been as prompt as Wright was with the 6th Corps, better results might have been obtained." Smith, *Command Conflicts*, 138–46. The seeming cosseting of General Wright is of interest, for there is nothing impressive about Wright's handling of his corps throughout the Overland Campaign, but he was often seemingly treated as beyond reproach. Perhaps Halleck's favoritism for Wright played a role, for Meade not only gave the lackluster Wright permanent command of the 6th Corps but also recommended him for promotion to major general.

14. Smith, *Command Conflicts*, 141–43; WAR Report, 36–37. General James Clay Rice had taken command of the 5th Corps's defense at Little Round Top upon the death of Strong Vincent. Though known to become rather overexcited during battle, Rice was a favorite among the officers and men.

15. OR 36, I, 4; Grant, *Memoirs* II, 354. Many years later, Grant admitted in his memoirs that his losses were heavy but repeated his self-congratulatory assertion that he didn't lose a whole organization like the enemy did. Matter, *If It Takes All Summer*, 267. The Confederate

generals captured were Edward "Allegheny" Johnson (USMA 1838) and George H. Steuart (USMA 1848).

16. Smith, *Command Conflicts*, 140–41. The fact that Hancock initially reported having lost 7,100 in his corps alone makes one suspect that the 2,043 he later reported again reflected orders to underreport casualties. Matter, *If It Takes All Summer*, 257; Meade, *Life*, 195; Charles A. Dana, *Recollections of the Civil War* (Lincoln: University of Nebraska Press, 1996), 199.

17. OR 36, I, 4; WAR Report, 37–38.

Chapter 23: The Fighting at Spotsylvania Continues

1. WAR Report, 38–39.
2. WAR Report, 39–40.
3. WAR Report, 41–42; Smith, *Command Conflicts*, 147–48.
4. OR 36, II, 816, 818. Meade eventually returned Roebling to Warren with plans for the battery locations on the 5th Corps's lines. This is another example of Meade's disapproval of any decisions Warren made without consulting him first. Smith, *Command Conflicts*, 148–49; WAR Report, 43–46.
5. OR 36, I, 600–601. Having brought the Marylanders forward double-quick, Roebling placed them on the right of the 1st Maine Heavy Artillery, while the Maryland right connected with Colonel Nathan T. Dushane's 1st Maryland Veteran Volunteers. WAR Report, 46–49. The Maryland brigade consisted of the 1st, 4th, 7th, and 8th Maryland regiments. Colonel John Howard Kitching's artillerymen, the 6th and 15th New York Heavy Artillery, were assigned to Warren's 5th Corps. The twenty-six-year-old Kitching would later be killed as a result of an injury at the Battle of Cedar Creek. General Robert Tyler had command of the 5th and 15th New York and the 1st Maine Heavies.
6. WAR Report, 50–51. General Henry Hunt was the Army of the Potomac's chief of artillery.
7. WAR Report, 49–52; Matter, *If It Takes All Summer*, 324–25. Another participant, the 1st Massachusetts Heavy Artillery, lost 398 men, some to unfortunate friendly fire from another heavy artillery unit, but some from Federal artillery. One of General Hunt's staff would report preventing one of Birney's batteries from firing into Tyler's men. Smith, *Command Conflicts*, 150; Grant, *Memoirs* II, 239–40; OR 36, II, 919–20; OR 36, III, 12. Roebling reported that he had also taken prisoners from Rodes's and Johnson's divisions of Ewell's corps. Those prisoners reported that General John Breckinridge's command had arrived to reinforce Lee. Warren also forwarded Roebling's observation that it would be very difficult to extricate Birney's division as ordered from their position on their right before morning. Warren also warned that the enemy was still present that night on his right, and weakening the force confronting them would likely bring on another attack.
8. Smith, *Command Conflicts*, 152; Emerson Gifford Taylor, *Gouverneur Kemble Warren: The Life and Letters of an American Soldier* (Boston: Houghton Mifflin, 1932), 172–75; Humphreys, *Virginia*, 115–18. Humphreys lists the total Federal losses—killed, wounded, missing, and sick—for the Wilderness and Spotsylvania as 37,335. OR 36, I, 3, 5; OR 36, II, 652–53.
9. WAR Report, 52–54. White House landing is on the Shenandoah's south branch.
10. OR 36, III, 57–58, 94; WAR Report, 54–55. The four branches of the Mattapony River—the Mat, the Ta, the Po, and the Ny—would become all too familiar to the Army of the Potomac during the Overland Campaign.

11. Grant, *Memoirs* II, 2; OR 36, III, 90–91; WAR Report, 56; Smith, *Command Conflicts*, 154–55, 235n9. After Sheridan's departure with his ten thousand–plus troopers, Meade was able to scrape up an estimated five cavalry regiments, mostly serving as headquarters guards. OR 36, III, 88. The recalcitrant cavalry commander was Lieutenant Colonel Edmund M. Pope of the 8th New York Cavalry. Pope, becoming sick just before Gettysburg, was taken prisoner from his sickbed when the enemy took the town of Funkstown. He was later exchanged and, on returning to the 8th New York, promoted to lieutenant colonel but returned to the Army of the Potomac too late to take part in Sheridan's expedition. Pope had served as General George A. Custer's assistant inspector general of the 8th New York Cavalry, and though Pope's failure to report the rebel wagon train and his refusal to attack an unguarded train amply demonstrate his incompetence, he would later be promoted to brigadier general of volunteers in the cavalry. J. Michael Miller, in *The North Anna Campaign: "Even to Hell Itself," May 21–26, 1864* (Lynchburg, VA: H. E. Howard, 1989), implies that the 5th Corps stood idly by, watching the enemy's train pass, but Roebling's account makes clear that the only force within striking distance and with the capacity to stop the wagon train was the reluctant Lieutenant Colonel Pope and his troopers.
12. Smith, *Command Conflicts*, 156–58; WAR Report, 58–59. When 5th Corps scouts pressed local inhabitants about the location of the Mat River, everyone they questioned said they had never heard of it. Diane Monroe Smith, *Chamberlain at Petersburg: The Charge at Fort Hell Gettysburg* (Gettysburg, PA: Thomas Publications, 2004), 15–16. With General Bartlett on the sick list, Colonel Joshua Chamberlain, commanding the 5th Corps's 3rd Brigade, 1st Division, pursued General John Chambliss's cavalry brigade and attempted to capture James Brethed's horse artillery.
13. WAR LB, 238, 241, 243–44. At the beginning of the campaign, the 5th Corps's strength was estimated at 23,000–24,000. Alongside Gouverneur, Emily's brother Robert ("Bob") served on Warren's staff.

CHAPTER 24: NORTH ANNA, TOTOPOTOMOY, AND COLD HARBOR

1. WAR LB, 244–45.
2. Smith, *Command Conflicts*, 158. General Alfred Thomas Archimedes Torbert, who had been on sick leave when Sheridan took the cavalry off on his expedition, was still serving with the Army of the Potomac. WAR Report, 59–60.
3. Smith, *Command Conflicts*, 158–60; Agassiz, *Meade's Headquarters*, 125–26.
4. OR 36, III, 158, 161; Smith, *Command Conflicts*, 158–60; WAR Report, 161–62; OR 36, I, 76–77; Eric J. Wittenberg, *Little Phil: A Reassessment of the Civil War Leadership of Gen. Philip H. Sheridan: Civil War Leadership of Gen. Philip H. Sheridan* (Washington, DC: Potomac Books, 2002), 27–28, 137.
5. OR 36, III, 159–60, 162–63. Roebling found a better crossing place for Burnside at Quarles Ford, but Grant's decision to retire from the North Anna brought that movement to a halt. WAR Report, 66–68; Smith, *Command Conflicts*, 161–62. Sheridan, in his fight at Haw's Shop, was dealing with Wade Hampton, the new commander of J. E. B. Stuart's cavalry.
6. WAR LB, 246–47; OR 36, III, 249.
7. Smith, *Command Conflicts*, 162–64; WAR Report, 69–70. Burnside also protested when asked to relieve Griffin's division when it was needed to defend Warren's left during an attack.
8. Smith, *Command Conflicts*, 162–65; WAR Report, 70–73.

9. OR 36, III, 342, 358–59; Smith, *Command Conflicts*, 165, 236n39; Louis J. Baltz III, *The Battle of Cold Harbor* (Lynchburg, VA: H. E. Howard, 1994), 46–54; OR 36, I, 84; WAR Report, 72–73. During the Overland Campaign, when the Confederates attacked one section of the Federal line, Army of the Potomac headquarters would often order a Federal assault somewhere else, wishfully thinking it would prove a distraction and take some of the heat off those initially attacked—in this case, Warren and the 5th Corps. It seldom worked.

10. OR 36, III, 447–48; WAR Report, 73–74; Smith, *Command Conflicts*, 166, 235–36n36. General Henry Hayes Lockwood (USMA 1836) would lead the 2nd Division of the 5th Corps for less than a month in 1864; he was dismissed by Warren, who judged him unfit to command a division. The newly arrived Lockwood had brought a contingent of former garrison troops out to the front and was assigned to command the newly constituted 4th Division of the 5th Corps. Roebling records the Army of the Potomac's destination as "Coal Harbor," OR 36, III, 727–28. Lockwood, in a protest to Army of the Potomac headquarters upon his removal, would place the blame upon Roebling, who he insisted had approved the positions where Roebling found Lockwood's division. Since Lockwood had failed to take up the positions assigned him by General Warren, it seems unlikely that Roebling would have been complicit in Lockwood's decisions.

11. WAR Report, 74–75; Smith, *Command Conflicts*, 167.

12. Smith, *Command Conflicts*, 168–70. There are indications that Grant had originally intended to send Smith to bolster the 2nd, 5th, and 9th Corps still on the Totopotomoy, making Smith's orders a matter not of misdirection but of Grant changing his mind.

13. Smith, *Command Conflicts*, 169–70; OR 36, III, 454; OR 1, 86; WAR Report, 73–77.

14. WAR Report, 75; Smith, *Command Conflicts*, 170; OR 36, III, 452; OR 36, I, 87–88.

15. Smith, *Command Conflicts*, 171–72; OR 36, II, 447–52; WAR Report, 74. Roebling's numerous reports to Warren that were forwarded to Army of the Potomac headquarters, providing Meade with information about the enemy's movement toward Cold Harbor. OR 36, III, 450.

16. WAR Report, 74–77; OR 36, II, 447–52; OR 36, III, 450, 486.

17. Meade, *Life*, 200–201.

18. Smith, *Command Conflicts*, 172–73; OR 36, I, 85; OR 36, II, 451–52.

19. Smith, *Command Conflicts*, 172–73; OR 36, III, 450, 486–87; Grant, *Memoirs* II, 265–66; OR 36, II, 447–52. On learning that Warren would be replacing Lockwood as a division commander, Meade made clear his desire for Warren to appoint Meade's friend Samuel Crawford to division command in the 5th Corps. Meade wrote, "An order will be sent in the morning relieving Brigadier-General Lockwood from command. You can now make a division for Crawford." Fulfilling Meade's wishes, Warren would have to cope with Crawford's ineptitude; the latter's bumbling would have fatal consequences for the 5th Corps and for Warren and his future as a commander.

CHAPTER 25: COLD HARBOR

1. Smith, *Command Conflicts*, 175.
2. Smith, *Command Conflicts*, 175–77; WAR Report, 77–80.
3. Smith, *Command Conflicts*, 176–77.
4. WAR Report, 80. See map on page 277.
5. WAR Report, 83.

6. Smith, *Command Conflicts*, 178–82; Meade, *Life*, 200–201.
7. Smith, *Command Conflicts*, 183–84.
8. Smith, *Command Conflicts*, 184–85; WAR Report, 84–85; Agassiz, *Meade's Headquarters*, 147.
9. Smith, *Command Conflicts*, 186; WAR Report, 85–86.
10. Smith, *Command Conflicts*, 186–87; OR 36, III, 610, 631.
11. Smith, *Command Conflicts*, 188; OR 36, III, 628.

CHAPTER 26: THE 5TH CORPS SCREENS GRANT'S MOVE TO THE JAMES

1. WAR Report, 87–88,
2. WAR Report, 88–89; Baltz, *Battle of Cold Harbor*, 196–99; Smith, *Command Conflicts*, 188–95. By June 11, Sheridan had been defeated at Trevilian Station, leaving Hunter, whom Sheridan was to have met at Charlottesville, to fend for himself.
3. Jordan, *Happiness*, 162; Diane Monroe Smith, *Chamberlain at Petersburg: The Charge at Fort Hell* (Gettysburg, PA: Thomas Publications, 2004), 32; WAR Report, 89; Boatner, *Civil War Dictionary*, 656. In April 1864, Robert Hoke and the Confederate ram *Albemarle* had attacked and captured the federal fort and garrison at Plymouth, North Carolina, capturing a considerable amount of supplies. Jefferson Davis promoted Hoke to major general for this victory.
4. Smith, *Petersburg*, 33; WAR Report, 90; Meade, *Life*, 202–3. It is said that many reporters, resentful of Crapsey's humiliation at Meade's hands, refused to mention Meade's name in their accounts for the rest of the campaign. "The Suicide of Ruffin," *New York Times*, June 22, 1865, https://www.nytimes.com/1865/06/22/archives/the-suicide-of-ruffin-the-man-who-fired-the-first-gun-on-fort.html. Edward Ruffin, the famous Confederate firebrand who fired the first artillery shot against Fort Sumter, lost everything in war, including his estate, "Roseneath." Smith, *Command Conflicts*, 189.
5. WAR Report, 90–92; Smith, *Petersburg*, 33. "Uncovering Long Bridge" would involve a Federal force sent around and behind to attack the rebel defenders of the bridge, while their comrades attacked on the enemy's front, making it altogether too hot for them to hold it.
6. Meade, *Life*, 202–3.
7. OR 36, II, 762.
8. WAR Report, 92–93; Wilson, *Under the Old Flag*, 397–401. Wilson elaborately embroidered his tale regarding Warren, saying that he later refused to shake Warren's hand and demanded an apology from him. Wilson also told of what he apparently thought was an amusing idea that he shared with Grant, a suggestion that they get Ely Parker, Grant's Native American military secretary, drunk and send him out to scalp some major generals. "Ulysses S. Grant Information Center: Up Close and Personal," College of St. Scholastica, https://libguides.css.edu/usgrant/home/upclose. Grant was known to become upset when anyone used profanity or told risqué stories. Wilson knew his man and how to manipulate him.
9. WAR Report, 93–94.
10. WAR Report, 95.
11. WAR Report, 95–96. Roebling, on page 100 of his report, incorrectly gave the date of Smith's James River passage as June 15. Hennessy, "I Dread the Spring." One delay regarding the completion of the pontoon bridge across the James was the necessity to dismantle

part of the bridge to create a gap to allow the boats carrying Baldy Smith's 18th Corps to Petersburg to pass down the river on June 14. Meade, *Life*, 204.

CHAPTER 27: THE ROAD TO PETERSBURG

1. Smith, *Command Conflicts*, 189; William G. Robertson, *The Petersburg Campaign: The Battle of Old Men and Young Boys, June 9, 1864* (Lynchburg, VA: H. E. Howard, 1989), 6–7; James G. Scott and Edward A. Wyatt IV, *Petersburg's Story* (Richmond: Dietz Press, 1960), 171, 177. Work on Petersburg's defenses, the Dimmock Line, was begun in 1862 by Confederate engineer Captain Charles Dimmock with a workforce of two hundred free and slave laborers. It consisted of fifty-five artillery batteries extending in a ten-mile arc east, south, and west of the city of Petersburg. While a Petersburg historian stresses that the fortifications of the Dimmock Line didn't achieve the standards that came to earthworks during Grant's "siege" in 1864 and 1865, they apparently were substantial enough to give Generals Baldy Smith and Quincy Gillmore pause.
2. OR 36, I, 15–18. Grant's April 2 instructions to Butler seem to clearly state that Butler should take and fortify City Point, and then await the arrival of the Army of the Potomac for joint operations. In a later report, Grant speaks of having given instructions, including verbal ones, to Butler that encouraged him to make a try for Richmond. Robertson, *Petersburg Campaign*, 8–11. While Butler was unwise to put off acting on his own before the Army of the Potomac arrived, Grant's duplicitous reports of his progress and successes no doubt helped mislead Butler.
3. Robertson, *Petersburg Campaign*, 31–33, 42–53, 55–81. Hinks was born in Bucksport, Maine. His name, spelled correctly, is "Hincks," but the *c* was deleted when he joined the U.S. Army in 1861. He went back to the original spelling in 1871 after he retired from the service. The German-born Kautz, though his cavalry brigade was seriously undermanned, provided valuable assistance to Warren and the 5th Corps, helping them avoid a surprise encounter with the enemy during their march to Petersburg. Scott and Wyatt, *Petersburg's Story*, 177–81; Walker, *History*, 524.
4. Smith, *Command Conflicts*, 192–94, 214; Boatner, *Civil War Dictionary*, 932. Sheridan's unexpected return to the Army of the Potomac also left his two other division commanders, Wilson and Kautz, in the lurch when their raid also failed and, hounded by the enemy, the retreating Federal troopers found that, contrary to their expectations, Reams Station was in the hands of the enemy. Nor did Sheridan obey Meade's orders to assist Wilson.
5. WAR Report, 100; Smith, *Command Conflicts*, 195; "Battle of Cold Harbor," National Park Service, http://www.nps.gov/history/online_bppls/civil_war_series/11/sec17.htm; Grant, *Memoirs* II, 294–95; Walker, *History*, 525–30. The 2nd Corps had found the situation when they reached the James much as Roebling described: "The means of crossing were very limited, and the landing places, wharves and roads were incomplete."
6. Smith, *Command Conflicts*, 199; Walker, *History of the Second Corps*, 528–29; Boatner, *Civil War Dictionary*, 168–69. Comstock, Grant's chief aide since November 1863, despite his sketchy topographic abilities, by the end of the war had been awarded for his service the ranks of brevet major general of volunteers and brevet brigadier general in the regular army.
7. Smith, *Command Conflicts*, 196–97; Marszalek, *Personal Memoirs of Ulysses S. Grant*, 593; Young, *Around the World with General Grant*, 124.
8. WAR Report, 96–97; Walker, *History*, 527; Smith, *Command Conflicts*, 196; Earl Hess, *In the Trenches at Petersburg* (Chapel Hill: University of North Carolina Press, 2009), 12–14.

A major criticism of Captain Charles Dimmock's design of the fortification surrounding Petersburg was that the works provided defense only from attackers making a frontal assault. The rear of each work was virtually unprotected and defenseless.

9. Smith, *Command Conflicts*, 196–97; Walker, *History*, 525–33. Hancock's physical condition was another factor during the Battle of Petersburg, for the severe wound at Gettysburg, after the hard service of the Overland Campaign, was reopened and debilitating, to the point that Hancock would soon relinquish command of the 2nd Corps.

10. Smith, *Command Conflicts*, 199–200; Meade, *Life*, 205–9; Walker, *History of the 2nd Corps*, 527–30.

11. WAR Report, 97.

12. WAR Report, 98–99; A. Wilson Greene, "Respect Earned through Blood," *Civil War Times Magazine*, December 2018, https://www.historynet.com/respect-earned-blood.htm. On June 15, 1864, Hinks's two brigades of U.S. Colored Troops captured the Dimmock Line's manned batteries, #6 through #11, by a series of frontal attacks and flanking movements. Roebling, like others who had not witnessed Hinks's assault, seemingly belittled what was, in fact, a remarkable display of good tactics and bravery. Jordan, *Happiness*, 167.

13. WAR Report, 98–99; Smith, *Petersburg*, 54n11, 55n12. Roebling's description of the Hagood Line, one the enemy threw together overnight on its withdrawal from a portion of the Dimmock Line, is of particular interest because of a recent challenge to Chamberlain's and others' accounts of 1st Brigade, 1st Division's assault at Rives Salient on June 18. Consider Earl Hess's description of a Dimmock Line fortification: large parapets twenty feet thick at the base and six feet wide at top with deep ditches in front fifteen feet wide and six feet deep. Hess, *In the Trenches*, 11. Also consider Roebling's description of what the rebels were able to throw together overnight for their new Hagood Line, which illustrates what they were able to construct the following night, when they had to repeat their withdrawal and dig in on their new Harris Line. It leads one to disbelieve a modern-day challenger's assertion, for it would have been impossible for an intelligent veteran like Chamberlain to mistake a weak position on the new Harris Line for a formidable fortification of the Dimmock Line. For Chamberlain's first-person account, see Smith, *Petersburg*, and "A More Detailed Look at Rasbach's Book," Diane Monroe Smith, http://www.dianemonroesmith.com/a-more-detailed-look-at-rasbachs-book. Peter Burchard, *One Gallant Rush: Robert Gould Shaw and His Brave Black Regiment* (New York: St. Martin's Press, 1965), 142–43. General Johnson Hagood, who laid out the new line, was part of Hoke's contingent brought from Bermuda Hundred to assist with the defense of Petersburg. Hagood is perhaps best remembered as the Confederate commander who, after the defeat of the 54th Massachusetts, U.S. Colored Troops, at Fortress Wagner, reported that ordinarily a Federal officer's body would be returned for burial, but in General Robert Gould Shaw's case, "We buried him with his niggers."

CHAPTER 28: THE BATTLE OF PETERSBURG

1. OR 40, II, 174; WAR Report, 99–101. Brigadier General James D. Dearing was a cadet at West Point when the war broke out, and he resigned just short of graduation to fight with the Confederacy. He was mortally wounded on April 6, 1865.

2. WAR Report, 101–2. General Samuel Wylie Crawford, 2nd Division, 5th Corps, was simply someone the exacting General G. K. Warren had to put up with regardless of how inept his performance. Crawford was a close friend of General Meade's and had led one of Meade's

former commands, the Pennsylvania Reserves; Meade had a real soft spot for him and the Pennsylvanians of his home state. See chapter 24, note 19, for evidence of Meade's preference and "suggestions" for Crawford's advancement. Smith, *Petersburg*, 43–45. At 1 a.m. on June 18, the enemy pulled back from the Hagood Line and started digging in on a new line, the Harris Line.

3. WAR Report, 103–4; OR 40, II, 174.
4. WAR Report, 103–5; Smith, *Petersburg*, 41–44.
5. WAR Report, 105–6; Smith, *Petersburg*, 45, 50–51n8, 53, 53n10. 55n12. Chamberlain had approached Cutler hoping that they could coordinate their attacks, a request Cutler clearly misunderstood. But Cutler also harbored considerable resentment toward the young colonel, who'd been given a substantial number of Cutler's men to make up his new 1st Brigade. OR 40, II, p 179. It is likely that Roebling was riding along the 5th Corps's entire front on this day, for he also reported that Crawford, on the 5th Corps's extreme right, was bringing up new batteries to a wheat field on his line.
6. WAR Report, 105–8; OR 40, II, 187; Smith, *Petersburg*, 53–67. Smith's *Chamberlain at Petersburg* is Joshua Chamberlain's first-person account of his brigade's assault at Rives Salient on June 18, 1864, with annotation and an introduction bringing it into the context of the Overland Campaign. The highly inaccurate Federal maps apparently named Poor Creek "Poo Creek," which would be amusing except for the terrible history of what took place there.
7. WAR Report, 106–8; Smith, *Petersburg*, 51n8; Scott, *Petersburg*, 28. Ironically, the walls of Colonel John Avery's house were covered with murals of the Revolutionary War battle that took place at Petersburg on April 25, 1781. Horatio Warren, *Two Reunions of the 142nd Regiment, Pa. Vols.: Including a History of the Regiment, Dedication of the Monument, a Description of the Battle of Gettysburg, also a Complete Roster of the Regiment* (Buffalo, NY: Courier Co., 1890), 37; WAR LB, 267. The renowned photographer Matthew Brady took a photograph of General Warren and his staff, but, as Roebling told his Emily, "Brady took the pictures of G.E. & staff, luckily I was absent on business and I am spared the pain of seeing myself perpetuated in my present appearance." Roebling had explained, "If you were to see me now I doubt whether you could be prevailed upon to look at me, much less kiss me—I am all dirty, ragged and I might say lousy—there isn't a brass button on my coat, I haven't had a shirt collar on since we left Culpeper and when my only shirt is washed I lie abed."
8. WAR LB, 265, 267–68; Agassiz, *Meade's Headquarters*, 147.
9. Smith, *Command Conflicts*, 207–8; OR 15, I, 25–27; Jordan, *Happiness*, 168–71. The contrast between David M. Jordan's and Emerson Taylor's biographies of G. K. Warren offers an example of the complicated dynamics and, perhaps, the perils and pitfalls of writing biography. While Taylor's work could be considered sympathetic to the trials of General Warren, Jordan's biography leaves one with the distinct feeling that, on some level, he really disliked his subject and was perhaps too willing to embrace the opinions of Warren's critics. An interesting example is that, upon Warren's pleas to Meade to choose maneuver as opposed to continually resorting to frontal assault on fortifications, Jordan comments, "One can easily sympathize with Meade in his patient tolerance of such a troubling subordinate." One suspects that the best assessment of General Warren and his performance as a commander lies in the sometimes murky middle between Taylor and Jordan.
10. Smith, *Command Conflicts*, 208–9; OR 15, I, 25; Taylor, *Warren*, 182–83; Jordan, *Happiness*, 168, 175.

CHAPTER 29: ROEBLING'S REDOUBT AND
THE EXPLODING OF BURNSIDE'S MINE

1. OR 40, II, 240; WAR Report, 10. Roebling mistakenly called Colonel William S. Tilton, who took over commend of Chamberlain's 1st Brigade, "Tilden." Since there was a Colonel Charles W. Tilden commanding the 16th Maine in Ayres's 2nd Division, this error demands correction. "Wilderness Union Order of Battle," Wikipedia, https://en.wikipedia .org/wiki/Wilderness_Union_order_of_battle. Colonel William S. Tilton, formerly in command of 22nd Massachusetts, Sweitzer's brigade, took command of the 1st Brigade, 1st Division, 5th Corps after its commander, Colonel Joshua Chamberlain, was seriously wounded on June 18, 1864. Colonel Tilton, who had not covered himself with glory at Gettysburg the previous year, when writing the report for Chamberlain's 1st Brigade for June 18, did not make clear just who was in command (it was Chamberlain) during the desperate attack on Rives Salient. No trace remains of Fort Sedgwick in modern-day Petersburg, but the remains of Fort Davis are still very visible on South Crater Road, formerly known as the Jerusalem Plank Road. It was originally named Fort Warren but was renamed in honor of Colonel P. Stearns Davis, 39th Massachusetts, killed on July 11 by an enemy artillery shell.
2. Walker, *History*, 544; Humphreys, *Virginia*, 228–29. Humphreys records the Federal 2nd Corps's loss as seventeen hundred, the discrepancy perhaps again attributable to underreporting. WAR Report, 110–11.
3. WAR LB, 268–71, 273–74, 293. While Emily and Washington discussed forlorn hopes for marrying sometime in the winter of 1864–1865, Washington made it clear that he couldn't contemplate marrying until the war was over. He cited the anguish Emily's brother and his commander, General Warren, experienced at being separated from his wife of little more than a year, and Washington declared, "I don't want to see you a soldier's wife. Your brother G.K. now spends half his waking hours in cursing the damned fate that keeps him away from his wife." OR 40, II, 333. With ample evidence that Meade's failures had resulted from sending one corps against the enemy at a time, Warren, despite his awareness that Meade wanted no advice from him, nonetheless implored Meade on June 23 to move against Lee with the entire Army of the Potomac. While Meade agreed to forward Warren's suggestion to Grant, he offered many objections to the plan.
4. WAR LB, 268–69, 295; Hess, *In the Trenches*, 39; WAR Report, 111–13; Meade, *Life*, 206–7. In his letters home following the final battle of the Overland Campaign at Petersburg, Meade acknowledged that his losses were severe: ninety-five hundred killed, wounded, or missing in the three-day fight. He believed that fifty days of marching and fighting had left the Army of the Potomac in a considerably weaker condition than when it had crossed the Rapidan. Meade declared, "I failed, and met with serious loss, principally owing to the moral condition of the army; for I am satisfied had these assaults been made on the 5th and 6th of May [the first days of the Overland Campaign] we should have succeeded with half the loss we met." He also acknowledged the effect of the loss of so many experienced officers, who were impossible to replace.
5. Boatner, *Civil War Dictionary*, 931–32; WAR Report, 113; "James Harrison Wilson," in Smith, *Command Conflicts*, 223.
6. Jordan, *Happiness*, 170–72.
7. WAR LB, 265, 275, 277, 279, 290, 292, 299–300. Roebling suggested that when he got his new buttons sewn on his coat, he'd be able to go incognito, for he was known along the line as the "three-buttoned major." Roebling also reported the far from admirable practice, in

this few days of quiet, of his and the men at 5th Corps headquarters amusing themselves by harassing Roebling's apparently intellectually challenged black servant. Another occupation to break the tedium, somewhat less disreputable, had the headquarters staff test two elephant beetles (*Megasoma elephas*, two to five inches) to see how much they could carry. Roebling commented, "They will carry all sorts of things on their back and are mighty strong: they don't smell very nicely though."

8. OR 40, II, 599; Jordan, *Happiness*, 273.

9. WAR Report, 113–14. Roebling's mention of the "advance position which Gen. Griffin had taken possession of in the charge of the 18th" refers to Sweitzer's brigade, which was operating with Crawford's division on the 9th Corps's left. OR 36, I, 523. A more accurate description of the future site of the Battle of the Crater would be the front upon which the 9th Corps fought on June 18.

10. WAR Report, 114–15. The upcoming Burnside assault referred to here by Roebling would take place at the end of July at the enemy position known as Elliott's or Pegram's Salient, where the 9th Corps fought on June 18. WAR LB, 278–79. Boatner, *Civil War Dictionary*, 249–50, 418; Meade, *Life*, 210, 220.

11. OR 40, III, 43, 294–95; OR 40, I, 454; Hess, *In the Trenches*, 56–57. While no sign remains of Fort Sedgwick/Hell, the embankments of Fort Davis are still very visible on the South Crater Road at Petersburg, the road formerly known as the Jerusalem Plank Road. Fort Davis was built to be manned by fifteen hundred men and to hold eight guns.

12. Meade, *Life*, 210–16, 219–21. When Meade approached Grant about the command at Washington, Grant told him that if any more troops were sent, he would send Meade. But when the time came to choose a man to take overall command of the campaign against Early in the valley, Grant sent his favorite, Sheridan. Meade would learn of Grant's perfidy when he read in the newspapers that Sheridan had been appointed to command the military division that Meade felt had been promised to him. The swiftness with which General Baldy Smith, formerly of Grant's inner circle, was put aside at this time must also have added to Meade's uneasiness. While it was believed that Butler was about to be removed from command of the Army of the James, when General Smith returned from sick leave, it was he who was relieved of command of the 18th Corps and sent away to New York. Meade also learned of a disgruntled Joe Hooker's resignation from Sherman's army when General O. O. Howard (nicknamed "Uh Oh Howard" by his troops) was appointed to command the Army of the Cumberland. WAR Report, 116. The 6th Corps left the Army of the Potomac on July 9 for City Point to embark for Washington.

13. WAR Report, 116–17.

14. OR 40, III, 43; WAR Report, 118–19; Meade, *Life*, 216–22. Meade's attention during the days preceding, during, and after the explosion of the mine were taken up with three matters: his hoped-for appointment to an independent command defending Washington against Early's raid, his optimistic focus upon Hancock's assault at Deep Bottom, and, in some ways seemingly the event of least importance to him, the exploding of the mine on July 30 and subsequent assault by the 9th Corps. The days after the Battle of the Crater were taken up with Meade's disappointment at Sheridan being appointed to the command that he felt he had been promised and his rage for what Meade saw as Burnside's negligent bungling of the assault on July 30. That unfortunate event would become known as the Battle of the Crater, for the wide hole left by the massive explosion upon the detonation in the mine. For the finding of the court of inquiry Meade demanded, see OR 40, I, 127–29; WAR LB, 291.

15. WAR Report, 120–21. General Edward Ord (USMA 1839), friend of Generals W. T. Sherman and Henry Halleck, had replaced General John McClernand when Grant relieved the latter at Vicksburg in 1863. In the summer of 1864, Ord was handed another plum assignment when he replaced William "Baldy" Smith as commander of the 18th Corps. Richard Kiper, *Major General John Alexander McClernand: Politician in Uniform* (Kent, OH: Kent University Press, 1999). Kiper provides ample evidence of Charles Dana's and James Harrison Wilson's ongoing efforts to discredit McClernand and have him removed from his command.
16. WAR Report, 121–22.
17. WAR Report, 122–23.
18. WAR Report, 123–24.
19. WAR Report, 124–25; Jordan, *Happiness*, 179–80; "Gouverneur K. Warren," in Smith, *Command Conflicts*, 222; Young, *Around the World with General Grant*.
20. WAR Report, 124–25. Though Meade was contemplating sending Ayres into the fray, the order was never given.
21. WAR Report, 125–28.
22. WAR LB, 305. Roebling focused blame for the failure of the 9th Corps's assault at the crater on the U.S. Colored Troops, but there is much blame to go around. Roebling was at Burnside's point of observation and did report a flood of black soldiers to the rear at one point after the initial advance by Ledlie's force. Or perhaps Roebling was reiterating the conventional wisdom being tossed about in the headquarters of the Army of the Potomac.

CHAPTER 30: DIGGING IN AND MANEUVERING AT PETERSBURG AND A STRIKE AT THE WELDON RAILROAD

1. WAR Report, 132–33. The Confederates did in fact explode a mine in front of the 18th Corps, but it had little effect.
2. WAR Report, 134. Page 134 of the report is mistakenly numbered 124.
3. WAR Report, 124–25; Armstrong, *Warrior in Two Camps*, 100. "The Ammunition Explosion at City Point—Terrible Effects," *Daily Dispatch*, August 17, 1864, Perseus Digital Library, http://www.perseus.tufts.edu/hopper/text?doc=Perseus%3Atext%3A2006 .05.1147%3Aarticle%3Dpos%3D3:

> Fifty-eight Yankees were killed and one hundred and twenty-six wounded by the ammunition explosion at City Point on the 9th instant. A correspondent of the New York Tribune, who witnessed it, says:
> Every frame-house in the town was jarred by the concussion alone to the extent of having its inside plastering knocked off, beside other damages by missiles, &c. Against the houses and other obstructions near the wharf, and even upon the hill, hundreds, and perhaps thousands, of broken, twisted and splintered muskets, and such debris, lay in drifts, like straw drifted by the wind; and all over the ground for at least a quarter of a mile from the scene of the explosion, shell, solid shot, grape, canister, musket and Minnie balls, pieces of shells, nails, screws, bolts and bolt-heads, and fragments of almost everything—wooden, iron and leaden— you can think of, are strewn and drifted like hail and chunks of ice immediately after a dreadful hail storm.
> Everywhere are seen the rents, dents, deep abrasions and scarred furrows of the iron and leaden storm. The thousandth part cannot be told.

My first thought was that an ammunition car had exploded just ahead of the one I was on, and that it would be of little use to try to escape the storm that had gone up and would come down—that one was about as safe in one place as another; and oh! how it did rain and hail all the terrible instruments of war.

It was not a railroad car, but the ammunition barge J. E. Kendrick, that had exploded from the careless handling of percussion shells or some other kind of ammunition, it is supposed. No one that was aboard of the boat remains to tell the tale of her destruction.

4. Meade, *Life*, 223.
5. WAR LB, 281.
6. Humphreys, *Virginia*, 268–73; WAR LB, 318. Meade was, as Roebling reported, not speaking to General Warren, commander of the 5th Corps, or General Burnside of the 9th Corps. The latter would be relieved of his command within the next few days, to be replaced by General John G. Parke.
7. Humphreys, *Virginia*, 272–73; WAR Report, 132–33; "Globe Tavern Union Order of Battle," Wikipedia, https://en.wikipedia.org/wiki/Globe_Tavern_Union_order_of_battle. While General Kautz's cavalry were guarding the Army of the Potomac's left flank, Colonel Samuel P. Spear commanded the Army of the James Cavalry Division, composed of the 1st District of Columbia and the 11th Pennsylvania Cavalry.
8. WAR Report, 133–36; Humphreys, *Virginia*, 274.
9. WAR Report, 136–38.
10. WAR Report, 136, 138–39; Humphreys, *Virginia*, 274.
11. WAR Report, 140–42; Humphreys, *Virginia*, 275; OR 42, II, 314–15. It seems likely that Warren had Roebling pay particular attention to Crawford's division, for Crawford had often failed him and would do so again in the future.
12. WAR Report, 142–44. The 6th and 7th Wisconsin weren't regiments to be trifled with, for though much whittled down with hard service, they were original regiments of the famed Iron Brigade.
13. WAR Report, 144–45. I've taken the liberty of correcting Roebling's misspelling of the name of 9th Corps division commander Orlando Willcox.
14. Humphreys, *Virginia*, 274–78; WAR Report, 146.
15. WAR Report, 146–48; Humphreys, *Virginia*, 277; OR 42, II, 310.

CHAPTER 31: HANGING ON TO THE WELDON RAILROAD

1. WAR Report, 148–50; OR 42, II, 343, 347–48. Roebling was apparently unaware that General Potter of the 9th Corps had advanced a skirmish line early that morning on his front without finding the enemy, but he explained that his right flank was in the air, and Potter was unsure just how far he should advance.
2. Humphreys, *Virginia*, 277; WAR Report, 150–52. Roebling reported that they learned afterward that the enemy had sixteen guns at the Flower house and twelve at the White house, all firing at one point. Roebling, who had experienced firsthand the enemy's shelling on the Federal line preceding Pickett's Charge, declared that the fire received at the Blick house that day equaled, if not surpassed, any at Gettysburg. Meanwhile, many of the enemy's shots fired from the Davis house ricocheted into Griffin's line, and while many of the enemy's shells didn't burst, they were being used effectively as solid shot. The enemy

brigade Roebling mistakenly identified as "Haywood's" was in fact "Hagood's," as identified by Humphreys. Roebling reported that as Daly reached for the flag, Hagood shot him in the side with a pistol and then ordered his men to flee. Jordan, *Happiness*, 185.

3. OR 42, II, 355, 358, 369; Jordan, *Happiness*, 185. Roebling completes his report on the Overland Campaign, written in the fall of 1864, by giving details of events of Warren and the 5th Corps's successful operation against the Weldon Railroad and celebrating their ability to fight off the enemy determined to dislodge them on August 21, 1864. Roebling proudly stated, "This day's work was a clear victory for us, achieved with trivial loss." Although Roebling described his report as "written in a severely official style the personal element being entirely wanting (this is what gives life & interest to everything)," it proved a most valuable tool for this grateful researcher and writer. Roebling provided one more gift of valuable information: a list of casualties for the 5th Corps during the Overland Campaign and the investment of Petersburg, drawn from lists of names of the killed, wounded, or missing assembled principally for hospital purposes, as opposed to reports, in which casualties were known to be underreported. Roebling concluded that the 5th Corps had lost 2,706 more men than had been officially reported. The final total for May 4 to October 27, 1864, was 606 officers and 14,841 men, for a grim total of 15,447.

4. Meade, *Life*, 224; Jordan, *Happiness*, 185.

5. Humphreys, *Virginia*, 278–83; OR 42, II, 489.

6. Jordan, *Happiness*, 188.

7. WAR LB, 327–30, 345.

8. WAR LB, 330–32, 337, 346. Roebling's friend, the resourceful Francis Walker, would later serve as president of MIT.

9. WAR LB, 334–36.

10. WAR LB, 339, 341, 348–49. Time would show that the majority of the soldiers in the Federal armies supported Abraham Lincoln over General George McClellan.

11. WAR LB, 349, 351–52. Interestingly, Roebling mentioned nothing of his continued scouting missions or picket line supervision to Emily in his letters, likely a purposeful omission to allay her continuing fears for his safety. Humphreys, *Virginia*, 308; OR 42, I, 512–13; OR 42, II, 840–21. Roebling and General Baxter's reconnaissance lost a dozen killed or wounded. By October 19, Sheridan had defeated General Early in the valley. The 6th Corps returned to the Army of the Potomac, as did Sheridan and his cavalry, contrary to his orders from Grant. Early's troops, commanded by General John B. Gordon, and Kershaw's division returned to the Army of Northern Virginia. Syphax, king of the Masaesylians in Numidia during the last quarter of the third century BCE, was defeated by a less favored enemy and eventually paraded through Rome as a captive in a Roman triumphal procession of prisoners. "Syphax," Livius, http://www.livius.org/articles/person/syphax.

12. WAR LB, 361–63, 365.

13. WAR LB, 363, 365. Marl, or marlstone, is a calcium carbonate—or lime-rich mud or mudstone that contains variable amounts of clays and silt.

14. WAR LB, 302, 368, 391–92. Interestingly, John's belief in hydropathy never waned, and his adamant refusal to allow any other sort of medical treatment after his injury on the Brooklyn Bridge building site led to his own painful death in 1869 from tetanus.

15. WAR LB, 368, 372.

CHAPTER 32: THE FIRST BATTLE OF HATCHER'S RUN AND THE HICKSFORD RAID

1. WAR LB, 368–69, 372; WAR LB, 386. Roebling's November 8, 1864, letter to Emily made his sentiments clear with his comment "Hurrah for Old Abe." Washington's lizard, to his surprise, returned several days later. He pondered the creature's apparent reluctance to be "stowed away in his hole for the winter, enjoying his torpidity at ease," but he imagined "the warm air of the room seems to have given him a lease of life for a few weeks longer."

   Cope was promoted to captain of volunteers on April 20, 1864, and served as aide-de-camp on the staff of Major General G. K. Warren and later as chief of engineers for Warren's 5th Corps. "Emmor Bradley Cope," Antietam on the Web, http://antietam.aotw.org/officers.php?officer_id=1194.
2. OR 42, I, 434–39; Hess, *In the Trenches*, 189–90. Hess, in his consideration of this expedition, quoted Meade's assessment of Grant, noting that the lieutenant general's main fault was "unflinching tenacity of purpose, which blinds him to opposition and obstacles." Hess also commented that, with the November elections just days away, Grant's risking a Federal disaster at the Petersburg front was no way to shore up support for the administration and the continuance of the war. Jordan, *Happiness*, 189, 198–99. In September, Warren had pleaded, largely in vain, with Army of the Potomac headquarters to give the large number of new men he had recently received a break from the heavy labor of building and strengthening fortifications to allow time to teach them to be soldiers.
3. OR 42, I, 434–37; Jordan, *Happiness*, 193. Slashing is when the trees cut down to create a clear field of fire are left on the ground in front of earthworks to create an obstruction for attackers. "Fortification Friday: Abattis and Slashings, Let Us Get a Clear View These Obstacles," *To the Sound of the Guns*, https://markerhunter.wordpress.com/tag/abattis. Richard J. Sommers, *Richmond Redeemed: The Siege at Petersburg* (Garden City, NY: Doubleday, 1981), 240.
4. OR 42, I, 438–39; OR 42, III, 402–3. Grant would angrily question Meade as to why Crawford had not come up to assist Hancock, claiming that Hancock's disaster would not have happened had Warren carried through on the orders Meade had repeatedly given him. By way of example of the "fog of war" that was in full force on this battlefield, consider the report of Major H. H. Bingham of the 2nd Corps, who was sent out to find General Crawford this day. Bingham found Crawford and later encountered Roebling, who had been unable to find Crawford. When Bingham tried to return to Crawford, he was captured by a party of some two hundred South Carolinian rebels, but, the night being exceedingly dark, he escaped. He reported back to General Hancock that he had failed in his mission to communicate with either General Crawford or Warren.
5. OR 42, III, 402–3; OR 42, I, 440–42. Roebling's report of his busy day at the front on October 27 is a revealing look at the service he rendered on a regular basis to his corps and to the Army of the Potomac. OR 42, I, 434–39. It is also of interest that Warren sent two very detailed maps with his report for October 27, commenting, "I accompany it by a map, made from our reconnaissances. If the operations should ever become a matter of criticism, the study of this map would be of importance in comprehending the difficulties of executing any design or meeting expectations previously formed." Hess, *In the Trenches*, 194. Warren's apprehensions were not misplaced, for Grant, apparently loath to admit that his plan had

miscarried, in his missive to Meade made clear his suspicion that Warren had not carried through on Meade's orders and had failed to see that Crawford went swiftly to Hancock's aid. The impossibility of getting Crawford to where Hancock was in time was, to Grant, seemingly, an inconsequential detail, and, as historian Hess points out, sending only two divisions of the much-battered 2nd Corps without nearby support into an unknown area, hostile both in conditions on the ground and in the enemy intent, was a costly mistake on Grant's part. The First Battle of Hatcher's Run is also known as the Battle of Boydton Plank Road.

6. OR 42, I, 442.
7. OR 42, I, 438–39; Jordan, *Happiness*, 199.
8. WAR LB, 373–75; Hess, *In the Trenches*, 194.
9. WAR LB, 385, 392–93, 299, 392, 396.
10. WAR LB, 397–400.
11. WAR LB, 402–7. This letter, mistakenly dated November 6, should be dated December 6 based on its contents. Hess, *In the Trenches*, 213–14.
12. WAR LB, 401; WAR's certificate for commission as lieutenant colonel, December 2, 1864, Rutgers Roebling Collection, Box 11, Folder 55.
13. Raymond Watkins, *The Hicksford Raid* (1978; rprt. Emporia, VA: Greensville County Historical Society, 1995), 3–4, 8.
14. OR 42, I, 443–44. Hicksford was a mere ten miles north of the North Carolina border. Hess, *In the Trenches*, 213–14; Watkins, *The Hicksford Raid*, 3, 6–14, 18–27. Hicksford historian Raymond Watkins suggests that some portion of the slaves who went to Petersburg after Warren's raid were carried off by the Federals, but, as they would pose a considerable impediment to the expedition, they more likely insisted on leaving with the Yankees.
15. OR 42, I, 445–46; Pullen, *Twentieth Maine*, 232–34; Watkins, *The Hicksford Raid*, 4–5, 15, 17–37, 61. Watkins reports that while there was applejack found on many farms, the 20th Maine hit the jackpot, finding twenty-five barrels of the potent brandy on one Benjamin Bailey's farm. Soon the whole brigade was filling their canteens with the stuff, and some of those sent to quell the party succumbed to temptation themselves. Forty-three men of the 3rd Brigade would be reported missing. Wade Hampton, who led the Confederate cavalry's defense against the Federal incursion, reported having taken 250–300 prisoners. As for the reported atrocities that the Federal soldiers on the Hicksford Raid believed were perpetrated upon their comrades, tangible proof, it seems, was augmented by inflated rumors, resulting in the wholesale destruction of farms and other buildings during the expedition's return to Petersburg.
16. OR 42, I, 445; OR 42, III, 965; Jordan, *Happiness*, 202–3; Watkins, *The Hicksford Raid*, 27–37.
17. WAR LB, 404–7.
18. WAR LB, 363, 392, 406–7; Jordan, *Happiness*, 203; WAR Pension Record, NA. Pension records indicate that his resignation took effect on January 21, 1865, though several forms date it to January 27, 1865.

Acknowledgments

First and foremost, I want to thank my husband, Ned, who tolerated years of my talking about Washington Roebling. But because of his sharing my passion for the Civil War and history in general, I couldn't possibly have a better partner with whom to share, discuss, argue, and consider all that matters than I have with my Ned. I also am greatly beholden to him for the maps that accompany this book, created after much research with great diligence and attention to detail.

A very long list of archivists, librarians, and others have made the research for this work possible. I've so much admiration for their collective dedication and public service for facilitating historical research.

All due gratitude to:

Rutgers University Special Collections and Archives: Curator of
    Manuscripts Albert King and librarians Edward Skipworth,
    Fernanda Perrone, Ronald Becker, Katie Anderson, David Kuzma,
    Helen van Rossum, and Arla Jejia
Rensselaer Polytechnic Institute, Folsom Library: Jenifer Monger
New York State Library: Head Librarian Fred Bassett and Senior
    Librarian P. J. Nastasi
Library of Congress: Patrick Kermwin and Bruce Kirby

And a special thank-you to:

Clare Davitt and Karen Alley Corbett, Bangor Public Library
John Hennessy, historian, National Park Service
Dennis Frye, historian, National Park Service
Clifford Zink, author of *The Roebling Legacy*
Susan Natale, archivist and friend extraordinaire

James Green, NASA, Civil War ballooning
Tony Harrison, naval historian, "From the Orlop Deck"
Chip Woolman, Mariners' Museum, Newport News
John Jackson, Special Collections, Virginia Tech

Last, but most certainly not least, I want to thank Stackpole Books, the long-revered publisher of Civil War scholarship, for their belief in and support for this project. Many thanks to Dave Reisch and Stephanie Otto, production editor Patricia Stevenson, and copyeditor extraordinaire Jen Kelland, whose professional expertise and kind patience have added so much to this book.

Selected Bibliography

ABBREVIATIONS USED IN ENDNOTES

JAR: John A. Roebling

JAR bio transcription: Washington Roebling, "Life of John A. Roebling, C.A.," transcription, Rutgers Roebling Collection, MS Box 10, folders 23–36

LoC: Library of Congress

Memoirs II: U. S. Grant, *Personal Memoirs of U. S. Grant*. Vol. 2. New York: Charles L. Webster, 1885.

NA: National Archives

OR: United States War Department, *The War of the Rebellion: A Compilation of the Official Records of the Union and Confederate Armies*. Series I. 53 vols. Washington, DC: Government Printing Office, 1880–1898.

USMA: United States Military Academy at West Point

WAR: Washington A. Roebling

WAR LB: Washington A. Roebling, Letterbook, Roebling Collection, Brooklyn Historical Society

WAR Report: Washington Roebling, "Report of the Operations of the 5th Corps, May 4 to Aug. 20, 1864," Gouverneur K. Warren Papers, New York State Library, Albany, New York

WAR Report to Meigs: Washington Roebling, Report to General M. C. Meigs, Rutgers MS Box 11, folder 58

ARTICLES AND ESSAYS

Anonymous. "Biography—Washington Roebling." *Smithsonian Associates Civil War E-Mail Newsletter* 3, no. 9. http://civil warstudies.ord/articles/Vkol_3/augustus-roebling.shtm (accessed January 26, 2014).

Bacon, Cyrus. "A Michigan Surgeon at Chancellorsville One Hundred Years Ago." *University of Michigan Medical School Bulletin* 29, no. 6 (November–December 1963): 315–31.

Billings, Elden E. "Letteres & Diaries." *Civil War Times Illustrated* (January 1963).

Caso, Frank. "Immigrant Entrepreneurship." Immigrantentrpreneurship.org. http://immigrantentrpreneurship.org/entry.php?rec=37 (accessed January 10, 2015).

Downey, Brian. "James Chatham Duane." Antietam on the Web. http://antietam.aotw.org/officers.php?officer_id=149 (accessed November 18, 2014).

———. "Washington Augustus Roebling." Antietam on the Web. http://antietam.aotw.org/officers.php?officer_id+1041 (accessed November 18, 2014).

Hennessy, [John]. "A Mystery: Roebling's 'Wire Bridge' on the Rappahannock." Mysteries & Conundrums. http://npsfrsp.wordpress.com/2010/07/11/a-mystery-roeblings-wire-bridge-on-the-rappahannock (accessed October 5, 2014).

Hennessy, John J. "I Dread the Spring: The Army of the Potomac Prepares for the Overland Campaign." In *The Wilderness Campaign*, ed. Gary Gallagher. Chapel Hill: University of North Carolina Press, 1997.

Henriksson, Anders, ed. "The Narrative of Friedrich Meyer." *Civil War Regiments* 6, no. 2 (1998): 1–22.

Jones, J. William. "Official Diary of First Corps A.M.V. While Commanded by Lieutenant-General R. H. Anderson, May 7–31, 1864." *Southern Historical Society Papers* 7 (January–December 1879).

Law, Evander M. "From the Wilderness to Cold Harbor." In *Battles and Leaders of the Civil War*, edited by Robert Underwood Johnson and Clarence C. Buel. Vol. 4. New York: Century Co., 1884.

Monroe, J. Albert. "The Rhode Island Artillery at the First Battle of Bull Run." *Personal Narratives of the Battles of the Rebellion Being Papers Read before the Rhode Island Soldiers and Sailors Historical Society* No. 2. Providence: Sidney S. Rider, 1878.

U.S. Corps of Topographical Engineers. "Gouverneur Kemble Warren: 1830–1882." TopoGSA. http://www.topogsa.org/b_warren.htm (accessed December 29, 2014).

Williams, Bob. "A Guided Tour to Petersburg's 'Fort Hell.'" Plowshares & Bayonets. http://26nc.org/blog/?p=177 (accessed November 24, 2014).

Zinc, Clifford. "Washington A. Roebling, the Civil War and Building the Brooklyn Bridge." *Wire Rope Exchange* (September–October 2013).

UNPUBLISHED SOURCES

Duane, James Chatham. Letterbook, University of Virginia, Small Special Collections Library.

Roebling, Washington A. 1863 Notebook, Roebling Collection, Rensselaer Polytechnic Institute, Folsom Library Special Collections.

———. Letterbook, Roebling Collection, Brooklyn Historical Society.

———. "Life of John A. Roebling, C.A." Rutgers University Library, Special Collections, Roebling Collection, MS Box 10, folders 23–36, ca. 1897 & 1907.

———. "Report of the Operations of the 5th Corps, May 4 to Aug. 20, 1864." Gouverneur K. Warren Papers, New York State Library.

ONLINE RESOURCES

Crowninshield, Caspar. "A Ball's Bluff Letter." *Civil War Monitor*. October 20, 2017. https://www.civilwarmonitor.com/blog/a-balls-bluff-letter.

"Disaster at Ball's Bluff, 21 October 1861." National Museum of the United States Army. July 17, 2014. https://armyhistory.org/disaster-at-balls-bluff-21-october-1861.

"Eddie Lincoln." Abraham Lincoln Research Site. http://rogerjnorton.com/Lincoln67.html.

Hawks, Steve A. "Timeline of the Department of Pennsylvania 1861." *Civil War in the East.* http://civilwarintheeast.com/us-armies/dept-pennsylvania.
"The Modern Battle of Bunker Hill." *New York Times.* July 18, 1861. http://www.nytimes.com/1861/07/18/news/the-modern-battle-of-bunker-hill.html.
Murray, Jennifer. *The Civil War Begins: Opening Clashes.* Washington, DC: Center of Military History, U.S. Army, 2012. https://history.army.mil/html/books/075/75-2/CMH_Pub_75-2.pdf.
Schreckengost, Gary J. "The Artillery Fight at the First Battle of Bull Run." *Field Artillery Journal.* July 2001. http://vcwsg.com/PDF%20Files/The%20Artillery%20Battle%20At%20The%20First%20Battle%20Of%20Bull%20Run.pdf.
Stonesifer, Ray P. "The Little Round Top Controversy: Gouverneur Warren, Strong Vincent and George Sykes." *Pennsylvania History: A Journal of Mid-Atlantic Studies* 35, no. 3 (July 1968): 225–30. https://www.jstor.org/stable/27771702?newaccount=true&read-now=1.
Trefousse, Hans L. "United States Congress Joint Committee on the Conduct of the War." Revolvy. https://www.revolvy.com/main/index.php?s=Joint_Committee_on_the_Conduct_of_the_War&item_type=topic.
"Vanderbilt." Naval History and Heritage Command. October 21, 2015. https://www.history.navy.mil/research/histories/ship-histories/danfs/v/vanderbilt.html.

BOOKS

155th Regimental Association. *Under the Maltese Cross: Antietam to Appomattox.* Pittsburgh, PA: Warner, 1910.
Agassiz, George R., ed. *Meade's Headquarters, 1863–1865: Letters of Colonel Theodore Lyman.* Boston: Atlantic Monthly Press, 1922.
Aldrich, Thomas M. *The History of Battery A First Regiment Rhode Island Light Artillery in the War to Preserve the Union, 1861–1865.* Providence: Snow & Farnham, 1904.
Anders, Curt. *Henry Halleck's War.* Carmel: Guild Press of Indiana, 1999.
Armstrong, William H. *Warrior in Two Camps.* Syracuse, NY: Syracuse University Press, 1978.
Badeau, Adam. *Military History of Ulysses S. Grant.* New York: D. Appleton, 1885.
Baltz, Louis J., III. *The Battle of Cold Harbor.* Lynchburg, VA: H. E. Howard, 1994.
Bearss, Edwin C., with J. Parker Hills. *Receding Tide: Vicksburg and Gettysburg: The Campaigns That Changed the Civil War.* Washington, DC: National Geographic, 2010.
Burchard, Peter. *One Gallant Rush: Robert Gould Shaw and His Brave Black Regiment.* New York: St. Martin's Press, 1965.
Burgess, Milton. *David Gregg: Pennsylvania Cavalryman.* State College, PA: Nittany Valley Offset, 1984.
Chamberlain, Joshua. *Passing of the Armies.* New York: Bantam Books, 1993.
Cooling, Benjamin Franklin. *Counter-thrust: From the Peninsula to the Antietam.* Lincoln: University of Nebraska Press, 2007.
Cox, Jacob Dolson. *Military Reminiscences of the Civil War.* Vol. 1. New York: Charles Scribner's Sons, 1900.
Crook, General George. *Gen. George Crook: His Autobiography.* Edited by Martin F. Schmitt. Norman: University of Oklahoma Press, 1986.
Crouch, Tom D. *The Eagle Aloft: Two Centuries of the Balloon in America.* Washington, DC: Smithsonian Institution Press, 1983.
Dana, Charles A. *Recollections of the Civil War.* Lincoln: University of Nebraska Press, 1996.

Davis, Major Geo. B. *Official Military Atlas of the Civil War*. Washington, DC: Government Printing Office, 1891–1895.

Fifth Massachusetts Battery Committee. *History of the Fifth Massachusetts Battery*. Boston: Luther E. Cowles, 1902.

Fishel, Edwin C. *The Secret War for the Union*. Boston: Houghton Mifflin, 1996.

Frye, Dennis. *Harpers Ferry under Fire: A Border Town in the American Civil War*. Virginia Beach, VA: Donning Publishing, 2012.

Gottfried, Bradley M. *The Maps of the Bristoe Station and Mine Run Campaigns: An Atlas of the Battles and Movements in the Eastern Theater after Gettysburg, Including Rappahannock Station, Kelly's Ford, and Mortons Ford, July 1863–February 1864*. El Dorado Hills, CA: Savas Beatie, 2013.

Graham, Martin F. *Mine Run: A Campaign of Lost Opportunities, October 21, 1863–May 1, 1864*. Lynchburg, VA: H. E. Howard, 1987.

Graham, Matthew J. *The Ninth Regiment New York Volunteers (Hawkins Zouaves)*. New York: E. P. Coby, 1900.

Grant, U. S. *Personal Memoirs of U. S. Grant*. New York: Konecky and Konecky, 1992.

———. *Personal Memoirs of U. S. Grant*. Vol. 2. New York: Charles L. Webster, 1885.

Griffin, Richard N., ed. *Three Years a Soldier: The Diary and Newspaper Correspondence of Private George Perkins, Sixth New York Independent Battery, 1861–1864*. Knoxville: University of Tennessee Press, 2006.

Henderson, William D. *The Road to Bristoe Station: Campaigning with Lee and Meade, August 1–October 20, 1863*. Lynchburg, VA: H. E. Howard, 1987.

Hennessy, John J. *The First Battle of Manassas: An End to Innocence, July 18–21, 1861*. Mechanicsburg, PA: Stackpole, 2015.

———. *Return to Bull Run: The Campaign and Battle of Second Manassas*. New York: Simon and Schuster, 1993.

Hess, Earl. *In the Trenches at Petersburg*. Chapel Hill: University of North Carolina Press, 2009.

Hoptak, John David. *The Battle of South Mountain*. Charleston, SC: History Press, 2011.

Horn, John. *The Destruction of the Weldon Railroad*. Lynchburg, VA: H. E. Howard, 1991.

———. *The Petersburg Campaign: June 1864–April 1865*. Conshohocken, PA: Combined Books, 1993.

Humphreys, Andrew A. *From Gettysburg to the Rapidan*. New York: Charles Scribner's Sons, 1883.

———. *The Virginia Campaign of 1864 and 1865*. New York: Charles Scribner's Sons, 1883.

Hussey, George A. *History of the Ninth Regiment New York State Militia*. New York: Veterans of the Regiment, 1889.

Hyde, Bill. *The Union Generals Speak*. Baton Rouge: Louisiana State University Press, 2003.

Jordan, David M. *Happiness Is Not My Companion*. Bloomington: Indiana University Press, 2001.

Keneally, Thomas. *American Scoundrel: The Life of the Notorious Civil War General Dan Sickles*. New York: Anchor Books, 2002.

Kennedy, Randall. *Nigger: The Strange Career of a Troublesome Word*. New York: Pantheon Books, 2002.

Kiper, Richard. *Major General John Alexander McClernand: Politician in Uniform*. Kent, OH: Kent University Press, 1999.

Lamb, Blaine. *The Extraordinary Life of Charles Pomeroy Stone*. Yardley, PA: Westholme, 2016.

Lapham, William B. *My Recollections of the War of the Rebellion*. Augusta, ME: Burleigh & Flynt, 1892.

Marszalek, John F. *Commander of All Lincoln's Armies: A Life of General Henry W. Halleck*. Cambridge, MA: Belknap Press of Harvard University, 2004.

———, ed. *The Personal Memoirs of Ulysses S. Grant: The Complete Annotated Edition*. Cambridge, MA: Harvard University Press, 2017.

McClellan, Carswell. *Notes on the Personal Memoirs of P. H. Sheridan*. Saint Paul: William Banning Jr., 1889.

———. *The Personal Memoirs and Military History of U. S. Grant versus the Record of the Army of the Potomac*. General Books, 2010.

McCullough, David. *The Great Bridge*. New York: Simon & Schuster, 1972.

Matter, William. *If It Takes All Summer*. Chapel Hill: University of North Carolina Press, 1988.

Meade, George G. *The Life and Letters of George Gordon Meade*. Vol. 2. New York: Scribner's Sons, 1913.

Miers, Earl S. *Wash Roebling's War*. Newark, DE: Curtis Paper Company, 1961.

Norton, Oliver Willcox. *The Attack and Defense of Little Round Top: Gettysburg, July 2, 1863*. Gettysburg. PA: Stan Clark Military Books, 1992.

Parson, Philip W. *The Union Sixth Army Corps in the Chancellorsville Campaign*. Jefferson, NC: McFarland, 2006.

Patterson, Robert. *A Narrative of the Campaign of the Valley of the Shenandoah in 1861*. Philadelphia: John Campbell, 1865.

Pennypacker, Isaac R. *General Meade*. New York: D. Appleton and Company, 1901.

Pfanz, Harry W. *Gettysburg: The Second Day*. Chapel Hill: Univeristy of North Carolina Press, 1987.

Phisterer, Frederick. *New York in the War of the Rebellion*. 3rd ed. Vols. 2 and 3. Albany: Lyon Co., 1912.

Priest, John Michael. *Before Antietam: The Battle for South Mountain*. Shippensburg, PA: White Mane, 1992.

Pullen, John J. *The Twentieth Maine*. Dayton, OH: Morningside, 1991.

Rafuse, Ethan S. *Corps Commanders in Blue*. Baton Rouge: Louisiana State University Press, 2014.

———. *George Gordon Meade and the War in the East*. Abilene, TX: McWhiney Foundation Press, 2003.

———. *McClellan's War: The Failure of Moderation in the Struggle for the Union*. Bloomington: Indiana University Press, 2005.

Robertson, William G. *The Petersburg Campaign: The Battle of Old Men and Young Boys, June 9, 1864*. Lynchburg, VA: H. E. Howard, 1989.

Roebling, Washington. *Instructions for Transport and Erection of Military Wire Suspension Bridge Equipage*. Quartermaster's Department, U.S. Army, 1862.

———. *Washington Roebling's Father: A Memoir of John A. Roebling*. Edited by Donald Sayenga. Reston, VA: American Society of Civil Engineers, 2009.

Schultz, Duane. *Most Glorious Fourth*. New York: W. W. Norton, 2002.

Schulz, John W. M. *The Engineer Battalion in the Civil War*. Washington, DC: Press of the Engineer School, 1910.

Schuyler, Hamilton. *The Roeblings: A Century of Engineers Bridge-Builders and Industrialists*. Princeton, NJ: Princeton University Press, 1931.

Schaff, Morris. *The Battle of the Wilderness*. Boston: Houghton Mifflin, 1910.

Shattuck, Charles H. *The Hamlet of Edwin Booth*. Urbana: University of Illinois Press, 1969.

Simon, John, ed. *The Papers of Ulysses S. Grant*. Vols. 4 and 5. Carbondale: Southern Illinois University Press, 1973.

———. *The Papers of Ulysses S. Grant*. Vol. 10. Carbondale: Southern Illinois University Press, 1982.

Small, Abner R. *The Sixteenth Maine Regiment in the War of the Rebellion*. Portland, ME: B. Thurston, 1886.

Smith, Diane Monroe. *Chamberlain at Petersburg: The Charge at Fort Hell*. Gettysburg, PA: Thomas Publications, 2004.

———. *Command Conflicts in Grant's Overland Campaign*. Jefferson, NC: McFarland, 2013.

———. *Fanny and Joshua*. Hanover, NH: University Press of New England, 2013.

Sommers, Richard J. *Richmond Redeemed: The Siege at Petersburg*. Garden City, NY: Doubleday, 1981.

Steere, Edward. *The Wilderness Campaign*. Harrisburg: Stackpole, 1960.

Steinman, D. B. *The Builders of the Bridge*. New York: Harcourt, Brace and Company, 1945.

Sumner, Merlin E., ed. *Diary of Cyrus B. Comstock*. Dayton, OH: Morningside, 1987.

Tap, Bruce. *Over Lincoln's Shoulder: The Committee on the Conduct of the War*. Lawrence: University Press of Kansas, 1998.

Taylor, Emerson Gifford. *Gouverneur Kemble Warren: The Life and Letters of an American Soldier*. Boston: Houghton Mifflin, 1932.

Titone, Nora. *My Thoughts Be Bloody*. New York: Free Press, 2010.

Toomey, Daniel C. *Hero at Front Royal*. Baltimore: Toomey Press, 2009.

Trexler, Harrison A. *The Confederate Ironclad "Virginia" ("Merrimac")*. Chicago: University of Chicago Press, 1938.

U.S. War Department, *The War of the Rebellion: A Compilation of the Official Records of the Union and Confederate Armies*. Series I. 53 vols. Washington, DC: Government Printing Office, 1880–1898.

Wainwright, Charles S. *A Diary of Battle*. New York: De Capo Press, 1998.

Walker, Francis A. *History of the Second Army Corps*. New York: Charles Scribner's Sons, 1891.

Warner, Ezra J. *Generals in Blue*. Baton Rouge: Louisiana State University Press, 1964.

Warren, Gouverneur K. *An Account of the Operations of the Fifth Army Corps at the Battle of Five Forks*. New York: D. Van Nostrand, 1866.

Warren, Horatio. *Two Reunions of the 142nd Regiment, Pa. Vols.: Including a History of the Regiment, Dedication of the Monument, a Description of the Battle of Gettysburg, also a Complete Roster of the Regiment*. Buffalo, NY: Courier Co., 1890.

Watkins, Raymond. *The Hicksford Raid*. 1978. Reprint, Emporia, VA: Greensville County Historical Society, 1995.

Weigold, Marilyn E. *Silent Builder: Emily Warren Roebling and the Brooklyn Bridge*. New York: Associated Faculty Press, 1984.

Welsh, Jack, MD. *Medical Histories of Union Generals*. Kent, OH: Kent State University Press, 1996.

Wilson, James Harrison. *Under the Old Flag*. Vol. 1. New York: D. Appleton, 1912.

Wittenberg, Eric. *Little Phil: A Reassessment of the Civil War Leadership of Gen. Philip H. Sheridan*. Washington, DC: Brassey's, Inc., 2002.

Wittenberg, Eric J., J. David Petruzzi, and Michael F. Nugent. *One Continuous Fight*. New York: Savas Beaty, 2008.

Young, Jesse Bowman. *The Battle of Gettysburg*. Dayton, OH: Morningside Bookshop, 1976.

Young, John Russell. *Around the World with General Grant*. New York: American News Co., 1879.

Zink, Clifford W. *The Roebling Legacy*. Princeton, NJ: Princeton Landmark Publications, 2011.

Zinn, Jack. *The Battle of Rich Mountain*. Parsons, WV: McClain Printing, 1971.

Index

Virginia, CSS (ironclad warship), 32,
40, 41–42, 43–44, 44*f*, 45, 383n1,
384nn2–3, 385n5
Virginia Central Railroad, 259, 260*f*
Virginia peninsula, 41*f*; McClellan's
force on, 32–39

Wade, Benjamin, 180, 186
Wadsworth, James, 187, 217*f*, 235;
and Wilderness, 201, 209, 214–15,
217–18
Wainwright, Charles S., 38, 187, 334–35
waiting: Roebling on, 7, 37–38, 195–96,
339; Warren on, 280
Walker, Francis, 160, 163, 172–73, 177,
220, 222, 336, 337*f*, 426n8
Wallkill of Newburgh (barge), 42–43
Warren, Emily (Chase). *See* Chase,
Emily
Warren, Emily (Roebling), 162, 188*f*,
196, 342, 349–50, 355*f*, 358*f*, 405n12;
background and character of, 184–85,
403n6; first meeting with Washington, 179–89; later life, 355–57, 362;
and marriage plans, 422n3, 348
Warren, Gouverneur K., 82, 140*f*, 152*f*;
and alcohol, 162, 194–95; and Bristoe
Station, 164–69; and Chancellorsville,
120, 125, 130; character of, 162, 276;
and Cold Harbor, 267–68, 270–78;
and Five Forks, 360–62; and Gettysburg, 143–45; and Grant, 209–10,
283, 319–20, 333–34, 414n13; and
Hatcher's Run, 343–46, 347; and
Hicksford Raid, 350–54; later life,
360–64; and lead-up to Gettysburg,
133–42; legacy of, 362, 363, 363*f*;
and Meade, 174–76, 178, 190, 194,
242–44, 248–49, 269, 304–5, 311–12,
341–42, 365–66; and Mine Run,
170–78; and North Anna, 259–61;
personal life, 138, 163, 397n7; and

Petersburg, 295, 297–321; promotion
of, 160; and reconnaissance, 157–58,
161–62; and reorganization, 182,
186–87, 190, 280; reputation of,
333, 335; and road to James River,
279–84; and Roebling, 160, 183, 211,
256, 350, 397n7; and Sheridan, 233,
360–61, 375–76; and Spotsylvania,
227–29, 231, 235, 237–43, 247–49,
251; and Totopotomoy, 262–63;
and Weldon Railroad, 324–42; and
Wilderness, 202, 204–6, 208–10; and
Wilson, 234, 418n8
Warren, Robert, 191, 195, 416n13
Washburne, Elihu B., 198, 245, 369, 373
Washington, DC: defenses of, 11, 51;
Early's raid and, 315, 323–24
Waterloo Bridge, 79
weather, 33–35, 173, 180, 187, 310,
352–53
Webb, Alexander, 151, 153*f*, 166, 399n9,
407n11
Weed, Stephen, 145, 146, 363, 398n2
Weldon Railroad, 311, 322, 324–31,
329*f*, 338*f*, 350–52; defense of,
332–42
West Point Battery, 20
White House, 252, 265, 288, 325
White Sulphur Springs, 67–68
Widow Tapp's Field, 215, 217
the Wilderness, 132, 198–224, 203*f*,
214*f*, 221*f*; aftermath of, 225–27; his-
toriography of, 199–200
Wilkenson, Morton S., 315
Willcox, Orlando, 217, 328–29, 330
Williamsburg, Battle of, 47
Williams House, 306, 326
Wilson, James H. "Harry," 189, 190,
200*f*, 230*f*, 400n1, 409n20; character
of, 212, 405n2; and Cold Harbor,
266, 275–78; and Grant, 370, 372,
373, 375, 411n7; and Petersburg,

About the Author

Diane Monroe Smith is the mother of two handsome sons and grandmother to three amazing grandsons. She and her husband, Civil War author Ned Smith, live in Maine in the winter and spend summers in the Canadian Maritimes (there really are only two seasons in this part of the world). At their summer home, they watch whales playing and feeding in their "front yard," the Bay of Fundy.

Diane is the author of three previous books, the first of which is *Fanny and Joshua: The Enigmatic Lives of Frances Caroline Adams and Joshua Lawrence Chamberlain* (with the second edition published in 2013). Her second book is a previously unpublished first-person account by Joshua Chamberlain of his and his brigade's assault at Rives Salient during the Battle of Petersburg in 1864. *Chamberlain at Petersburg: The Charge at Fort Hell* was released in 2004. Diane's research provided extensive annotation and, with Ned Smith's well-researched maps, put Chamberlain's account into its proper context—that of the Overland Campaign.

Diane's third book was the natural outcome of her extensive research and writing on the 5th Corps, Army of the Potomac. *Command Conflicts in Grant's Overland Campaign: Ambition and Animosity in the Army of the Potomac* brought Washington Roebling and his corps commander, General Gouverneur Warren, ever more prominently to Diane's attention, and the story of the dramatic roles they played in the Federals' hard war to defeat the defenders of the rebellion demanded to be told.

Visit the author at her website: dianemonroesmith.com.